Library of Southern Civilization
Lewis P. Simpson, Editor

THE IDEOLOGY OF SLAVERY

THE IDEOLOGY
OF SLAVERY

Proslavery Thought in the Antebellum South, 1830–1860

Edited, with an Introduction, by DREW GILPIN FAUST

Louisiana State University Press, Baton Rouge and London

Copyright © 1981 by Louisiana State University Press
All rights reserved
Manufactured in the United States of America

Designer: Patricia Douglas Crowder
Typeface: Linotron 202 Sabon
Typesetter: G & S Typesetters, Inc.

LIBRARY OF CONGRESS CATALOGING IN PUBLICATION DATA

The Ideology of slavery.

(Library of Southern civilization)
Bibliography: p.
Contents: Abolition of Negro slavery / Thomas Roderick Dew—
Memoir on slavery / William Harper—A brief examination of
scripture testimony on the institution of slavery / Thornton
Stringfellow—[etc.]
1. Slavery—Southern States—History—Sources. 2. Southern
States—History—1775–1865—Sources. 3. Afro-Americans—
History—To 1863—Sources. I. Faust, Drew Gilpin. II. Series.
E449.126   975'.00496073   81-3755
ISBN 0–8071–0855–3
ISBN 0–8071–0892–8 (pbk.)

CONTENTS

Preface ix

INTRODUCTION 1
The Proslavery Argument in History

I. THOMAS RODERICK DEW 21
Abolition of Negro Slavery

II. WILLIAM HARPER 78
Memoir on Slavery

III. THORNTON STRINGFELLOW 136
*A Brief Examination of Scripture Testimony
on the Institution of Slavery*

IV. JAMES HENRY HAMMOND 168
Letter to an English Abolitionist

V. JOSIAH C. NOTT 206
*Two Lectures on the Natural History
of the Caucasian and Negro Races*

VI. HENRY HUGHES 239
Treatise on Sociology

VII. GEORGE FITZHUGH 272
Southern Thought

*Selected Bibliography of Secondary Works
on the Proslavery Argument* 301

PREFACE

The pages that follow attempt to portray the development, mature essence, and ultimate fragmentation of proslavery thought during the era of its greatest importance in the American South. Although recent years have witnessed an intensification of interest in the antebellum defense of slavery, students and scholars have not had convenient access to texts that could provide a basis for serious study of the proslavery argument. I have tried here to place some of the most significant nineteenth-century proslavery writings within a framework of twentieth-century scholarly understanding by providing an introduction, head notes, and a bibliography of relevant secondary material.

The introduction establishes a context for the selections that follow by presenting both a history of the defense of slavery and a historiographical survey of writing on proslavery thought. The texts themselves have been reproduced with a minimum of abridgement, although some editing was necessary to make a one-volume anthology feasible. For the most part, I restricted my omissions to eliminating some of the interminable examples these nineteenth-century authors liked to offer in support of each assertion within their arguments. In several cases, I chose to include lesser-known works by standard authors because these could be reproduced without substantial editorial intervention. I felt that, insofar as possible, I should allow slavery's defenders to speak for themselves. Original spelling and punctuation, even when inconsistent, have been retained. The Selected Bibliography that closes the volume is designed to serve as a comprehensive guide to the historical literature on the proslavery theorists and their arguments.

I have been aided in compiling this anthology by a variety of scholars and friends. Peter Kolchin, Larry Tise, and Bertram Wyatt-Brown generously provided me access to their unpublished work. Lewis Simpson and Beverly Jarrett of Louisiana State University Press had the idea for the volume in the

first place, and helped shape the book with clear-headed and useful suggestions. Carolyn Kappes, Margaret Fisher Dalrymple, Marlene Heck, and
Janet Tighe worked hard to keep the text free from error. Charles Rosenberg
and Paul and Barbara Rosenkrantz set a scholarly tone that inspired me to
come home from the beach and finish the project. To all I am grateful.

THE IDEOLOGY OF SLAVERY

INTRODUCTION
The Proslavery Argument in History

The controversy over slavery in the antebellum United States did not end with abolition of the South's peculiar institution. In the century that has followed Appomattox, historians have debated the sources and meaning of the slavery agitation nearly as vigorously as early nineteenth-century Americans argued about human bondage itself. But a disproportionate amount of this scholarly attention has been devoted to antislavery movements and ideologies. Whereas studies of abolitionism have established it as both a product and an index of fundamental aspects of nineteenth-century culture, historical treatment of proslavery has emphasized its aberrant qualities, identifying it as the evanescent product of the unique civilization that flourished in the South during the last three decades before the Civil War. Many scholars have felt uncomfortable contending with zealous defenses of a social system that the twentieth century judges abhorrent, and, like David Donald, they have found the proslavery movement "astonishing."[1]

In recent years, however, interpretations of proslavery thought have shifted. Perhaps more accustomed to the notion of a timeless and geographically extensive American racism, scholars have begun to place proslavery within a wider context, to regard it as more than simply a distasteful manifestation of a collective paranoia gripping the South in the years before the Civil War. Historians have come to view the proslavery argument less as evidence of moral failure and more as a key to wider patterns of beliefs and values. The defense of human bondage, they recognize, was perhaps more important as an effort to construct a coherent southern social philosophy than as a political weapon of short-lived usefulness during the height of sectional conflict. In defending what they repeatedly referred to as the "cornerstone" of their

---

1. David Donald, "The Proslavery Argument Reconsidered," *Journal of Southern History*, XXXVII (1971), 3. For a useful summary of the extensive literature on abolition, see James Brewer Stewart, *Holy Warriors: The Abolitionists and American Slavery* (New York: Hill and Wang, 1976), and Ronald G. Walters, *The Antislavery Appeal: American Abolitionism After 1830* (Baltimore: Johns Hopkins University Press, 1976).

social order, slavery's apologists were offering posterity an unusual opportunity to examine the world view of articulate southerners, their sources of social legitimation, and their self-conscious definition of themselves.[2] Slavery became a vehicle for the discussion of fundamental social issues—the meaning of natural law, the conflicting desires for freedom and order, the relationship between tradition and progress, the respective roles of liberty and equality, dependence and autonomy. "The question of negro slavery," one apologist recognized in 1856, "is implicated with all the great social problems of the current age."[3] Addressing topics of deepest import to Americans North and South, the proslavery argument embodied the South's particular perspective on those philosophical, moral, and social dilemmas confronting the nation as a whole. "Proslavery thought," as one recent scholar has remarked, "was nothing more or less than thought about society."[4]

A significant aspect of the reorientation of modern scholarship toward a widening interpretation of proslavery's significance has been a growing interest in its persistence over time. Although a few scholars of the 1930s and 1940s noted proslavery's early origins,[5] most historians continued to associate the defense of slavery with a movement of the South away from Jeffersonian liberalism in the late 1820s and 1830s. After abolitionist William Lloyd Garrison began to denounce slavery in *The Liberator* in 1831, these scholars explained, the South rapidly abandoned its Revolutionary American heritage and took up the almost polar opposite position of proslavery reactionism.[6]

2. The reference to slavery as the "cornerstone" of the southern social order has most frequently been attributed to an 1861 speech of Alexander Stephens, but contemporary southerners recognized the origin of the phrase in a speech by George McDuffie of 1836. See James Henry Hammond to M. C. M. Hammond, July 23, 1859, in James Henry Hammond Papers, Library of Congress. For other examples of the use of this concept, see Hammond, "Hammond's Letters on Slavery," in *The Pro-Slavery Argument as Maintained by the Most Distinguished Writers of the Southern States* (Charleston: Walker, Richards & Co., 1852), 111; George Frederick Holmes, "Slavery and Freedom," *Southern Quarterly Review*, I (1856), 87, 92; Edmund Ruffin, *The Political Economy of Slavery* (Washington: L. Towers, 1857), 5, 23.

3. Holmes, "Slavery and Freedom," 95.

4. Larry Edward Tise, "Proslavery Ideology: A Social and Intellectual History of the Defense of Slavery in America, 1790–1840" (Ph.D. dissertation, University of North Carolina, 1975), 57.

5. See especially William Sumner Jenkins, *Pro-Slavery Thought in the Old South* (1935; reprint ed., Gloucester, Mass.: Peter Smith, 1960); William B. Hesseltine, "Some New Aspects of the Pro-Slavery Argument," *Journal of Negro History*, XXI (1936), 1–15; Kenneth M. Stampp, "An Analysis of T. R. Dew's *Review of the Debate in the Virginia Legislature," Journal of Negro History*, XXVII (1942), 380–87.

6. See Charles A. and Mary R. Beard, *The Rise of American Civilization* (New York: Macmillan, 1927); Albert Bushnell Hart, *Slavery and Abolition, 1831–1841* (New York: Harper &

Recent work, however, has revised this chronology, exploring in new detail the significance of proslavery doctrines during the colonial period.[7] Acknowledging a brief period of quiescence during the egalitarian ferment of the Revolutionary years, this interpretation chronicles a reemergence as early as 1808 of a proslavery literature that grew steadily in volume and vehemence throughout the remainder of the antebellum period. This writing, moreover, was not restricted to the South. One of the earliest slavery debates took place in colonial Massachusetts;[8] northerners continued publicly to defend slavery in significant numbers through the time of the Civil War. Britons in England and the West Indies also justified slavery throughout the eighteenth and early nineteenth centuries, and these arguments served as useful sources for American advocates of human bondage.[9]

This broadened chronology and geography of proslavery contains important implications for the understanding of the movement and of the Old

Bros., 1906); Clement Eaton, *The Growth of Southern Civilization, 1790–1860* (New York: Harper & Row, 1961).

7. See Tise, "Proslavery Ideology"; Larry Morrison, "The Proslavery Argument in the Early Republic, 1790–1830" (Ph.D. dissertation, University of Virginia, 1975); Robert McColley, *Slavery in Jeffersonian Virginia* (Urbana: University of Illinois Press, 1964); Frederika Teute Schmidt and Barbara Ripel Wilhelm, "Early Proslavery Petitions in Virginia," *William and Mary Quarterly*, 3rd. ser., XXX (1973), 133–46; Rena Vassar, "William Knox's Defense of Slavery [1768]," *Proceedings of the American Philosophical Society*, CXIV (1970), 310–26; Anne C. Loveland, "Richard Furman's 'Questions on Slavery,'" *Baptist History and Heritage*, X (1975), 177–81; Stephen J. Stein, "George Whitfield on Slavery: Some New Evidence," *Church History*, XLII (1973), 243–56; Joseph C. Burke, "The Proslavery Argument and the First Congress," *Duquesne Review*, XIV (1969), 3–15; Peter Joseph Albert, "The Protean Institution: The Geography, Economy, and Ideology of Slavery in Post-Revolutionary Virginia" (Ph.D. dissertation, University of Maryland, 1976). Winthrop Jordan also treats the early appearance of racist ideas in particular in *White over Black: American Attitudes Toward the Negro, 1550–1812* (Chapel Hill: University of North Carolina Press, 1968).

8. John Saffin, *A Brief and Candid Answer to a late printed sheet, entitled The Selling of Joseph. . . .* (Boston, n.p., 1701).

9. Many scholars have noted northern manifestations of proslavery thought, but this aspect of the argument has not been given much consideration in general treatments until recently. See Adelaide Avery Lyons, "The Religious Defense of Slavery in the North," *Trinity College Historical Society Papers*, XIII (1919), 5–34; Henry Clyde Hubbart, "Pro-Southern Influence in the Free West, 1840–1865," *Mississippi Valley Historical Review*, XX (1933), 45–62; Howard C. Perkins, "The Defense of Slavery in the Northern Press on the Eve of the Civil War," *Journal of Southern History*, IX (1943), 501–531; Joel H. Silbey, "Pro-Slavery Sentiment in Iowa, 1836–1861," *Iowa Journal of History*, LV (1957), 289–318; Larry Edward Tise, "The Interregional Appeal of Proslavery Thought: An Ideological Profile of the Antebellum American Clergy," *Plantation Society*, I (1979), 58–72. See Tise, "Proslavery Ideology," for discussion of the proslavery argument in Britain and the West Indies. For an interesting new comparative perspective, see Peter Kolchin, "In Defense of Servitude: American Proslavery and Russian Proserfdom Arguments, 1760–1860," *American Historical Review*, 85, No. 4 (October, 1980), 809–827.

South itself. Some scholars in the past have tended to regard the defense of slavery as a product of southern guilt, an effort by slaveholders to assuage consciences riddled with shame about violations of America's democratic creed. Recent attention to the colonial origins and wide extension of proslavery views suggests the existence of a strong alternative tradition of social and even moral legitimation upon which antebellum southerners might draw. Less philosophically and morally isolated than Charles Sellers and W. J. Cash would have us think, southerners may have felt far less guilty and ambivalent as well.[10]

But emphasis on the extensiveness of proslavery thought through time and space has not diminished scholarly interest in the role of the argument in the South during the last three decades of the antebellum period. Even historians insisting upon its early origins and wide diffusion recognize its increased significance in these years. During this era, the slavery controversy not only became a matter of survival for the southern way of life; it served for Americans generally as a means of reassessing the profoundest assumptions on which their world was built.

Although proslavery thought demonstrated remarkable consistency from the seventeenth century on, it became in the South of the 1830s, forties, and fifties more systematic and self-conscious; it took on the characteristics of a formal ideology with its resulting social movement. The intensification of proslavery argumentation produced an increase in conceptual organization and coherence within the treatises themselves, which sought methodically to enumerate all possible foundations for human bondage—"a *discussion on Slavery in all its bearings*," as one southern apologist explained, "in the lights of History, Political Economy, Moral Philosophy, Political Science, Theology, Social Life, Ethnology and International Law."[11] At the same time, more structured arrangements developed among the apologists and their publishers for the production and distribution of these tracts. South-

10. Wilbur J. Cash, *The Mind of the South* (New York: Alfred Knopf, 1941); Charles G. Sellers, Jr., "The Travail of Slavery," in Charles G. Sellers (ed.), *The Southerner as American* (Chapel Hill: University of North Carolina Press, 1960), 40–71. See also William W. Freehling, *Prelude to Civil War: The Nullification Controversy in South Carolina, 1816–1836* (New York: Harper and Row, 1966), and Ralph E. Morrow, "The Proslavery Argument Revisited," *Mississippi Valley Historical Review*, XLVII (1961), 79–94.

11. E. N. Elliott to James Henry Hammond, September 15, 1859, in Hammond Papers, Library of Congress. Elliott was the editor of *Cotton Is King and Pro-Slavery Arguments* (Augusta: Pritchard, Abbott & Loomis, 1860), a collection of proslavery classics.

erners united to call upon the region's finest minds for defenses of slavery, to discuss with one another the appropriate contents and goals for their writings, and to arrange their wide dissemination in newspapers, pamphlets, and even book-sized collections of previously printed favorites. One publisher explained his intention of producing an anthology of arguments on fine paper "fit to take its place in the Library or Drawing Room, and to serve as a Text Book on the subject, so that every one in our community may have at hand good strong arguments . . . coming in a respectable shape and in good style it will attract much more attention than if simply sent in pamphlet form." [12] The need for a vigorous southern publishing industry became particularly obvious as a result of these efforts to diffuse proslavery views, and the defense of the peculiar institution had an important impact upon southern letters. "We shall be indebted," one southern intellectual and proslavery essayist proclaimed, "to the continuance and asperity of this controversy for the creation of a genuine Southern literature. . . . For out of this slavery agitation has sprung not merely essays on slavery, valuable and suggestive as these have been, but also the literary activity, and the literary movement which have lately characterized the intellect of the South." [13]

Whereas earlier proslavery writers had attracted little attention, the South now rewarded her defenders with acclaim. Francis Lieber, a German emigré with little sympathy for the peculiar institution of his adopted South, remarked bitterly that "nothing would give me greater renown than a pamphlet written . . . in favor of slavery." [14] After a long and unrewarding career as an agricultural essayist, Edmund Ruffin found that "I have had more notice taken of my late pamphlet [on slavery] than of anything I ever wrote before." [15]

Current scholarship regards the change in southern writings about slavery in the 1830s as more one of style and tone than of substance. Southerners did not move from an anti- to a proslavery position. Slaveholders were

12. Joseph Walker to James Henry Hammond, May 20, 1848, in Hammond Papers, Library of Congress. Walker published *The Pro-Slavery Argument*, which the Charleston *Courier* (May 26, 1853) greeted as a "thesaurus of facts and arguments" on the slavery question.

13. George Frederick Holmes, "Bledsoe on Liberty and Slavery," *De Bow's Review*, XXI (1856), 133.

14. Francis Lieber, quoted in Daniel Walker Hollis, *University of South Carolina: South Carolina College* (Columbia: University of South Carolina Press, 1951), 183.

15. Edmund Ruffin, Diary, January 29, 1859, in Edmund Ruffin Papers, Library of Congress.

less troubled about *whether* slavery was right than precisely *why* it was right and how its justice could best be demonstrated. Unsympathetic to the Perfectionism embraced by many of their abolitionist counterparts, proslavery advocates always saw evils in slavery, as they were sure they would in any terrestrial system of society and government. All earthly arrangements, they believed, necessarily required men to cope as best they could with sin; it was the relative merits of social systems, their comparative success in dealing with inherent evil, that should be discussed. As William Harper explained in his *Memoir on Slavery*, "the condition of our whole existence is but to struggle with evils—to compare them—to choose between them, and so far as we can, to mitigate them. To say that there is evil in any institution, is only to say that it is human." With the intensification of the slavery controversy, however, apologists began to acknowledge the institution's shortcomings less openly and to consider only the positive aspects of the system. "I see great evils in slavery," George Fitzhugh confessed to a friend, "but I think in a controversial work I ought not to admit them." [16]

Antebellum southerners themselves recognized and justified their heightened involvement in slavery's defense in the years after 1830. In spite of "speculative doubts by which the slave-owners were troubled," a Virginian observed in 1856, "the general sentiment among them . . . had always tenaciously maintained the sanctity and inviolability of slavery, but they have not arrived at a clear comprehension of the reasons by which slavery is justified and proved to be right and expedient, without the aid of the . . . treatises which the controversy still raging has called forth." Southerners, Mississippian Henry Hughes agreed, could successfully defend slavery only when they learned "to give the reasons for it." "Few of our own people," a South Carolinian advocate similarly complained, "understand it in its philosophical and economical bearing." These explanations suggest, as historian Ralph Morrow argued in 1961, that proslavery writings were directed primarily at other southerners. "We think it hardly to be expected," one apologist candidly admitted in 1843, "that anything which can be said at this late date will at all diminish the wrongheaded fanaticism and perverse

---

16. William Harper, *Memoir on Slavery, read before the Society for the Advancement of Learning at its annual meeting in Columbia, 1837* (Charleston: James S. Burges, 1838), 8; George Fitzhugh to George Frederick Holmes, 1855, in George Frederick Holmes Papers, Manuscript Division, William R. Perkins Library, Duke University.

intolerance of the Northern abolitionists." Northern antislavery had progressed "past the cure of argument."[17]

This concern with the sources and impact of proslavery writing within the South has generated new interest in the authors of proslavery tracts and in the nature of their lives within the southern social order. The psychological "guiltomania" interpretations of Sellers and Cash represent one aspect of this trend. David Donald offered a somewhat different but related perspective, combining sociological with psychological explanation by exploring the particular social locations of a group of slavery's southern defenders. "All," he found, were "unhappy men." But their "personal problems" had a social dimension and were even a direct result of "their place in southern society." Frustrated by their own failure to rise to positions of prominence in the South, slavery's apologists sought to compensate for their relegation to the "fringes of society"; they "looked back with longing to an earlier day of the Republic when men like themselves—their own ancestors—had been leaders in the South."[18]

Since Donald presented his ideas in a brief 1970 presidential address to the Southern Historical Association, other scholars have inquired more closely into the biographical questions he raised. Larry Edward Tise associated proslavery with the clergy in a study of 275 proslavery ministers and explored as well the institutions and experiences that exposed these men to the Federalist influences so evident in their writings. Although Federalism as a political force disappeared well before the 1830s, many of its conservative principles and hierarchical social assumptions, Tise noted, were perpetuated in the proslavery argument. The relationship of proslavery and social role has also been examined by Drew Gilpin Faust, who has suggested that the argument served as a vehicle for expression of alienation by the South's neglected intellectuals. The logic by which these advocates justified the right of whites to hold blacks in bondage, she argued, inevitably implied the social superiority of intellectuals as well. In taking up the public defense of the peculiar institution, the southern thinker thus sought to advance his partic-

17. George Frederick Holmes, "Slavery and Freedom," 132; Henry Hughes, "New Duties of the South," *Southern Reveille*, November 18, 1854, clipping in Henry Hughes Scrapbook, Mississippi Department of Archives and History, Jackson, Mississippi. This quotation was kindly provided me by Bertram Wyatt-Brown. William J. Grayson, to James Henry Hammond, November 3, 1849, in Hammond Papers, Library of Congress; George Frederick Holmes, "On Slavery and Christianity," *Southern Quarterly Review*, III (1843), 252.
18. Donald, "The Proslavery Argument Reconsidered," 12, 11, 12.

ular values and to define for himself a respected social role within a culture known for its inhospitality to letters.[19]

These studies assumed a significant relationship between social role and the particular details of the ideology invoked to legitimate it, and consequently undertook to reassess the contents of proslavery thought in light of these new sociological concerns. William Sumner Jenkins' pioneering study of proslavery in 1935 had definitively classified and explored the most familiar species of arguments. As late as 1971, David Donald still found that "the substance of the proslavery argument has little interest." Nevertheless, changing conceptions about the relationship of society and ideology arising in part from the impact of Eugene Genovese's Marxism and in part from shifting concerns of intellectual history have prompted a renewed interest in the contents and symbolic structure of the arguments themselves and in the nature of their development in the three decades before the Civil War.[20]

Many scholars have long acknowledged Thomas Roderick Dew's *Review of the Debate in the Virginia Legislature* as a herald of this new post-1830 era in proslavery ideology. Prompted by legislative discussion of emancipation in the winter of 1831–32, Dew's essay sought to establish the impracticality of the antislavery sentiments that had swept the state after Nat Turner's slave uprising left more than sixty whites dead in Virginia's Southside. Dew himself proclaimed his argument to be a new departure in proslavery writing, and his pragmatic tone was to serve as the inspiration for the inductive mode of almost all proslavery tracts henceforth. Rejecting the deductive principles of the Lockean contractual social theory that had influ-

19. Tise, "Proslavery Ideology," and "The Interregional Appeal of Proslavery Thought." On proslavery clergy, see also Jack P. Maddex, Jr., "Proslavery Millennialism: Social Eschatology in Antebellum Southern Calvinism," *American Quarterly*, XXXI (1979), 46–62, and Jack P. Maddex, Jr., "'The Southern Apostasy' Revisited: The Significance of Proslavery Christianity," *Marxist Perspectives*, II (Fall, 1979), 132–41. See also Drew Gilpin Faust, "A Southern Stewardship: The Intellectual and the Proslavery Argument," *American Quarterly*, XXXI (1979), 63–80; Drew Gilpin Faust, *A Sacred Circle: The Dilemma of the Intellectual in the Old South, 1840–1860* (Baltimore: Johns Hopkins University Press, 1977).

20. Jenkins, *The Proslavery Argument in the Old South*; Donald, "The Proslavery Argument Reconsidered," 4; Eugene Genovese, *The World the Slaveholders Made: Two Essays in Interpretation* (New York: Pantheon, 1969), Genovese's concern with planter "hegemony" has focused fresh interest on ideology in the Old South. Other historians have been influenced by anthropological studies of belief systems to regard ideology in new ways. Anthropologist Clifford Geertz has been especially influential. In the realm of proslavery historiography specifically, see Tise, "Proslavery Ideology"; Faust, *A Sacred Circle*; Kenneth Greenberg, "Revolutionary Ideology and the Proslavery Argument: The Abolition of Slavery in Antebellum South Carolina," *Journal of Southern History*, XLII (1976), 365–84.

enced the Founding Fathers, Dew embraced the conservative organic view of social order that had been implicit in proslavery thought from its earliest beginnings. Social institutions and arrangements evolved slowly over time, he believed, and could not be beneficially altered by abrupt human intervention. Like the proslavery advocates that followed him, Dew called upon his audience to study society as it had existed through the ages and to derive social principles and bases for action from these empirical observations. Theoretical notions of equality could not controvert the striking differences in men's capacities evident to any impartial observer. Idealized conceptions of justice—such as those of the abolitionists—could never serve as reliable bases for social organization. It was all very well, Dew counseled his fellow Virginians, to admit the abstract evils of slavery, but the relative dangers of the alternatives—abolition with or without colonization—were far greater.[21]

Dew called upon southerners to recognize the implications of their own social order and to assume responsibility for it. "One generation," as historian Eugene Genovese has remarked about the South in the years after the Revolution, "might be able to oppose slavery and favor everything it made possible, but the next had to choose sides."[22] Dew was important because he demonstrated the implausibility of straddling the issue any longer, of maintaining the stance of relativism that many southerners had found so comfortable during the Revolutionary era and its aftermath. As antislavery sentiment began to strengthen in the years after the Missouri debates of 1818–20, it was impossible any longer to endeavor to reconcile the North to the existence of the peculiar institution by conceding slavery's shortcomings. Once the issue was joined, Dew proclaimed, the South must acknowledge her commitment to her way of life and come out firmly on the proslavery side; the South must recognize that her superficial flirtation with the Revolutionary ideology of liberty and equality could be no more than just that.

Although Dew inaugurated a new era in proslavery, a flood of defenses did not appear at once. Only when northern abolitionists in 1835 inundated the South with antislavery propaganda sent through the federal mails did

21. Thomas R. Dew, *Review of the Debate in the Virginia Legislature of 1831 and 1832* (Richmond: T. W. White, 1832). This essay was an expansion of "Abolition of Negro Slavery," *American Quarterly Review*, XII (1832), 189–265, and was later reprinted in *The Pro-Slavery Argument*, 287–490.
22. Genovese, *The World the Slaveholders Made*, 133.

southerners respond in force, exhibiting a new vehemence in their defenses of their way of life. The attack from the North made southern mobilization an immediate necessity, and latent proslavery feeling was quickly translated into action.

In the course of the next decade, slavery's apologists would, in their collective oeuvre, develop a comprehensive defense of the peculiar institution that invoked the most important sources of authority in their intellectual culture and associated slavery with the fundamental values of their civilization. Their specific arguments showed striking continuity with earlier proslavery positions, elaborating rather than contradicting existing writing. The defenses of slavery of this period were, in addition, remarkably consistent with one another. While one advocate might specialize in religious arguments and another in the details of political economy, most acknowledged, accepted, and sometimes repeated the conclusions of their fellow apologists. The high level of conformity within proslavery thought was not accidental. Consistency was seen as the mark of strength and the emblem of truth. "Earlier and later writers," the editor of a collection of proslavery classics remarked proudly in 1860, "stood on substantially the same ground, and take the same general views of the institution." [23]

To ensure this uniformity, slavery's apologists articulated a series of what we might regard as rules guiding the post-1835 proslavery movement. Endeavoring to avoid the "domain of sectional controversy and political warfare," the defenders of slavery sought broader arguments and wider appeal. [24] Basing their essays in "sober and cautious reflection" upon "purely scientific principles" with "no appeal to passion or to sordid interest," the South's proslavery theorists hoped to attract those who "wished for argument instead of abuse." Many of the South's apologists communicated with one another about their essays and ideas, so that the mature proslavery argument might well be seen as a community product. [25]

As a result of this group criticism and evaluation, there emerged what could be considered a proslavery mainstream. The Bible served as the core of this defense. In the face of abolitionist claims that slavery violated the

23. E. N. Elliott, "Introduction," in *Cotton Is King*, xii.
24. George Frederick Holmes, "The Failure of Free Societies," *Southern Literary Messenger*, XXI (1855), 129.
25. *Ibid.*; Albert Taylor Bledsoe, "Liberty and Slavery; or, Slavery in the Light of Political Philosophy," in *Cotton Is King*, 274; Charleston *Courier*, May 26, 1853. See chart of personal interactions among slavery's defenders in Faust, "A Southern Stewardship," 68.

principles of Christianity, southerners demonstrated with ever more elaborate detail that both Old and New Testaments sanctioned human bondage. God's Chosen People had been slaveholders; Christ had made no attack on the institution; his disciple Paul had demonstrated a commitment to maintaining it.[26]

But for an age increasingly enamored of the vocabulary and methods of natural science, biblical guidance was not enough. The accepted foundations for truth were changing in European and American thought, as intellectuals sought to apply the rigor of science to the study of society and morality, as well as the natural world. The proslavery argument accordingly called not only upon divine revelation, the traditional source and arbiter of truth, but sought at the same time to embrace the positivistic standards increasingly accepted for the assessment of all social problems. Man could and must, these authors contended, determine his social and moral duties scientifically, through the examination of God's will revealed in nature and in history. A subspecies of general social thought, the defense of slavery assumed the methods and arguments of broader social theories and reflected an intellectual perspective that in these years first began to regard "social science" as a discrete and legitimate domain of human learning. Reverend Thornton Stringfellow would devise a proslavery theory designed to be at once "Scriptural and Statistical"; George Fitzhugh would write a *Sociology for the South*; Henry Hughes's proslavery tract would appear in the guise of *A Treatise on Sociology* in which the author's striving for relevance and legitimacy beyond the confines of the Old South even led him to replace the term *slavery* with that of *warranteeism*.[27]

But most advocates did not go so far. Sociology was not yet the academic discipline it has since become; moral science—from which sociology would later emerge—still remained the central framework for social analysis in

26. A. B. Longstreet, *Letters on the Epistle of Paul to Philemon* (Charleston: B. Jenkins, 1845); Howell Cobb, *A Scriptural Examination of the Institution of Slavery in the United States* (Perry, Ga.: Printed for the author, 1856); Thornton Stringfellow, "The Bible Argument, or Slavery in the Light of Divine Revelation," in *Cotton Is King*, 461–546.

27. For the impact of the emergence of "social science" upon the career of one of slavery's defenders, see Neal C. Gillespie, *The Collapse of Orthodoxy: The Intellectual Ordeal of George Frederick Holmes* (Charlottesville: University of Virginia Press, 1972). See also H. G. and Winnie Leach Duncan, "The Development of Sociology in the Old South," *American Journal of Sociology*, XXXIX (1934), 649–56. Thornton Stringfellow, *Scriptural and Statistical Views in Favor of Slavery* (Richmond: J. W. Randolph, 1856); George Fitzhugh, *Sociology for the South or the Failure of Free Society* (Richmond: A. Morris, 1854); Henry Hughes, *Treatise on Sociology: Theoretical and Practical* (Philadelphia: Lippincott, Grambo & Co., 1854).

colleges and among the educated both North and South. Thus the mainstream of proslavery argument sought to imbed the peculiar institution within the legitimating context of nineteenth-century moral philosophy, with its emphasis on man's duties and responsibilities and its invocation of historical precedent as guide for future action.[28]

Turning to the past as a catalog of social experiments, slavery's defenders discovered that from the time of Greece and Rome, human bondage had produced the world's greatest civilizations. The peculiar institution, they argued, was not so very peculiar, but had provided the social foundation for man's greatest achievements. Moreover, the experience of the ages showed the fundamental principles of the American Revolution to be sadly misguided. Social law as revealed in history demonstrated that men had not in reality been created equal and free, as Jefferson had asserted; this was a mistaken view arising from erroneous modes of abstract and deductive thought. Nature produced individuals strikingly unequal in both qualities and circumstances. "Scientific" truths demonstrated through empirical study prescribed a hierarchically structured society reproducing nature's orderly differentiations. The Revolutionary concepts of natural law were thus replaced by the tenets of social organicism; the prestige of modern science served to legitimate tradition and conservatism in a manner that held implications far wider than the boundaries of the slavery controversy.[29]

Such an approach to social order stressed the importance of man's duties rather than his rights. And for rhetorical purposes, it was often the duties of masters, rather than those of slaves, that apologists chose to emphasize. Within the organic community of a slave society, they argued, the master could not ignore the human obligation to care for his bondsman. "Fed, clothed, protected," the slave was far better off, William J. Grayson proclaimed, than the northern factory worker whose employer had no interest in his health or even his survival. "Free but in name," northern laborers had liberty only to starve. As William Harper argued, there existed "some form

28. On the emergence of social science from moral philosophy, see Gladys Bryson, "The Emergence of Social Sciences from Moral Philosophy," *International Journal of Ethics*, XLII (1932), 304–323; on moral science, see Donald H. Meyer, *The Instructed Conscience: The Shaping of the American National Ethic* (Philadelphia: University of Pennsylvania Press, 1972).
29. See Thomas Cooper, "Slavery," *Southern Literary Journal*, I (1835), 188; James Henry Hammond, "Law of Nature—Natural Rights—Slavery," MS in Tucker-Coleman Papers, Manuscript Department, Earl Gregg Swem Memorial Library, College of William and Mary, Williamsburg, Virginia; J. P. Holcombe, "Is Slavery Consistent with Natural Law?" *Southern Literary Messenger*, XXVII (1858), 408.

of slavery in all ages and countries." [30] It was always necessary, Abel Upshur explained, "that one portion of mankind shall live upon the labor of another portion." Every civilization needed what James Henry Hammond dubbed a "mud-sill" class to do the menial labor of society. [31] The southern system of human bondage, they argued, simply organized this interdependence and inequality in accordance with principles of morality and Christianity.

The humanitarian arrangements of slavery, the southerners proclaimed, contrasted favorably with the avaricious materialism of the "miscalled" free society of the North. Whereas the Yankees cared only about the wealth that their operatives might produce, southerners accepted costly responsibility for the human beings whom God had "entrusted" to them. A number of defenders even maintained, like Harper, that "slave labor can never be so cheap as what is called free labor." Nevertheless, Hammond piously advised, slavery's moral purposes dictated that "we must . . . content ourselves with . . . the consoling reflection that what is lost to us is gained to humanity." The proslavery argument asserted its opposition to the growing materialism of the age and offered the model of evangelical stewardship as the best representation of its labor system. The master was God's surrogate on earth; the southern system institutionalized the Christian duties of charity in the master and humility in the slave. "You have been chosen," Nathaniel Beverley Tucker declared to his fellow slaveholders, "as the instrument, in the hand of God, for accomplishing the great purpose of his benevolence." [32] The nineteenth-century concern with philanthropy, defenders of slavery argued, was most successfully realized in the South's system of

30. William J. Grayson, "The Hireling and the Slave," in Eric L. McKitrick (ed.), *Slavery Defended: The Views of the Old South* (Englewood Cliffs, N.J.: Prentice-Hall, 1963), 66, 68. On the notion of rights and duties, see W. T. Hamilton, D.D., *The Duties of Masters and Slaves Respectively: Or Domestic Servitude as Sanctioned by the Bible* (Mobile: F. A. Brooks, 1845), and James Henley Thornwell, *The Rights and Duties of Masters: A Sermon Preached at the Dedication of a Church Erected in Charleston for the Benefit and Instruction of the Coloured Population* (Charleston: Walker and James, 1850). On social organicism, see Theodore Dwight Bozeman, "Joseph LeConte: Organic Science and a 'Sociology for the South,'" *Journal of Southern History*, XXXIX (1973), 565–82.

31. Abel P. Upshur, "Domestic Slavery," *Southern Literary Messenger*, V (1839), 685; James Henry Hammond, Speech in the Senate, March 4, 1858, *Congressional Globe*, 35th Cong., 1st Sess., App., 71.

32. Harper, "Slavery in the Light of Social Ethics," 569; Hammond, "Hammond's Letters," 122; Nathaniel Beverley Tucker, *A Series of Lectures on the Science of Government Intended to Prepare the Student for the Study of the Constitution of the United States* (Philadelphia: Carey and Hart, 1845), 349.

human bondage. Reflecting the lessons of human experience through the ages, as well as the prescriptions of both divine and natural order, slavery seemed unassailable. The truths of science, religion, and history united to offer proslavery southerners ready support for their position.

But by the 1850s, challenges to the unity of proslavery ideology had begun to appear. In large part, these emerging rifts mirrored wider intellectual currents. Forms of knowledge and legitimation long assumed to be necessarily compatible were everywhere displaying nagging contradictions. Most significant was an increasingly unavoidable conflict between the claims of science and those of the Scriptures. Rather than supporting and amplifying the truths of biblical revelation, science seemed to many midcentury thinkers already a threat to the conclusions of other modes of knowledge; challenges had begun to appear to the nineteenth century's holistic conception of truth.[33]

But in the proslavery argument, as in patterns of American thought more generally, these inconsistencies were to remain largely dormant; comparatively little overt strife between religion and science appeared before the Civil War, for most Americans voiced confidence that the achievement of greater understanding would eventually reveal an underlying compatibility. So, too, southerners defending slavery sought to minimize the impact of philosophical contradictions in order to maintain the strength that derived from proslavery unity. "There is no forked tongue in the language of learned men—whether physician or divine," one proslavery scientist insisted. "Truth is the same whether uttered by one or the other—the phraseology may differ but truth is an unit."[34]

By the end of the antebellum period, however, even those recognizing the necessity for unity and consistency sometimes found it difficult to make their views conform to the moral-philosophical mainstream of proslavery thought. The emergence of ethnology by the late 1840s as a recognized science of racial differences was to pose inevitable difficulties for the Fundamentalist bases on which the proslavery movement had been built. On the

---

33. On these changes, see Charles C. Gillespie, *Genesis and Geology* (Cambridge: Harvard University Press, 1951); Theodore Dwight Bozeman, *Protestants in an Age of Science: The Baconian Ideal and Antebellum American Religious Thought* (Chapel Hill: University of North Carolina Press, 1977); Charles E. Rosenberg, *No Other Gods: On Science and Social Thought in America* (Baltimore: Johns Hopkins University Press, 1976).

34. Samuel Cartwright to William S. Forwood, March 24, 1858, in William S. Forwood Papers, Trent Collection, Duke Medical Library, Duke University, Durham, North Carolina.

other hand, scientific validation of Negro inferiority offered an alluring and seemingly irrefutable argument to those favoring the social suborindation of blacks in slavery. "The mission of Ethnology," as one southern proponent declared, "is to vindicate the great truths on which the institutions of the South are founded."[35] Yet theories that urged the existence of two permanently separate and unequal races of men directly challenged Genesis and its assertion that all humans were descended from a single set of common parents. The dilemma implicit in this conflict of knowledge and values was neatly illustrated in the personal dilemma of Josiah Nott. A leading southern spokesman for racial science, he was anxious to deemphasize challenges to religious orthodoxy, yet equally desirous of establishing the validity of his own field. The pressure for unity in the proslavery movement influenced Nott to suppress overt antagonism toward religion, and as a result the Alabama physician dotted his writings with protestations of his devotion to sacred truth. "No one can have more positive distaste than myself for religious or any other controversy," Nott proclaimed, insisting that he used his "best efforts to avoid unpleasant collisions." Science and revealed religion, he asserted, would necessarily be consistent if their truths were properly ascertained. "The works of God form one great chain, of which revealed religion is but a link; and while the Bible, on one hand, has shed a flood of light on Ethnology, this in turn has afforded immense aid to Biblical criticism."[36]

Ultimately, however, Nott was unable to fulfill the expectations for conformity held by the proslavery mainstream. Irascible and somewhat belligerent, Nott translated a latent hostility toward religion in general into an open assault upon the clergy as the purveyors of false doctrines. While he piously proclaimed his devotion to revelation, he mercilessly attacked its clerical interpreters. Such a position, he thought, would offer the possibility of establishing scientific principles without directly undermining religion; conflicts between ethnology and the Bible could be reconciled without challenging the unity of all truth. Science and religion were consistent, he maintained, but ministers were clearly fallible and in challenging science misinterpreted the divine word.

For the most part, Nott's audience did not perceive his subtle distinction

---

35. Samuel Cartwright to William S. Forwood, February 13, 1861, in *ibid.*
36. Josiah C. Nott, *Two Lectures on the Connection Between the Biblical and Physical History of Man* (1849; reprint ed., New York: Negro Universities Press, 1969), 7, 14.

between anticlericalism and antireligionism. Nott provoked violent controversy, and clerical defenders of slavery moved to affirm the unity of the human race and of proslavery ideology by disproving his polygenist theories. To many, Nott seemed to be causing altogether unnecessary difficulties. He and his associate George Gliddon, one critic remarked, had "involved their cause with the discussion of the inspiration, authenticity, authorship & translation of Scripture, to such an extent that their work looks more like a labored attempt to annihilate that volume than to discuss mooted questions in ethnology." [37]

Most defenders of slavery sought to use the scientific prestige of ethnology to enhance their position without becoming ensnared by the difficulties it presented; they were eager to sidestep the problems Nott addressed head-on. George Frederick Holmes, long sympathetic to the notion of race as a major determinant of human civilization, nevertheless advised fellow southerners that the truths of ethnology remained "enveloped . . . in all the mist of obscurity. I should steer a cautious middle course between the extreme views on this subject." Edmund Ruffin found that despite great potential value, ethnology offered "more amusement than reliable information," and George Fitzhugh bluntly declared that if forced to choose between the Bible and ethnology, southerners had best stick to the Holy Writ. [38] Although most proslavery advocates did not admit the inherent conflict so openly, in practice they followed Fitzhugh's advice. Racial arguments had been a part of proslavery thought since its earliest manifestations in the colonial period. The impact of ethnology was chiefly to enlarge and systematize this facet of the argument and to offer a variety of skull measurements, geological and anthropological "facts" as incontrovertible evidence for the mainstream

37. S. W. Butler to W. S. Forwood, June 26, 1857, in Forwood Papers. Like many of Nott's nineteenth-century readers, William Stanton also failed to distinguish between Nott's anticlericalism and antireligionism and greatly overstated the level of conflict between religion and science in the 1850s. Nevertheless, Stanton's study of the rise of ethnology is the most complete to date. See *The Leopard's Spots: Scientific Attitudes Toward Race in America, 1815–1859* (Chicago: University of Chicago Press, 1960). For the attack upon Nott, see Moses Ashley Curtis, "The Unity of the Races," *Southern Quarterly Review,* VII (1845), 372–448, and John Bachman, *The Doctrine of the Unity of the Human Race Examined on the Principles of Science* (Charleston: C. Canning, 1850). Note that Bachman, a Lutheran clergyman, invoked the "principles of science."

38. George Frederick Holmes to Daniel Whitaker, September 25, 1844, in George Frederick Holmes Letterbook, Holmes Papers; Edmund Ruffin, January 10, 1864, in Diary, Ruffin Papers; George Fitzhugh, "Southern Thought," *De Bow's Review,* XXIII (1857), 347.

position. Nature was invoked to provide additional support for the moral justifications that remained the core of the proslavery argument.[39]

The intricacies of racial and ethnological arguments were not the only difficulties confronting the mainstream of proslavery thinkers. Conformity and unanimity within the movement were occasionally threatened by departures from the prescribed style, as well as the substance of proslavery tracts. In their effort to present the defense of slavery as a part of the transcendent truths of religion and science, many apologists believed that a tone of dispassionate inquiry was an absolute necessity. Polemics would injure rather than advance the ultimate goals of the proslavery cause. "Christian candor and fairness of argument," one apologist insisted, were the emblems of "the search after truth."[40] When Josiah Nott replied angrily to attacks upon his ethnological assertions, the *Southern Quarterly Review* was quick to chastise him, proclaiming the tone of his work "unfortunate."[41] But the most vigorous criticism from the proslavery mainstream was directed against

39. In a recent reassessment of proslavery thought, historian George Fredrickson has portrayed the role of racial defenses quite differently, proclaiming the existence of significant opposition between racial and moral-philosophical rationalizations for the South's system of human bondage. Instead of proslavery unity, he found two distinct proslavery arguments, one in the aristocratic seaboard South and one in the more democratic Southwest. These latter egalitarian areas, he asserted, were unsympathetic to the hierarchical views of slavery's moral-philosophical defenders; racial arguments could provide the only convincing foundation for human bondage within the Old Southwest's "herrenvolk democracy." There is little evidence for these geographical differences in proslavery sentiment. A best-selling collection of defenses of slavery edited by E. N. Elliott of Mississippi included the most famous hierarchical arguments and emphasized the consistency of all proslavery thought; eastern apologists devoted considerable attention to racial justifications in their own tracts; seaboard and southwestern defenders exchanged pamphlets and essays and eagerly sought each other's advice. Fredrickson may err in regarding the mainstream proslavery position as uncongenial to the more democratic Southwest. As early as 1936, William B. Hesseltine made a convincing case that proslavery was motivated in large part by a desire to promote the loyalty of nonslaveholding whites, and he contended that all proslavery theories were designed to be attractive to these common folk. Even though the arguments "carried but little promise to the lower classes," he remarked, they "sufficed to draw a line of demarkation between the exploited groups of the South." The complex factors that kept the southern yeoman loyal to the region's master class may also have attracted them to the proslavery argument. Slavery, its defenders insisted, made republicanism and white freedom possible. Because blacks served as the necessary "mud-sill" class, whites all enjoyed enhanced liberty. George M. Fredrickson, *The Black Image in the White Mind: The Debate on Afro-American Character and Destiny, 1817–1914* (New York: Harper and Row, 1971); William B. Hesseltine, "Some New Aspects of the Pro-Slavery Argument," 11. On the position of the yeoman, see Eugene Genovese, "Yeoman Farmers in a Slaveholders Democracy," *Agricultural History*, XLIX (1975), 331–42.
40. E. N. Elliott, "Concluding Remarks," in *Cotton Is King*, 897.
41. "Critical Notices," *Southern Quarterly Review*, XVI (1849), 265.

George Fitzhugh, whose "extravagant heresies" sparked an outburst of protests from other apologists.[42]

A Virginian who began publishing well after the main lines of proslavery theory had been defined, Fitzhugh proclaimed himself the first true defender of slavery, the first to have "vindicated slavery in the abstract." He was the only southerner vigorously to advocate slavery as the most desirable arrangement for white as well as black labor, and the only apologist to transform the discussion of slavery into an unremitting attack on free labor and capital. But while presented in extreme form, his arguments were basically derived from those of the theorists who had preceded him and had been developing a general defense of slavery for decades. Fitzhugh's assault upon northern and British wage slavery and his discussion of the sorry plight of free workers, for example, had been a popular argument since Robert Walsh's comparison of southern slavery and European free labor in 1819. But it was Fitzhugh's outspoken tone and aggressive style that drew even more attention than the substance of his essays. His contemporaries regarded him as something of a crackpot.[43]

Fitzhugh candidly acknowledged that his involvement in proslavery was far from dispassionate or disinterested. "Confessing myself the greatest egoist in the world," Fitzhugh hoped to attract attention and promote book sales by self-consciously making his work "odd, eccentric, extravagant, and disorderly."[44] Southerners reviewing his books deplored their "utter recklessness of both statement and expression." George Frederick Holmes, whom Fitzhugh admired as the proslavery advocate with views closest to his own, found his discussions "incendiary and dangerous," and Edmund Ruffin pronounced Fitzhugh's views "absurd."[45]

Never included in the anthologies of proslavery classics of his own era, Fitzhugh's work has been often reprinted in ours, and he has attracted lavish attention from present-day historians. This modern interest in Fitzhugh may in part be a result of his very unrepresentativeness. In their perception

42. Holmes, "Slavery and Freedom," 65.
43. George Fitzhugh to George Frederick Holmes, March 27, 1855, in Holmes Papers; Robert Walsh, *An Appeal from the Judgments of Great Britain Respecting the United States of America* (Philadelphia: Mitchell, Ames and White, 1819).
44. George Fitzhugh to George Frederick Holmes, 1855, in Holmes Papers.
45. George Frederick Holmes, February 21, 1857, in Diary, Holmes Papers; Edmund Ruffin, October 26, 1858, in Diary, Ruffin Papers.

of the proslavery argument as aberrant and "astonishing,"[46] historians have turned to its most extreme, provocative, and even outrageous presentation. Many politically motivated northerners of the mid-nineteenth century chose a similar course, pointing to Fitzhugh's arguments as proof of the impassable gulf separating North and South. There is even evidence that Abraham Lincoln himself turned to Fitzhugh's writing for the portrait of intersectional opposition that led him to conclude that the nation was a "house divided."[47] It was much easier for nineteenth-century northerners, as it is for modern Americans as well, to discount an argument that is "odd, extravagant and disorderly" than to confront the ways in which the mainstream proslavery position drew upon basic values of Western civilization shared by the North and the South to justify human bondage.

Yet Eugene Genovese has argued persuasively for Fitzhugh's importance as a "ruthless and critical theorist who spelled out the logical outcome of slaveholders' philosophy and laid bare its essence."[48] Fitzhugh's attacks upon capitalism and free labor, he has asserted, were necessary corollaries to the defense of slavery. Because Fitzhugh was extreme, he was able to articulate the unspoken—and even unrecognized—assumptions on which proslavery rested.

Genovese was careful not to argue for Fitzhugh's representativeness. Indeed, other southerners and other proslavery advocates endeavored to refute what Genovese has called the "logical outcome" of their own philosophy. As they sought to avoid the implicit conflicts of religion and ethnology, so too they eschewed Fitzhugh's all-out attack upon civilization as it was developing in the nineteenth-century capitalist West. Fitzhugh's "opposition to interest or capital" one defender summarily dismissed as "foolish."[49] In hoping to save southern civilization as they knew it, southerners sought to perpetuate rather than resolve the inconsistencies between their prebourgeois labor system and the bourgeois world market in which it flourished.

---

46. Donald, "The Proslavery Argument Reconsidered," 3.

47. Arthur C. Cole presents evidence for the direct influence of Fitzhugh on Lincoln's "house divided" speech. See Cole, *Lincoln's House Divided Speech* (Chicago: University of Chicago Press, 1923).

48. Genovese, *The World the Slaveholders Made*, 129. Part of Genovese's attraction to Fitzhugh arises, of course, from the hostility to capitalism that this Marxist historian shares with the nineteenth-century southerner.

49. Edmund Ruffin, October 21, 1858, in Diary, Ruffin Papers.

The mainstream of the South's defenders had to dissociate themselves from Fitzhugh, for he showed them to be caught in a paradox at a time when they could ill afford the luxury of the self-examination and questioning necessary for its resolution. Yet this was a paradox that did not envelop the South alone. The paternalism of much of the North's industry, the ideas of evangelical stewardship underlying its widespread reform movements, indeed the strength of northern proslavery sentiment itself bespoke the existence of a similar conflict above the Mason-Dixon line between antimaterialist, prebourgeois values and the "cash-nexus" at the center of the modern civilization fast emerging.[50] The paradoxes that the proslavery argument encountered and unwittingly exposed—conflicts of tradition and modernity, of human and material values, of science with religion—were but further evidence of the argument's centrality within nineteenth-century American culture. These were problems in social philosophy and values confronting all Americans of this era, and unassailable solutions were as scarce in the North as in the South.

While we can continue to abhor the system of human bondage that flourished in the Old South, there is much we can learn from a more dispassionate examination of the arguments used to defend it. We have sought to distance the slaveholders and their creed, to define them as very unlike ourselves. Yet their processes of rationalization and self-justification were not so very different from our own, or from those of any civilization of human actors. The persistence of modern racism is but one forceful reminder of the ways that human beings always view the world in terms of inherited systems of belief and explanation that only partially reflect the reality they are meant to describe. By understanding how others have fashioned and maintained their systems of meaning, we shall be better equipped to evaluate, criticize, and perhaps even change our own.

50. The nature of this conflict between tradition and modernity has been a central concern in the extensive historical literature on the nineteenth-century North, and especially on evangelicalism and reform. For two examples, see Marvin Meyers, *The Jacksonian Persuasion* (Stanford: Stanford University Press, 1960), and Clifford S. Griffin, *Their Brothers Keepers: Moral Stewardship in the United States, 1800–1865* (New Brunswick: RutgersUniversity Press, 1960).

I. THOMAS RODERICK DEW
Abolition of Negro Slavery

"The seal has now been broken. . . ."

Thomas Roderick Dew was born in 1802 in Tidewater Virginia to a plantation-owning family that had been in America since the mid-seventeenth century. In 1818, he enrolled at the College of William and Mary, where he quickly rose to the top of his class. Dew continued through the M.A. degree, then departed for Europe in 1824 in an effort to improve his failing health. Upon his return to Virginia in 1826, he was made a professor of political law at his alma mater, where he taught history, political economy, law, and the philosophy of the human mind. Dew was deeply concerned with political and social questions and published essays on internal improvements, usury law, the tariff, and the proper relation of the sexes. In 1831 he served as a delegate to a Philadelphia Free Trade Convention, where he met such champions of southern rights as William Harper, who, like Dew, became a prominent defender of slavery.[1]

When Nat Turner's rebellion frightened the Virginia legislature into a heated debate over emancipation in 1831–32, Dew, as a slaveholder, intellectual, and social commentator, took up his pen to respond. His *Review of the Debate in the Virginia Legislature of 1831–2* was widely acclaimed and thenceforth recognized as an overture to the outpouring of proslavery writings that followed in the three decades after its publication. Dew was rewarded by his fellow Virginians with the presidency of William and Mary in

1. Information on Dew's life is available in the Dew Family Papers, Manuscript Division, Earl Gregg Swem Memorial Library, College of William and Mary, Williamsburg, Virginia; Stephen S. Mansfield, "Thomas Roderick Dew: Defender of the Southern Faith" (Ph.D. dissertation, University of Virginia, 1968). See also H. Marshall Booker, "Thomas Roderick Dew: Forgotten Virginian," *Virginia Cavalcade*, XIX (1969), 20–29; James C. Hite and Ellen J. Hall, "The Reactionary Evolution of Economic Thought in Antebellum Virginia," *Virginia Magazine of History and Biography*, LXXX (1972), 476–88; and Alison Harrison Goodyear Freehling, "Drift Toward Dissolution: The Virginia Slavery Debate of 1831–1832" (Ph.D. dissertation, University of Michigan, 1974).

1836. For the remaining decade of his life, he continued his work as a scholar and public essayist. In 1846, Dew died on his honeymoon trip to Paris.

The essay below, which appeared in the *American Quarterly Review* of September, 1832, under the title "Abolition of Negro Slavery," was the first published version of what was to become Dew's classic work.[2] A few months later, the essay was reprinted in an expanded pamphlet form.[3] Because the Virginia legislative debate had itself attracted so much public attention, excerpts from Dew's work were widely reprinted throughout the South. As a result, his pamphlet had an impact never achieved by earlier defenders of slavery. Even two decades later, the essay still seemed of sufficient importance to merit inclusion in a collection of classic defenses of slavery, *The Pro-Slavery Argument as Maintained by the Most Distinguished Writers of the Southern States.*[4]

Notable as the inaugural effort in the post-1830 proslavery movement, the version below demonstrated a new depth of commitment to slavery. In its insistence that emancipation and colonization were impossible, it brought widespread attention throughout the region to a position previously enunciated by only a few southerners.[5] Yet at the same time, it was a traditional work, for it concentrated on the immediate situation of the South, and of Virginia particularly, to a far greater extent than would later writings. Moreover, Dew seemed uncertain whether to accept or to challenge the notion of slavery as an evil that ought ultimately to be eradicated, and he therefore alternated between the two positions in the course of his essay. His own preference seems to have been that the Virginia economy develop naturally in such a way as to attract free labor and thus render slav-

2. Thomas R. Dew, "Abolition of Negro Slavery," *American Quarterly Review*, XII (1832), 189–265.

3. Thomas R. Dew, *Review of the Debate in the Virginia Legislature of 1831 and 1832* (Richmond: T. W. White, 1832). See Kenneth M. Stampp, "An Analysis of Thomas R. Dew's *Review of the Debate in the Virginia Legislature,*" *Journal of Negro History*, XXVII (1942), 380–87.

4. *The Pro-Slavery Argument as Maintained by the Most Distinguished Writers of the Southern States* (Charleston: Walker, Richards & Co., 1852), 287–490.

5. These were generally from Deep South states. See, for example, Whitemarsh Seabrook, *A Concise View of the Critical Situation and Future Prospects of the Slave-Holding States, in Relation to their Colored Population* (Charleston: A. E. Miller, 1825), and Thomas Cooper, *Two Essays: 1) On the Foundation of Civil Government 2) On the Constitution of the United States* (Columbia: D. and J. M. Faust, 1826).

ery no longer necessary. But the essay never directly addressed the possibility of an ultimate withering away of the peculiar institution. Dew's attitude toward the doctrines of natural rights was equally confused. While basically affirming the Revolutionary heritage, he nevertheless sought to curtail the legitimate right of rebellion, thus manifesting the South's growing disenchantment with the legacy of the Founding Fathers. Political economist at heart, the Virginian dwelt more on the rights of property as justification for human bondage than would his followers, who turned increasingly to what they saw as the disinterested and therefore nobler rationalizations of moral stewardship. Subsequent versions of this essay themselves reflected the rapid development and change within proslavery thought toward a more broad-gauged and confident stand. Like his successors in the proslavery movement, Dew would devote more attention to transcendent justifications for human bondage by appealing beyond the exigencies confronting the South to more general—and, he hoped, more compelling—systems of legitimation, such as religion, moral philosophy, and the sciences of both the natural and social world.[6]

Abolition of Negro Slavery.

In looking to the texture of the population of our country, there is nothing so well calculated to arrest the attention of the observer as the existence of negro slavery throughout a large portion of the confederacy; a race of people differing from us in colour and in habits, and vastly inferior in the scale of civilization, have been increasing and spreading—"growing with our growth and strengthening with our strength"—until they have become intertwined with every fibre of society. Go through our southern states, and every where you see the negro slave by the side of the white man, you find him alike in the mansion of the rich, the cabin of the poor, the workshop of the mechanic, and the field of the planter. Upon the contemplation of a population framed like this, a curious and interesting ques-

6. In later versions, what appears here as the last section, "Injustice and Evils of Slavery," was expanded and placed in a more prominent position. This was, of course, the portion dealing with biblical and other general justifications of slavery beyond the specific Virginia situation.

tion readily suggests itself to the inquiring mind. Can these two distinct races of people, now living together as master and servant, be ever separated? Can the black be sent back to his African home? or will the day ever arrive when he can be liberated from this thraldom, and mount in the scale of civilization and rights to an equality with the white? This is a question of truly momentous character: it involves the whole framework of society, contemplates a separation of its elements, or a radical change in their relation, and requires for its adequate investigation the most complete and profound knowledge of the nature and sources of national wealth and political aggrandizement, an acquaintance with the elastic and powerful spring of population, and the causes which invigorate or paralyze its energies. It requires a clear perception of the varying rights of man amid all the changing circumstances by which he may be surrounded, and a profound knowledge of all the principles, passions, and susceptibilities, which make up the moral nature of our species, and according as they are acted upon by adventitious circumstances, alter our condition, and produce all that wonderful variety of character which so strongly marks and characterizes the human family. Well, then, does it behoove even the wisest statesman to approach this august subject with the utmost circumspection and diffidence; its wanton agitation even is pregnant with mischief, but rash and hasty action threatens, in our opinion, the whole southern country with irremediable ruin. The evil of *yesterday's* growth may be extirpated *to-day*, and the vigour of society may heal the wound; but that which is the growth of *ages* may require *ages* to remove. The Parliament of Great Britain, with all its philanthropic zeal, guided by the wisdom and eloquence of such statesmen as Chatham, Fox, Burke, Pitt, Canning, and Brougham, has never yet seriously agitated this question, in regard to the West India possessions. Revolutionary France, actuated by the most intemperate and phrenetic zeal for liberty and equality, attempted to legislate the free people of colour in the Island of St. Domingo into all the rights and privileges of the whites; and but a season afterwards, convinced of her madness, she attempted to retrace her steps, when it was too late; the deed had been done, the bloodiest and most shocking insurrection ever recorded in the annals of history had broken out, and the whole island was involved in frightful carnage and anarchy, and France in the end has been stript of "the brightest jewel in her crown,"—the fairest and most valuable of all her colonial possessions. Since the revolution, France, Spain, and Portugal, large owners of colonial possessions, have not only not abol-

24

ished slavery in their colonies, but have not even abolished the slave trade in practice.

In our southern slave-holding country, the question of emancipation had never been seriously discussed in any of our legislatures, until the whole subject, under the most exciting circumstances, was, during the last winter, brought up for discussion in the Virginia legislature, and plans of partial or total abolition were earnestly pressed upon the attention of that body. It is well known, that during the last summer, in the county of Southampton in Virginia, a few slaves, led on by Nat Turner, rose in the night, and murdered in the most inhuman and shocking manner between sixty and seventy of the unsuspecting whites of that county. The news of course was rapidly diffused, and with it consternation and dismay were spread throughout the state, destroying for a time all feeling of security and confidence, and even when subsequent development had proven, that the conspiracy had originated with a fanatic negro preacher, (whose confessions prove beyond a doubt mental aberration,) and that this conspiracy embraced but few slaves, all of whom had paid the penalty of their crimes, still the excitement remained, still the repose of the commonwealth was disturbed, for the ghastly horrors of the Southampton tragedy could not immediately be banished from the mind. *Rumour*, with her thousand tongues, was busily engaged in spreading tales of disaffection, plots, insurrections, and even massacres, which frightened the timid, and harassed and mortified the whole of the slave-holding population. During this period of excitement, when reason was almost banished from the mind, and the imagination was suffered to conjure up the most appalling phantoms, and picture to itself a crisis in the vista of futurity, when the overwhelming numbers of the blacks would rise superior to all restraint, and involve the finest portion of our land in universal ruin and desolation, we are not to wonder that even in the lower part of Virginia many should have seriously inquired, if this supposed monstrous evil could not be removed from her bosom. Some looked to the removal of the free people of colour, by the efforts of the Colonization Society, as an antidote to all our ills; some were disposed to strike at the root of the evil, to call on the general government for aid, and by the labours of *Hercules* to extirpate the curse of slavery from the land; and others again, who could not bear that Virginia should stand towards the general government (whose unconstitutional action she had ever been foremost to resist) in the attitude of a suppliant, looked forward to the legislative action of the state as capa-

25

ble of achieving the desired result. In this degree of excitement and apprehension, the legislature met, and plans for abolition were proposed and earnestly advocated in debate.

Upon the impropriety of this debate we beg leave to make a few observations. Any scheme of abolition proposed so soon after the Southampton tragedy, would necessarily appear to be the result of that most inhuman massacre. Suppose the negroes, then, to be really anxious for their emancipation, no matter on what terms, would not the extraordinary effect produced on the legislature by the Southampton insurrection, in all probability have a tendency to excite another? And we must recollect, from the nature of things, no plan of abolition could act suddenly on the whole mass of slave population in the state. . . . Waiting, then, one year or more until the excitement could be allayed, and the empire of reason could once more have been established, would surely have been productive of no injurious consequences, and in the mean time a legislature could have been selected which would much better have represented the views and wishes of their constituents on this vital question. Virginia could have ascertained the sentiments and wishes of other slave-holding states, whose concurrence, if not absolutely necessary, might be highly desirable, and should have been sought after and attended to, at least as a matter of state courtesy. Added to this, the texture of the legislature was not of that character calculated to ensure the confidence of the people in a movement of this kind. If ever there was a question debated in a deliberative body, which called for the most exalted talent, the longest and most tried experience, the utmost circumspection and caution, a complete exemption from prejudice and undue excitement where both are apt to prevail, an ardent and patriotic desire to advance the vital interests of the state, uncombined with all mere desire for vain and ostentatious display, and with no view to party or geographical divisions, that question was the question of the *abolition* of *slavery* in the Virginia legislature. "*Grave* and *reverend* seniors," "the very fathers of the republic," were indeed required for the settlement of one of such magnitude. It appears, however, that the legislature was composed of an unusual number of young and inexperienced members, elected in the month of April previous to the Southampton massacre, and at a time of profound tranquillity and repose, when of course the people were not disposed to call from their retirement their most distinguished and experienced citizens.

We are very ready to admit, that in point of ability and eloquence, the

26

debate transcended our expectations. One of the leading political papers in the state remarked—"We have never heard any debate so eloquent, so sustained, and in which so great a number of speakers had appeared, and commanded the attention of so numerous and intelligent an audience. Day after day multitudes throng to the capital, and have been compensated by eloquence which would have illustrated Rome or Athens." But however fine might have been the rhetorical display, however ably some isolated points might have been discussed, still we affirm, with confidence, that no enlarged, wise, and practical plan of operations, was proposed by the abolitionists. We will go further, and assert that their arguments, in most cases, were of a wild and intemperate character, based upon false principles, and assumptions of the most vicious and alarming kind, subversive of the rights of property and the order and tranquillity of society, and portending to the whole slave-holding country—if they ever shall be followed out in practice—inevitable and ruinous consequences. Far be it, however, from us, to accuse the abolitionists in the Virginia legislature of any settled malevolent design to overturn or convulse the fabric of society. We have no doubt that they were acting conscientiously for the best; but it often happens that frail imperfect man, in the too ardent and confident pursuit of imaginary good, runs upon his utter destruction.

We have not formed our opinion lightly upon this subject; we have given to the vital question of abolition the most mature and intense consideration which we are capable of bestowing, and we have come to the conclusion—a conclusion which seems to be sustained by facts and reasoning as irresistible as the demonstration of the mathematician—that every plan of emancipation and deportation which we can possibly conceive, is *totally* impracticable. We shall endeavour to prove, that the attempt to execute these plans can only have a tendency to increase all the evils of which we complain, as resulting from slavery. If this be true, then the great question of abolition will necessarily be reduced to the question of emancipation, with a permission to remain, which we think can easily be shown to be subversive of the interests, security, and happiness, of both the blacks and whites, and consequently hostile to every principle of expediency, morality, and religion. We have heretofore doubted the propriety even of too frequently agitating, especially in a public manner, the questions of abolition, in consequence of the injurious effects which might be produced on the slave population. But the Virginia legislature, in its zeal for discussion, boldly set aside all prudential considerations of this kind, and openly and publicly debated the subject before the whole world. The seal has now been broken, the example has been set from a high quarter; we shall, therefore, waive all considerations of a prudential character which have heretofore restrained us, and boldly grapple with the abolitionists on this great question. We fear not the result, so far as truth, justice, and expediency alone are concerned. But we must be permitted to say, that we do most deeply dread the effects of misguided philanthropy, and the intrusion, in this matter, of those who have no interest at stake, and who have not that intimate and minute knowledge of the whole subject so absolutely necessary to wise action.

In our study, we began the examination of this subject with a general inquiry into the origin of slavery in ancient and modern times, and proceeded to a consideration of the slave trade, by which slavery has been introduced into the United States. We indicated the true sources of slavery, and the principles upon which it rests, in order that the value of those arguments founded on the maxims that "all men are born equal," that "slavery in the abstract is wrong," that "the slave has a natural right to regain his liberty," and so forth, might be fully appreciated. We endeavoured to show that those maxims may be and generally are inapplicable and mischievous, and that something else is requisite to convert slavery into freedom, than the mere enunciation of abstract truths divested of all adventitious circumstances and relations. But this first principal division of our subject proved so voluminous that we have been obliged to set it aside for the present, in order to obtain room for the more pressing and important topics of the great question which we undertook to treat. Upon these we enter, therefore, at once, and inquire seriously and fairly whether there be means by which our country may get rid of negro slavery.

Plans for the Abolition of Slavery.

Under this head we will consider, first, those schemes which propose abolition and deportation, and secondly, those which contemplate emancipation without deportation. 1st. In the late Virginia legislature, where the subject of slavery underwent the most thorough discussion, all seemed to be perfectly agreed in the necessity of removal in case of emancipation. Several members from the lower counties, which are deeply interested in this question, seemed to be sanguine in their anticipations of the final success of some project of emancipation and deportation to Africa, the original home of the negro. "Let us translate them," said one of the most respected and able members of the Legislature, (Gen. Broadnax,) "to those realms from which, in evil times, under inauspicious influences, their fathers were unfortunately abducted.—Mr. Speaker, the idea of restoring these people to the region in which nature had planted them, and to whose climate she had fitted their constitutions—the idea of benefiting not only our condition and their condition by the removal, but making them the means of carrying back to a great continent, lost in the profoundest depths of savage barbarity, unconscious of the existence even of the God who created them, not only the arts and comforts and multiplied advantages of civilized life, but what is of more value than all, a knowledge of true religion—intelligence of a Redeemer—is one of the grandest and noblest, one of the most expansive and glorious ideas which ever entered into the imagination of man. The conception, whether to the philosopher, the statesman, the philanthropist, or the Christian, of rearing up a colony which is to be the nucleus around which future emigration will concenter, and open all Africa to civilization and commerce, and science and arts and religion—when Ethiopia shall stretch out her hands, indeed, is one which warms the heart with delight." (*Speech of Gen. Broadnax of Dinwiddie*, pp. 36 and 37.) We fear that this splendid vision, the creation of a brilliant imagination, influenced by the pure feelings of a philanthropic and generous heart, is destined to vanish at the severe touch of analysis. Fortunately for reason and common sense, all these projects of deportation may be subjected to the most rigid and accurate calculations, which are amply sufficient to dispel all doubt, even in the minds of the most sanguine, as to their practicability.

We take it for granted that the right of the owner to his slave is to be respected, and consequently that he is not required to emancipate him, unless his full value is paid by the state. Let us then, keeping this in view, proceed to the very simple calculation of the expense of emancipation and deportation in Virginia. The slaves, by the last census (1830) amounted within a small fraction to 470,000; the average value of each one of these is $200; consequently the whole aggregate value of the slave population of Virginia in 1830, was $94,000,000, and allowing for the increase since, we cannot err far in putting the present value at $100,000,000. The assessed value of all the houses and lands in the state amounts to $206,000,000, and these constitute the material items in the wealth of the state, the whole personal property besides bearing but a very small proportion to the value of slaves, lands, and houses. Now, do not these very simple statistics speak volumes upon this subject? It is gravely recommended to the state of Virginia to give up a species of property which constitutes nearly one-third of the wealth of the whole state, and almost one-half of that of Lower Virginia, and with the remaining two-thirds to encounter the additional enormous expense of transportation and colonization on the coast of Africa. But the loss of $100,000,000 of property is scarcely the half of what Virginia would lose, if the immutable laws of nature could suffer (as fortunately they cannot) this tremendous scheme of colonization to be carried into full effect. Is it not population which makes our lands and houses valuable? Why are lots in Paris and London worth more than the silver dollars which it might take to cover them? Why are lands of equal fertility in England and France worth more than those of our Northern States, and those again worth more than Southern soils, and those in turn worth more than the soils of the distant West? It is the presence or absence of population which alone can explain the fact. It is in truth the slave labour in Virginia which gives value to her soil and her habitations—take away this and you pull down the atlas that upholds the whole system—eject from the state the whole slave population, and we risk nothing in the prediction, that on the day in which it shall be accomplished, the worn soils of Virginia will not bear the paltry price of the government lands in the West, and the Old Dominion will be a "waste howling wilderness,"—"the grass shall be seen growing in the streets, and the foxes peeping from their holes."

But the favourers of this scheme say they do not contend for the sudden emancipation and deportation of the whole black population;—they would send off only the increase, and thereby keep down the population to its present amount, while the whites increasing at their usual rate would finally become relatively so numerous as to render the presence of the blacks among us for ever afterwards entirely harmless. This scheme, which at first to the unreflecting seems plausible, and much less wild than the project of sending off the whole, is nevertheless impracticable and visionary, as we think a few remarks will prove. It is computed that the annual increase of the slaves and free coloured population of Virginia is about six thousand. Let us first, then, make a calculation of the expense of purchase and transportation. At $200 each, the six thousand will amount in value to $1,200,000. At $30 each, for transportation, which we shall soon see is too little, we have the whole expense of purchase and transportation

$1,380,000, an expense to be annually incurred by Virginia to keep down her black population to its present amount. And let us ask, is there any one who can seriously argue that Virginia can incur such an annual expense as this for the next twenty-five or fifty years, until the whites have multiplied so greatly upon the blacks, as in the *opinion* of the *alarmists* for ever to quiet the fears of the community? Vain and delusive hope, if any was ever wild enough to entertain it! . . .

But this does not develop to its full extent the monstrous absurdity of this scheme. There is a view of it yet to be taken, which seems not to have struck very forcibly any of the speakers in the Virginia legislature, but which appears to us of itself perfectly conclusive against this whole project. We have made some efforts to obtain something like an accurate account of the number of negroes every year carried out of Virginia to the south and southwest. We have not been enabled to succeed completely; but from all the information we can obtain, we have no hesitation in saying, that upwards of six thousand are yearly exported to other states. Virginia is in fact a *negro* raising state for other states; she produces enough for her own supply and six thousand for sale. Now, suppose the government of Virginia enters the slave market, resolved to purchase six thousand for emancipation and deportation, is it not evident that it must overbid the southern seeker, and thus take the very slaves who would have gone to the south? The very first operation then of this scheme, provided slaves be treated as property, is to arrest the current which has been hitherto flowing to the south, and to accumulate the evil in the state. As sure as the moon in her transit over the meridian arrests the current which is gliding to the ocean, so sure will the action of the Virginia government, in an attempt to emancipate and send off 6000 slaves, stop those who are annually going out of the state; and when 6000 are sent off in any one year, (which we never expect to see) it will be found on investigation that they are those who would have been sent out of the state by the operation of our slave trade, and to the utter astonishment and confusion of our abolitionists, the black population will be found advancing with its usual rapidity—the only operation of the scheme being to substitute our government, *alias ourselves*, as purchasers, instead of the planters of the south. This is a view which every legislator in the state should take. He should beware lest in his zeal for action, this efflux, which is now so salutary to the state, and such an abundant source of wealth, be suddenly dried up, and all the evils of slavery be increased instead of diminished. If government really could enter with capital and zeal enough into the boundless project, we might even in a few years see the laws of nature reversed, and the tide of slavery flowing from the south into Virginia, to satisfy the philanthropic demand for colonization. The only means which the government could use to prevent the above described effect, would be either arbitrarily to fix the price of slaves below their market value, which would be a clear violation of the right of property, (which we shall presently notice,) or to excite a feeling of insecurity and apprehension as to this kind of property, and thus dispose the owner to part with it at less than its true value:— but surely no statesman would openly avow such an object, although it must be confessed that some of the speakers even who contended that slaves should ever be treated as property, avowed sentiments which were well calculated to produce such a result.

It is said, however, that the southern market will at all events be closed against us, and consequently that the preceding argument falls to the ground. To this we answer, that as long as the demand to the south exists, the supply will be furnished in some way or other, if our government do not unwisely tamper with the subject. Bryan Edwards has said, that "an attempt to prevent the introduction of slaves into the West Indies, would be like churning the winds, or giving laws to the ocean." We may with truth affirm, that an attempt to prevent a circulation of this kind of property through the slave-holding states of our confederacy, would be equally if not more impracticable. But there is a most striking illustration of this now exhibiting before our eyes—the Southampton massacre produced great excitement and apprehension throughout the slave-holding states, and two of them, hitherto the largest purchasers of Virginia slaves, have interdicted their introduction under severe penalties. Many in our state looked forward to an immediate fall in the price of slaves from this cause—and what has been the result? Why, wonderful to relate, Virginia slaves are now higher than they have been for many years past—and this rise in price has no doubt been occasioned by the number of southern purchasers who have visited our state, under the belief that Virginians had been frightened into a determination to get clear of their slaves at all events; and we are, consequently, at this moment, exporting slaves more rapidly, through the operation of the internal slave trade, than for many years past.

Let us now examine a moment into the object proposed to be accomplished by this scheme. It is contended that free labour is infinitely superior

32

to slave labour in every point of view, and therefore that it is highly desirable to exchange the latter for the former, and that this will be gradually accomplished by emancipation and deportation; because the vacuum occasioned by the exportation of the slaves will be filled up by the influx of freemen from the north and other portions of the Union—and thus, for every slave we lose, it is contended we shall receive in exchange a free labourer, much more productive and more moral. If we are not greatly mistaken, this, on analysis, will be found to be a complete specimen of that arithmetical *school boy* reasoning, which has ever proved so deceptive in politics, and so ruinous in its practical consequences. We shall canvass, before concluding this review, the general assertion, that free labour is superior in cheapness and productiveness to slave labour; but for the present we will allow all that is asserted on this head, and that it is very desirable on our part to make the exchange of slave for free labour. Let us now see whether this plan of abolition and transportation be calculated to effect it; and in order that we may fully examine the project in this point of view, we will endeavour first to trace out its operation on the slave population, and then on the white.

Since the publication of the celebrated work of Dr. Malthus on the "principle of population," the knowledge of the causes which affect its condition and increase, is much more widely diffused. It is now well known to every studier of political economy, that in the wide range of legislation, there is nothing more dangerous than too much tampering with the elastic and powerful *spring* of population.

The energies of goverment are for the most part feeble or impotent when arrayed against its action. It is this procreative power of the human species, either exerted or dormant, which so frequently brushes away *in reality* the visionary fabrics of the philanthropists, and mars the cherished plots and schemes of statesmen. Euler has endeavoured to prove, by some calculations, that the human species, under the most favourable circumstances, is capable of doubling itself once in twelve years. In our western country, the progress of population has, in many extensive districts, been so rapid as to show, in our opinion most conclusively, that it is capable of doubling itself once in fifteen years without the aid of emigration. The whole of our population, since the independence of the United States, has shown itself fully capable of duplication in periods of twenty-five years, without the accession from abroad. In some portions of our country the population is stationary, in others but very slowly advancing. We will assume then for the two extremes in our country, the stationary condition on the one side, and such increase on the other as to give rise to a duplication every fifteen years. Now as throughout the whole range comprehended between these extremes, population is capable of exerting various degrees of energy, it is very evident that the statesman who wishes to increase or diminish population, must look cautiously to the effect of his measures on its spring, and see how this will be acted on. If for example his object be to lessen the number of a slowly increasing population, he must be convinced that his plan does not stimulate the procreative energies of society to produce more than he is capable of taking away; or if his object be to increase the numbers, take heed lest his project deaden and paralyze the source of increase so much as to more than counter-balance any effort of his. Now looking at the texture of the Virginia population, the desideratum is to diminish the blacks and increase the whites. Let us see how the scheme of emancipation and deportation will act. We have already shown that the first operation of the plan, if slave property were rigidly respected and never taken without full compensation, would be to put a stop to the efflux from the state through other channels; but this would not be the only effect. Government entering into the market with individuals, would elevate the price of slaves beyond their natural value, and consequently the raising of them would become an object of primary importance throughout the whole state. We can readily imagine that the price of slaves might become so great that each master would do all in his power to encourage marriage among them—would allow the females almost entire exemption from labour, that they might the better breed and nurse—and would so completely concentrate his efforts upon this object, as to neglect other schemes and less productive sources of wealth. Under these circumstances the prolific African might no doubt be stimulated to press hard upon one of the limits above stated, doubling his numbers in fifteen years; and such is the tendency which our abolition schemes, if ever seriously engaged in, will most undoubtedly produce; they will be certain to stimulate the procreative powers of that very race which they are aiming to diminish; they will enlarge and invigorate the very monster which they are endeavouring to stifle, and realize the beautiful but melancholy fable of Sisyphus, by an eternal renovation of hope and disappointment. If it were possible for Virginia to purchase and send off annually for the next twenty-five or fifty years, 12,000 slaves, we should have very little hesitation in affirming, that the number of slaves in Virginia would not be at all lessened by the

34

operation, and at the conclusion of the period such habits would be generated among our blacks, that for a long time after the cessation of the drain,
population might advance so rapidly as to produce among us all the calamities and miseries of an over crowded people. . . .

But our opponents perhaps may be disposed to answer, that this increase
of slavery from the stimulus to the black population afforded by the colonization abroad, ought not to be objected to on our own principles, since
each slave will be worth two hundred dollars or more. This answer would
be correct enough if it were not that the increase of the blacks is effected at
our expense both as to wealth and numbers; and to show this, we will now
proceed to point out the operation of the scheme under consideration upon
the white population. Malthus has clearly shown that population depends
on the *means of subsistence*, and will, under ordinary circumstances, increase to a level with them. Now by means of subsistence we must not only
comprehend the necessaries of life, such as food, clothing, shelter, &c., but
likewise such conveniences, comforts, and even luxuries, as the habits of the
society may render it essential for all to enjoy. Whatever then has a tendency
to destroy the wealth and diminish the aggregate capital of society, has the
effect, as long as the *standard of comfort* remains the same, to check the
progress of the population.

It is sure to discourage matrimony, and cause children to be less carefully
attended to, and to be less abundantly supplied. The heavy burthens which
have hitherto been imposed on Virginia, through the operation of Federal
exactions, together with the *high standard* of comfort prevalent throughout
the whole state, (about which we shall by and by make a few observations)
have already imposed checks upon the progress of the white population of
the state. If not one single individual were to emigrate from the state of Virginia, it would be found, so inert has become the principle of increase in the
state, that the population would not advance with the average rapidity of
the American people. Now, under these circumstances, an imposition of an
additional burthen of $1,380,000 for the purpose of purchase and deporta-
tion of slaves, would add so much to the taxes of the citizens—would sub-
tract so much from the capital of the state, and increase so greatly the em-
barrassments of the whole population, that fewer persons would be enabled
to support families, and consequently to get married. This great tax, added
to those we are already suffering under, would weigh like an incubus upon
the whole state—it would operate like the blighting hand of Providence that

should render our soil barren and our labour unproductive. It would diminish the value of the *fee simple* of Virginia, and not only check the natural increase of population within the commonwealth, but would make every man desirous of quitting the scenes of his home and his infancy, and fleeing from the heavy burthen which would for ever keep him and his children buried in the depths of poverty. His sale of negroes would partly enable him to emigrate; and we have little doubt, that whenever this wild scheme shall be seriously commenced, it will be found that more whites than negroes will be banished by its operation from the state. And there will be this lamentable difference between those who are left behind; a powerful stimulus will be given to the procreative energies of the blacks, while those of the whites will be paralyzed and destroyed. Every emigrant from among the whites will create a vacuum not to be supplied—every removal of a black will stimulate to the generation of another. . . .

It is almost useless to inquire whether this deportation of slaves to Africa would, as some seem most strangely to anticipate, invite the whites of other states into the commonwealth. Who would be disposed to enter a state with worn out soil and a black population mortgaged to the payment of millions per annum, for the purpose of emancipation and deportation, when in the West the most luxuriant soils, unencumbered with heavy exactions, could be purchased for the paltry sum of $1.25 per acre?

Where, then, is that multitude of whites to come from, which the glowing fancy of orators has sketched out as flowing into and filling up the vacuum created by the removal of slaves? The fact is—throughout the whole debate in the Virginia legislature, the speakers seemed to consider the increase of population as a sort of fixed quantity, which would remain the same under the endless change of circumstance, and consequently that every man exported from among the blacks, lessened *pro tanto* exactly the black population, and that the whites, moving on with their usual speed, would fill the void; which certainly was an erroneous supposition, and manifested an almost unpardonable inattention to the wonderful *elasticity* of the powerful spring of population. The removal of inhabitants, accompanied with great loss of productive labour and capital, so far from leaving the residue in a better situation, and disposing them to increase and multiply, produces the directly opposite effect; it deteriorates the condition of society, and deadens the spring of population. . . .

Against most of the great difficulties attendant on the plan of emancipation above examined, it was impossible for the abolitionists entirely to close their eyes; and it is really curious to pause a moment and examine some of the reflections and schemes by which Virginia was to be reconciled to the plan. We have been told that it would not be necessary to purchase all the slaves sent away—that many would be surrendered by their owners without an equivalent. "There are a number of slave-holders," (said one who has all the lofty feeling and devoted patriotism which have hitherto so proudly characterized Virginia,) "at this very time, I do not speak from vain conjecture, but from what I know from the best information, and this number would continue to increase, who would voluntarily surrender their slaves, if the state would provide the means of colonizing them elsewhere. And there would be again another class, I have already heard of many, while they could not afford to sacrifice the entire value of their slaves, would cheerfully compromise with the state for half of their value." In the first place, we would remark that the gentleman's anticipation would certainly prove delusive—the surrender of a very few slaves would enhance the importance and value of the residue, and make the owner much more reluctant to part with them. Let any farmer in Lower Virginia ask himself how many he can spare from his plantation—and he will be surprised to see how few can be dispensed with. If that intelligent gentleman, from the storehouse of his knowledge, would but call up the history of the past, he would see that *mere philanthropy*, with all her splendid boastings, has never yet accomplished one great scheme; he would find the remark of that great judge of human nature, the illustrious author of the Wealth of Nations, that no people had the generosity to liberate their slaves until it became their interest to do so, but too true. . . .

But it is strange indeed that gentlemen have never reflected, that the pecuniary loss to the state, will be precisely the same, whether the negroes be purchased or gratuitously surrendered. In the latter case the burthen is only shifted from the whole state to that portion where the surrender is made— thus if we own $10,000 worth of this property, and surrender the whole to government, it is evident that we lose the amount of $10,000; and if the whole of Lower Virginia could at once be induced to give up all of this property, and it could be sent away, the only effect of this generosity and self devotion would be to inflict the *blow* of *desolation* more exclusively on this portion of the state. . . . Can it be genuine philanthropy to persuade them *alone* to step forward and bear the whole burthen?

Again; some have attempted to evade the difficulties by seizing on the increase of the negroes after a certain time. Thus Mr. Randolph's plan proposed that all born after the year 1840, should be raised by their masters to the age of eighteen for the female and twenty-one for the male, and then hired out, until the neat sum arising therefrom amounted to enough to send them away. Scarcely any one in the legislation—we believe not even the author himself—entirely approved of this plan. It is obnoxious to the objections we have just been stating against voluntary surrender. It proposes to saddle the slave-holder with the whole burthen; it infringes directly the rights of property; it converts the fee simple possession of this kind of property into an estate for years; and it only puts off the great sacrifice required of the state to 1840, when most of the evils will occur that have already been described. In the mean time it destroys the value of slaves, and with it all landed possessions—checks the productions of the state, imposes (when 1840 arrives) upon the master the intolerable and grievous burthen of raising his young slaves to the ages of eighteen and twenty-one, and then liberating them to be hired out under the superintendence of government (the most miserable of all managers,) until the proceeds arising therefrom shall be sufficient to send them away. If any man at all conversant with political economy should ever anticipate the day when this shall happen, we can only say that his faith is great indeed, enough to remove mountains, and that he has studied in a totally different school from ourselves.

Again; we entirely agree with the assertion of Mr. Brown, one of the ablest and most promising of Virginia's sons, that the ingenuity of man, if exerted for the purpose, could not devise a more efficient mode of producing discontent among our slaves, and thus endangering the peace of the community. There are born annually of this population about 20,000 children. Those which are born before the year 1840 are to be slaves; those which are born after that period are to be free at a certain age. These two classes will be reared together; they will labour together, and commune together. It cannot escape the observation of him who is doomed to servitude, that although of the same colour and born of the same parents, a far different destiny awaits his more fortunate brother—as his thoughts again and again revert to the subject, he begins to regard himself as the victim of injustice. Cheerfulness and contentment will flee from his bosom, and the most harmless and happy creature that lives on earth, will be transformed into a dark designing and desperate rebel. (*Brown's Speech, pp.* 8 *and* 9.)

There are some again who exhaust their ingenuity in devising schemes for taking off the breeding portion of the slaves to Africa, or carrying away the sexes in such disproportions as will in a measure prevent those left behind from breeding. All of these plans merit nothing more than the appellation of *vain juggling legislative conceits*, unworthy of a wise statesman and a moral man. If our slaves are ever to be sent away in any systematic manner, *humanity* demands that they should be carried in families. The voice of the world would condemn Virginia if she sanctioned any plan of deportation by which the male and female, husband and wife, parent and child, were systematically and relentlessly separated. . . .

There is $100,000,000 of slave property in the state of Virginia, and it matters but little how you destroy it, whether by the slow process of the cautious *practitioner*, or with the frightful despatch of the self confident *quack*; when it is gone, no matter how, the deed will be done, and Virginia will be a desert.

We shall now proceed to examine briefly the most dangerous of all the wild doctrines advanced by the abolitionists in the Virginia legislature, and the one which, no doubt, will be finally acted upon, if ever this business of emancipation shall be seriously commenced. *It was contended that property is the creature of civil society, and is subject to its action even to destruction.* But lest we may misrepresent, we will give the language of the gentleman who first boldly and exultingly announced it. "My views are briefly these," said Mr. Faulkner; "they go to the foundation upon which the social edifice rests—property is the creature of civil society.—So long as that property is not dangerous to the good order of society, it may and will be tolerated. But, sir, so soon as it is ascertained to jeopardize the peace, the happiness, the good order, nay the very existence of society, from that moment the right by which they hold their property is gone, society ceases to give its consent, the condition upon which they are permitted to hold it is violated, their right ceases. . . .

We find that the highly obnoxious doctrine just spoken of, was not entertained by the gentleman from Berkeley alone, but was urged to an equally offensive extent by Mr. M'Dowell, who is supposed by his friends to have made the most able and eloquent speech in favour of abolition. He says, "when it [property] loses its utility, when it no longer contributes to the personal benefits and wants of its holders in any equal degree with the expense or the risk or the danger of keeping it, much more when it jeopards the security of the public;—when this is the case, then the original purpose for which it is authorized is lost, its character of property in the just and beneficial sense of it is gone, and it may be regulated without private injustice, in any manner which the general good of the community, by whose laws it was licensed, may require." (*M'Dowell's Speech, see Richmond Whig, 24th March 1832.*). . . .

The doctrine of these gentlemen, so far from being true in its application, is not true in theory. The great object of government is the protection of property:—from the days of the patriarchs down to the present time, the great desideratum has been to find out the most efficient mode of protecting property. There is not a government at this moment in Christendom, whose peculiar practical character is not the result of the state of property.

No government can exist which does not conform to the state of property;—it cannot make the latter conform entirely to the government;—an attempt to do it would and ought to revolutionize any state. The great difficulty in forming the government of any country arises almost universally from the state of property, and the necessity of making it conform to that state; and it was the state of property in Virginia which really constituted the whole difficulty in the late convention. There is a right which these gentlemen seem likewise to have had in their minds, which writers on the law of nations call the right of *eminent* or *transcendental domain*; that right by which, in an exigency, the government or its agents may seize on persons or property, to be used for the general weal. Now, upon this there are two suggestions which at once present themselves.—First, that this right only occurs in cases of real exigency; and secondly, that the writers of our national law—and the Constitution of the United States expressly sanctions the principle—say, that no property can be thus taken without full and fair compensation.

These gentlemen, we hope to prove conclusively before finishing, have failed to show the *exigency*; and even if they have proved that, they deny the right of compensation, and upon what principle? why, that the whole state is not competent to afford it, and may therefore justly *abate* the *nuisance.* And is it possible that a burthen, in this Christian land, is most unfeelingly and remorselessly to be imposed upon a portion of the state, which, by the very confession of the gentlemen who urge it, could not be borne by the whole without inevitable ruin? But it was the main object of their speeches to show, that slave property is valueless, that it is a burthen, a

40

nuisance to the owner; and they seemed most anxious to enlighten the poor ignorant farmers on this point, who hold on with such pertinacity to this kind of property, which is inflicting its bitterest sting upon them. Now, is it not enough for the slave-holder to reply, that the circumstance of the slave bearing the price of two hundred dollars in the market, is an evidence of his value with every one acquainted with the elements of political economy; that, generally speaking, the market value of the slave is even less than his real value; for no one would like to own and manage slaves unless equally or more profitable than other kinds of investments in the same community; and if this or that owner may be pointed out as ruined by this species of property, might we not point to merchants, mechanics, lawyers, doctors, and divines, all of whom have been ruined by their several pursuits; and must all these employments be abated as *nuisances*, to satisfy the crude, un-digested theories of tampering legislators? . . .

The fact is, it is always a most delicate and dangerous task for one set of people to legislate for another, without any community of interests. It is sure to destroy the great principle of responsibility, and in the end to lay the weaker interest at the mercy of the stronger. It subverts the very end for which all governments are established, and becomes intolerable, and con-sequently against the fundamental rights of man, whether prohibited by the constitution or not. . . .

In fine, we would say, these doctrines are "nuisances," and if we were dis-posed to retaliate, would add that they ought to be "abated." We will close our remarks on this dangerous doctrine, by calling upon Western Virginia and the non-slave-holders of Eastern Virginia, not to be allured by this syren song. It is as delusive as it may appear fascinating; all the sources of wealth and departments of industry, all the great interests of society, are really interwoven with one another—they form an indissoluble chain; a blow at any part quickly vibrates through the whole length—the destruc-tion of one interest involves another. Destroy agriculture, destroy tillage, and the ruin of the farmer will draw down ruin upon the mechanic, the mer-chant, the sailor, and the manufacturer—they must all escape together from the land of desolation.

We hope we have now satisfactorily proved the impracticability of send-ing off the whole of our slave population, or even the annual increase; and we think we have been enabled to do this by pointing out only one half of the difficulties which attend the scheme. We have so far confined our atten-

41

tion to the expense and difficulty of purchasing the slaves, and sending them across the ocean. We have now to look a little to the recipient or territory to which the blacks are to be sent; and if we know any thing of the history and nature of colonization, we shall be completely upheld in the assertion, that the difficulties on this score are just as great and insurmountable as those which we have shown to be attendant on the purchase and deportation. We shall be enabled to prove, if we may use the expression, *a double impracticability* attendant on all these schemes.

The impossibility of colonizing the blacks.

The whole subject of colonization is much more difficult and intricate than is generally imagined, and the difficulties are often very different from what would, on slight reflection, be anticipated. They are of three kinds, physical, moral, and national. The former embraces unhealthy climate or want of proper seasoning, a difficulty of procuring subsistence and the conveniences of life, ignorance of the adaptations and character of the soils, want of habitations, and the necessity of living together in multitudes for the purposes of defence, whilst purposes of agriculture require that they should live as dispersed as possible. The moral difficulties arise from a want of adaptation on the part of the new colonists to their new situation, want of conformity in habits, manners, tempers, and dispositions, producing a heterogeneous mass of population, uncemented and unharmonizing. Lastly, the difficulties of a national character embrace all the causes of altercation and rupture between the colonists and neighbouring tribes or nations; all these dangers, difficulties, and hardships, are much greater than generally believed. Every new colony requires the most constant attention, the most cautious and judicious management in both the number and character of the emigrants, a liberal supply of both capital and provisions, together with a most watchful and paternal government on the part of the mother country, which may defend it against the incursions and depredations of warlike or savage neighbours. Hence the very slow progress made by all colonies in their first settlement. . . .

And in the first place we would remark, that almost all countries, especially those in southern and tropical latitudes, are extremely unfavourable to life when first cleared and cultivated. Almost the whole territory of the United States and South America, offer a conclusive illustration of this fact. We are daily witnessing, in the progress of tillage in our country, the visita-

42

tion of diseases of the most destructive kind, over regions hitherto entirely exempt; our bilious fevers, for example, seem to travel in great measure with the progress of opening, clearing, and draining of the country. Now, when we turn our attention to Africa, on which continent all agree that we must colonize, if at all, we find almost the whole continent possessing an insalubrious climate under the most favourable circumstances; and, consequently, we may expect this evil will be enhanced during the incipient stages of society, at any given point, while the progress of clearing, draining, and tilling is going forward. All the travellers through Africa agree in their descriptions of the general insalubrity of the climate. Park and Buffon agree in stating, that longevity is very rare among the negroes. At forty they are described as wrinkled and gray haired, and few of them survive the age of fifty-five or sixty; a Shungalla woman, says Bruce, at twenty-two, is more wrinkled and deformed by age, than a European at sixty; this short duration of life is attributable to the climate, for in looking over the returns of the census in our country, we find a much larger proportional number of cases of longevity among the blacks than the whites. "If accurate registers of mortality," says Malthus, (and no one was more indefatigable in his researches, or more capable of drawing accurate conclusions) "were kept among these nations (African), I have little doubt, that including the mortality from wars, one in seventeen or eighteen, at least, dies annually, instead of one in thirty-four or thirty-six, as in the generality of European states." The sea coast is described as being generally much more unhealthy than the interior. "Perhaps it is on this account chiefly," says Park, "that the interior countries abound more with inhabitants than the maritime districts." The deleterious effects of African climate, are of course much greater upon those accustomed to different latitudes and not yet acclimated. It is melancholy, indeed, to peruse the dreadful hardships and unexampled mortality attendant upon those companies which have from time to time, actuated by the most praiseworthy views, penetrated into the interior of Africa.

It is difficult to say, which has presented most obstacles to the inquisitive traveller, the suspicion and barbarity of the natives, or the dreadful insalubrity of the climate. Now, it is to this continent, the original home of our blacks, to this destructive climate we propose to send the slave of our country, after the lapse of ages has completely inured him to our colder and more salubrious continent. It is true, that a territory has already been secured for the Colonization Society of this country, which is said to enjoy an unusually

43

healthful climate. Granting that this may be the case, still when we come to examine into the capacity of the purchased territory for the reception of emigrants, we find that it only amounts to about 10,000 square miles, not a seventh of the superficies of Virginia. When other sites are fixed upon, we may not, and cannot expect to be so fortunate;—are not the most healthy districts in Africa the most populous, according to Park and all travellers? Will not these comparatively powerful nations, in all probability relinquish their territory with great reluctance? Will not our lot be consequently cast on barren sands or amid pestilential atmospheres, and then what exaggerated tales and false statements must be made if we would reconcile the poor blacks to a change of country pregnant with their fate?

But we believe that the very laudable zeal of many conscientious philanthropists has excited an overweening desire to make our colony in Liberia, in every point of view, appear greatly superior to what it is. . . .

We have said enough to show that the Continent of Africa, and its coasts particularly, are extremely unhealthy—that the natives themselves are not long lived—and that unacclimated foreigners are in most imminent danger. That there may be some healthy points on the sea shore, and salubrious districts in the interior, and that Liberia may be fortunately one of them, we are even willing to admit—but then we know that generally the most insalubrious portions will fall into our possession, because those of an opposite character are already too densely populated to be deserted by the natives—and consequently, let us view the subject as we please, we shall have this mighty evil of unhealthy climate to overcome. We have seen already, in the past history of our colony, that the slightest blunder, in landing on an unhealthy coast, in exposure to a deadly night air, or in neglecting the necessary precautions during the period of acclimating, has proved most frightfully fatal to both blacks and whites. Suppose now, that instead of the one or two hundred sent by the Colonization Society, Virginia should actually send out six thousand—or if we extend our views to the whole United States, that sixty thousand should be annually exported, accompanied of course by some hundreds of whites, what an awful fatality might we not occasionally expect? The chance for blundering would be infinitely increased, and if some ships might fortunately distribute their cargoes with the loss of few lives, others again might lose all their whites and a fourth or more of the blacks, as we know has already happened; and although this fatality might arise from blunder or accident, yet would it strike the imagination of men—and that which may be kept comparatively concealed now, would, when the number of emigrants swelled to such multitudes, produce alarm and consternation. We look forward confidently to the day, if this wild scheme should be persevered in for a few years, when the poor African slave, on bended knees, might implore a remission of that fatal sentence which would send him to the land of his forefathers. . . . If Virginia should send out 6000 emigrants to Africa, and much more, if the United States should send 60,000, the whole colony would inevitably perish, if the wealth of the mother country was not exhausted for their supply. . . .

So far we have been attending principally to the difficulties of procuring subsistence; but the habits and moral character of our slaves present others of equal importance and magnitude. Doctor Franklin says that one of the reasons why we see so many fruitless attempts to settle colonies at an immense public and private expense by several of the powers of Europe, is that the moral and mechanical habits adapted to the mother country, are frequently not so to the new settled one, and to external events, many of which are unforeseen, and that it is to be remarked that none of the English colonies became any way considerable, till the necessary manners were born and grew up in the country. Now, with what peculiar and overwhelming force does this remark apply to our colonization of liberated blacks? We are to send out thousands of these, taken from a state of slavery and ignorance, unaccustomed to guide and direct themselves, void of all the attributes of free agents, with dangerous notions of liberty and idleness, to elevate them at once to the condition of freemen, and invest them with the power of governing an empire, which will require more wisdom, more prudence, and at the same time more firmness than ever government required before. We are enabled to support our position by a quotation from an eloquent supporter of the American colonization scheme. "Indeed," said the Rev. Mr. Bacon, at the last meeting of the American Colonization Society, "it is something auspicious, that in the earlier stages of our undertaking, there has not been a general rush of emigration to the colony. In *any single year* since Cape Montserado was purchased, the influx of *a thousand emigrants* might have been fatal to our enterprise.—The new comers into any community must always be a *minority*, else every arrival is a *revolution*; they must be a *decided minority*, easily absorbed into the system and mingled with the mass, else the community is constantly liable to convulsion. Let 10,000 *foreigners, rude and ignorant*, be landed at once in this District (of Columbia,) and

45

what would be the result? Why you must have an armed force here to keep the peace;—so *one thousand* now landing *at once* in our colony, might be its ruin."

The fact is, the *true* and *enlightened* friends of colonization, must reprobate all those chimerical schemes proposing to deport any thing like the increase of one state, and more particularly of the whole United States. The difficulty just explained, has already been severely felt in Liberia, though hitherto supplied very scantily with emigrants, and those generally the most exemplary of the free blacks: thus in 1828 it was the decided opinion of Mr. Ashmun, "that for at least two years to come, a much more discriminating selection of settlers must be made, than ever has been—even in the first and second expeditions by the Elizabeth and Nautilus in 1820 and 21, or that the prosperity of the colony will *inevitably* and *rapidly decline.*" Now when to all these difficulties we add the prospect of frequent wars with the natives of Africa, the great expense we must incur to support the colony, and the anomalous position of Virginia, an *imperium in imperio*, holding an empire abroad, we do not see how the whole scheme can be pronounced any thing less than a *stupendous piece of folly.*

Some have supposed that the circumstance of the Africans being removed a stage or two above the savages of North America, will render the colonization of Africa much easier than that of America:—we draw directly the opposite conclusion. The Indians of North America had nowhere taken possession of the soil; they were wanderers over the face of the country; their titles could be extinguished for slight considerations; and it is ever melancholy to reflect that their habits of improvidence and of intoxication, and even their cruel practices in war, have all been (such has been for them the woeful march of events,) favourable to the rapid increase of the whites, who have thus been enabled to exterminate the *red men.*

The natives of Africa exist in the rude agricultural state, much more numerously than the natives of America. Their titles to land will be extinguished with much more difficulty and expense. The very first contact with our colony will carry to them the whole art and implements of war. As our colonists spread and press upon them, border wars will arise; and in vain will the attempt be made to extirpate the African nations, as we have the Indian tribes: every inhabitant of Liberia who is taken prisoner by his enemy, will be consigned, according to the universal practice of Africa, to the most wretched slavery either in Africa or the West Indies. And what will our

46

colony do? Must they murder, while their enemies enslave? Oh, no, it is too cruel, and will produce barbarizing and exterminating wars. Will they spare the prisoners of war? No! There does not and never will exist a people on earth, who would tamely look on and see their wives, mothers, brothers, and sisters, ignominiously enslaved, and not resent the insult. What, then, will be done? Why, they will be certain to enslave too; and if domestic slavery should be interdicted in the colony, it would be certain to encourage the slave trade; and if we could ever look forward to the time when the slave trade should be destroyed, then the throwing back of this immense current upon Africa would inundate all the countries of that region. . . .

Let, then, the real philanthropist ponder over these things, and tremble for the fate of colonies which may be imprudently planted on the African soil. The history of the world has too conclusively shown, that two races, differing in manners, customs, language, and civilization, can never harmonize upon a footing of equality. One must rule the other, or exterminating wars must be waged. In the case of the savages of North America, we have been successful in exterminating them; but in the case of African nations, we do think, from a view of the whole subject, that our colonists will most probably be the victims; but the alternative is almost equally shocking, should this not be the case. They must, then, be the exterminators or enslavers of all the nations of Africa with which they come into contact. The whole history of colonization, indeed, presents one of the most gloomy and horrific pictures to the imagination of the genuine philanthropist which can possibly be conceived. The many Indians who have been murdered, or driven in despair from the haunts and hunting grounds of their fathers—the heathen driven from his heritage, or hurried into the presence of his God in the full blossom of all his heathenish sins—the cruel slaughter of Ashantees—the murder of Burmese—all, *all* but too eloquently tell the misery and despair portended by the advance of civilization to the savage and the pagan, whether in America, Africa, or Asia. In the very few cases where the work of desolation ceased, and a commingling of races ensued, it has been found that the civilized man has sunk down to the level of barbarism, and there has ended the mighty work of civilization! Such are the melancholy pictures which sober reason is constrained to draw of the future destinies of our colony in Africa. And what, then, will become of that grand and glorious idea of carrying religion, intelligence, industry, and the arts, to the already wronged and injured Africa? It is destined to vanish, and prove worse

47

than mere delusion. The rainbow of promise will be swept away, and we shall awake at last to all the sad realities of savage warfare and increasing barbarism. We have thus stated some of the principal difficulties and dangers accompanying a scheme of colonization, upon a scale as large as proposed in the Virginia legislature. We have said enough to show, that if we ever send off 6000 per annum, we must incur an expense far beyond the purchase money.

The expense of deportation to Africa we have estimated at thirty dollars; but when there is taken into the calculation the further expense of collecting in Virginia, of feeding, protecting, &c., in Africa, the amount swells beyond all calculation. Mr. Tazewell, in his able Report on the colonization of free people of colour on the African coast, represents this expense as certainly amounting to one hundred dollars; and judging from actual experience, was disposed to think two hundred dollars would fall below the fair estimate. If the Virginia scheme shall ever be adopted, we have no doubt that both these estimates will fall below the real expense. The annual cost of removing 6000, instead of being $1,380,000, will swell beyond $2,400,000, an expense sufficient to destroy the entire value of the whole property of Virginia. Voltaire, in his Philosophical Dictionary, has said, that such is the inherent and preservative vigour of nations, that governments cannot possibly ruin them; that almost all governments which had been established in the world had made the attempt, but had failed. If the sage of France had lived in our days, he would have had a receipt furnished by some of our philanthropists, by which this work might have been accomplished! We read in holy writ of one great emigration from the land of Egypt, and the concomitant circumstances should bid us well beware of an imitation, unless assisted by the constant presence of Jehovah. Ten plagues were sent upon the land of Egypt before Pharaoh would consent to part with the Israelites, the productive labourers of his kingdom. But a short time convinced him of the heavy loss which he sustained by their removal, and he gave pursuit; but God was present with the Israelites—He parted the waters of the Red Sea for *their* passage, and closed them over the Egyptians—He led on his chosen people through the wilderness, testifying his presence in a pillar of fire by night and a cloud of smoke by day—He supplied them with manna in their long journey, sending a sufficiency on the sixth for that and the seventh day. When they were thirsty the rocks poured forth waters, and when they finally arrived in the land of promise, after the loss of a genera-

48

tion, the mysterious will of heaven had doomed the tribes of Canaan to destruction; fear and apprehension confounded all their counsels; their battlements sunk down at the trumpet's sound; the native hosts, under heaven's command, were all slaughtered; and the children of Israel took possession of the habitations and property of the slaughtered inhabitants. The whole history of this emigration beautifully illustrates the great difficulties and hardships of removal to foreign lands of multitudes of people.

But, say some, if Virginia cannot accomplish this work, let us call upon the general government for aid—let Hercules be requested to put his shoulders to the wheels, and roll us through the formidable *quagmire* of our difficulties. Delusive prospect! Corrupting scheme! We will throw all constitutional difficulties out of view, and ask if the federal government can be requested to undertake the expense for Virginia, without encountering it for the whole slave-holding population? And then, whence can be drawn the funds to purchase more than 2,000,000 of slaves, worth at the lowest calculation $400,000,000; or if the increase alone be sent off, can Congress undertake annually to purchase at least 60,000 slaves at an expense of $12,000,000, and deport and colonize them at an expense of twelve or fifteen millions more? But the fabled hydra would be more than realized in this project. We have no doubt that if the United States in good faith should enter into the slave markets of the country, determined to purchase up the whole annual increase of our slaves, so unwise a project, by its artificial demand, would immediately produce a rise in this property, throughout the whole southern country, of at least 33⅓ per cent. It would stimulate and invigorate the *spring* of black population, which, by its tremendous action, would set at naught the puny efforts of man, and like the Grecian matron, unweave in the night what had been woven in the day. We might well calculate upon an annual increase of at least four and half per cent. upon our two millions of slaves, if ever the United States should create the artificial demand which we have just spoken of; and then, instead of an increase of 60,000, there will be 90,000, bearing the average price of $300 each, making the enormous annual expense of purchase alone $27,000,000!—and difficulties, too, on the side of the colony, would more than enlarge with the increase of the evil at home. Our Colonization Society has been more than fifteen years at work; it has purchased, according to its friends, a district of country as congenial to the constitution of the black as any in Africa; it has, as we have seen, frequently over-supplied the colony with emigrants; and mark the *result*, for it is worthy of all observation, there are not now more than 2000 or 2500 inhabitants in Liberia! And these are alarmed lest the Southampton insurrection may cause such an emigration as to inundate the colony. When, then, in the lapse of time, can we ever expect to build up a colony which can receive sixty or ninety thousand slaves per annum? And if this should ever arrive, what guarantee could be furnished us that their ports would always be open to our emigrants? Would law or compact answer? Oh, no! Some legislator, in the plenitude of his wisdom, might arise, who could easily and *truly* persuade his countrymen that these annual importations of blacks were *nuisances*, and that the laws of God, whatever might be those of men, would justify their abatement. And the drama would be wound up in this land of promise and expectation, by turning the cannon's mouth against the liberated emigrant and deluded philanthropist. The scheme of colonizing our blacks on the coast of Africa, or any where else, by the United States, is thus seen to be more stupendously absurd than even the Virginia project. King Canute, the Dane, seated on the sea shore, and ordering the rising flood to recede from his royal feet, was not guilty of more vanity and presumption than the government of the United States would manifest, in the vain effort of removing and colonizing the annual increase of our blacks.

We have thus examined fully this scheme of emancipation and deportation, and trust we have satisfactorily shown, that the whole plan is utterly impracticable, requiring an expense and sacrifice of property far beyond the entire resources of the state and federal governments. We shall now proceed to inquire, whether we can emancipate our slaves with permission that they remain among us.

Emancipation without deportation.

We candidly confess that we look upon this last mentioned scheme as much more practicable and likely to be forced upon us, than the former. We consider it at the same time so fraught with danger and mischief both to the whites and blacks—so utterly subversive of the welfare of the slave-holding country, in both an economical and moral point of view, that we cannot, upon any principle of right or expediency, give it our sanction. Almost all the speakers in the Virginia legislature seemed to think there ought to be no emancipation without deportation. Mr. Clay, too, in his celebrated Colonization speech of 1830, says, "If the question were submitted whether there should be immediate or gradual emancipation of all the slaves in the United States, without their removal or colonization, painful as it is to express the opinion, *I have no doubt that it would be unwise to emancipate them.* I believe, that the *aggregate* of evils which would be engendered in society, upon the supposition of general emancipation, and of the liberated slaves remaining principally among us, would be greater than *all* the evils of slavery, great as they unquestionably are." Even the northern philanthropists themselves admit, generally, that there should be no emancipation without removal. Perhaps, then, under these circumstances, we might have been justified in closing our review with a consideration of the colonization scheme; but as we are anxious to survey this subject fully in all its aspects, and to demonstrate upon every ground the complete justification of the whole southern country in a further continuance of that system of slavery which has been originated by no fault of theirs, and continued and increased contrary to their most earnest desires and petitions, we have determined briefly to examine this scheme likewise. As we believe the scheme of deportation *utterly* impracticable, we have come to the conclusion that in the present great question, the real and the decisive line of conduct is either *abolition without removal*, or a *steady perseverance* in the system now established. . . .

The great ground upon which we shall rest our argument on this subject is, *that the slaves, in both an economical and moral point of view, are entirely unfit for a state of freedom among the whites*; and we shall produce such proofs and illustrations of our position, as seem to us perfectly conclusive. That condition of our species from which the most important consequences flow, says Mr. Mill the Utilitarian, is the necessity of labour for the supply of the fund of our necessaries and conveniences. It is this which influences, perhaps, more than any other, even our moral and religious character, and determines more than every thing else besides, the social and political state of man. It must enter into the calculations of not only the political economist, but even of the metaphysician, the moralist, the theologian, and politician.

We shall therefore proceed at once to inquire what effect would be produced upon the slaves of the South in an economical point of view, by emancipation with permission to remain—whether the *voluntary* labour of the freedman would be as great as the *involuntary* labour of the slave? Fortunately for us this question has been so frequently and fairly subjected to

51

the test of experience, that we are no longer left to vain and fruitless conjecture. Much was said in the legislature of Virginia about superiority of free labour over slave, and perhaps under certain circumstances this might be true; but in the present instance, the question is between *the relative amounts of labour which may be obtained from slaves before and after their emancipation.* Let us then first commence with our country, where it is well known to every body, that slave labour is vastly more efficient and productive, than the labour of free blacks. Taken as a whole class, the latter must be considered the most worthless and indolent of the citizens of the United States. It is well known that throughout the whole extent of our Union, they are looked upon as the very *drones* and *pests* of society. Nor does this character arise from the disabilities and disfranchisement by which the law attempts to guard against them. In the non-slave-holding states, where they have been more elevated by law, this kind of population is in a worse condition and much more troublesome to society, than in the slave-holding, and especially in the planting states. . . .

From these facts it would require no great sagacity to come to the conclusion, that slave cannot be converted into free labour without imminent danger to the prosperity and wealth of the country where the change takes place—and in this particular it matters not what may be the colour of the slave. . . . It is because there is an inherent and intrinsic cause at work, which will produce its effect under all circumstances. In the free black, the principle of idleness and dissipation triumphs over that of accumulation and the desire to better our condition; the animal part of the man gains the victory over the *moral*; and he consequently prefers sinking down into the listless inglorious repose of the brute creation, to rising to that energetic activity which can only be generated amid the multiplied, refined, and artificial wants of civilized society. The very conception which nine slaves in ten have of liberty, is that of idleness and sloth with the enjoyment of plenty; and we are not to wonder that they should hasten to practise upon their theory so soon as liberated. But the experiment has been sufficiently tried to prove most conclusively that the free black will work nowhere except by compulsion.

St. Domingo is often spoken of by philanthropists and schemers; the trial has there been made upon a scale sufficiently grand to test our opinions, and we are perfectly willing to abide the result of the experiment. . . .

There has been a gradual diminution of the amount of the products of Hayti since 1822. In 1825 the whole value of exports was about $8,000,000, more than $1,000,000 less than in 1822, and the revenue of the island was not equal to the public expenditure. Is not this fair experiment for forty years, under more favourable circumstances than any reasonable man had a right to anticipate, sufficient to convince and overwhelm the most sceptical as to the unproductiveness of slave labour converted into free labour? . . .

We have now, we think, proved our position that slave labour in an economical point of view, is far superior to free negro labour; and have no doubt that if an immediate emancipation of the negroes were to take place, the whole southern country would be visited with an immediate general famine, from which the productive sources of all the other states of the Union could not deliver them.

It is now easy for us to demonstrate the second point in our argument—that the slave is not only *economically* but *morally* unfit for freedom. And first, idleness and consequent want, are of themselves sufficient to generate a catalogue of vices of the most mischievous and destructive character. Look to the penal prosecutions of every country, and mark the situation of those who fall victims to the laws. And what a frightful proportion do we find among the indigent and idle classes of society! Idleness generates want—want gives rise to temptation—and strong temptation makes the villain. The most appropriate prayer for frail imperfect man, is, "lead us not into temptation." Mr. Archer of Virginia well observed in a speech before the Colonization Society, that "the free blacks were destined by an insurmountable barrier—to the want of occupation—thence to the want of food—thence to the distresses which ensue that want—thence to the settled deprivation which grows out of those distresses, and is nursed at their bosoms; and this condition *was not casualty but fate.* The evidence was not speculation in political economy—it was geometrical demonstration."

We are not to wonder that this class of citizens should be so depraved and immoral. An idle population will always be worthless; and it is a mistake to think that they are only worthless in the Southern States, where it is erroneously supposed the slavery of a portion of their race depresses them below their condition in the free states: on the contrary, we are disposed rather to think their condition better in the slave than the free states. Mr. Everett, in a speech before the Colonization Society, during the present year, says, "they (the free blacks) form in Massachusetts about one-seventy-fifth part of the population; *one-sixth of the convicts in our prisons are of this class.*" The average number of annual convictions in the state of Virginia, estimated by the late Governor Giles, from the penitentiary reports, up to 1829, is seventy-one for the whole population—making one in every sixteen thousand of the white population, one in every twenty-two thousand of the slaves, and one for every five thousand of the free coloured people. Thus, it will be seen, that crimes among the free blacks are more than three times as numerous as among the whites, and four and a half times more numerous than among the slaves. But although the free blacks have thus much the largest proportion of crime to answer for, yet the proportion is not so great in Virginia as in Massachusetts. Although they are relatively to the other classes more numerous, making the one-thirtieth of the population of the state, not one-eighth of the whole number of convicts are from among them in Virginia, while in Massachusetts there is one-sixth. We may infer, then, they are not so degraded and vicious in Virginia, a slave-holding state, as in Massachusetts, a non-slave-holding state. But there is one fact to which we invite particularly the attention of those philanthropists who have the elevation of southern slaves so much at heart—*that the slaves in Virginia furnish a much smaller annual proportion of convicts than the whites, and among the latter a very large proportion of the convicts consist of foreigners or citizens of other states.*

There is one disadvantage attendant upon free blacks, in the slave-holding states, which is not felt in the non-slave-holding. In the former they corrupt the slaves, encourage them to steal from their masters by purchasing from them, and they are, too, a sort of moral conductor by which the slaves can better organize and concert plans of mischief among themselves.

So far we have been speaking of the evils resulting from mere idleness; but there are other circumstances which must not be omitted in an enumeration of the obstacles to emancipation. The blacks have now all the habits and feelings of slaves, the whites have those of masters; the prejudices are formed and mere legislation cannot remove them. "Give me," said a wise man, "the formation of the habits and manners of a people, and I care not who makes the laws." Declare the negroes of the South free to-morrow, and vain will be your decree until you have prepared them for it; you depress, instead of elevating. The law would, in every point of view, be one of the most cruel and inhumane which could possibly be passed. The law would make them freemen, and custom or prejudice, we care not which you call it, would degrade them to the condition of slaves; and soon should we see, that "it is happened unto them, according to the true proverb, the dog is turned to his own vomit again, and the sow that was washed to her wallowing in the mire." . . . We must never endeavour to elevate beyond what circumstances will allow. It is better that each one should remain in society in the condition in which he has been born and trained, and not to mount too fast without preparation. Hence, in the southern states the condition of the free blacks is better than in the northern; in the latter he is told that he is a freeman and entirely equal to the white, and prejudice assigns to him a degraded station—light is furnished him by which to view the interior of the fairy palace which is fitted up for him, and custom expels him from it, after the law has told him it was his. He consequently leads a life of endless mortification and disappointment. Tantalus like, he has frequently the cup to his lips, and imperious custom dashes it untasted from him. In the southern states, law and custom more generally coincide; the former makes no profession which the latter does not sanction, and consequently the free black has nothing to grieve and disappoint him.

We have already said, in the course of this review, that if we were to liberate the slaves, we could not, in fact, alter their condition—they would still be virtually slaves; talent, habit, and wealth, would make the white the master still, and the emancipation would only have the tendency to deprive him of those sympathies and kind feelings for the black which now characterize him. Liberty has been the heaviest curse to the slave, when given too soon; we have already spoken of the eagerness and joy with which the negroes of Mr. Steele, in Barbadoes, returned to a state of slavery. The east of Europe affords hundreds of similar instances. In 1791, Stanislaus Augustus, preparing a hopeless resistance to the threatened attack of Russia, in concert with the states, gave to Poland a constitution which established the complete personal freedom of the peasantry. The boon has never been recalled, and what was the consequence? "Finding," (says Jones, in his volume on Rents,) "their dependence on their proprietors for subsistence remained undiminished, the peasants showed no very grateful sense of the boon bestowed upon them; they feared they should now be deprived of all claim upon the proprietors for assistance, when calamity or infirmity overtook them. It is only since they have discovered that the *connexion* between them and the owners of the estates on which they reside *is little altered in practice*, and that their old masters very generally *continue*, from expediency or humanity, the occasional aid they formerly lent them, that they have become *reconciled* to their new character of freemen." . . .

Let us for a moment revert to the black republic of Hayti, and we shall see that the negroes have gained nothing by their bloody revolution. Mr. Franklin, who derives his information from personal inspection, gives the following account of the present state of the island:—"Oppressed with the weight of an overwhelming debt, contracted without an equivalent, with an empty treasury, and destitute of the way and means for supplying it; the soil almost neglected, or at least very partially tilled; without commerce or credit. Such is the present state of the republic; and it seems almost impossible that, under the system which is now pursued, there should be any melioration of its condition, or that it can arrive at any very high state of improvement. Hence, there appears every reason to apprehend that it *will recede into irrecoverable insignificance, poverty, and disorder.*" (p. 265.) And the great mass of the Haytiens are virtually in a state of as abject slavery as when the island was under the French dominion. The government soon found it absolutely necessary to establish a system of compulsion in all respects as bad, and more intolerable, than when slavery existed. . . . And here is the boasted freedom of the negroes of St. Domingo;—the appalling vocabulary of "overseer," "driver," "pass," &c., is not even abolished. Slavery to the government and its military officers is substituted for private slavery; the black master has stepped into the shoes of the white; and we all know that he is the most cruel of masters, and more dreaded by the negro than any of the ten plagues of Egypt. We are well convinced, that there is not a single negro in the commonwealth of Virginia who would accept such *freedom*; and yet the happiest of the human race are constantly invited to sigh for such freedom, and to sacrifice all their happiness in the vain wish. But it is not necessary further to multiply examples; enough has already been said, we hope, to convince the most sceptical of the great disadvantage to the slave himself, of freedom, when he is not prepared for it. It is unfortunate, indeed, that prejudiced and misguided philanthropists so often assert as *facts*, what, on investigation, turns out not only false, but even hostile to the very theories which they are attempting to support by them. . . .

Indeed, it is a calamity to mankind, that zealous and overheated philanthropists will not suffer the truth to circulate, when believed hostile to their visionary schemes. . . . "There is a time for all things," and nothing in this world should be done before its time. An emancipation of our slaves would check at once that progress of improvement, which is now so manifest among them. The whites would either gradually withdraw, and leave whole districts or settlements in their possession, in which case they would sink rapidly in the scale of civilization; or the blacks, by closer intercourse, would bring the whites down to their level. In the contact between the civilized and uncivilized man, all history and experience show, that the former will be sure to sink to the level of the latter. In these cases it is always easier to descend than ascend, and nothing will prevent the *facilis descensus* but slavery. The great evil, however, of these schemes of emancipation, remains yet to be told. They are admirably calculated to excite plots, murders, and insurrections; whether gradual or rapid in their operation, this is the inevitable tendency. In the former case, you disturb the quiet and contentment of the slave who is left unemancipated; and he becomes the midnight murderer to gain that fatal freedom whose blessings he does not comprehend. In the latter case, want and invidious distinction will prompt to revenge. Two totally different races, as we have before seen, cannot easily harmonize together; and although we have no idea that any organized plan of insurrection or rebellion can ever secure for the black the superiority, even when free, yet his idleness will produce want and worthlessness, and his very worthlessness and degradation will stimulate him to deeds of rapine and vengeance; he will oftener engage in plots and massacres, and thereby draw down on his devoted head the vengeance of the provoked whites. But one limited massacre is recorded in Virginia history; let her liberate her slaves, and every year you would hear of insurrections and plots, and every day would perhaps record a murder; the melancholy tale of Southampton would not alone blacken the page of our history, and make the tender mother shed the tear of horror over her babe as she clasped it to her bosom; others of a deeper die would thicken upon us; those regions where the brightness of polished life has dawned and brightened into full day, would relapse into darkness, thick and full of horrors. . . . Do not all these appalling examples but too eloquently tell the consequences of emancipation, and bid us well beware how we enter on any system which will be almost certain to bring down ruin and degradation on both the whites and the blacks?

But in despite of all the reasoning and illustrations which can be urged, the example of the northern states of our confederacy and the west of Europe afford, it is thought by some, conclusive evidence of the facility of changing the slave into the freeman. As to the former, it is enough to say that paucity of numbers, uncongenial climate, and the state of agriculture to the north, together with the great demand of slaves to the south, alone accomplished the business. In reference to the west of Europe, it was the rise of the towns, the springing up of a middle class, and a change of agriculture, which gradually and silently effected the emancipation of the slaves, in a great measure through the operation of the selfish principle itself. Commerce and manufactures arose in the western countries, and with them sprang up a middle class of freemen, in the cities and the country too, which gradually and imperceptibly absorbed into its body all the slaves. But for this middle class, which acted as the *absorbent*, the slaves could not have been liberated with safety or advantage to either party. Now, in our southern country, there is no body of this kind to become *the absorbent*, nor are we likely to have such a body, unless we look into the vista of the future, and imagine a time when the south shall be to the north, what England now is to Ireland, and will consequently be *overrun* with northern labourers, underbidding *the means of subsistence* which will be furnished to the negro; then *perhaps* such a labouring class, devoid of all pride and habits of lofty bearing, *may* become a proper *recipient* or *absorbent* for emancipated slaves. But even then we fear the effects of difference of colour. The slave of Italy or France could be emancipated or escape to the city, and soon all records of his former state would perish, and he would gradually sink into the mass of freemen around him. But unfortunately the emancipated black carries a mark which no time can erase; he forever wears the indelible symbol of his inferior condition; *the Ethiopian cannot change his skin, nor the leopard his spots.*

In Greece and Rome, and we imagine it was so during the feudal ages, the domestic slaves were frequently among the most learned, virtuous, and intelligent members of society. Terence, Phaedrus, Esop, and Epictetus were all slaves. They were frequently taught all the arts and sciences, in order that they might be more valuable to their masters. . . . There was no obstacle, therefore, to the emancipation of such men as these (except as to the fool,) either on the score of colour, intelligence, habits, or any thing else— the *body* of freemen could readily and without difficulty or danger absorb them. Not so now—nor ever will it be in all time to come, with our blacks. With these remarks, we shall close our examination of the plans by which it has been or may be proposed to get rid of slavery. If our arguments are sound, and reasonings conclusive, we have shown they are all wild and visionary, calculated to involve the South in ruin and degradation: and we now most solemnly call upon the statesman and the patriot, the editor and the philanthropist, to pause, and consider well, before they move in this dangerous and delicate business. But a few hasty and fatal steps in advance, and the work may be irretrievable. For Heaven's sake then let us pause, and recollect, that on this subject, so pregnant with the safety, happiness, and prosperity of millions, we shall be doomed to realize the fearful motto, "nulla vestigia retrorsum."

There are some who, in the plenitude of their folly and recklessness, have likened the cause of the blacks to Poland and France, and have *darkly hinted* that the same aspirations which the generous heart breathes for the cause of bleeding, suffering Poland, and revolutionary France, must be indulged for the *insurrectionary blacks*. And has it come at last to this? that the hellish plots and massacres of Dessalines, Gabriel, and Nat Turner, are to be compared to the noble deeds and devoted patriotism of Lafayette, Kosciusko, and Schrynecki? There is an absurdity in this conception, which so outrages reason and the most common feelings of humanity, as to render it unworthy of serious patient refutation. But we will, nevertheless, for a moment examine it, and we shall find, on their own principles, if such reasoners have any principles, that their conception is entirely fallacious. The true theory of the right of revolution we conceive to be the following: no men or set of men are justifiable in attempting a revolution which must *certainly* fail; or if successful must produce *necessarily a much worse state* of things than the pre-existent order. We have not the right to plunge the dagger into the monarch's bosom merely because he is a monarch—we must be sure it is the *only means* of dethroning a tyrant and giving peace and happiness to an aggrieved and suffering people. Brutus would have had no right to kill Caesar if he could have foreseen the consequences. If France and Poland had been peopled with a race of serfs and degraded citizens, totally unfit for freedom and self-government, and Lafayette and Kosciusko could have known it, they would have been *parricides* instead of *patriots*, to have roused such ignorant and unhappy wretches to engage in a revolution whose object they could not comprehend, and which would inevitably involve them in all the horrors of relentless carnage and massacre. No man has ever yet contended that the blacks could gain their liberty and an ascendency over the whites by wild insurrections; no one has ever imagined that they could do more than bring down, by their rash and barbarous achievements, the vengeance of the infuriated whites upon their devoted heads. Where then is the analogy to Poland and to France, lands of generous achievement, of learning, and of high and noble purposes, and with people capable of self-government? We shall conclude this branch of our subject with the following splendid extract from a speech of Mr. Canning, which should at least make the rash legislator more distrustful of his specifics.

"In dealing with a negro we must remember that we are dealing with a being possessing the form and strength of a man, but the intellect only of a child. To turn him loose in the manhood of his physical passions, but in the infancy of his uninstructed reason, would be to raise up a creature resembling the splendid fiction of a recent romance; the hero of which constructs a human form with all the physical capabilities of man, and with the thews and sinews of a giant, but being unable to impart to the work of his hands a perception of right and wrong, he finds too late that he has only created a more than mortal power of doing mischief, and himself recoils from the monster which he has made. What is it we have to deal with? is it an evil of yesterday's origin? with a thing which has grown up in our time—of which we have watched the growth—measured the extent—and which we have ascertained the means of correcting or controlling? No, we have to deal with an evil which is the growth of centuries and of tens of centuries; which is almost coeval with the deluge; which has existed under different modifications since man was man. Do gentlemen, in their passion for legislation, think, that after only thirty years discussion, they can now at once manage as they will the most unmanageable perhaps of all subjects? or do we forget, sir, that in fact not more than thirty years have elapsed since we first presumed to approach even the outworks of this great question? Do we, in the ardour of our nascent reformation, forget that during the ages which this system has existed, no preceding generation of legislators has ventured to touch it with a reforming hand; and have we the vanity to flatter ourselves that we can annihilate it at a blow? No Sir, No!—If we are to do good it is not to be done by sudden and violent measures." Let the warning language of Mr. Canning be attended to in our legislative halls, and all rash and intemperate legislation avoided. We will now proceed to the last division of our subject, and examine a little into the injustice and evils of slavery, with

60

the view of ascertaining if we are really exposed to those dangers and horrors which many seem to anticipate in the current of time.

Injustice and Evils of Slavery.

1st. It is said slavery is wrong, in the *abstract* at least, and contrary to the spirit of Christianity. To this we answer as before, that any question must be determined by its circumstances, and if, as really is the case, we cannot get rid of slavery without producing a greater injury to both the masters and slaves, there is no rule of conscience or revealed law of God which *can* condemn us. The physician will not order the spreading cancer to be extirpated, although it will eventually cause the death of his patient, because he would thereby hasten the fatal issue. So if slavery had commenced even contrary to the laws of God and man, and the sin of its introduction rested upon our hands, and it was even carrying forward the nation by slow degrees to final ruin—yet if it were *certain* that an attempt to remove it would only hasten and heighten the final catastrophe—that it was in fact a "vulnus immedicabile" on the body politic, which no legislation could safely remove, then, we would not only not be bound to attempt the extirpation, but we would stand guilty of a high offence in the sight of both God and man, if we should rashly make the effort. But the original sin of introduction rests not on our heads, and we shall soon see that all those dreadful calamities which the false prophets of our day are pointing to, will never in all probability occur. With regard to the assertion, that slavery is against the spirit of Christianity, we are ready to admit the general assertion, but deny most positively that there is any thing in the Old or New Testament, which would go to show that slavery, when once introduced, ought at all events to be abrogated, or that the master commits any offence in holding slaves. The Children of Israel themselves were slave-holders, and were not condemned for it. When they conquered the land of Canaan they made one whole tribe "hewers of wood and drawers of water," and they were at that very time under the special guidance of Jehovah; they were permitted expressly to purchase slaves of the heathens, and keep them as an inheritance for their posterity—and even the Children of Israel might be enslaved for six years. When we turn to the New Testament, we find not one single passage at all calculated to disturb the conscience of an honest slave-holder. No one can read it without seeing and admiring that the meek and humble Saviour of the world in no instance meddled with the established institutions of mankind—he came to save a fallen world, and not to excite the black passions of men and array them in deadly hostility against each other. From no one did he turn away; his plan was offered alike to all—to the monarch and the subject—the rich and the poor the master and the slave. He was born in the Roman world, a world in which the most galling slavery existed, a thousand times more cruel than the slavery in our own country—and yet he nowhere encourages insurrection—he nowhere fosters discontent—but exhorts *always* to implicit obedience and fidelity. What a rebuke does the practice of the Redeemer of mankind imply upon the conduct of some of his nominal disciples of the day, who seek to destroy the contentment of the slaves, to rouse their most deadly passions, to break up the deep foundations of society, and to lead on to a night of darkness and confusion! "Let every man (says Paul,) abide in the same calling wherein he is called. Art thou called *being* a servant? care not for it; but if thou mayest be made free use *it* rather." (1 *Corinthians*, vii. 20, 21.) Again; "Let as many servants as are under the yoke, count their own masters worthy of all honour, that the name of God and his doctrines be not blasphemed; and they that have believing masters, let them not despise *them*, because they are brethren, but rather do them service, because they are faithful and beloved partakers of the benefit. These things teach and exhort." (1 *Tim*. vi. 1, 2.) Servants are even commanded in Scripture to be faithful and obedient to unkind masters. "Servants, (says Peter,) be subject to your masters with all fear; not only to the good and gentle, but to the froward. For what glory is it if when ye shall be buffeted for your faults ye take it patiently; but if when ye do well and suffer for it, ye take it patiently, this is acceptable with God." (1 *Peter*, ii. 18, 20.) These, and many other passages in the New Testament, most convincingly prove, that slavery in the Roman world was nowhere charged as a fault or crime upon the holder, and everywhere is the most implicit obedience enjoined.

We beg leave, before quitting this topic, to address a few remarks to those who have conscientious scruples about the holding of slaves, and therefore consider themselves under an obligation to break all the ties of friendship and kindred—dissolve all the associations of happier days, to flee to a land where this evil does not exist. We cannot condemn the conscientious actions of mankind, but we must be permitted to say, that if the assumption even of these pious gentlemen be correct, we do consider their conduct as very unphilosophical, and we will go further still, we look upon it as even immoral upon their own principles. Let us admit that slavery is an evil, and what then? why it has been entailed upon us by no fault of ours, and must we shrink from the charge which devolves upon us, and throw the slave in consequence into the hands of those who have no scruples of conscience—those who will not perhaps treat him so kindly? No! this is not philosophy, it is not morality; we must recollect that the unprofitable man was thrown into utter darkness. To the slave-holder has truly been intrusted the five talents. Let him but recollect the exhortation of the Apostle—"Masters, give unto your servants that which is just and equal; knowing that ye also have a master in Heaven; " and in the final day he shall have nothing on this score with which his conscience need be smitten, and he may expect the welcome plaudit—"Well done thou good and faithful servant, thou hast been faithful over a few things, I will make thee ruler over many things; enter thou into the joy of the Lord." . . .

2dly. *But it is further said that the moral effects of slavery are of the most deleterious and hurtful kind;* and as Mr. Jefferson has given the sanction of his great name to this charge, we shall proceed to examine it with all that respectful deference to which every sentiment of so pure and philanthropic a heart is justly entitled.

"The whole commerce between master and slave," says he, "is a perpetual exercise of the most boisterous passions—the most unremitting despotism on the one part, and degrading submission on the other. Our children see this, and learn to imitate it, for man is an imitative animal—this quality is the germ of education in him. From his cradle to his grave, he is learning what he sees others do. If a parent had no other motive, either in his own philanthropy or self love, for restraining the intemperance of passion towards his slave, it should always be a sufficient one that his child is present. But generally it is not sufficient. The parent storms, the child looks on, catches the lineaments of wrath, puts on the same airs in the circle of smaller slaves, gives a loose to his worst of passions, and thus nursed, educated, and daily exercised in the worst of tyranny, cannot but be stamped by it with odious peculiarities." Now we boldly assert that the fact does not bear Mr. Jefferson out in his conclusions. He has supposed the master in a continual passion—in the constant exercise of the most odious tyranny, and the child, a creature of imitation, looking on and learning. But is not this master sometimes kind and indulgent to his slaves? does he not mete out to

63

them, for faithful service, the reward of his cordial approbation? Is it not his interest to do it? and when thus acting humanely, and speaking kindly, where is the child, the creature of imitation, that he does not look on and learn? We may rest assured, in this intercourse between a good master and his servant, more good than evil *may* be taught the child, the exalted principles of morality and religion may thereby be sometimes indelibly inculcated upon his mind, and instead of being reared a selfish contracted being, with nought but self to look to—he acquires a more exalted benevolence, a greater generosity and elevation of soul, and embraces for the sphere of his generous actions a much wider field. Look to the slave-holding population of our country, and you everywhere find them characterized by noble and elevated sentiment, by humane and virtuous feelings. We do not find among them that cold, contracted, calculating *selfishness*, which withers and repels every thing around it, and lessens or destroys all the multiplied enjoyments of social intercourse. Go into our national councils, and ask for the most generous, the most disinterested, the most conscientious, and the least unjust and oppressive in their principles, and see whether the slave-holder will be past by in the selection. Edwards says that slavery in the West Indies seems to awaken the laudable propensities of our nature, such as "frankness, sociability, benevolence, and generosity. In no part of the globe is the virtue of hospitality more prevalent than in the British sugar islands. The gates of the planter are always open to the reception of his guests—to be a stranger is of itself a sufficient introduction."

Is it not a fact, known to every man in the South, that the most *cruel masters* are those who have been unaccustomed to slavery. It is well known that northern gentlemen who marry southern heiresses, are much severer masters than southern gentlemen. And yet, if Mr. Jefferson's reasoning were correct, they ought to be much milder: in fact, it follows from his reasoning, that the authority which the father is called on to exercise over his children, must be seriously detrimental; and yet we know that this is not the case; that on the contrary, there is nothing which so much humanizes and softens the heart, as this *very authority*; and there are none, even among those who have no children themselves, so disposed to pardon the follies and indiscretion of youth, as those who have seen most of them, and suffered greatest annoyance. There may be many cruel relentless masters, and there are unkind and cruel fathers too; but both the one and the other make all those around them shudder with horror. We are disposed to think that their ex-

64

ample in society tends rather to strengthen, than weaken the principle of benevolence and humanity.

Let us now look a moment to the slave, and contemplate *his* position. Mr. Jefferson has described him as hating, rather than loving his master, and as losing, too, all that *amor patriae* which characterizes the true patriot. We assert again, that Mr. Jefferson is not borne out by the fact. We are well convinced that there is nothing but the mere relations of husband and wife, parent and child, brother and sister, which produce a closer tie, than the relation of master and servant. We have no hesitation in affirming, that throughout the whole slave-holding country, the slaves of a good master are his warmest, most constant, and most devoted friends; they have been accustomed to look up to him as their supporter, director, and defender. Every one acquainted with southern slaves, knows that the slave rejoices in the elevation and prosperity of his master; and the heart of no one is more gladdened at the successful debut of young master or miss on the great theatre of the world, than that of either the young slave who has grown up with them, and shared in all their sports, and even partaken of all their delicacies—or the aged one who has looked on and watched them from birth to manhood, with the kindest and most affectionate solicitude, and has ever met from them all, the kind treatment and generous sympathies of feeling tender hearts.

Gilbert Stuart, in his History of Society, says that the time when the vassal of the feudal ages was most faithful, most obedient, and most interested in the welfare of his master, was precisely when his dependence was most complete, and when, consequently, he relied upon his lord for every thing. When the feudal tenure was gradually changing, and the law was interposing between landlord and tenant, the close tie between them began to dissolve, and with it, the kindness on one side, and the affection and gratitude on the other, waned and vanished. From all this, we are forced to draw one important inference—that it is dangerous to the happiness and well being of the slave, for either the imprudent philanthropist to attempt to interpose too often, or the rash legislator to obtrude his regulating edicts, between master and slave. They only serve to render the slave more intractable and unhappy, and the master more cruel and unrelenting. And we call upon the reverend clergy, whose examples should be pure, and whose precepts should be fraught with wisdom and prudence, to beware, lest in their zeal for the black, they suffer too much of the passion and prejudice of the human heart to mingle with those pure principles by which they should be governed. Let them beware of "what spirit they are of." "No sound," says Burke, "ought to be heard in the church, but the healing voice of Christian charity. Those who quit their proper character, to assume what does not belong to them, are for the most part ignorant of the character they assume, and of the character they leave off. Wholly unacquainted with the world in which they are so fond of meddling, and inexperienced in all its affairs, on which they pronounce with so much confidence, they have nothing of politics but the *passions* they excite. Surely the church is a place where one day's truce ought to be allowed to the dissensions and animosities of mankind."

In the debate in the Virginia legislature, no speaker *insinuated even*, we believe that the slaves in Virginia were not treated kindly; and all too agreed that they were most abundantly fed, and we have no doubt but that they form the happiest portion of our society. A merrier being does not exist on the face of the globe than the negro slave of the United States. . . .

3dly. *It has been contended that slavery is unfavourable to a republican spirit*: but the whole history of the world proves that this is far from being the case. In the ancient republics of Greece and Rome, where the spirit of liberty glowed with most intensity, the slaves were more numerous than the freemen. Aristotle, and the great men of antiquity, believed slavery necessary to keep alive the spirit of freedom. In Sparta, the freeman was even forbidden to perform the offices of slaves, lest he might lose the spirit of independence. In modern times, too, liberty has always been more ardently desired by slave-holding communities. "Such," says Burke, "were our Gothic ancestors; such, in our days, were the Poles; and such will be all masters of slaves who are not slaves themselves."—"These people of the southern (American) colonies are much more strongly, and with a higher and more stubborn spirit, attached to liberty, than those of the northward." And from the time of Burke down to the present day, the southern states have always borne this same honourable distinction. Burke says, "it is because freedom is to them not only an enjoyment, but a kind of rank and privilege." Another, and perhaps more efficient cause, of this, is the perfect spirit of equality so prevalent among the whites of all the slave-holding states. Jack Cade, the English reformer, wished all mankind to be brought to one common level. We believe slavery, in the United States, has accomplished this, in regard to the whites, as nearly as can be expected or even desired in this world. The menial and low offices being all performed by the

blacks, there is at once taken away the greatest cause of distinction and separation of the ranks of society. The man to the north will not shake hands
familiarly with his servant, and converse, and laugh, and dine with him, no
matter how honest and respectable he may be. But go to the south, and you
will find that no white man feels such inferiority of rank as to be unworthy
of association with those around him. The same thing is observed in the
West Indies. "Of the character common to the white residents of the West
Indies, it appears to me," says Edwards, "that the leading feature is an independent spirit, and a display of *conscious equality* throughout all ranks and
conditions. The poorest white person seems to consider himself nearly on a
level with the richest; and emboldened by this idea, approaches his employer with extended hand, and a freedom, which, in the countries of Europe, is seldom displayed by men in the lower orders of life towards their
superiors." And it is this spirit of equality which is both the generator and
preserver of the genuine spirit of liberty.

4thly. *Insecurity of the whites, arising from plots, insurrections, &c.,
among the blacks.* This is the evil, after all, let us say what we will, which
really operates most powerfully upon the schemers and emancipating philanthropists of those sections where slaves constitute the principal property.
Now, if we have shown, as we trust we have, that the scheme of deportation
is utterly impracticable, and that emancipation, with permission to remain,
will produce all these horrors in *still greater degree*, it follows that this evil
of slavery, allowing it to exist in all its latitude, would be no argument for
legislative action, and therefore we might well rest contented with this issue; but as we are anxious to exhibit this whole subject in its true bearings,
and as we do believe that this evil has been most strangely and causelessly
exaggerated, we have determined to examine it a moment, and point out its
true extent. It seems to us, that those who insist most upon it, commit the
enormous error of looking upon every slave in the whole slave-holding
country as actuated by the most deadly enmity to the whites, and possessing
all that reckless, fiendish temper, which would lead him to murder and as-
sassinate the moment the opportunity occurs. This is far from being true;
the slave, as we have already said, generally loves the master and his family;
and few indeed there are, who can coldly plot the murder of men, women,
and children; and if they do, there are fewer still who can have the villany to
execute. We can sit down and imagine that all the negroes in the south have
conspired to rise on a certain night, and murder all the whites in their re-

67

spective families; we may suppose the secret to be kept, and that they have the physical power to exterminate; and yet, we say the whole is *morally impossible*. No insurrection of this kind can ever occur where the blacks are as much civilized as they are in the United States. Savages and Koromantyn slaves can commit such deeds, because their whole life and education have prepared them, and they glory in the achievement; but the negro of the United States has imbibed the principles, the sentiments, and feelings of the white; in one word, he is civilized—at least, comparatively; his whole education and course of life are at war with such fell deeds. Nothing, then, but the most subtle and poisonous principles, sedulously infused into his mind, can break his allegiance, and transform him into the midnight murderer. Any man who will attend to the history of the Southampton massacre, must at once see, that the cause of even the partial success of the insurrectionists, was the very circumstance that there was no extensive plot, and that Nat, a demented fanatic, was under the impression that heaven had enjoined him to liberate the blacks, and had made its manifestations by loud noises in the air, an eclipse, and by the greenness of the sun. It was these signs which determined *him*, and ignorance and superstition, together with implicit confidence in Nat, determined a few others, and thus the bloody work began. So fearfully and reluctantly did they proceed to the execution, that we have no doubt but that if Travis, the first attacked, could have waked whilst they were getting into his house, or could have shot down Nat or Will, the rest would have fled, and the affair would have terminated *in limine*.

We have read with great attention the history of the insurrections in St. Domingo, and have no hesitation in affirming, that to the reflecting mind, that whole history affords the most complete evidence of the difficulty and almost impossibility of succeeding in these plots, even under the most favourable circumstances. It would almost have been a *moral miracle*, if that revolution had not succeeded. The French revolution had kindled a blaze throughout the world. The society of the *Amis des Noirs* (the friends of the blacks,) in Paris, had educated and disciplined many of the mulattoes, who were almost as numerous as the whites in the island. The National Assembly, in its mad career, declared these mulattoes to be equal in all respects to the whites, and gave them the same privileges and immunities as the whites. During the ten years, too, immediately preceding the revolution, more than 200,000 negroes were imported into the island from Africa. It is a well known fact, that newly imported negroes are always greatly more dangerous than those born among us; and of those importations a very large proportion consisted of Koromantyn slaves, from the Gold Coast, who have all the savage ferocity of the North American Indian. And lastly, the whites themselves, disunited and strangely inharmonious, would nevertheless have suppressed the insurrections, although the blacks and mulattoes were nearly *fifteen-fold* their numbers, if it had not been for the constant and too fatal interference of France. The great sin of that revolution rests on the *National Assembly*, and should be an awful warning to every legislature to beware of too much tampering with so delicate and difficult a subject as an alteration of the fundamental relations of society.

But there is another cause which will render the success of the blacks for ever impossible in the South, as long as slavery exists. It is, that, in modern times especially, wealth and talent must ever rule over *mere* physical force. During the feudal ages, the vassals never made a settled concerted attempt to throw off the yoke of the lord or landed proprietor; and the true reason was, they had neither property nor talent, and consequently the power, under these circumstances, could be placed nowhere else than in the hands of the lords; but so soon as the *tiers etat* arose, with commerce and manufactures, there was something to struggle for, and the *crise des revolutions*, (the crisis of revolutions,) was the consequence. No connected, persevering, and well concerted movement, ever takes place, in modern times, unless for the sake of property. Now, the property, talent, concert, and we may add habit, are all with the whites, and render their continued superiority absolutely certain, if they are not meddled with, no matter what may be the disproportion of numbers. We look upon these insurrections in the same light that we do the murders and robberies which occur in society, and in a slave-holding state, they are a sort of substitute for the latter; the robbers and murderers in what are called free states, are generally the poor and needy, who rob for money; negro slaves rarely murder or rob for this purpose; they have no inducement to do it—the fact is, the whole capital of the South is pledged for their maintenance. Now, there is no doubt but that the common robberies and murders, for money, take off, in the aggregate, more men, and destroy more property than insurrections among the slaves; the former are the result of fixed causes *eternally* at work, the latter of occasional causes which are rarely, *very rarely*, in action. Accordingly, if we should look to the whole of our southern population, and compare the average number of deaths, by the hands of assassins, with the numbers elsewhere, we would be astonished to find them perhaps as few or fewer than in any other population of equal amount on the globe. In the city of London there is, upon an average, a murder or a house-breaking and robbery every night in the year, which is greater than the amount of deaths by murders, insurrections, &c., in our whole southern country; and yet the inhabitant of London walks the streets and sleeps in perfect confidence, and why should not we who are in fact in much less danger? These calamities in London, very properly give rise to the establishment of a police, and the adoption of precautionary measures; and so they should in our country, and every where else. And if the Virginia legislature had turned its attention more to this subject during its last session, we think, with all due deference, it would have redounded much more to the advantage of the state than the intemperate discussion which was gotten up.

But it is agreed on almost all hands, that the danger of insurrection now is not very great; but a time must arrive, it is supposed by many, when the dangers will infinitely increase, and either the one or the other race must necessarily be exterminated. "I do believe," said one in the Virginia legislature, "and such must be the judgment of every reflecting man, that unless something is done in time to obviate it, the day must arrive when scenes of inconceivable horror must inevitably occur, and one of these two races of human beings will have their throats cut by the other." Another gentleman anticipates the dark day when a negro legislature would be in session in the capital of the Old Dominion! . . .

But we have none of these awful forebodings. We do not look to the time when the throats of one race must be cut by the other; on the contrary, we have no hesitation in affirming, and we think we can prove it too, that in 1929, taking Mr. Clay's own statistics, we shall be much more secure from plots and insurrections, than we are at this moment. It is an undeniable fact, that in the increase of population, the power and security of the dominant party always increase *much more* than in proportion to the relative augmentation of their numbers. One hundred men can much more easily keep an equal number in subjection than fifty, and a million would rule a million more certainly and securely than any lesser number. The dominant can only be overturned by concert and harmony among the subject party, and the greater the relative numbers on both sides, the more impossible does this concert on the part of the subjected become. A police, too, of the same *rela-*

tive numbers, is much more efficient amid a numerous population, than a very sparse one. . . .

Let us apply these principles to our own case; and for the sake of simplicity we will take a country of a mixed population of twenty thousand, viz. blacks ten thousand, and whites as many:—the patrol which they can keep out, would, according to our rule, be two hundred—double both sides, and the patrol would be four hundred, quadruple and it would be eight hundred—now a patrol of eight hundred would be much more efficient than the two hundred, though they were, relatively to the numbers kept in order, exactly the same; and the same principle is applicable to the progress of population in the whole slave-holding country. In 1929, our police will be much more efficient than now, if the two castes preserve any thing like the same relative numbers. We believe it would be better for the whites that the negro population should double, if they added only one half more to their numbers, than that they should remain stationary on both sides. Hence an insuperable objection to all these deporting schemes—they cannot diminish the relative proportion of the blacks to the whites, but on the contrary increase it, while they check the augmentation of the population as a whole, and consequently lessen the security of the dominant party. We do not fear the increase of the blacks, for that very increase adds to the wealth of society, and enables it to keep up the police. This is the true secret of the security of the West Indies and Brazil. In Jamaica, the blacks are eight fold the whites; throughout the extensive empire of Brazil, they are three to one. Political prophets have been prophesying for fifty years past, that the day would speedily arrive, when all the West Indies would be in the possession of the negroes; and the danger is no greater now, than it was at the commencement. We sincerely believe the blacks never will get possession, unless through the mad interference of the mother countries, and *even* then we are doubtful whether they can conquer the whites. Now, we have nowhere in the United States, the immense disproportion between the two races observed in Brazil and the West Indies, and we are not like to have it in all time to come. We have no data, therefore, upon which to anticipate that dreadful crisis, which so torments the imagination of some.

But our population returns have been looked to, and it has been affirmed that they show a steady increase of blacks, which will finally carry them in all proportion beyond the whites, and that this will be particularly the case in Eastern Virginia. We have no fears on this score either: even if it were true, the danger would not be very great. With the increase of the blacks, we can afford to enlarge the police; and we will venture to say, that with the hundredth man at our disposal, and faithful to us, we would keep down insurrection in any large country on the face of the globe. But the speakers in the Virginia legislature, in our humble opinion, made most unwarrantable inferences from the census returns. They took a period between 1790 and 1830, and judged exclusively from the aggregate results of that whole time. Mr. Brown pointed out their fallacy, and showed that there was but a small portion of the period in which the blacks had rapidly gained upon the whites, but during the residue they were most rapidly losing their high relative increase, and would, perhaps, in 1840, exhibit an augmentation less than the whites. But let us go a little back—in 1740 the slaves in South Carolina, says Marshall, were three times the whites, the danger from them was greater then than it ever has been since, or ever will be again. There was an insurrection in that year, which was put down with the utmost ease, although instigated and aided by the Spaniards. The slaves in Virginia, at the same period, were much more numerous than the whites. Now suppose some of those *peepers* into futurity could have been present, would they not have predicted the speedy arrival of the time when the blacks, running ahead of the whites in numbers, would have destroyed their security? In 1763, the black population of Virginia was 100,000, and the white 70,000. In South Carolina, the blacks were 90,000, and the whites 40,000. Comparing these with the returns of 1740, our prophets, could they have lived so long, might have found some consolation in the greater relative increase of the whites. Again, when we see in 1830, that the blacks in both states have fallen in numbers below the whites, our prophets, were they alive, might truly be pronounced *false*. (*See Holmes's Annals, and Marshall's Life of Washington*, on this subject.)

We are happy to see that the legislature of Virginia, during the last session, incorporated a company to complete the James river and Kanhawa improvements, and that the city of Richmond has so liberally contributed by her subscriptions, as to render the project almost certain of success. It is this great improvement which is destined to revolutionize the financial condition of the Old Dominion, and speed her on more rapidly in wealth and numbers, than she has ever advanced before: the snail pace at which she has hitherto been crawling, is destined to be converted into the giant's stride, and this very circumstance, of itself, will defeat all the gloomy predictions about the blacks. The first effect of the improvement will be to raise up larger towns in the eastern portion of the state. Besides other manifold advantages which these towns will diffuse, they will have a tendency to draw into them the capital and free labourers of the north, and in this way to destroy the proportion of the blacks. Baltimore is now an exemplification of this fact, which by its mighty agency is fast making Maryland a non-slaveholding state. Again, the rise of cities in the lower part of Virginia, and increased density of population, will render the division of labour more complete, break down the large farms into small ones, and substitute, in a great measure, the garden for the plantation cultivation; consequently, less slave and more free labour will be requisite, and in due time the abolitionists will find this most lucrative system working to their heart's content, increasing the prosperity of Virginia, and diminishing the evils of slavery without those impoverishing effects which all other schemes must *necessarily* have. We hope then that those gentlemen who have so perseveringly engaged in urging forward this great scheme of improvement, will not falter until the work is accomplished, and they will have the consolation of seeing that its moral effects will be no less salutary than the physical.

5thly, and lastly. *Slave labour is unproductive, and the distressed condition of Virginia and the whole South is owing to this cause.* Our limits will not allow us to investigate fully this assertion, but a very partial analysis will enable us to show that the truth of the general proposition upon which the conclusion is based, depends on circumstances, and that those circumstances do not apply to our southern country. The ground assumed by Smith and Storch, who are the most able supporters of the doctrine of the superior productiveness of free labour, is that each one is actuated by a desire to accumulate when free, and this desire produces much more efficient and constant exertions than can possibly be expected from the feeble operation of fear upon the slave. We are, in the main, converts to this doctrine, but must be permitted to limit it by some considerations. It is very evident, when we look to the various countries in which there is free labour alone, that a vast difference in its productiveness is manifested. The English operative we are disposed to consider the most productive labourer in the world, and the Irish labourer, in his immediate neighbourhood, is not more than equal to the southern slave—the Spanish and even Italian labourers are inferior. Now, how are we to account for this great difference? It will be found *mainly* to depend upon the operation of two great principles, and *secondarily* upon attendant circumstances. These two principles are the desire to accumulate and better our condition, and a desire to indulge in idleness and inactivity.

We have already seen that the principle of idleness triumphed over the desire for accumulation among the savages of North and South America, among the African nations, among the blacks of St. Domingo, &c., and nothing but the strong arm of authority could overcome its operation. In southern countries, idleness is very apt to predominate, even under the most favourable circumstances, over the desire to accumulate, and slave labour, consequently, in such countries, is most productive. Again, staple-growing states are, *caeteris paribus*, more favourable to slave labour than manufacturing states. Slaves in such countries may be worked in bodies under the eye of a superintendent, and made to perform more labour than freemen. There is no instance of the successful cultivation of the sugar cane by free labour. St. Domingo, once the greatest sugar-growing island in the world, makes now scarcely enough for her own supply. We very much doubt even whether slave labour be not best for all southern agricultural countries. Humboldt, in his New Spain, says he doubts whether there be a plant on the globe so productive as the banana, and yet these banana districts, strange to tell, are the poorest and most miserable in all South America, because the people only labour a little to support themselves, and spend the rest of their time in idleness. There is no doubt but slave labour would be the most productive kind in these districts. We doubt whether the extreme south of the United States, and the West India islands, would ever have been cultivated to the same degree of perfection as now, by any other than slave labour.

But it is said free labour becomes cheaper than slave labour, and finally extinguishes it, as has actually happened in the West of Europe; this we are ready to admit, but think it was owing to a change in the tillage, and the rise of manufactures and commerce, to which free labour alone is adapted. As a proof of this, we can cite the populous empire of China, and the eastern nations generally, where slave labour has stood its ground against free labour, although the population is denser, and the proportional means of subsistence more scanty than anywhere else on the face of the globe. How is

74

this to be accounted for, let us ask? Does it not prove, that under some circumstances, slave labour is as productive as free? We would as soon look to
China to test this principle, as any other nation on earth. Again, looking to
the nations of antiquity, if the Scriptural accounts are to be relied on, the
number of inhabitants in Palestine must have been more than 6,000,000; at
which rate, Palestine was at least, when taking into consideration her limited territory, five times as populous as England. Now we know that the
tribes of Judah and Israel both used slave labour, and it must have been exceedingly productive, for we find the two Kings of Judah and Israel bringing
into the field no less than 1,200,000 chosen men; and Jehosaphat, the son of
Asa, had an army consisting of 1,160,000; and what a prodigious force
must he have commanded, had he been sovereign of all the tribes! Nothing
but the most productive labour could ever have supported the immense armies which were then led into the field. . . .

But the southern states, and particularly Virginia, have been compared
with the non-slave-holding states, and pronounced far behind them in the
general increase of wealth and population; and this, it is said, is a decisive
proof of the inferiority of slave labour in this country. We are sorry we have
not the space for a thorough investigation of this assertion, but we have no
doubt of its fallacy. Look to the progress of the colonies before the establishment of the federal government, and you find the slave-holding were the
most prosperous and the most wealthy. The north dreaded the formation of
the confederated government, *precisely* because of its *poverty*. This is an
historic fact. It stood to the south, as Scotland did to England at the period
of the Union; and feared lest the south, by its superior wealth, supported by
this very *slave labour*, which, all of a *sudden*, has become so unproductive,
should abstract the little wealth which it possessed. Again, look to the exports at the present time of the whole confederacy, and what do we see—
why, that one-third of the states, and those *slave-holding* too, furnish two-
thirds of the whole exports!! But although this is now the case, we are still
not prosperous. Let us ask them two simple questions; 1st. How came the
south, for two hundred years, to prosper with her slave labour, if so very
unproductive and ruinous? and 2dly. How does it happen, that her exports
are so great even now, and that her prosperity is nevertheless on the decline?
Painful as the accusation may be to the heart of the true patriot, we are
forced to assert, that the unequal operation of the federal government has

principally achieved it. The north has found that it could not compete with the south in agriculture, and has had recourse to the system of duties, for the purpose of raising up the business of manufactures. This is a business in which the slave labour cannot compete with northern, and in order to carry this system through, a coalition has been formed with the west, by which a large portion of the federal funds are to be spent in that quarter for internal improvements. These duties act as a discouragement to southern industry, which furnishes the exports by which the imports are purchased, and a bounty to northern labour, and the partial disbursements of the funds increase the pressure on the south to a still greater degree. It is not slave labour then which has produced our depression, but it is the action of the federal government which is ruining slave labour. . . .

There are other causes too, which have operated in concert with the federal government, to depress the south. The climate is unhealthy, and upon an average, perhaps one-tenth of the labour is suspended during the sickly months. There is a great deal of travelling too, from this cause, to the north, which abstracts the capital from the south, and spreads it over the north; and added to all this, the *standard of comfort* is much higher in the slave-holding than the non-slave-holding states. All these circumstances together, are surely sufficient to account for the depressed condition of the south, without asserting that slave labour is valueless. But we believe all other causes as "dust in the balance," when compared with the operation of the federal government.

How does it happen that Louisiana, with a greater proportional number of slaves than any other state in the Union, with the most insalubrious climate, with one-fourth of her white population spread over the more northern states in the sickly season, and with a higher *standard of comfort* than perhaps any other state in the Union, is nevertheless one of the most rapidly flourishing in the whole southern country? The true answer is, she has been so fortunately situated as to be able to reap the fruits of federal protection. "Midas's wand" has touched her, and she has reaped the golden harvest. There is no complaint there of the unproductiveness of slave labour.

But it is time to bring this long article to a close; it is upon a subject which we have most reluctantly discussed; but, as we have already said, the example was set from a higher quarter; the seal has been broken, and we therefore determined to enter fully into the discussion. If our positions be true, and it does seem to us they may be sustained by reasoning almost as conclusive as the demonstration of the mathematician, it follows, that the time for emancipation has not yet arrived, and perhaps it never will. We hope sincerely, that the intelligent sons of Virginia will ponder well before they move—before they enter into a scheme which will destroy more than half Virginia's wealth, and drag her down from her proud and elevated station among the mean things of the earth.

II. WILLIAM HARPER
Memoir on Slavery

". . . an institution which has interwoven itself with every fibre
of the body politic; which has formed the habits of our society,
and is consecrated by the usage of generations."

William Harper was born in Antigua in 1790, the son of a Presbyterian minister who moved with his family to Charleston in 1799. Young
Harper graduated from South Carolina College in 1808 and was admitted
to the bar in 1813. After army service in the War of 1812, Harper opened a
law office in Columbia. In 1818 he moved to Missouri, where he soon became chancellor, the highest legal officer of the territory, then, after the admission of Missouri to the Union, of the state. In 1823 he returned to South
Carolina and in 1826 served briefly in the U.S. Senate. In 1828 he represented Charleston in the state legislature and was elected speaker of the
lower house, where he became leader of an antitariff coalition. Even when
he left the legislature to become chancellor of South Carolina later the same
year, Harper remained politically active and was an ardent supporter of
Nullification. As an appeals court judge from 1830–35, Harper wrote decisions noted for their powerful presentation of the states' rights position. In
1835, Harper left the bench to reassume the position of state chancellor. He
continued to speak and write on sectional issues until his death in 1847.[1]

Harper's *Memoir on Slavery* was originally an anniversary oration delivered in Columbia in 1837 before the South Carolina Society for the Advancement of Learning. The speech was printed in pamphlet form early in
1838. Two years before, after northerners had begun to escalate their abolitionist attacks, Harper had made an address to the same organization in
which he called upon southerners to undertake a detailed inquiry into the
complicated questions surrounding the rising controversy over slavery. Ap-

---

1. On Harper's life, see J. G. DeR. Hamilton, "William Harper," *Dictionary of American
Biography*, ed. Allen Johnson and Dumas Malone (New York: Charles Scribner's Sons, 1932),
IV, 287; Charleston *Courier*, October 15, 1847.

parently, the South Carolinian took his own advice to heart, for his *Memoir* represented a careful examination of the issues and a confident advocacy of the institution not evident in his earlier oration.[2]

Whereas Thomas Dew had dealt chiefly with the immediate circumstances of slavery in Virginia, Harper began his essay with the sweeping statement that slavery "exists over far the greater portion of the inhabited earth." Far from being a peculiar institution, human bondage must be "deeply founded in the nature of man and the exigencies of human society." Harper declared his intention to broaden the appeal of the proslavery argument by going beyond the "present position of the Slave-Holding States" to consider slavery as "a naked, abstract question." Harper attacked the Revolutionary heritage with its "well-sounding but unmeaning verbiage of natural equality and inalienable rights" and rejected another of the favorite doctrines of the Founding Fathers by arguing for the inherent and permanent inequality of blacks apart from any environmental influence. While launching a direct assault upon the misguidedness of northern reform and philanthropy, Harper insisted that social improvement could result only from individual moral uplift and could never come from precipitous tampering with institutions that had evolved over time. Slavery, he proclaimed, was essential to the South and "the habits of our society." Far from being an evil to be extirpated, slavery was the "sole cause of civilization." Demonstrating a new level of assertiveness and self-assurance, Harper's essay was reprinted in 1852 in *The Pro-Slavery Argument as Maintained by the Most Distinguished Writers of the Southern States* and in the 1860 collection of proslavery classics, *Cotton is King and Pro-Slavery Arguments.*[3]

Memoir on Slavery

The institution of domestic slavery exists over far the greater portion of the inhabited earth. Until within a very few centuries, it may be said to have existed over the whole earth—at least in all those portions of it

2. William Harper, *Anniversary Oration. South Carolina Society for the Advancement of Learning* (Washington, D.C.: Duff Green, 1836); William Harper, *Memoir on Slavery, Read Before the Society for the Advancement of Learning of South Carolina at Its Annual Meeting at Columbia, 1837* (Charleston: James S. Burges, 1838).
3. William Harper, "Memoir on Slavery," *The Pro-Slavery Argument as Maintained by the Most Distinguished Writers of the Southern States* (Charleston: Walker, Richards & Co.,

which had made any advances towards civilization. We might safely conclude then that it is deeply founded in the nature of man and the exigencies of human society. Yet, in the few countries in which it has been abolished—claiming, perhaps justly, to be farthest advanced in civilization and intelligence, but which have had the smallest opportunity of observing its true character and effects—it is denounced as the most intolerable of social and political evils. Its existence, and every hour of its continuance, is regarded as the crime of the communities in which it is found. Even by those in the countries alluded to, who regard it with the most indulgence or the least abhorrence—who attribute no criminality to the present generation—who found it in existence, and have not yet been able to devise the means of abolishing it, it is pronounced a misfortune and a curse injurious and dangerous always, and which must be finally fatal to the societies which admit it. This is no longer regarded as a subject of argument and investigation. The opinions referred to are assumed as settled, or the truth of them as self-evident. If any voice is raised among ourselves to extenuate or to vindicate, it is unheard. The judgment is made up. We can have no hearing before the tribunal of the civilized world.

Yet, on this very account, it is more important that we, the inhabitants of the slave holding States of America, insulated as we are, by this institution, and cut off, in some degree, from the communion and sympathies of the world by which we are surrounded, or with which we have intercourse, and exposed continually to their animadversions and attacks, should thoroughly understand this subject and our strength and weakness in relation to it. If it be thus criminal, dangerous and fatal; and if it be possible to devise means of freeing ourselves from it, we ought at once to set about the employing of those means. It would be the most wretched and imbecile fatuity, to shut our eyes to the impending dangers and horrors, and "drive darkling down the current of our fate," till we are overwhelmed in the final destruction. If we are tyrants, cruel, unjust, oppressive, let us humble ourselves and repent in the sight of Heaven, that the foul stain may be cleansed, and we enabled to stand erect as having common claims to humanity with our fellow men.

But if we are nothing of all this; if we commit no injustice or cruelty; if

1852), 1–98; William Harper, "Slavery in the Light of Social Ethics," *Cotton Is King and Pro-Slavery Arguments* (Augusta: Pritchard, Abbott & Loomis, 1860), 547–626.

the maintenance of our institutions be essential to our prosperity, our character, our safety, and the safety of all that is dear to us, let us enlighten our minds and fortify our hearts to defend them.

It is a somewhat singular evidence of the indisposition of the rest of the world to hear any thing more on this subject, that perhaps the most profound, original and truly philosophical treatise, which has appeared within the time of my recollection, seems not to have attracted the slightest attention out of the limits of the slave holding States themselves. If truth, reason and conclusive argument, propounded with admirable temper and perfect candour, might be supposed to have an effect on the minds of man, we should think this work would have put an end to agitation on the subject. The author has rendered inappreciable service to the South in enlightening them on the subject of their own institutions, and turning back that monstrous tide of folly and madness which, if it had rolled on, would have involved his own great State along with the rest of the slave holding States in a common ruin. But beyond these, he seems to have produced no effect whatever. The denouncers of Slavery, with whose productions the press groans, seem to be unaware of his existence—unaware that there is reason to be encountered, or argument to be answered. They assume that the truth is known and settled, and only requires to be enforced by denunciation. . . .

President Dew has shown that the institution of Slavery is a principal cause of civilization. Perhaps nothing can be more evident than that it is the sole cause. If any thing can be predicated as universally true of uncultivated man, it is that he will not labour beyond what is absolutely necessary to maintain his existence. Labour is pain to those who are unaccustomed to it, and the nature of man is averse to pain. Even with all the training, the helps and motives of civilization, we find that this aversion cannot be overcome in many individuals of the most cultivated societies. The coercion of Slavery alone is adequate to form man to habits of labour. Without it, there can be no accumulation of property, no providence for the future, no taste for comforts or elegancies, which are the characteristics and essentials of civilization. He who has obtained the command of another's labour, first begins to accumulate and provide for the future, and the foundations of civilization are laid. We find confirmed by experience that which is so evident in theory. Since the existence of man upon the earth, with no exception whatever, either of ancient or modern times, every society which has attained civilization, has advanced to it through this process.

Will those who regard Slavery as immoral, or crime in itself, tell us that man was not intended for civilization, but to roam the earth as a biped brute? That he was not to raise his eyes to Heaven, or be conformed in his nobler faculties to the image of his Maker? Or will they say that the Judge of all the earth has done wrong in ordaining the means by which alone that end can be attained? It is true that the Creator can make the wickedness as well as the wrath of man to praise him, and bring forth the most benevolent results from the most atrocious actions. But in such cases, it is the motive of the actor alone which condemns the action. The act itself is good, if it promotes the good purposes of God, and would be approved by him, if that result only were intended. Do they not blaspheme the providence of God who denounce as wickedness and outrage, that which is rendered indispensable to his purposes in the government of the world? Or at what stage of the progress of society will they say that Slavery ceases to be necessary, and its very existence becomes sin and crime? I am aware that such argument would have little effect on those with whom it would be degrading to contend—who pervert the inspired writings—which in some parts expressly sanction Slavery, and throughout indicate most clearly that it is a civil institution, with which religion has no concern—with a shallowness and presumption not less flagrant and shameless than his, who would justify murder from the text, "and Phineas arose and executed judgment."

There seems to be something in this subject, which blunts the perceptions, and darkens and confuses the understandings and moral feelings of men. Tell them that, of necessity, in every civilized society, there must be an infinite variety of conditions and employments, from the most eminent and intellectual, to the most servile and laborious; that the negro race, from their temperament and capacity, are peculiarly suited to the situation which they occupy, and not less happy in it than any corresponding class to be found in the world; prove incontestably that no scheme of emancipation could be carried into effect without the most intolerable mischiefs and calamities to both master and slave, or without probably throwing a large and fertile portion of the earth's surface out of the pale of civilization—and you have done nothing. They reply, that whatever may be the consequence, you are bound to do *right*; that man has a right to himself, and man cannot have a property in man; that if the negro race be naturally inferior in mind and character, they are not less entitled to the rights of humanity; that if they are happy in their condition, it affords but the stronger evidence of their degradation, and renders them still more objects of commiseration. They repeat, as the fundamental maxim of our civil policy, that all men are born free and equal, and quote from our Declaration of Independence, "that men are endowed by their Creator with certain inalienable *rights*, among which are life, liberty, and the pursuit of happiness."

It is not the first time that I have had occasion to observe that men may repeat with the utmost confidence, some maxim or sentimental phrase, as self-evident or admitted truth, which is either palpably false or to which, upon examination, it will be found that they attach no definite idea. Notwithstanding our respect for the important document which declared our independence, yet if any thing be found in it, and especially in what may be regarded rather as its ornament than its substance—false, sophistical or unmeaning, that respect should not screen it from the freest examination.

All men are born free and equal. Is it not palpably nearer the truth to say that no man was ever born free, and that no two men were ever born equal? Man is born in a state of the most helpless dependence on others. He continues subject to the absolute control of others, and remains without many of the civil, and all of the political privileges of his society, until the period which the laws have fixed, as that at which he is supposed to attain the maturity of his faculties. Then inequality is further developed, and becomes infinite in every society, and under whatever form of government. Wealth and poverty, fame or obscurity, strength or weakness, knowledge or ignorance, ease or labor, power or subjection, mark the endless diversity in the condition of men.

But we have not arrived at the profundity of the maxim. This inequality is in a great measure the result of abuses in the institutions of society. They do not speak of what exists, but of what ought to exist. Every one should be left at liberty to obtain all the advantages of society which he can compass, by the free exertion of his faculties, unimpeded by civil restraints. It may be said that this would not remedy the evils of society which are complained of. The inequalities to which I have referred, with the misery resulting from them, would exist in fact under the freest and most popular form of government that man could devise. But what is the foundation of the bold dogma so confidently announced? Females are human and rational beings. They may be found of better faculties and better qualified to exercise political privileges and to attain the distinctions of society than many men; yet who complains of the order of society by which they are excluded from them?

83

For I do not speak of the few who would desecrate them; do violence to the nature which their Creator has impressed upon them; drag them from the position which they necessarily occupy for the existence of civilized society, and in which they constitute its blessing and ornament—the only position which they have ever occupied in any human society—to place them in a situation in which they would be alike miserable and degraded. Low as we descend in combatting the theories of presumptuous dogmatists, it cannot be necessary to stoop to this. A youth of eighteen may have powers which cast into the shade those of any of his more advanced contemporaries. He may be capable of serving or saving his country, and if not permitted to do so now, the occasion may have been lost forever. But he can exercise no political privilege or aspire to any political distinction. It is said that of necessity, society must exclude from some civil and political privileges those who are unfitted to exercise them, by infirmity, unsuitableness of character, or defect of discretion; that of necessity there must be some general rule on the subject, and that any rule which can be devised will operate with hardship and injustice on individuals. This is all that can be said and all that need be said. It is saying, in other words, that the privileges in question are no matter of natural right, but to be settled by convention, as the good and safety of society may require. If society should disfranchise individuals convicted of infamous crimes, would this be an invasion of natural right? Yet this would not be justified on the score of their moral guilt, but that the good of society required, or would be promoted by it. We admit the existence of a moral law, binding on societies as on individuals. Society must act in good faith. No man or body of men has a right to inflict pain or privation on others, unless with a view, after full and impartial deliberation, to prevent a greater evil. If this deliberation be had, and the decision made in good faith, there can be no imputation of moral guilt. Has any politician contended that the very existence of governments in which there are orders privileged by law, constitutes a violation of morality; that their continuance is a crime, which men are bound to put an end to without any consideration of the good or evil to result from the change? Yet this is the natural inference from the dogma of the natural equality of men as applied to our institution of slavery—an equality not to be invaded without injustice and wrong, and requiring to be restored instantly, unqualifiedly, and without reference to consequences.

This is sufficiently common-place, but we are sometimes driven to common-place. It is no less a false and shallow than a presumptuous philosophy, which theorizes on the affairs of men as of a problem to be solved by some unerring rule of human reason, without reference to the designs of a superior intelligence, so far as he has been pleased to indicate them, in their creation and destiny. Man is born to subjection. Not only during infancy is he dependent and under the control of others; at all ages, it is the very bias of his nature, that the strong and the wise should control the weak and the ignorant. So it has been since the days of Nimrod. The existence of some form of Slavery in all ages and countries, is proof enough of this. He is born to subjection as he is born in sin and ignorance. To make any considerable progress in knowledge, the continued efforts of successive generations, and the diligent training and unwearied exertions of the individual are requisite. To make progress in moral virtue, not less time and effort, aided by superior help, are necessary; and it is only by the matured exercise of his knowledge and his virtue, that he can attain to civil freedom. Of all things, the existence of civil liberty is most the result of artificial institution. The proclivity of the natural man is to domineer or to be subservient. A noble result indeed, but in the attaining of which, as in the instances of knowledge and virtue, the Creator, for his own purposes, has set a limit beyond which we cannot go.

But he who is most advanced in knowledge, is most sensible of his own ignorance, and how much must forever be unknown to man in his present condition. As I have heard it expressed, the further you extend the circle of light, the wider is the horizon of darkness. He who has made the greatest progress in moral purity, is most sensible of the depravity, not only of the world around him, but of his own heart and the imperfection of his best motives, and this he knows that men must feel and lament so long as they continue men. So when the greatest progress in civil liberty has been made, the enlightened lover of liberty will know that there must remain much inequality, much injustice, much *Slavery*, which no human wisdom or virtue will ever be able wholly to prevent or redress. As I have before had the honor to say to this Society, the condition of our whole existence is but to struggle with evils—to compare them—to choose between them, and so far as we can, to mitigate them. To say that there is evil in any institution, is only to say that it is human.

And can we doubt but that this long discipline and laborious process, by which men are required to work out the elevation and improvement of their individual nature and their social condition, is imposed for a great and benevolent end? Our faculties are not adequate to the solution of the mystery, why it should be so; but the truth is clear, that the world was not intended for the seat of universal knowledge or goodness or happiness or freedom.

Man has been endowed by his Creator with certain inalienable rights, among which are life, liberty and the pursuit of happiness. What is meant by the *inalienable* right of liberty? Has any one who has used the words ever asked himself this question? Does it mean that a man has no right to alienate his own liberty—to sell himself and his posterity for slaves? This would seem to be the more obvious meaning. When the word *right* is used, it has reference to some law which sanctions it, and would be violated by its invasion. It must refer either to the general law of morality or the law of the country—the law of God or the law of man. If the law of any country permitted it, it would of course be absurd to say that the law of that country was violated by such alienation. If it have any meaning in this respect, it must mean that though the law of the country permitted it, the man would be guilty of an immoral act who should thus alienate his liberty. A fit question for schoolmen to discuss, and the consequences resulting from its decision as important as from any of theirs. Yet who will say that the man pressed by famine and in prospect of death, would be criminal for such an act? Self-preservation as is truly said, is the first law of nature. High and peculiar characters, by elaborate cultivation, may be taught to prefer death to Slavery, but it would be folly to prescribe this as a duty to the mass of mankind.

If any rational meaning can be attributed to the sentence I have quoted, it is this:—That the society, or the individuals who exercise the powers of government, are guilty of a violation of the law of God or of morality, when by any law or public act, they deprive men of life or liberty, or restrain them in the pursuit of happiness. Yet every government does, and of necessity must, deprive men of life and liberty for offences against society. Restrain them in the pursuit of happiness! Why all the laws of society are intended for nothing else but to restrain men from the pursuit of happiness, according to their own ideas of happiness or advantage—which the phrase must mean if it means any thing. And by what right does society punish by the loss of life or liberty? Not on account of the moral guilt of the criminal—not by impiously and arrogantly assuming the prerogative of the Almighty, to dispense justice or suffering, according to moral desert. It is for its own protection—it is the right of self-defence. If there existed the blackest moral turpitude, which by its example or consequences, could be of no evil to society, government would have nothing to do with that. If an action, the most harmless in its moral character, could be dangerous to the security of society, society would have the perfect right to punish it. If the possession of a black skin would be otherwise dangerous to society, society has the same right to protect itself by disfranchising the possessor of civil privileges, and to continue the disability to his posterity, if the same danger would be incurred by its removal. Society inflicts these forfeitures for the security of the lives of its members; it inflicts them for the security of their property, the great essential of civilization; it inflicts them also for the protection of its political institutions; the forcible attempt to overturn which, has always been justly regarded as the greatest crime; and who has questioned its right so to inflict? "Man cannot have property in man"—a phrase as full of meaning as, "who slays fat oxen should himself be fat." Certainly he may, if the laws of society allow it, and if it be on sufficient grounds, neither he nor society do wrong.

And is it by this—as we must call it, however recommended to our higher feelings by its associations—well-sounding, but unmeaning verbiage of natural equality and inalienable rights, that our lives are to be put in jeopardy, our property destroyed, and our political institutions overturned or endangered? If a people had on its borders a tribe of barbarians, whom no treaties or faith could bind, and by whose attacks they were constantly endangered, against whom they could devise no security, but that they should be exterminated or enslaved; would they not have the right to enslave them, and keep them in slavery so long as the same danger would be incurred by their manumission? If a civilized man and a savage were by chance placed together on a desolate island, and the former, by the superior power of civilization, would reduce the latter to subjection, would he not have the same right? Would this not be the strictest self-defence? I do not now consider, how far we can make out a similar case to justify our enslaving of the negroes. I speak to those who contend for inalienable rights, and that the existence of slavery always, and under all circumstances, involves injustice and crime.

As I have said, we acknowledge the existence of a moral law. It is not necessary for us to resort to the theory which resolves all right into force. The existence of such a law is imprinted on the hearts of all human beings.

But though its existence be acknowledged, the mind of man has hitherto been tasked in vain to discover an unerring standard of morality. It is a common and undoubted maxim of morality, that you shall not do evil that good may come. You shall not do injustice or commit an invasion of the rights of others, for the sake of a greater ulterior good. But what is injustice, and what are the rights of others? And why are we not to commit the one or invade the others? It is because it inflicts pain or suffering, present or prospective, or cuts them off from enjoyment which they might otherwise attain. The Creator has sufficiently revealed to us that *happiness* is the great end of existence, the sole object of all animated and sentient beings. To this he has directed their aspirations and efforts, and we feel that we thwart his benevolent purposes when we destroy or impede that happiness. This is the only *natural* right of man. All other rights result from the conventions of society, and these, to be sure, we are not to invade, whatever good may appear to us likely to follow. Yet are we in no instance to inflict pain or suffering, or disturb enjoyment for the sake of producing a greater good? Is the madman not to be restrained who would bring destruction on himself or others? Is pain not to be inflicted on the child, when it is the only means by which he can be effectually instructed to provide for his own future happiness? Is the surgeon guilty of wrong who amputates a limb to preserve life? Is it not the object of all penal legislation, to inflict suffering for the sake of greater good to be secured to society?

By what right is it that man exercises dominion over the beasts of the field; subdues them to painful labour, or deprives them of life for his sustenance or enjoyment? They are not rational beings. No, but they are the creatures of God, sentient beings, capable of suffering and enjoyment, and entitled to enjoy according to the measure of their capacities. Does not the voice of nature inform every one, that he is guilty of wrong when he inflicts on them pain without necessity or object? If their existence be limited to the present life, it affords the stronger argument for affording them the brief enjoyment of which it is capable. It is because the greater good is effected; not only to man but to the inferior animals themselves. The care of man gives the boon of existence to myriads who would never otherwise have enjoyed it, and the enjoyment of their existence is better provided for while it lasts. It belongs to the being of superior faculties to judge of the relations which shall subsist between himself and inferior animals, and the use he shall make of them; and he may justly consider himself, who has the greater capacity of enjoyment, in the first instance. Yet he must do this conscientiously, and no doubt, moral guilt has been incurred by the infliction of pain on these animals, with no adequate benefit to be expected. I do no disparagement to the dignity of human nature, even in its humblest form, when I say that on the very same foundation, with the difference only of circumstance and degree, rests the right of the civilized and cultivated man, over the savage and ignorant. It is the order of nature and of God, that the being of superior faculties and knowledge, and therefore of superior power, should control and dispose of those who are inferior. It is as much in the order of nature, that men should enslave each other, as that other animals should prey upon each other. I admit that he does this under the highest moral responsibility, and is most guilty if he wantonly inflicts misery or privation on beings more capable of enjoyment or suffering than brutes, without necessity or any view to the greater good which is to result. If we conceive of society existing without government, and that one man by his superior strength, courage or wisdom, could obtain the mastery of his fellows, he would have a perfect right to do so. He would be morally responsible for the use of his power, and guilty if he failed to direct them so as to promote their happiness as well as his own. Moralists have denounced the injustice and cruelty which have been practiced towards our aboriginal Indians, by which they have been driven from their native seats and exterminated, and no doubt with much justice. No doubt, much fraud and injustice has been practised in the circumstances and the manner of their removal. Yet who has contended that civilized manner of their removal. Yet who has contended that civilized man had no moral right to possess himself of the country? That he was bound to leave this wide and fertile continent which is capable of sustaining uncounted myriads of a civilized race, to a few roving and ignorant barbarians? Yet if any thing is certain, it is certain that there were no means by which he could possess the country, without exterminating or enslaving them. Savage and civilized man cannot live together, and the savage can only be tamed by being enslaved or by having slaves. By enslaving alone could he have preserved them. . . .

If we should refer to the common moral sense of mankind, as determined by their conduct in all ages and countries, for a standard of morality, it would seem to be in favor of Slavery. The will of God, as determined by utility, would be an infallible standard, if we had an unerring measure of utility. The Utilitarian Philosophy, as it is commonly understood, referring only to the animal wants and employments, and physical condition of man, is utterly false and degrading. If a sufficiently extended definition be given to utility, so as to include every thing that may be a source of enjoyment or suffering, it is for the most part useless. How can you compare the pleasures resulting from the exercise of the understanding, the taste and the imagination, with the animal enjoyments of the senses—the gratification derived from a fine poem with that from a rich banquet? How are we to weigh the pains and enjoyments of one man highly cultivated and of great sensibility, against those of many men of blunter capacity for enjoyment or suffering? And if we could determine with certainty in what utility consists, we are so short sighted with respect to consequences—the remote results of our best considered actions, are so often wide of our anticipations, or contrary to them, that we should still be very much in the dark. But though we cannot arrive at absolute certainty with respect to the utility of actions, it is always fairly matter of argument. Though an imperfect standard, it is the best we have, and perhaps the Creator did not intend that we should arrive at perfect certainty with regard to the morality of many actions. If after the most careful examination of consequences that we are able to make, with due distrust of ourselves, we impartially, and in good faith, decide for that which appears likely to produce the greatest good, we are free from moral guilt. And I would impress most earnestly, that with our imperfect and limited faculties, and short sighted as we are to the future, we can rarely, very rarely indeed, be justified in producing considerable present evil or suffering, in the expectation of remote future good—if indeed this can ever be justified.

In considering this subject, I shall not regard it in the first instance in reference to the present position of the Slave-Holding States, or the difficulties which lie in the way of their emancipating their Slaves, but as a naked, abstract question—whether it is better that the institution of praedial and domestic Slavery should, or should not exist in civilized society. And though some of my remarks may seem to have such a tendency, let me not be understood as taking upon myself to determine that it is better that it should exist. God forbid that the responsibility of deciding such a question should ever be thrown on me or my countrymen. But this I will say, and not without confidence, that it is in the power of no human intellect to establish the contrary proposition—that it is better it should not exist. This is probably known but to one being, and concealed from human sagacity.

90

There have existed in various ages, and we now see existing in the world, people in every stage of civilization, from the most barbarous to the most refined. Man, as I have said, is not born to civilization. He is born rude and ignorant. But it will be, I suppose, admitted that it is the design of his Creator that he should attain to civilization: That religion should be known, that the comforts and elegancies of life should be enjoyed, that letters and arts should be cultivated, in short, that there should be the greatest possible development of moral and intellectual excellence. It can hardly be necessary to say any thing of those who have extolled the superior virtues and enjoyments of savage life—a life of physical wants and sufferings, of continual insecurity, of furious passions and depraved vices. Those who have praised savage life, are those who have known nothing of it, or who have become savages themselves. But as I have said, so far as reason or universal experience instruct us, the institution of slavery is an essential process in emerging from savage life. It must then produce good, and promote the designs of the Creator.

I add further, *that Slavery anticipates the benefits of civilization, and retards the evils of civilization.* The former has been as fully established by a writer of great power of thought . . . that it is hardly necessary to urge it. [He refers here to James Boardman, the anonymous author of *England and America.*—EDITOR] Property—the accumulation of capital, as it is commonly called, is the first element of civilization. But to accumulate, or to use capital to any considerable extent, the combination of labor is necessary. In early stages of society, when people are thinly scattered over an extensive territory, the labor necessary to extensive works, cannot be commanded. Men are independent of each other. Having the command of abundance of land, no one will submit to be employed in the service of his neighbor. No one, therefore, can employ more capital than he can use with his own hands, or those of his family, nor have an income much beyond the necessaries of life. There can, therefore, be little leisure for intellectual pursuits, or means of acquiring the comforts or elegancies of life. It is hardly necessary to say however, that if a man has the command of slaves, he may combine labor, and use capital to any required extent, and therefore accumulate wealth. He shows that no colonies have been successfully planted without some sort of Slavery. So we find the fact to be. It is only in the Slave-Holding States of our confederacy, that wealth can be acquired by agriculture—

91

which is the general employment of our whole country. Among us, we know that there is no one, however humble his beginning, who with persevering industry, intelligence, and orderly and virtuous habits, may not attain to considerable opulence. So far as wealth has been accumulated in the States which do not possess Slaves, it has been in cities by the pursuits of commerce, or lately, by manufactures. But the products of Slave labor furnish more than two-thirds of the materials of our foreign commerce, which the industry of those States is employed in transporting and exchanging; and among the Slave-Holding States is to be found the great market for all the productions of their industry, of whatever kind. The prosperity of those States, therefore, and the civilization of their cities, have been for the most part created by the existence of Slavery. Even in the cities, but for a class of population, which our institutions have marked as servile, it would be scarcely possible to preserve the ordinary habitudes of civilized life, by commanding the necessary menial and domestic service.

Every stage of human society, from the most barbarous to the most refined, has its own peculiar evils to mark it as the condition of mortality; and perhaps there is none but omnipotence who can say in which the scale of good or evil most preponderates. We need say nothing of the evils of savage life. There is a state of society elevated somewhat above it, which is to be found in some of the more thinly peopled portions of our own country— the rudest agricultural state— . . .

But let us take another stage in the progress—which to many will appear to offer all that is desirable in existence, and realize another Utopia. Let us suppose a state of society in which all shall have property, and there shall be no great inequality of property—in which society shall be so much condensed as to afford the means of social intercourse, without being crowded, so as to create difficulty in obtaining the means of subsistence—in which every family that chooses may have as much land as will employ its own hands, while others may employ their industry in forming such products as it may be desirable to exchange with them. Schools are generally established, and the rudiments of education universally diffused. Religion is taught, and every village has its church, neat though humble, lifting its spire to Heaven. Here is a situation apparently the most favorable to happiness. I say *apparently*, for the greatest source of human misery is not in external circumstances, but in men themselves—in their depraved inclinations, their

wayward passions and perverse wills. Here is room for all the petty competition, the envy, hatred, malice and dissimulation, that torture the heart in
what may be supposed the most sophisticated states of society; and though
less marked and offensive, there may be much of the licentiousness.

But apart from this, in such a condition of society, if there is little suffering, there is little high enjoyment. The even flow of life forbids the high excitement which is necessary for it. If there is little vice, there is little place for
the eminent virtues, which employ themselves in controlling the disorders
and remedying the evils of society, which like war and revolution, call forth
the highest powers of man, whether for good or for evil. If there is little
misery, there is little room for benevolence. . . . In short, it is plain that in
such a state of society, the moral and intellectual faculties cannot be cultivated to their highest perfection.

But whether that which I have described be the most desirable state of
society or no, it is certain that it cannot continue. Mutation and progress is
the condition of human affairs. Though retarded for a time by extraneous
or accidental circumstances, the wheel must roll on. The tendency of population is to become crowded, increasing the difficulty of obtaining subsistence. There will be some without any property except the capacity for labor. This they must sell to those who have the means of employing them,
thereby swelling the amount of their capital, and increasing inequality. The
process still goes on. The number of laborers increases until there is a difficulty in obtaining employment. Then competition is established. The re-
muneration of the laborer becomes gradually less and less; a larger and
larger proportion of the product of his labor goes to swell the fortune of the
capitalist; inequality becomes still greater and more invidious, until the process ends in the establishment of such a state of things, as the same author
describes as now existing in England. After a most imposing picture of her
greatness and resources; of her superabounding capital, and all-pervading
industry and enterprize; of her public institutions for purposes of art, learning and benevolence; her public improvements, by which intercourse is fa-
cilitated, and the convenience of man subserved; the conveniences and luxuries of life enjoyed by those who are in possession of fortune, or have
profitable employments; of all, in short, that places her at the head of modern civilization, he proceeds to give the reverse of the picture. And here I
shall use his own words. "The laboring class compose the bulk of the peo-

ple; the great body of the people; the vast majority of the people—these are the terms by which English writers and speakers usually describe those whose only property is their labor."

"Of comprehensive words, the two most frequently used in English politics, are distress and pauperism. After these, of expressions applied to the state of the poor, the most common are vice and misery, wretchedness, sufferings, ignorance, degradation, discontent, depravity, drunkenness, and the increase of crime; with many more of the like nature."

He goes on to give the details of this inequality and wretchedness, in terms calculated to sicken and appal one to whom the picture is new. This inequality, this vice, this misery, this *Slavery*, is the price of England's civilization. . . .

It is the competition for employment, which is the source of this misery of society, that gives rise to all excellence in art and knowledge. When the demand for labor exceeds the supply, the services of the most ordinarily qualified laborer will be eagerly retained. When the supply begins to exceed, and competition is established, higher and higher qualifications will be required, until at length when it becomes very intense, none but the most consummately skilful can be sure to be employed. Nothing but necessity can drive men to the exertions which are necessary so to qualify themselves. But it is not in arts, merely mechanical alone, that this superior excellence will be required. It will be extended to every intellectual employment; and though this may not be the effect in the instance of every individual, yet it will fix the habits and character of the society, and prescribe every where, and in every department, the highest possible standard of attainment.

But how is it that the existence of Slavery as with us, will retard the evils of civilization? Very obviously. It is the intense competition of civilized life, that gives rise to the excessive cheapness of labor, and the excessive cheapness of labor is the cause of the evils in question. Slave labor can never be so cheap as what is called free labor. Political economists have established as the natural standard of wages in a fully peopled country, the value of the laborer's subsistence. I shall not stop to inquire into the precise truth of this proposition. It certainly approximates the truth. Where competition is intense, men will labor for a bare subsistence, and less than a competent subsistence. The employer of free laborers obtains their services during the time of their health and vigor, without the charge of rearing them from infancy, or supporting them in sickness or old age. This charge is imposed on the employer of Slave labor, who, therefore, pays higher wages, and cuts off the

94

principal source of misery—the wants and sufferings of infancy, sickness, and old age. Laborers too will be less skilful, and perform less work—enhancing the price of that sort of labor. The poor laws of England are an attempt—but an awkward and empirical attempt—to supply the place of that which we should suppose the feelings of every human heart would declare to be a natural obligation—that he who has received the benefit of the laborer's services during his health and vigor, should maintain him when he becomes unable to provide for his own support. They answer their purpose, however, very imperfectly, and are unjustly, and unequally imposed. There is no attempt to apportion the burden according to the benefit received—and perhaps there could be none. This is one of the evils of their condition.

In periods of commercial revulsion and distress, like the present, the distress, in countries of free labor, falls principally on the laborers. In those of Slave labor, it falls almost exclusively on the employer. In the former, when a business becomes unprofitable, the employer dismisses his laborers or lowers their wages. But with us, it is the very period at which we are least able to dismiss our laborers; and if we would not suffer a further loss, we cannot reduce their wages. To receive the benefit of the services of which they are capable, we must provide for maintaining their health and vigor. In point of fact, we know that this is accounted among the necessary expenses of management. If the income of every planter of the Southern States, were permanently reduced one half, or even much more than that, it would not take one jot from the support and comforts of the Slaves. And this can never be materially altered, until they shall become so unprofitable that Slavery must be of necessity abandoned. It is probable that the accumulation of individual wealth will never be carried to quite so great an extent in a Slave-Holding country, as in one of free labor; but a consequence will be, that there will be less inequality and less suffering.

Servitude is the condition of civilization. It was decreed, when the command was given, "be fruitful, and multiply and replenish the earth, and subdue it," and when it was added, "in the sweat of thy face shalt thou eat bread." And what human being shall arrogate to himself the authority to pronounce that our form of it is worse in itself, or more displeasing to God than that which exists elsewhere? Shall it be said that the servitude of other countries grows out of the exigency of their circumstances, and therefore society is not responsible for it? But if we know that in the progress of things it is to come, would it not seem the part of wisdom and foresight, to make provision for it, and thereby, if we can, mitigate the severity of its evils? But the fact is not so. Let any one who doubts, read the book to which I have several times referred, and he may be satisfied that it was forced upon us by the extremest exigency of circumstances, in a struggle for very existence. Without it, it is doubtful whether a white man would be now existing on this continent—certain, that if there were, they would be in a state of the utmost destitution, weakness and misery. It was forced on us by necessity, and further fastened upon us, by the superior authority of the mother country. I, for one, neither deprecate nor resent the gift. Nor did we institute Slavery. The Africans brought to us had been, speaking in the general, slaves in their own country, and only underwent a change of masters. In the countries of Europe, and the States of our Confederacy, in which Slavery has ceased to exist, it was abolished by positive legislation. If the order of nature has been departed from, and a forced and artificial state of things introduced, it has been, as the experience of all the world declares, by them and not by us.

That there are great evils in a society where slavery exists, and that the institution is liable to great abuse, I have already said. To say otherwise, would be to say that they were not human. But the whole of human life is a system of evils and compensations. We have no reason to believe that the compensations with us are fewer, or smaller in proportion to the evils, than those of any other condition of society. Tell me of an evil or abuse; of an instance of cruelty, oppression, licentiousness, crime or suffering, and I will point out, and often in five fold degree, an equivalent evil or abuse in countries where Slavery does not exist!

Let us examine without blenching, the actual and alleged evils of Slavery, and the array of horrors which many suppose to be its universal concomitants. It is said that the Slave is out of the protection of the law; that if the law purports to protect him in life and limb, it is but imperfectly executed; that he is still subject to excessive labor, degrading blows, or any other sort of torture, which a master pampered and brutalized by the exercise of arbitrary power, may think proper to inflict; he is cut off from the opportunity of intellectual, moral, or religious improvement, and even positive enactments are directed against his acquiring the rudiments of knowledge; he is cut off forever from the hope of raising his condition in society, whatever may be his merit, talents, or virtues, and therefore deprived of the strongest

96

incentive to useful and praiseworthy exertion; his physical degradation begets a corresponding moral degradation; he is without moral principle, and
addicted to the lowest vices, particularly theft and falsehood; if marriage be
not disallowed, it is little better than a state of concubinage, from which
results general licentiousness, and the want of chastity among females—this
indeed is not protected by law, but is subject to the outrages of brutal lust;
both sexes are liable to have their dearest affections violated; to be sold like
brutes; husbands to be torn from wives, children from parents;—this is the
picture commonly presented by the denouncers of Slavery.

It is a somewhat singular fact, that when there existed in our State no law
for punishing the murder of a slave, other than a pecuniary fine, there were,
I will venture to say, at least ten murders of freemen, for one murder of a
slave. Yet it is supposed they are less protected, or less secure than their
masters. Why they are protected by their very situation in society, and
therefore less need the protection of law. With any other person than their
master, it is hardly possible for them to come into such sort of collision as
usually gives rise to furious and revengeful passions; they offer no temptation to the murderer for gain; against the master himself, they have the security of his own interest, and by his superintendence and authority, they
are protected from the revengeful passions of each other. I am by no means
sure that the cause of humanity has been served by the change in jurispru-
dence, which has placed their murder on the same footing with that of a
freeman. The change was made in subserviency to the opinions and clamor
of others, who were utterly incompetent to form an opinion on the subject;
and a wise act is seldom the result of legislation in this spirit. From the fact
which I have stated, it is plain that they less need protection. Juries are,
therefore, less willing to convict, and it may sometimes happen that the
guilty will escape all punishment. *Security* is one of the compensations of
their humble position. We challenge the comparison, that with us there
have been fewer murders of Slaves, than of parents, children, apprentices,
and other murders, cruel and unnatural, in society where Slavery does not
exist.

But short of life or limb, various cruelties may be practised as the passions of the master may dictate. To this the same reply has been often
given—that they are secured by the master's interest. If the state of Slavery
is to exist at all, the master must have, and ought to have, such power of

punishment as will compel them to perform the duties of their station. And is not this for their advantage as well as his? No human being can be contented, who does not perform the duties of his station. Has the master any temptation to go beyond this? If he inflicts on him such punishment as will permanently impair his strength, he inflicts a loss on himself, and so if he requires of him excessive labor. Compare the labor required of the Slave, with those of the free agricultural, or manufacturing laborer in Europe, or even in the more thickly peopled portions of the non-Slave-Holding States of our Confederacy—though these last are no fair subjects of comparison—they enjoying, as I have said, in a great degree, the advantages of Slavery along with those of an early and simple state of society. Read the English Parliamentary reports, on the condition of the manufacturing operatives, and the children employed in factories. And such is the impotence of man to remedy the evils which the condition of his existence has imposed on him, that it is much to be doubted whether the attempts by legislation to, improve their situation, will not aggravate its evils. They resort to this excessive labor as a choice of evils. If so, the amount of their compensation will be lessened also with the diminished labor; for this is a matter which legislation cannot regulate. Is it the part of benevolence then to cut them off even from this miserable liberty of choice? Yet would these evils exist in the same degree, if the laborers were the *property* of the master—having a direct interest in preserving their lives, their health and strength? Who but a drivelling fanatic, has thought of the necessity of protecting domestic animals from the cruelty of their owners? And yet are not great and wanton cruelties practised on these animals? Compare the whole of the cruelties inflicted on Slaves throughout our Southern country, with those elsewhere, inflicted by ignorant and depraved portions of the community, on those whom the relations of society put into their power—of brutal husbands on their wives; of brutal parents—subdued against the strongest instincts of nature to that brutality by the extremity of their misery—on their children; of brutal masters on apprentices. And if it should be asked, are not similar cruelties inflicted, and miseries endured in your society? I answer in no comparable degree. The class in question are placed under the control of others, who are interested to restrain their excesses of cruelty or rage. Wives are protected from their husbands, and children from their parents. And this is no inconsiderable compensation of the evils of our system; and would so appear, if we could form any conception of the immense amount of misery which is elsewhere thus inflicted. The other class of society, more elevated in their position, are also (speaking of course in the general) more elevated in character, and more responsible to public opinion.

But besides the interest of their master, there is another security against cruelty. The relation of Master and Slave, when there is no mischievous interference between them, is as the experience of all the world declares, naturally one of kindness. As to the fact, we should be held interested witnesses, but we appeal to universal nature. Is it not natural that a man should be attached to that which is *his own*, and which has contributed to his convenience, his enjoyment, or his vanity? This is felt even towards animals, and inanimate objects. How much more towards a being of superior intelligence and usefulness, who can appreciate our feelings towards him, and return them? Is it not natural that we should be interested in that which is dependent on us for protection and support? Do not men every where contract kind feelings towards their dependents? Is it not natural that men should be more attached to those whom they have long known—whom, perhaps, they have reared or been associated with from infancy—than to one with whom their connexion has been casual and temporary? What is there in our atmosphere or institutions, to produce a perversion of the general feelings of nature? To be sure, in this as in all other relations, there is frequent cause of offence or excitement—on one side, for some omission of duty, on the other, on account of reproof or punishment inflicted. But this is common to the relation of parent and child; and I will venture to say that if punishment be justly inflicted—and there is no temptation to inflict it unjustly—it is as little likely to occasion permanent estrangement or resentment as in that case. Slaves are perpetual children. It is not the common nature of man, unless it be depraved by his own misery, to delight in witnessing pain. It is more grateful to behold contented and cheerful beings, than sullen and wretched ones. That men are sometimes wayward, depraved and brutal, we know. That atrocious and brutal cruelties have been perpetrated on Slaves, and on those who were not Slaves, by such wretches, we also know. But that the institution of Slavery has a natural tendency to form such a character, that such crimes are more common, or more aggravated than in other states of society, or produce among us less surprise and horror, we utterly deny, and challenge the comparison. Indeed I have little hesitation in saying, that if full evidence could be obtained, the comparison would result in our favor, and that the tendency of Slavery is rather to humanize than to brutalize. . . .

It is true, as suggested by President Dew—with the exception of the ties of close consanguinity, it forms one of the most intimate relations of society. And it will be more and more so, the longer it continues to exist. The harshest features of Slavery were created by those who were strangers to Slavery—who supposed that it consisted in keeping savages in subjection by violence and terror. The severest laws to be found on our statute book, were enacted by such, and such are still found to be the severest masters. As society becomes settled, and the wandering habits of our countrymen altered, there will be a larger and larger proportion of those who were reared by the owner, or derived to him from his ancestors, and who therefore will be more and more intimately regarded, as forming a portion of his family.

It is true that the Slave is driven to labor by stripes; and if the object of punishment be to produce obedience or reformation, with the least permanent injury, it is the best method of punishment. But is it not intolerable, that a being formed in the image of his Maker, should be degraded by *blows*? This is one of the perversions of mind and feeling, to which I shall have occasion again to refer. Such punishment would be degrading to a freeman, who had the thoughts and aspirations of a freeman. In general it is not degrading to a Slave, nor is it felt to be so. The evil is the bodily pain. Is it degrading to a child? Or if in any particular instance it would be so felt, it is sure not to be inflicted—unless in those rare cases which constitute the startling and eccentric evils, from which no society is exempt, and against which no institutions of society can provide.

The Slave is cut off from the means of intellectual, moral, and religious improvement, and in consequence his moral character becomes depraved, and he addicted to degrading vices. The Slave receives such instruction as qualifies him to discharge the duties of his particular station. The Creator did not intend that every individual human being should be highly cultivated, morally and intellectually, for as we have seen, he has imposed conditions on society which would render this impossible. There must be general mediocrity, or the highest cultivation must exist along with ignorance, vice, and degradation. But is there in the aggregate of society, less opportunity for intellectual and moral cultivation, on account of the existence of Slavery? We must estimate institutions from their aggregate of good or evil. I

100

refer to the views which I have before expressed to this society. It is by the existence of Slavery, exempting so large a portion of our citizens from the necessity of bodily labor, that we have a greater proportion than any other people, who have leisure for intellectual pursuits, and the means of attaining a liberal education. If we throw away this opportunity, we shall be morally responsible for the neglect or abuse of our advantages, and shall most unquestionably pay the penalty. But the blame will rest on ourselves, and not on the character of our institutions.

I add further, notwithstanding that *equality* seems to be the passion of the day, if, as Providence has evidently decreed, there can be but a certain portion of intellectual excellence in any community, it is better that it should be *unequally* divided. It is better that a part should be fully, and highly cultivated, and the rest utterly ignorant. To constitute a society, a variety of offices must be discharged, from those requiring but the lowest degree of intellectual power, to those requiring the very highest, and it should seem that the endowments ought to be apportioned according to the exigencies of the situation. In the course of human affairs, there arise difficulties which can only be comprehended, or surmounted by the strongest native power of intellect, strengthened by the most assiduous exercise, and enriched with the most extended knowledge—and even these are sometimes found inadequate to the exigency. The first want of society is—leaders. . . . The whole of society receives the benefit of the exertions of a mind of extraordinary endowments. Of all communities, one of the least desirable, would be that in which imperfect, superficial, half-education should be universal. The first care of a State which regards its own safety, prosperity and honor, should be, that when minds of extraordinary power appear, to whatever department of knowledge, art or science, their exertions may be directed, the means should be provided of their most consummate cultivation. Next to this, that education should be as widely extended as possible.

Odium has been cast upon our legislation, on account of its forbidding the elements of education to be communicated to Slaves. But in truth what injury is done to them by this? He who works during the day with his hands, does not read in intervals of leisure for his amusement, or the improvement of his mind—or the exceptions are so very rare, as scarcely to need the being provided for. Of the many Slaves whom I have known capable of reading, I have never known one to read any thing but the Bible, and this task they impose on themselves as matter of duty. Of all methods of

101

religious instruction, however, this, of reading for themselves would be the most inefficient—their comprehension is defective, and the employment is to them an unusual and laborious one. There are but very few who do not enjoy other means, more effectual for religious instruction. There is no place of worship opened for the white population, from which they are excluded. I believe it a mistake, to say that the instructions there given are not adapted to their comprehension, or calculated to improve them. If they are given as they ought to be—practically, and without pretension, and are such as are generally intelligible to the free part of the audience, comprehending all grades of intellectual capacity, they will not be unintelligible to Slaves. I doubt whether this be not better than instruction, addressed specially to themselves—which they might look upon as a device of the master's, to make them more obedient and profitable to himself. Their minds, generally, shew a strong religious tendency, and they are fond of assuming the office of religious instructors to each other; and perhaps their religious notions are not much more extravagant than those of a large portion of the free population of our country. I am not sure that there is a much smaller proportion of them, than of the free population, who make some sort of religious profession. It is certainly the master's *interest* that they should have proper religious sentiments, and if he fails in his duty towards them, we may be sure that the consequences will be visited not upon them, but upon him.

If there were any chance of their elevating their rank and condition in society, it might be matter of hardship, that they should be debarred those rudiments of knowledge which open the way to further attainments. But this they know cannot be, and that further attainments would be useless to them. Of the evil of this, I shall speak hereafter. A knowledge of reading, writing, and the elements of arithmetic, is convenient and important to the free laborer, who is the transactor of his own affairs, and the guardian of his own interests—but of what use would they be to the slave? These alone do not elevate the mind or character, if such elevation were desirable.

If we estimate their morals according to that which should be the standard of a free man's morality, then I grant they are degraded in morals—though by no means to the extent which those who are unacquainted with the institution seem to suppose. We justly suppose, that the Creator will require of man, the performance of the duties of the station in which his Providence has placed him, and the cultivation of the virtues which are adapted

102

to their performance; that he will make allowance for all imperfection of knowledge, and the absence of the usual helps and motives which lead to self correction and improvement. The degradation of morals relates principally to loose notions of honesty leading to petty thefts; to falsehood and to licentious intercourse between the sexes. Though with respect even to these, I protest against the opinion which seems to be elsewhere entertained, that they are universal, or that slaves, in respect to them, might not well bear a comparison with the lowest laborious class of other countries. But certainly there is much dishonesty leading to petty thefts. It leads, however, to nothing else. They have no contracts or dealings which might be a temptation to fraud, nor do I know that their characters have any tendency that way. They are restrained by the constant, vigilant, and interested superintendence which is exercised over them, from the commission of offences of greater magnitude—even if they were disposed to them—which I am satisfied they are not. Nothing is so rarely heard of, as an atrocious crime committed by a slave; especially since they have worn off the savage character which their progenitors brought with them from Africa. Their offences are confined to petty depredations, principally for the gratification of their appetites, and these for reasons already given, are chiefly confined to the property of their owner, which is most exposed to them. They could make no use of a considerable booty, if they should obtain it. It is plain that this is a less evil to society in its consequences and example, than if committed by a freeman, who is master of his own time and actions. With reference to society then, the offence is less in itself—and may we not hope that it is less in the sight of God. A slave has no hope that by a course of integrity, he can materially elevate his condition in society, nor can his offence materially depress it, or affect his means of support, or that of his family. Compared to the freeman, he has no character to establish or to lose. He has not been exercised to self-government, and being without intellectual resources, can less resist the solicitations of appetite. Theft in a freeman is a crime; in a slave, it is a vice. I recollect to have heard it said, in reference to some question of a slave's theft which was agitated in a Court, "Courts of Justice have no more to do with a slave's stealing, than with his lying—that is a matter for the domestic forum." It was truly said—the theft of a slave is no offence against society. Compare all the evils resulting from this, with the enormous amount of vice, crime and depravity, which in an European, or one of our Northern cities, disgusts the moral feelings, and render life and property insecure. So

103

with respect to his falsehood. I have never heard or observed, that slaves have any peculiar proclivity to falsehood, unless it be in denying, or concealing their own offences, or those of their fellows. I have never heard of falsehood told by a slave for a malicious purpose. Lies of vanity are sometimes told, as among the weak and ignorant of other conditions. Falsehood is not attributed to an individual charged with an offence before a Court of Justice, who pleads *not guilty*—and certainly the strong temptation to escape punishment, in the highest degree extenuates, if it does not excuse, falsehood told by a *slave*. If the object be to screen a fellow slave, the act bears some semblance of fidelity, and perhaps truth could not be told without breech of confidence. I know not how to characterize the falsehood of a slave.

It has often been said by the denouncers of Slavery, that marriage does not exist among slaves. It is difficult to understand this, unless wilful falsehood were intended. We know that marriages are contracted; may be, and often are, solemized with the forms usual among other classes of society, and often faithfully adhered to during life. The law has not provided for making those marriages indissoluble, nor could it do so. If a man abandons his wife, being without property, and being both property themselves, he cannot be required to maintain her. If he abandons his wife, and lives in a state of concubinage with another, the law cannot punish him for bigamy. It may perhaps be meant that the chastity of wives is not protected by law from the outrages of violence. I answer, as with respect to their lives, that they are protected by manners, and their position. Who ever heard of such outrages being offered? At least as seldom, I will venture to say, as in other communities of different forms of polity. One reason doubtless may be, that often there is no disposition to resist. Another reason also may be, that there is little temptation to such violence, as there is so large a proportion of this class of females who set little value on chastity, and afford easy gratification to the hot passions of men. It might be supposed, from the representations of some writers, that a slave-holding country were one wide stew for the indulgence of unbridled lust. Particular instances of intemperate and shameless debauchery are related, which may perhaps be true, and it is left to be inferred that this is the universal state of manners. Brutes and shameless debauchees there are in every country; we know that if such things are related as general or characteristic, the representation is false. . . . It is true that in this respect the morals of this class are very loose, (by no means so

104

universally so as is often supposed,) and that the passions of men of the superior caste, tempt and find gratification in the easy chastity of the females. This is evil, and to be remedied, if we can do so, without the introduction of greater evil. But evil is incident to every condition of society, and as I have said, we have only to consider in which institution it most predominates.

Compare these prostitutes of our country, (if it is not injustice to call them so,) and their condition with those of other countries—the seventy thousand prostitutes of London, or of Paris, or the ten thousand of New York, or our other Northern cities. Take the picture given of the first from the author whom I have before quoted. "The laws and customs of England, conspire to sink this class of English women into a state of vice and misery, below that which necessarily belongs to their condition. Hence, their extreme degradation, their troopers' oaths, their love of gin, their desperate recklessness, and the shortness of their miserable lives."

"English women of this class, or rather girls, for few of them live to be women, die like sheep with the rot; so fast that soon there would be none left, if a fresh supply were not obtained equal to the number of deaths. But a fresh supply is always obtained without the least trouble: seduction easily keeps pace with prostitution or mortality. Those that die are, like factory children that die, instantly succeeded by new competitors for misery and death." There is no hour of a summer's or a winter's night, in which there may not be found in the streets a ghastly wretch, expiring under the double tortures of disease and famine. Though less aggravated in its features, the picture of prostitution in New York or Philadelphia would be of like character.

In such communities, the unmarried woman who becomes a mother, is an outcast from society—and though sentimentalists lament the hardship of the case, it is justly and necessarily so. She is cut off from the hope of useful and profitable employment, and driven by necessity to further vice. Her misery, and the hopelessness of retrieving, render her desperate, until she sinks into every depth of depravity, and is prepared for every crime that can contaminate and infest society. She has given birth to a human being, who, if it be so unfortunate as to survive its miserable infancy, is commonly educated to a like course of vice, depravity and crime.

Compare with this the female slave under similar circumstances. She is not a less useful member of society than before. If shame be attached to her

105

conduct, it is such shame as would be elsewhere felt for a venial impropriety. She has not impaired her means of support, nor materially impaired her character, or lowered her station in society; she has done no great injury to herself, or any other human being. Her offspring is not a burden, but an acquisition to her owner; his support is provided for, and he is brought up to usefulness; if the fruit of intercourse with a freeman, his condition is, perhaps, raised somewhat above that of his mother. Under these circumstances, with imperfect knowledge, tempted by the strongest of human passions—unrestrained by the motives which operate to restrain, but are so often found insufficient to restrain the conduct of females elsewhere, can it be matter of surprise that she should so often yield to the temptation? Is not the evil less in itself, and in reference to society—much less in the sight of God and man. As was said of theft—the want of chastity, which among females of other countries, is sometimes vice, sometimes crime—among the free of our own, much more aggravated; among slaves, hardly deserves a harsher turn than that of weakness. I have heard of complaint made by a free prostitute, of the greater countenance and indulgence shewn by society towards colored persons of her profession, (always regarded as of an inferior and servile class, though individually free,) than to those of her own complexion. The former readily obtain employment; are even admitted into families, and treated with some degree of kindness and familiarity, while any approach to intercourse with the latter is shunned as contamination. The distinction is habitually made, and it is founded on the unerring instinct of nature. The colored prostitute is, in fact, a far less contaminated and depraved being. Still many, in spite of temptation, do preserve a perfectly virtuous conduct, and I imagine it hardly ever entered into the mind of one of these, that she was likely to be forced from it by authority or violence.

It may be asked, if we have no prostitutes from the free class of society among ourselves. I answer in no assignable proportion. With general truth, it might be said, that there are none. When such a case occurs, it is among the rare evils of society. And apart from other and better reasons, which we believe to exist, it is plain that it must be so, from the comparative absence of temptation. Our brothels, comparatively very few—and these should not be permitted to exist at all—are filled, for the most part, by importation from the cities of our confederate States, where Slavery does not exist. In return for the benefits which they receive from our Slavery, along with tariffs, libels, opinions moral, religious, or political—they furnish us also with a supply of thieves and prostitutes. Never, but in a single instance, have I heard of an imputation on the general purity of manners, among the free females of the slave-holding States. Such an imputation, however, and made in coarse terms, we have never heard here—*here* where divorce was never known—where no Court was ever polluted by an action for criminal conversation with a wife—where it is related rather as matter of tradition, not unmingled with wonder, that a Carolinian woman of education and family, proved false to her conjugal faith—an imputation deserving only of such reply as self-respect would forbid us to give, if respect for the author of it did not. And can it be doubted, that this purity is caused by, and is a compensation for the evils resulting from the existence of an enslaved class of more relaxed morals?

It is mostly the warm passions of youth, which give rise to licentious intercourse. But I do not hesitate to say, that the intercourse which takes place with enslaved females, is less depraving in its effects, than when it is carried on with females of their own caste. In the first place, as like attracts like, that which is unlike repels; and though the strength of passion be sufficient to overcome the repulsion, still the attraction is less. He feels that he is connecting himself with one of an inferior and servile caste, and that there is something of degradation in the act. The intercourse is generally casual; he does not make her habitually an associate, and is less likely to receive any taint from her habits and manners. He is less liable to those extraordinary fascinations, with which worthless women sometimes entangle their victims, to the utter destruction of all principle, worth and vigor of character. The female of his own race offers greater allurements. The haunts of vice often present a shew of elegance and various luxury tempts the senses. They are made an habitual resort, and their inmates associates, till the general character receives a taint from the corrupted atmosphere. Not only the practice is licentious, but the understanding is sophisticated; the moral feelings are bewildered, and the boundaries of virtue and vice confused. Where such licentiousness very extensively prevails, society is rotten to the heart.

But is it a small compensation for the evils attending the relation of the sexes among the enslaved class, that they have universally the opportunity of indulging the first instinct of nature, by forming matrimonial connexions? What painful restraint—what constant effort to struggle against the strongest impulses, are habitually practised elsewhere, and by other classes?

And they must be practised, unless greater evils would be encountered. On the one side, all the evils of vice, with the miseries to which it lends—on the other, a marriage cursed and made hateful by want—the sufferings of children, and agonizing apprehensions concerning their future fate. Is it a small good, that the slave is free from all this? He knows that his own subsistence is secure, and that his children will be in as good a condition as himself. To a refined and intellectual nature, it may not be difficult to practise the restraint of which I have spoken. But the reasoning from such to the great mass of mankind, is most fallacious. To these, the supply of their natural and physical wants, and the indulgence of the natural domestic affections, must, for the most part, afford the greatest good of which they are capable. To the evils which sometimes attend their matrimonial connexions, arising from their looser morality, slaves, for obvious reasons, are comparatively insensible. I am no apologist of vice, nor would I extenuate the conduct of the profligate and unfeeling, who would violate the sanctity of even these engagements, and occasion the pain which such violations no doubt do often inflict. Yet such is the truth, and we cannot make it otherwise. We know, that a woman's having been before a mother, is very seldom indeed an objection to her being made a wife. I know perfectly well how this will be regarded by a class of reasoners or declaimers, as imposing a character of deeper horror on the whole system; but still, I will say, that if they are to be exposed to the evil, it is mercy that the sensibility to it should be blunted. Is it no compensation also for the vices incident to Slavery, that they are, to a great degree, secured against the temptation to greater crimes, and more atrocious vices, and the miseries which attend them; against their own disposition to indolence, and the profligacy which is its common result?

But if they are subject to the vices, they have also the virtues of slaves. Fidelity—often proof against all temptation—even death itself—an eminently cheerful and social temper—what the Bible imposes as a duty, but which might seem an equivocal virtue in the code of modern morality—submission to constituted authority, and a disposition to be attached to, as well as to respect those whom they are taught to regard as superiors. They may have all the knowledge which will make them useful in the station in which God has been pleased to place them, and may cultivate the virtues which will render them acceptable to him. But what has the slave of any country to do with heroic virtues, liberal knowledge, or elegant accomplishments? It is for the master; arising out of his situation—imposed on him as

108

duty—dangerous and disgraceful if neglected—to compensate for this, by his own more assiduous cultivation, of the more generous virtues, and liberal attainments.

It has been supposed one of the great evils of Slavery, that it affords the slave no opportunity of raising himself to a higher rank in society, and that he has, therefore, no inducement to meritorious exertion, or the cultivation of his faculties. The indolence and carelessness of the slave, and the less productive quality of his labor, are traced to the want of such excitement. The first compensation for this disadvantage, is his security. If he can rise no higher, he is just in the same degree secured against the chances of falling lower. It has been sometimes made a question whether it were better for man to be freed from the perturbations of hope and fear, or to be exposed to their vicissitudes. But I suppose there could be little question with respect to a situation, in which the fears must greatly predominate over the hopes. And such, I apprehend, to be the condition of the laboring poor in countries where Slavery does not exist. If not exposed to present suffering, there is continual apprehension for the future—for themselves—for their children—of sickness and want, if not of actual starvation. They expect to improve their circumstances! Would any person of ordinary candor, say that there is one in a hundred of them, who does not well know, that with all the exertion he can make, it is out of his power materially to improve his circumstances? I speak not so much of menial servants, who are generally of a superior class, as of the agricultural and manufacturing laborers. They labor with no such view. It is the instinctive struggle to preserve existence, and when the superior efficiency of their labor over that of our slaves is pointed out, as being animated by a free man's hopes, might it not well be replied—it is because they labor under a sterner compulsion. The laws interpose no obstacle to their raising their condition in society. 'Tis a great boon—but as to the great mass, they know that they never will be able to raise it—and it should seem not very important in effect, whether it be the interdict of law, or imposed by the circumstances of the society. One in a thousand is successful. But does his success compensate for the sufferings of the many who are tantalized, baffled, and tortured in vain attempts to attain a like result? If the individual be conscious of intellectual power, the suffering is greater. Even where success is apparently attained, he sometimes gains it but to die—or with all capacity to enjoy it exhausted—worn out in the struggle with fortune. If it be true that the African is an inferior variety of

109

the human race, of less elevated character, and more limited intellect, is it not desirable that the inferior laboring class should be made up of such, who will conform to their condition without painful aspirations, and vain struggles?

The slave is certainly liable to be sold. But, perhaps, it may be questioned, whether this is a greater evil than the liability of the laborer, in fully peopled countries, to be dismissed by his employer, with the uncertainty of being able to obtain employment, or the means of subsistence elsewhere. With us, the employer cannot dismiss his laborer without providing him with another employer. His means of subsistence are secure, and this is a compensation for much. He is also liable to be separated from wife or child—though not more frequently, that I am aware of, than the exigency of their condition compels the separation of families among the laboring poor elsewhere—but from native character and temperament, the separation is much less severely felt. And it is one of the compensations, that he may sustain these relations without suffering a still severer penalty for the indulgence.

The love of liberty is a noble passion—to have the free, uncontrolled disposition of ourselves, our words and actions. But alas! it is one in which we know that a large portion of the human race can never be gratified. It is mockery, to say that the laborer any where has such disposition of himself—though there may be an approach to it in some peculiar, and those, perhaps, not the most desirable, states of society. But unless he be properly disciplined and prepared for its enjoyment, it is the most fatal boon that could be conferred—fatal to himself and others. If slaves have less freedom of action than other laborers, which I by no means admit, they are saved in a great degree from the responsibility of self-government, and the evils springing from their own perverse wills. Those who have looked most closely into life, and know how great a portion of human misery is derived from these sources—the undecided and wavering purpose—producing ineffectual exertion, or indolence with its thousand attendant evils—the wayward conduct—intemperance of profligacy—will most appreciate this benefit. The line of a slave's duty is marked out with precision, and he has no choice but to follow it. He is saved the double difficulty, first of determining the proper course for himself, and then of summoning up the energy which will sustain him in pursuing it.

If some superior power should impose on the laborious poor of any other country—this as their unalterable condition—you shall be saved from the torturing anxiety concerning your own future support, and that of your children, which now pursues you through life, and haunts you in death—you shall be under the necessity of regular and healthful, though not excessive labor—in return, you shall have the ample supply of your natural wants—you may follow the instinct of nature in becoming parents, without apprehending that this supply will fail yourselves or your children—you shall be supported and relieved in sickness, and in old age, wear out the remains of existence among familiar scenes and accustomed associates, without being driven to beg, or to resort to the hard and miserable charity of a work house—you shall of necessity be temperate, and shall have neither the temptation nor opportunity to commit great crimes, or practice the more destructive vices—how inappreciable would the boon be thought! And is not this a very near approach to the condition of our slaves? The evils of their situation they but lightly feel, and would hardly feel at all, if they were not sedulously instructed into sensibility. Certain it is, that if their fate were at the absolute disposal of a council of the most enlightened philanthropists in christendom, with unlimited resources, they could place them in no situation so favorable to themselves, as that which they at present occupy. But whatever good there may be, or whatever mitigation of evil, it is worse than valueless, because it is the result of *Slavery*. . . .

There is something in this word *Slavery* which seems to partake of the qualities of the insane root, and distempers the minds of men. That which would be true in relation to one predicament, they misapply to another, to which it has no application at all. Some of the virtues of a freeman would be the vices of slaves. To submit to a blow, would be degrading to a freeman, because he is the protector of himself. It is not degrading to a slave—neither is it to a priest or a woman. And is it a misfortune that it should be so? The freeman of other countries is compelled to submit to indignities hardly more endurable than blows—indignities to make the sensitive feelings shrink, and the proud heart swell; and this very name of freeman, gives them double rancour. If when a man is born in Europe, it were certainly foreseen that he was destined to a life of painful labor—to obscurity, contempt and privation—would it not be mercy that he should be reared in ignorance and apathy, and trained to the endurance of the evils he must encounter? It is not certainly foreseen as to any individual, but it is foreseen as to the great mass of those born of the laboring poor; and it is for the mass, not for the exception, that the institutions of society are to provide. Is it not better that the character and intellect of the individual should be suited to the station which he is to occupy? Would you do a benefit to the horse or the ox, by giving him a cultivated understanding or fine feelings? So far as the mere laborer has the pride, the knowledge, or the aspirations of a freeman, he is unfitted for his situation, and must doubly feel its infelicity. If there are sordid, servile, and laborious offices to be performed, is it not better that there should be sordid, servile, and laborious beings to perform them? If there were infallible marks by which individuals of inferior intellect, and inferior character, could be selected at their birth—would not the interests of society be served, and would not some sort of fitness seem to require, that they should be selected for the inferior and servile offices? And if this race be generally marked by such inferiority, is it not fit that they should fill them?

I am well aware that those whose aspirations are after a state of society from which evil shall be banished, and who look in life for that which life will never afford, contemplate that all the offices of life may be performed without contempt or degradation—all be regarded as equally liberal, or equally respected. But theorists cannot control nature and bend her to their views, and the inequality of which I have before spoken is deeply founded in nature. . . .

What is the essential character of *Slavery*, and in what does it differ from the *servitude* of other countries? If I should venture on a definition, I should say that where a man is compelled to labor at the will of another, and to give him much the greater portion of the product of his labor, there *Slavery* exists; and it is immaterial by what sort of compulsion the will of the laborer is subdued. It is what no human being would do without some sort of compulsion. He cannot be compelled to labor by blows. No—but what difference does it make, if you can inflict any other sort of torture which will be equally effectual in subduing the will? if you can starve him, or alarm him for the subsistence of himself or his family? And is it not under this compulsion that the *freeman* labors? I do not mean in every particular case, but in the general. Will any one be hardy enough to say that he is at his own disposal, or has the government of himself? True, he may change his employer if he is dissatisfied with his conduct towards him; but this is a privilege he would in the majority of cases gladly abandon, and render the connexion between them indissoluble. There is far less of the interest and attachment in his relation to his employer, which so often exists between the master and the slave, and mitigates the condition of the latter. An intelligent English traveller has characterized as the most miserable and degraded of all beings, "a masterless slave." And is not the condition of the laboring poor of other countries too often that of masterless slaves? . . .

That they are called free, undoubtedly aggravates the sufferings of the slaves of other regions. They see the enormous inequality which exists, and feel their own misery, and can hardly conceive otherwise, than that there is some injustice in the institutions of society to occasion these. They regard the apparently more fortunate class as oppressors, and it adds bitterness, that they should be of the same name and race. They feel indignity more acutely, and more of discontent and evil passion is excited; they feel that it is mockery that calls them free. Men do not so much hate and envy those who are separated from them by a wide distance, and some apparently impassible barrier, as those who approach nearer to their own condition, and with whom they habitually bring themselves into comparison. The slave with us is not tantalized with the name of freedom, to which his whole condition gives the lie, and would do so if he were emancipated to-morrow. The African slave sees that nature herself has marked him as a separate—and if left to himself, I have no doubt he would feel it to be an inferior—race, and interposed a barrier almost insuperable to his becoming a member of the same society, standing on the same footing of right and privilege with his master.

That the African negro is an inferior variety of the human race, is, I think, now generally admitted, and his distinguishing characteristics are such as peculiarly mark him out for the situation which he occupies among us. And these are no less marked in their original country, than as we have daily occasion to observe them. The most remarkable is their indifference to personal liberty. In this they have followed their instincts since we have any knowledge of their continent, by enslaving each other; but contrary to the experience of every other race, the possession of slaves has no material effect in raising the character, and promoting the civilization of the master. Another trait is the want of domestic affections, and insensibility to the ties of kindred. In the travels of the Landers, after speaking of a single exception, in the person of a woman who betrayed some transient emotion in passing by the country from which she had been torn as a slave, the authors add: "that Africans, generally speaking, betray the most perfect indifference on losing their liberty, and being deprived of their relatives, while love of

113

country is equally a stranger to their breasts, as social tenderness or domestic affection." "Marriage is celebrated by the nations as unconcernedly as possible; a man thinks as little of taking a wife, as of cutting an ear of corn—affection is altogether out of the question." They are, however, very submissive to authority, and seem to entertain great reverence for chiefs, priests, and masters. No greater indignity can be offered an individual, than to throw approbrium on his parents. On this point of their character, I think I have remarked, that, contrary to the instinct of nature in other races, they entertain less regard for children than for parents, to whose authority they have been accustomed to submit. Their character is thus summed up by the travellers quoted, "the few opportunities we have had of studying their characters, induce us to believe that they are a simple, honest, inoffensive, but weak, timid, and cowardly race. They seem to have no social tenderness, very few of those amiable private virtues which could win our affections, and none of those public qualities that claim respect or command admiration. The love of country is not strong enough in their bosoms to incite them to defend it against a despicable foe; and of the active energy, noble sentiments, and contempt of danger which distinguishes the North American tribes and other savages, no traces are to be found among this slothful people. Regardless of the past, as reckless of the future, the present alone influences their actions. In this respect, they approach nearer to the nature of the brute creation, than perhaps any other people on the face of the globe." Let me ask if this people do not furnish the very material out of which slaves ought to be made, and whether it be not an improving of their condition to make them the slaves of civilized masters. There is a variety in the character of the tribes. Some are brutally, and savagely ferocious and bloody, whom it would be mercy to enslave. From the travellers' account, it seems not unlikely that the negro race is tending to extermination, being daily encroached on, and overrun by the superior Arab race. It may be, that when they shall have been lost from their native seats, they may be found numerous, and in no unhappy condition, on the continent to which they have been transplanted.

The opinion which connects form and features with character and intellectual power, is one so deeply impressed on the human mind, that perhaps there is scarcely any man who does not almost daily act upon it, and in some measure verify its truth. Yet in spite of this intimation of nature, and though the anatomist and physiologist may tell them that the races differ in every bone and muscle, and in the proportion of brain and nerves, yet there are some, who with a most bigoted and fanatical determination to free themselves from what they have prejudged to be prejudice, will still maintain that this physiognomy, evidently tending to that of the brute when compared to that of the Caucasian race, may be enlightened by as much thought, and animated by as lofty sentiment. We who have the best opportunity of judging, are pronounced to be incompetent to do so, and to be blinded by our interest and prejudices—often by those who have no opportunity at all—and we are to be taught to distrust or disbelieve that which we daily observe, and familiarly know, on such authority. Our prejudices are spoken of. But the truth is, that, until very lately, since circumstances have compelled us to think for ourselves, we took our opinions on this subject, as on every other, ready formed from the country of our origin. And so deeply rooted were they, that we adhered to them, as most men will do to deeply rooted opinions, even against the evidence of our own observation, and our own senses. If the inferiority exists, it is attributed to the apathy and degradation produced by Slavery. Though of the hundreds of thousand scattered over other countries, where the laws impose no disability upon them, none has given evidence of an approach to even mediocrity of intellectual excellence, this too is attributed to the Slavery of a portion of their race. They are regarded as a servile caste, and degraded by opinion, and thus every generous effort is repressed. Yet though this should be the general effect, this very estimation is calculated to produce the contrary effect in particular instances. It is observed by Bacon, with respect to deformed persons and eunuchs, that though in general there is something of perversity in the character, the disadvantage often leads to extraordinary displays of virtue and excellence. "Whosoever hath any thing fixed in his person that doth induce contempt, hath also a perpetual spur in himself, to rescue and deliver himself from scorn." So it would be with them, if they were capable of European aspirations—genius, if they possessed it, would be doubly fired with noble rage to rescue itself from this scorn. Of course, I do not mean to say that there may not be found among them some of superior capacity to many white persons; but that great intellectual powers are, perhaps, never found among them, and that in general their capacity is very limited, and their feelings animal and coarse—fitting them peculiarly to discharge the lower, and merely mechanical offices of society. . . .

Slavery, as it is said in an eloquent article published in a Southern periodi-

115

cal work, to which I am indebted for other ideas, "has done more to elevate a degraded race in the scale of humanity; to tame the savage; to civilize the barbarous; to soften the ferocious; to enlighten the ignorant, and to spread the blessings of christianity among the heathen, than all the missionaries that philanthropy and religion have ever sent forth." Yet unquestionable as this is, and though human ingenuity and thought may be tasked in vain to devise any other means by which these blessings could have been conferred, yet a sort of sensibility which would be only mawkish and contemptible, if it were not mischievous, affects still to weep over the wrongs of "injured Africa." Can there be a doubt of the immense benefit which has been conferred on the race, by transplanting them from their native, dark, and barbarous regions, to the American Continent and Islands? There, three-fourths of the race are in a state of the most deplorable personal Slavery. And those who are not, are in a scarcely less deplorable condition of political Slavery, to barbarous chiefs—who value neither life nor any other human right, or enthralled by priests to the most abject and atrocious superstitions. . . .

We believe that the tendency of Slavery is to elevate the character of the master. No doubt the character—especially of youth—has sometimes received a taint and premature knowledge of vice, from the contact and association with ignorant and servile beings of gross manners and morals. Yet still we believe that the entire tendency is to inspire disgust and aversion towards their peculiar vices. It was not without a knowledge of nature, that the Spartans exhibited the vices of slaves by way of negative example to their children. We flatter ourselves that the view of this degradation, mitigated as it is, has the effect of making probity more strict, the pride of character more high, the sense of honor more strong, than is commonly found where this institution does not exist. Whatever may be the prevailing faults or vices of the masters of slaves, they have not commonly been understood to be those of dishonesty, cowardice, meanness or falsehood. And so most unquestionably it ought to be. Our institutions would indeed be intolerable in the sight of God and man, if, condemning one portion of society to hopeless ignorance and comparative degradation, they should make no atonement by elevating the other class by higher virtues, and more liberal attainments—if, besides degraded slaves, there should be ignorant, ignoble, and degraded freemen. There is a broad and well marked line, beyond which no slavish vice should be regarded with the least toleration or allowance. One class is cut off from all interest in the State—that abstraction so potent to the feelings of a generous nature. The other must make compensation by increased assiduity and devotion to its honor and welfare. The love of wealth—so laudable when kept within proper limits, so base and mischievous when it exceeds them—so infectious in its example—an infection to which I fear we have been too much exposed—should be pursued by no arts in any degree equivocal, or at any risk of injustice to others. So surely as there is a just and wise governor of the universe, who punishes the sins of nations and communities, as well as of individuals, so surely shall we suffer punishment, if we are indifferent to that moral and intellectual cultivation of which the means are furnished to us, and to which we are called and incited by our situation.

I would to heaven I could express, as I feel, the conviction how necessary this cultivation is, not only to our prosperity and consideration, but to our safety and very existence. We, the slave-holding States, are in a hopeless minority in our own confederated republic—to say nothing of the great confederacy of civilized States. It is admitted, I believe, not only by slave-holders, but by others, that we have sent to our common councils more than our due share of talent, high character and eloquence. Yet in spite of all these most strenuously exerted, measures have been sometimes adopted which we believed to be dangerous and injurious to us, and threatening to be fatal. What would be our situation, if, instead of these, we were only represented by ignorant and grovelling men, incapable of raising their views beyond a job or petty office, and incapable of commanding hearing or consideration. May I be permitted to advert—by no means invidiously—to the late contest carried on by South-Carolina against Federal authority, and so happily terminated by the moderation which prevailed in our public counsels. I have often reflected, what one circumstance, more than any other, contributed to the successful issue of a contest, apparently so hopeless, in which one weak and divided state was arrayed against the whole force of the Confederacy—unsustained, and uncountenanced, even by those who had a common interest with her. It seemed to me to be, that we had for leaders an unusual number of men of great intellectual power, co-operating cordially and in good faith, and commanding respect and confidence at home and abroad, by elevated and honorable character. . . .

I am sure that it is unnecessary to say to an assembly like this, that the conduct of the master to his slave should be distinguished by the utmost humanity. That we should indeed regard them as wards and dependants on our kindness, for whose well being in every way we are deeply responsible. This is no less the dictate of wisdom and just policy, than of right feeling. It is wise with respect to the services to be expected from them. I have never heard of an owner whose conduct in their management was distinguished by undue severity, whose slaves were not in a great degree worthless to him. A cheerful and kindly demeanor, with the expression of interest in themselves and their affairs, is, perhaps, calculated to have a better effect on them, than what might be esteemed more substantial favors and indulgencies. Throughout nature, attachment is the reward of attachment. It is wise too in relation to the civilized world around us, to avoid giving occasion to the odium which is so industriously excited against ourselves and our institutions. For this reason, public opinion should, if possible, bear even more strongly and indignantly than it does at present, on masters who practise any wanton cruelty on their slaves. The miscreant who is guilty of this, not only violates the law of God and of humanity, but as far as in him lies, by bringing odium upon, endangers the institutions of his country, and the safety of his countrymen. He casts a shade upon the character of every individual of his fellow-citizens, and does every one of them a personal injury. So of him who indulges in any odious excess of intemperate or licentious passion. It is detached instances of this sort, of which the existence is, perhaps, hardly known among ourselves, that, collected with pertinacious and malevolent industry, affords the most formidable weapons to the mischievous zealots, who array them as being characteristic of our general manners and state of society.

I would by no means be understood to intimate, that a vigorous, as well as just government, should not be exercised over slaves. This is part of our duty towards them, no less obligatory than any other duty, and no less necessary towards their well being than to ours. I believe that at least as much injury has been done and suffering inflicted by weak and injudicious indulgence, as by inordinate severity. He whose business is to labor, should be made to labor, and that with due diligence, and should be vigorously restrained from excess or vice. This is no less necessary to his happiness than to his usefulness. The master who neglects this, not only makes his slaves unprofitable to himself, but discontented and wretched—a nuisance to his neighbors and to society.

I have said that the tendency of our institution is to elevate the female character, as well as that of the other sex, and for similar reasons. In other states of society, there is no well defined limit to separate virtue and vice. There are degrees of vice from the most flagrant and odious, to that which scarcely incurs the censure of society. Many individuals occupy an unequivocal position; and as society becomes accustomed to this, there will be a less peremptory requirement of purity in female manners and conduct; and often the whole of the society will be in a tainted and uncertain condition with respect to female virtue. Here, there is that certain and marked line, above which there is no toleration or allowance for any approach to license of manners or conduct, and she who falls below it, will fall far below even the slave. How many will incur this penalty?

And permit me to say that this elevation of the female character is no less important and essential to us, than the moral and intellectual cultivation of the other sex. It would indeed be intolerable, if, when one class of the society is necessarily degraded in this respect, no compensation were made by the superior elevation and purity of the other. Not only essential purity of conduct, but the utmost purity of manners, and I will add, though it may incur the formidable charge of affectation or prudery,—a greater severity of decorum than is required elsewhere, is necessary among us. Always should be strenuously resisted the attempts which have been sometimes made to introduce among us the freedom of foreign European, and especially of continental manners. This freedom, the remotest in the world from that which sometimes springs from simplicity of manners is calculated and commonly intended to confound the outward distinctions of virtue and vice. It is to prepare the way for licentiousness—to produce this effect—that if those who are clothed with the outward color and garb of vice, may be well received by society, those who are actually guilty may hope to be so too. It may be said, that there is often perfect purity where there is very great freedom of manners. And, I have no doubt, this may be true in particular instances, but it is never true of any *society* in which this is the general state of manners. What guards can there be to purity, when every thing that *may possibly* be done innocently, is habitually practised; when there can be no impropriety which is not vice. And what must be the depth of the depravity when there is a departure from that which they admit as principle. . . .

I have before said that free labor is cheaper than the labor of slaves, and so far as it is so, the condition of the free laborer is worse. But I think President Dew has sufficiently shown that this is only true of Northern countries.

It is matter of familiar remark that the tendency of warm climates is to relax the human constitution and indispose to labor. The earth yields abundantly—in some regions almost spontaneously—under the influence of the sun, and the means of supporting life are obtained with but slight exertion; and men will use no greater exertion than is necessary to the purpose. This very luxuriance of vegetation, where no other cause concurs, renders the air less salubrious, and even when positive malady does not exist, the health is habitually impaired. Indolence renders the constitution more liable to these effects of the atmosphere, and these again aggravate the indolence. Nothing but the coercion of slavery can overcome the repugnance to labor under these circumstances, and by subduing the soil, improve and render wholesome the climate.

It is worthy of remark that there does not now exist on the face of the earth, a people in a tropical climate, or one approaching to it, where slavery does not exist, that is in a state of high civilization, or exhibits the energies which mark the progress towards it. . . . In short, the uncontradicted experience of the world is, that in Southern States where good government and predial and domestic slavery are found, there are prosperity and greatness; where either of these conditions is wanting, degeneracy and barbarism. The former however is equally essential in all climates and under all institutions. And can we suppose it to be the design of the creator, that these regions, constituting half of the earth's surface, and the more fertile half and more capable of sustaining life, should be abandoned forever to depopulation and barbarism? Certain it is that they will never be reclaimed by the labour of freemen. In our own country, look at the lower valley of the Mississippi, which is capable of being made a far greater Egypt. In our own state, there are extensive tracts of the most fertile soil, which are capable of being made to swarm with life. These are at present pestilential swamps, and valueless, because there is abundance of other fertile soil in more favorable situations, which demand all and more than all the labour which our country can supply. Are these regions of fertility to be abandoned at once and forever to the alligator and tortoise—with here and there perhaps a miserable, shivering, crouching *free* black savage? Does not the finger of heaven itself seem to point to a race of men—not to be enslaved by us but already enslaved, and who will be in every way benefitted by the change of masters—to whom such climate is not uncongenial, who though disposed to indolence are yet patient and capable of labor, on whose whole features, mind and character, nature has indelibly written—slave;—and indicate that we should avail ourselves of these in fulfilling the first great command to subdue and replenish the earth.

It is true that this labor will be dearer than that of northern countries, where under the name of freedom, they obtain cheaper and perhaps better slaves. Yet it is the best we can have, and this too has its compensation. We see it compensated at present by the superior value of our agricultural products. And this superior value they must probably always have. The Southern climate admits of a greater variety of productions. Whatever is produced in Northern climates, the same thing, or something equivalent, may be produced in the Southern. But the Northern have no equivalent for the products of Southern climates. The consequence will be, that the products of Southern regions will be demanded all over the civilized world. The agricultural products of Northern regions are chiefly for their own consumption. They must therefore apply themselves to the manufacturing of articles for luxury, elegance, convenience or necessity,—which requires cheap labor—for the purpose of exchanging them with their Southern neighbors. Thus nature herself indicates that agriculture should be the predominating employment in Southern countries, and manufactures in Northern. Commerce is necessary to both—but less indispensable to the Southern, which produce within themselves a greater variety of things desirable to life. They will therefore have somewhat less of the commercial spirit. We must avail ourselves of such labor as we can command. The slave must labour and is innured to it; while the necessity of energy in his government, of watchfulness, and of preparation and power to suppress insurrection, added to the moral force derived from the habit of command, may help to prevent the degeneracy of the master.

The task of keeping down insurrection is commonly supposed, by those who are strangers to our institutions, to be a very formidable one. Even among ourselves; accustomed as we have been to take our opinions on this as on every other subject, ready formed from those whom we regarded as instructors, in the teeth of our own observation and experience, fears have been entertained which are absolutely ludicrous. We have been supposed to be nightly reposing over a mine, which may at any instant explode to our destruction. The first thought of a foreigner sojourning in one of our cities, who is awakened by any nightly alarm, is of servile insurrection and massacre. Yet if any thing is certain in human affairs, it is certain and from the

121

most obvious considerations, that we are more secure in this respect than any civilized and fully peopled society upon the face of the earth. In every such society, there is a much larger proportion than with us, of persons who have more to gain than to lose by the overthrow of government, and the embroiling of social order. It is in such a state of things that those who were before at the bottom of society, rise to the surface. From causes already considered, they are peculiarly apt to consider their sufferings the result of injustice and misgovernment, and to be rancorous and embittered accordingly. They have every excitement therefore of resentful passion, and every temptation which the hope of increased opulence, or power or consideration can hold out, to urge them to innovation and revolt. Supposing the same disposition to exist in equal degree among our slaves, what are their comparative means or prospect of gratifying it? The poor of other countries are called free. They have, at least, no one interested to exercise a daily and nightly superintendence and control over their conduct and actions. Emissaries of their class may traverse, unchecked, every portion of the country, for the purpose of organizing insurrection. From the greater intelligence, they have greater means of communicating with each other. They may procure and secrete arms. It is not alone the ignorant, or those who are commonly called the poor, that will be tempted to revolution. There will be many disappointed men and men of desperate fortune—men perhaps of talent and daring—to combine them and direct their energies. Even those in the higher ranks of society who contemplate no such result, will contribute to it, by declaiming on their hardships and rights.

With us, it is almost physically impossible, that there should be any very extensive combination among the slaves. It is absolutely impossible that they should procure and conceal efficient arms. Their emissaries traversing the country, would carry their commission on their foreheads. If we suppose among them an individual of sufficient talent and energy to qualify him for a revolutionary leader, he could not be so extensively known as to command the confidence, which would be necessary to enable him to combine and direct them. Of the class of freemen, there would be no individual so poor or degraded (with the exception perhaps of here and there a reckless and desperate outlaw and felon) who would not have much to lose by the success of such an attempt; every one therefore would be vigilant and active to detect and suppress it. Of all impossible things, one of the most

122

impossible would be a successful insurrection of our slaves, originating with themselves.

Attempts at insurrection have indeed been made—excited, as we believe, by the agitation of the abolitionists and declaimers on slavery; but these have been in every instance promptly suppressed. We fear not to compare the riots, disorder, revolt and bloodshed which have been committed in our own, with those of any other civilized communities, during the same lapse of time. And let it be observed under what extraordinary circumstances our peace has been preserved. For the last half century, one half of our population has been admonished in terms the most calculated to madden and excite, that they are the victims of the most grinding and cruel injustice and oppression. We know that these exhortations continually reach them, through a thousand channels which we cannot detect, as if carried by the birds of the air—and what human being, especially when unfavorably distinguished by outward circumstances, is not ready to give credit when he is told that he is the victim of injustice and oppression? In effect, if not in terms, they have been continually exhorted to insurrection. The master has been painted a criminal, tyrant and robber, justly obnoxious to the vengeance of God and man, and they have been assured of the countenance and sympathy, if not of the active assistance of all the rest of the world. We ourselves have in some measure pleaded guilty to the impeachment. It is not long since a great majority of our free population, servile to the opinions of those whose opinions they had been accustomed to follow, would have admitted slavery to be a great evil, unjust and indefensible in principle, and only to be vindicated by the stern necessity which was imposed upon us. Thus stimulated by every motive and passion which ordinarily actuate human beings—not as to a criminal enterprize, but as to something generous and heroic—what has been the result? A few imbecile and uncombined plots—in every instance detected before they broke out into action, and which perhaps if undetected would never have broken into action. One or two sudden, unpremeditated attempts, frantic in their character, if not prompted by actual insanity, and these instantly crushed. As it is, we are not less assured of safety, order and internal peace than any other people; and but for the pertinacious and fanatical agitation of the subject, would be much more so. . . .

It has commonly been supposed, that this institution will prove a source of weakness in relation to military defence against a foreign enemy. I will venture to say that in a slave holding community, a larger military force may be maintained permanently in the field, than in any State where there are not slaves. It is plain that almost the whole of the able bodied free male population, making half of the entire able bodied male population, may be maintained in the field, and this without taking in any material degree from the labour and resources of the country. In general the labor of our country is performed by slaves. In other countries, it is their laborers that form the material of their armies. What proportion of these can be taken away without fatally crippling their industry and resources? In the war of the revolution, though the strength of our state was wasted and paralyzed by the unfortunate divisions which existed among ourselves, yet it may be said with general truth, that every citizen was in the field and acquired much of the qualities of the soldier.

It is true that this advantage will be attended with its compensating evils and disadvantages; to which we must learn to submit, if we are determined on the maintenance of our institutions. We are, as yet, hardly at all aware how little the maxims and practices of modern civilized governments will apply to us. Standing armies, as they are elsewhere constituted, we cannot have; for we have not, and for generations cannot have the materials out of which they are to be formed. If we should be involved in serious wars, I have no doubt but that some sort of conscription, requiring the services of all citizens for a considerable term, will be necessary. Like the people of Athens, it will be necessary that every citizen should be a soldier, and qualified to discharge efficiently the duties of a soldier. It may seem a melancholy consideration, that an army so made up should be opposed to the disciplined mercenaries of foreign nations. But we must learn to know our true situation. But may we not hope, that made up of superior materials, of men having home and country to defend; inspired by higher pride of character, of greater intelligence and trained by an effective, though honorable discipline, such an army will be more than a match for mercenaries. The efficiency of an army is determined by the qualities of its officers, and may we not expect to have a greater proportion of men better qualified for officers, and possessing the true spirit of military command. And let it be recollected that if there were otherwise reason to apprehend danger from insurrection, there will be the greatest security when there is the largest force on foot

124

within the country. Then it is that any such attempt would be most instantly and effectually crushed. . . .

President Dew has very fully shown how utterly vain are the fears of those, who though there may be no danger for the present, yet apprehend great danger for the future, when the number of slaves shall be greatly increased. He has shown that the large and more condensed the society becomes, the easier it will be to maintain subordination, supposing the relative numbers of the different classes to remain the same—or even if there should be a very disproportionate increase of the enslaved class. Of all vain things, the vainest and that in which man most shows his impotence and folly, is the taking upon himself to provide for a very distant future—at all events by any material sacrifice of the present. Though experience has shown that revolutions and political movements—unless when they have been conducted with the most guarded caution and moderation—have generally terminated in results just the opposite of what was expected from them, the angry ape will still play his fantastic tricks, and put in motion machinery, the action of which he no more comprehends or foresees than he comprehends the mysteries of infinity. The insect that is borne upon the current, will fancy that he directs its course. Besides the fear of insurrection and servile war, there is also alarm lest when their numbers shall be greatly increased, their labor will become utterly unprofitable, so that it will be equally difficult for the master to retain and support them, or to get rid of them. But at what age of the world is this likely to happen? At present, it may be said that almost the whole of the Southern portion of this continent is to be subdued to cultivation; and in the order of providence, this is the task allotted to them. For this purpose, more labour will be required for generations to come than they will be able to supply. When that task is accomplished, there will be many objects to which their labour may be directed. . . .

When the demand for agricultural labour shall be fully supplied, then of course the labour of slaves will be directed to other employments and enterprises. Already it begins to be found, that in some instances it may be used as profitable in works of public improvement. As it becomes cheaper and cheaper, it will be applied to more various purposes and combined in larger masses. It may be commanded and combined with more facility than any other sort of labour; and the labourer, kept in stricter subordination, will be less dangerous to the security of society than in any other country, which is crowded and overstocked with a class of what are called free laborers. Let it be remembered that all the great and enduring monuments of human art and industry—the wonders of Egypt—the everlasting works of Rome—were created by the labor of slaves. There will come a stage in our progress when we shall have facilities for executing works as great as any of these—more useful than the pyramids—not less magnificent than the Sea of Moeris. What the end of all is to be; what mutations lie hid in the womb of the distant future; to what convulsions our societies may be exposed—whether the master, finding it impossible to live with his slaves, may not be compelled to abandon the country to them—of all this it were presumptuous and vain to speculate.

I have hitherto, as I proposed, considered it as a naked, abstract question of the comparative good and evil of the institution of slavery. Very far different indeed is the practical question presented to us, when it is proposed to get rid of an institution which has interwoven itself with every fibre of the body politic; which has formed the habits of our society, and is consecrated by the usage of generations. If this be not a vicious prescription, which the laws of God forbid to ripen into right, it has a just claim to be respected by all tribunals of man. If the negroes were now free and it were proposed to enslave them, then it would be incumbent on those who proposed the measure to show clearly that their liberty was incompatible with the public security. When it is proposed to innovate on the established state of things, the burden is on those who propose the innovation, to show that advantage will be gained from it. There is no reform, however necessary, wholesome or moderate, which will not be accompanied with some degree of inconvenience, risque or suffering. Those who acquiesce in the state of things which they found existing, can hardly be thought criminal. But most deeply criminal are they who give rise to the enormous evil with which great revolutions in society are always attended, without the fullest assurance of the greater good to be ultimately obtained. But if it can be made to appear, even probably, that no good will be obtained, but that the results will be evil and calamitous as the process, what can justify such innovations? No human being can be so mischievous—if acting consciously, none can be so wicked, as those who finding evil in existing institutions, rush blindly upon change, unforeseeing and reckless of consequences, and leaving it to chance or fate to determine whether the end shall be improvement, or greater and more

126

intolerable evil. Certainly the instincts of nature prompt to resist intolerable oppression. For this resistance no rule can be prescribed, but it must be left to the instincts of nature. To justify it however the insurrectionists should at least have a reasonable probability of success, and be assured that their condition will be improved by success. But most extraordinary is it, when those who complain and clamor, are not those who are supposed to feel the oppression, but persons at a distance from them, and who can hardly at all appreciate the good or evil of their situation. It is the unalterable condition of humanity, that men must achieve civil liberty for themselves. The assistance of allies has sometimes enabled nations to repel the attacks of foreign power; never to conquer liberty as against their own internal government.

In one thing I concur with the abolitionists; that if emancipation is to be brought about, it is better that it should be immediate and total. But let us suppose it to be brought about in any manner, and then enquire what would be the effects.

The first and most obvious effect, would be to put an end to the cultivation of our great southern staple. And this would be equally the result, if we suppose the emancipated negroes to be in no way distinguished from the free laborers of other countries, and that their labour would be equally effective. In that case, they would soon cease to be laborers for hire, but would scatter themselves over our unbounded territory, to become independent land owners themselves. The cultivation of the soil on an extensive scale, can only be carried on where there are slaves, or in countries superabounding with free labour. No such operations are carried on in any portions of our own country where there are not slaves. Such are carried on in England, where there is an overflowing population and intense competition for employment. And our institutions seem suited to the exigences of our respective situations. There, a much greater number of labourers is required at one season of the year than at another, and the Farmer may enlarge or diminish the quantity of labour he employs, as circumstance may require. Here, about the same quantity of labour is required at every season, and the planter suffers no inconvenience from retaining his labourers throughout the year. Imagine an extensive rice or cotton plantation cultivated by free laborers, who might perhaps *strike* for an increase of wages, at a season when the neglect of a few days would insure the destruction of the whole crop. Even if it were possible to procure laborers at all, what planter would venture to carry on his operations under such circumstances? I need hardly say that these staples cannot be produced to any extent where the proprietor of the soil cultivates it with his own hands. He can do little more than produce the necessary food for himself and his family.

And what would be the effect of putting an end to the cultivation of these staples, and thus annihilating at a blow, two thirds or three fourths of our foreign commerce? Can any sane mind contemplate such a result without terror? I speak not of the utter poverty and misery to which we ourselves would be reduced, and the desolation which would overspread our own portion of the country. Our slavery has not only given existence to millions of slaves within our own territories, it has given the means of subsistence and therefore existence to millions of freemen in our confederate States; enabling them to send forth their swarms, to overspread the plains and forests of the West and appear as the harbingers of civilization. The products of the industry of those States are in general similar to those of the civilized world, and are little demanded in their markets. By exchanging them for ours, which are every where sought for, the people of these States are enabled to acquire all the products of art and industry, all that contributes to convenience or luxury, or gratifies the taste or the intellect, which the rest of the world can supply. Not only on our own continent, but on the other, it has given existence to hundreds of thousands, and the means of comfortable subsistence to millions. A distinguished citizen of our own state, than whom none can be better qualified to form an opinion, has lately stated that our great staple, cotton, has contributed more than any thing else of later times to the progress of civilization. By enabling the poor to obtain cheap and becoming clothing, it has inspired a taste for comfort, the first stimulus to civilization. Does not *self defence* then demand of us, steadily to resist the abrogation of that which is productive of so much good? It is more than self defence. It is to defend millions of human beings, who are far removed from us, from the intensest suffering, if not from being struck out of existence. It is the defence of human civilization.

But this is but a small part of the evil which would be occasioned. After President Dew, it is unnecessary to say a single word on the practicability of colonizing our slaves. The two races, so widely seperated from each other by the impress of nature, must remain together in the same country. Whether it be accounted the result of prejudice or reason, it is certain that the two races will not be blended together so as to form a homogenous population. To one who knows any thing of the nature of man and human society, it would

128

be unnecessary to argue that this state of things cannot continue, but that one race must be driven out by the other, or exterminated, or again enslaved. I have argued on the supposition that the emancipated negroes would be as efficient as other free laborers. But whatever theorists, who know nothing of the matter, may think proper to assume, we well know that this would not be so. We know that nothing but the coercion of slavery can overcome their propensity to indolence, and that not one in ten would be an efficient laborer. Even if this disposition were not grounded in their nature, it would be a result of their position. I have somewhere seen it observed, that to be degraded by opinion, is a thousand fold worse, so far as the feelings of the individual are concerned, than to be degraded by the laws. *They* would be thus degraded, and this feeling is incompatible with habits of order and industry. Half our population would at once be paupers. Let an inhabitant of New York or Philadelphia conceive of the situation of their respective States, if one half of their population consisted of free negroes. The tie which now connects them being broken, the different races would be estranged from each other, and hostility would grow up between them. Having the command of their own time and actions, they could more effectually combine insurrection and provide the means of rendering it formidable. Released from the vigilant superintendence which now restrains them, they would infallibly be led from petty to greater crimes, until all life and property would be rendered insecure. Aggression would beget retaliation, until open war—and that a war of extermination were established. From the still remaining superiority of the white race, it is probable that they would be the victors, and if they did not exterminate, they must again reduce the others to slavery—when they could be no longer fit to be either slaves or freemen. It is not only in self defence, in defence of our country and of all that is dear to us, but in defence of the slaves themselves that we refuse to emancipate them.

If we suppose them to have political privileges, and to be admitted to the elective franchise, still worse results may be expected. . . . It is already known, that if there be a class unfavorably distinguished by any peculiarity from the rest of society, this distinction forms a tie which binds them to act in concert, and they exercise more than their due share of political power and influence—and still more, as they are of inferior character and looser moral principle. Such a class form the very material for demagogues to work with. Other parties court them and concede to them. So it would be with the free blacks in the case supposed. They would be used by un-principled politicians, of irregular ambition, for the advancement of their schemes, until they should give them political power and importance beyond even their own intentions. They would be courted by excited parties in their contests with each other. At some time, they may perhaps attain political ascendency, and this is more probable, as we may suppose that there will have been a great emigration of whites from the country. Imagine the government of such legislators. Imagine then the sort of laws that will be passed, to confound the invidious distinction which has been so long as-sumed over them, and if possible to obliterate the every memory of it. These will be resisted. The blacks will be tempted to avenge themselves by oppres-sion and proscription of the white race, for their long superiority. Thus mat-ters will go on, until universal anarchy, or kakistocracy, the government of the worst, is fully established. I am persuaded that if the spirit of evil should devise to send abroad upon the earth all possible misery, discord, horror and atrocity, he could contrive no scheme so effectual as the emancipation of negro slaves within our country.

The most feasible scheme of emancipation, and that which I verily believe would involve the least danger and sacrifice, would be that the *entire* white population should emigrate, and abandon the country to their slaves. Here would be triumph to philanthrophy. This wide and fertile region would be again restored to ancient barbarism—to the worst of all barbarism—bar-barism corrupted and depraved by intercourse with civilization. And this is the consummation to be wished, upon a *speculation*, that in some distant future age, they may become so enlightened and improved, as to be capable of sustaining a position among the civilized races of the earth. But I believe moralists allow men to defend their homes and their country, even at the expense of the lives and liberties of others.

Will any philanthropist say that the evils, of which I have spoken, would be brought about only by the obduracy, prejudices and overweening self es-timation of the whites in refusing to blend the races by marriage, and so create an homogenous population. But what if it be not prejudice, but truth, and nature, and right reason, and just moral feeling? As I have before said, throughout the whole of nature, like attracts like, and that which is unlike repels. What is it that makes so unspeakably loathsome, crimes not to be named, and hardly alluded to? Even among the nations of Europe, so nearly homogenous, there are some peculiarities of form and feature, mind and

130

character, which may be generally distinguished by those accustomed to observe them. Though the exceptions are numerous, I will venture to say that not in one instance in a hundred, is the man of sound and unsophisticated tastes and propensities so likely to be attracted by the female of a foreign stock, as by one of his own, who is more nearly conformed to himself. Shakspeare spoke the language of nature, when he made the senate and people of Venice attribute to the effect of witchcraft, Desdemona's passion for Othello—though, as Coleridge has said, we are to conceive of him not as a negro, but as a high bred, Moorish Chief.

If the negro race, as I have contended, be inferior to our own in mind and character, marked by inferiority of form and features, then ours would suffer deterioration from such intermixture. What would be thought of the moral conduct of the parent who should voluntarily transmit disease, or fatuity, or deformity to his offspring? If man be the most perfect work of the creator, and the civilized European man the most perfect variety of the human race, is he not criminal who would desecrate and deface God's fairest work, estranging it further from the image of himself, and conforming it more nearly to that of the brute. I have heard it said as if it afforded an argument, that the African is as well satisfied of the superiority of his own complexion, form and features, as we can be of ours. If this were true, as it is not, would any one be so recreant to his own civilization, as to say that his opinion ought to weigh against ours—that there is no universal standard of truth and grace and beauty—that the Hottentot Venus may perchance possess as great perfection of form as the Medicean? It is true, the licentious passions of men overcome the natural repugnance, and find transient gratification in intercourse with females of the other race. But this is a very different thing from making her the associate of life, the companion of the bosom and the hearth. Him who would contemplate such an alliance for himself, or regard it with patience, when proposed for a son or daughter or sister, we should esteem a degraded wretch—with justice, certainly, if he were found among ourselves—and the estimate would not be very different if he were found in Europe. It is not only in defence of ourselves, of our country and of our own generation, that we refuse to emancipate our slaves, but to defend our posterity and race from degeneracy and degradation.

Are we not justified then in regarding as criminals, the fanatical agitators whose efforts are intended to bring about the evils I have described. It is sometimes said that their zeal is generous and disinterested, and that their motives may be praised, though their conduct be condemned. But I have little faith in the good motives of those who pursue bad ends. It is not for us to scrutinize the hearts of men, and we can only judge of them by the tendency of their actions. There is much truth in what was said by Coleridge. "I have never known a trader in philanthropy who was not wrong in heart somehow or other. Individuals so distinguished, are usually unhappy in their family relations—men not benevolent or beneficent to individuals, but almost hostile to them, yet lavishing money and labor and time on the race—the abstract notion." The prurient love of notoriety actuates some. There is much luxury in sentiment, especially if it can be indulged at the expense of others, and if there be added some share of envy or malignity, the temptation to indulgence is almost irresistible. But certainly they may be justly regarded as criminal, who obstinately shut their eyes and close their ears to all instruction with respect to the true nature of their actions.

It must be manifest to every man of sane mind that it is impossible for them to achieve ultimate success; even if every individual in our country, out of the limits of the slave holding states, were united in their purposes. They cannot have even the miserable triumph of St. Domingo—of advancing through scenes of atrocity, blood and massacre, to the restoration of barbarism. They may agitate and perplex the world for a time. They may excite to desperate attempts and particular acts of cruelty and horror, but these will always be suppressed or avenged at the expense of the objects of their truculent philanthropy. But short of this, they can hardly be aware of the extent of the mischief they perpetrate. As I have said, their opinions, by means to us inscrutable, do very generally reach our slave population. What human being, if unfavorably distinguished by outward circumstances, is not ready to believe when he is told that he is the victim of injustice? Is it not cruelty to make men restless and dissatisfied in their condition, when no effort of theirs can alter it? The greatest injury is done to their characters, as well as to their happiness. Even if no such feelings or designs should be entertained or conceived by the slave, they will be attributed to him by the master, and all his conduct scanned with a severe and jealous scrutiny. Thus distrust and aversion are established, where, but for mischievous interference, there would be confidence and good will, and a sterner control is exercised over the slave who thus becomes the victim of his cruel advocates.

An effect is sometimes produced on the minds of slave holders, by the publications of the self styled philanthropists, and their judgments staggered and consciences alarmed. It is natural that the oppressed should hate the oppressor. It is still more natural that the oppressor should hate his victim. Convince the master that he is doing injustice to his slave, and he at once begins to regard him with distrust and malignity. It is a part of the constitution of the human mind, that when circumstances of necessity or temptation induce men to continue in the practice of what they believe to be wrong, they become desperate and reckless of the degree of wrong. I have formerly heard of a master who accounted for his practising much severity upon his slaves, and exacting from them an unusual degree of labor, by saying that the thing (slavery) was altogether wrong, and therefore it was well to make the greatest possible advantage out of it. This agitation occasions some slave holders to hang more loosely on their country. Regarding the institution as of questionable character, condemned by the general opinion of the world, and one which must shortly come to an end, they hold themselves in readiness to make their escape from the evil which they anticipate. Some sell their slaves to new masters (always a misfortune to the slave) and remove themselves to other societies, of manners and habits uncongenial to their own. And though we may suppose that it is only the weak and the timid who are liable to be thus affected, still it is no less an injury and public misfortune. Society is kept in an unquiet and restless state, and every sort of improvement is retarded.

Some projectors suggest the education of slaves, with a view to prepare them for freedom—as if there were any method of a man's being educated to freedom, but by himself. The truth is however, that supposing that they are shortly to be emancipated, and that they have the capacities of any other race, they are undergoing the very best education which it is possible to give. They are in the course of being taught habits of regular and patient industry, and this is the first lesson which is required. I suppose that their most zealous advocates would not desire that they should be placed in the high places of society immediately upon their emancipation, but that they should begin their course of freedom as laborers, and raise themselves afterwards as their capacities and characters might enable them. But how little would what are commonly called the rudiments of education, add to their qualifications as laborers? But for the agitation which exists however, their education would be carried further than this. There is a constant tendency in our society to extend the sphere of their employments, and consequently to give them the information which is necessary to the discharge of those employments. And this for the most obvious reason, it promotes the master's interest. How much would it add to the value of a slave, that he should be capable of being employed as a clerk, or be able to make calculations as a mechanic? In consequence, however, of the fanatical spirit which has been excited, it has been thought necessary to repress this tendency by legislation, and to prevent their acquiring the knowledge of which they might make a dangerous use. If this spirit were put down, and we restored to the consciousness of security, this would be no longer necessary, and the process of which I have spoken would be accelerated. Whenever indications of superior capacity appeared in a slave, it would be cultivated; gradual improvement would take place, until they might be engaged in as various employments as they were among the ancients—perhaps even liberal ones. Thus, if in the adorable providence of God, at a time and in a manner which we can neither foresee nor conjecture, they are to be rendered capable of freedom and to enjoy it, they would be prepared for it in the best and most effectual, because in the most natural and gradual manner. But fanaticism hurries to its effect at once. I have heard it said, God does good, but it is by imperceptible degrees; the Devil is permitted to do evil, and he does it in a hurry. The beneficent processes of nature are not apparent to the senses. You cannot see the plant grow or the flower expand. The volcano, the earthquake and the hurricane do their work of desolation in a moment. Such would be the desolation, if the schemes of fanatics were permitted to have effect. They do all that in them lies to thwart the beneficent purposes of providence. The whole tendency of their efforts is to aggravate present suffering and to cut off the chance of future improvement, and in all their bearings and results, have produced, and are likely to produce, nothing but "pure, unmixed, dephlegmated, defecated evil."

If Wilberforce or Clarkson were living, and it were enquired of them "can you be sure that you have promoted the happiness of a single human being?" I imagine that, if they considered conscientiously, they would find it difficult to answer in the affirmative. If it were asked "can you be sure that you have not been the cause of suffering, misery and death to thousands,"—when we recollect that they probably stimulated the exertions of the *amis des noirs* in France and that through the efforts of these, the horrors of St. Domingo were perpetrated. I think they must hesitate long to return a decided negative. It might seem cruel, if we could, to convince a man who has devoted his life to what he esteemed a good and generous purpose, that he

134

has been doing only evil—that he has been worshipping a horrid fiend, in the place of the true God. But fanaticism is in no danger of being convinced. It is one of the mysteries of our nature, and of the divine government, how utterly disproportioned to each other, are the powers of doing evil and of doing good. The poorest and most abject instrument, that is utterly imbecile for any purpose of good, seems sometimes endowed with almost the powers of omnipotence for mischief. A mole may inundate a province—a spark from a forge may conflagrate a city—a whisper may separate friends, a rumor may convulse an empire—but when we would do benefit to our race or country, the purest and most chastened motives, the most patient thought and labor, with the humblest self distrust, are hardly sufficient to assure us that the results may not disappoint our expectations, and that we may not do evil instead of good. But are we therefore to refrain from efforts to benefit our race and country? By no means: but these motives, this labour and self distrust are the only conditions upon which we are permitted to hope for success. Very different indeed is the course of those, whose precipitate and ignorant zeal would overturn the fundamental institutions of society, uproar its peace and endanger its security, in pursuit of a distant and shadowy good, of which they themselves have formed no definite conception— whose atrocious philosophy would sacrifice a generation—and more than one generation—for any hypothesis.

III. THORNTON STRINGFELLOW
A Brief Examination of Scripture Testimony on the Institution of Slavery

"... we shall be seen cleaving to the Bible and taking all our decisions about this matter from its inspired pages."

Thornton Stringfellow was born in Fauquier County, Virginia, in 1788, and except for a brief period of residence in South Carolina lived in Fauquier and nearby Culpeper counties all his life.[1] Son of a slaveholder who owned nearly a thousand acres of land, Stringfellow appeared to his contemporaries as "a man of high social position."[2]

Under the influence of his parents, who were evangelical Baptists, Stringfellow experienced an emotional conversion at the age of twenty-three. In 1814 he was ordained as a Baptist minister and took charge of several congregations in Fauquier County. Viewing himself as God's steward, Stringfellow was active in a host of reform and benevolent activities, including the Sunday School movement, domestic and foreign missions, temperance, and, ultimately, the proslavery crusade. "The guardianship and control of the black race, by the white," he argued, "is an indispensable Christian duty, to which we must yet look, if we would secure the well-being of both races."[3] Stringfellow called upon the "Southern section as a whole"[4] to serve as missionary for his cause, and thus in 1846 he eagerly supported the separation of the southern Baptist church from its northern counterpart. During the remaining years of the antebellum period, Stringfellow worked to convert

1. On the life of Thornton Stringfellow, see Drew Gilpin Faust, "Evangelicalism and the Meaning of the Proslavery Argument: The Reverend Thornton Stringfellow of Virginia," *Virginia Magazine of History and Biography*, LXXXV (1977), 3–17. Most of Stringfellow's personal papers were destroyed, but a diary remains in the possession of the family.
2. Richmond *Religious Herald*, March 18, 1869.
3. Thornton Stringfellow, *Scriptural and Statistical Views in Favor of Slavery* (Richmond: J. W. Randolph, 1856), 105.
4. Richmond *Religious Herald*, November 6, 1856.

136

the slaves in his own congregation and continued to publish tracts on slavery. Moving beyond the somewhat limited scope of his original biblical exegesis, Stringfellow undertook a historical study of the origins of human bondage and an improbably empirical analysis of religious devotion North and South based in comparison of regional church attendance statistics.⁵ When the Civil War broke out, Stringfellow found his two-thousand acre property near Fredericksburg under almost constant military threat. In 1863 he and his wife were held prisoners in their home for several months while Union armies supplied themselves from his plantation. Even when his seventy slaves ran away to the Yankees, however, Stringfellow's faith in the justice and benevolence of human bondage did not falter. But his health began to fail, and he remained almost constantly bedridden until his death in 1869.

The selection below originally appeared in the Richmond *Religious Herald* in 1841 as a response to a debate over slavery undertaken by two prominent Baptist divines, Francis Wayland, president of Brown University, and Richard Fuller of South Carolina. Reprinted in pamphlet form some years later, *A Brief Examination of Scripture Testimony on the Institution of Slavery* set forth the biblical arguments for human bondage more fully and more systematically than had any previous proslavery treatment.⁶ Stringfellow specifically sought to counter the "bitter fruits" and "false doctrines" of abolitionism by setting forth the details of God's response to slavery in both the Old and New Testaments. The Virginian also devoted considerable attention to refuting the abolitionist contention that the "servitude" discussed in the Bible was contractual in nature and thus markedly different from involuntary slavery in the South. Stringfellow intended "to prove the term servant to be identical in the import of its essential particulars with the term slave among us" and to demonstrate as well biblical sanction for the physical chastisement of bondsmen. The essay also demonstrated String-

5. Stringfellow, *Scriptural and Statistical Views*; Stringfellow, *Slavery: Its Origin, Nature and History . . . Considered in the Light of Bible Teachings, Moral Justice, and Political Wisdom* (Alexandria: Virginia Sentinel Office, 1860).

6. Richmond *Religious Herald*, February 25, 1841; Stringfellow, *A Brief Examination of Scripture Testimony on the Institution of Slavery. In an essay first published in the Religious Herald and republished by request; With Remarks on a letter of Elder Galusha of New York to Dr. Richard Fuller of South Carolina* (Washington, D.C.: Congressional Globe Office, 1850). Only the first section of the pamphlet is included here; the *Remarks* have been omitted.

fellow's notion of the South as a purer, more righteous civilization than the North. In its call for a withdrawal from northern moral pollution, it might be seen to justify the 1846 division of the Baptist church into sectional wings.

Stringfellow's essays were widely hailed as "vastly the best" religious defenses of slavery, and one of his works was chosen to represent the scriptural argument for human bondage in the 1860 proslavery anthology *Cotton is King and Pro-Slavery Arguments*.[7]

A Brief Examination of Scripture Testimony on the Institution of Slavery

In an Essay, first published in the Religious Herald, and republished by request

Locust Grove, *Culpeper Co., Va.*, 1841.

Brother Sands:

Circumstances exist among the inhabitants of these United States, which make it proper that the Scriptures should be carefully examined by Christians in reference to the institution of Slavery, which exists in several of the States, with the approbation of those who profess unlimited subjection to God's revealed will.

It is branded by one portion of people, who take their rules of moral rectitude from the Scriptures, as a great sin; nay, the greatest of sins that exist in the nation. And they hold the obligation to exterminate it, to be paramount to all others.

If slavery be thus sinful, it behooves all Christians who are involved in the sin, to repent in dust and ashes, and wash their hands of it, without consulting with flesh and blood. Sin in the sight of God is something which God in his Word makes known to be wrong, either by perceptive prohibition, by principles of moral fitness, or examples of inspired men, contained in the

---

7. William C. Preston to Waddy Thompson, August 10, 1857, in Waddy Thompson Papers, South Caroliniana Library, University of South Carolina, Columbia. See also James Henry Hammond to William Gilmore Simms, June 11, 1852, in James Henry Hammond Papers, Library of Congress; Edmund Ruffin, August 2, 1859, in Diary, Edmund Ruffin Papers, Library of Congress. Thornton Stringfellow, "The Bible Argument: or, Slavery in the Light of Divine Revelation," *Cotton Is King and Pro-Slavery Arguments* (Augusta: Pritchard, Abbott & Loomis, 1860), 459–546.

sacred volume. When these furnish no law to condemn human conduct, there is no transgression. Christians should produce a "thus saith the Lord," both for what they condemn as sinful, and for what they approve as lawful, in the sight of Heaven.

It is to be hoped, that on a question of such vital importance as this to the peace and safety of our common country, as well as to the welfare of the church, we shall be seen cleaving to the Bible and taking all our decisions about this matter from its inspired pages. With men from the North, I have observed for many years a palpable ignorance of the divine will, in reference to the institution of slavery. I have seen but a few, who made the Bible their study, that had obtained a knowledge of what it did reveal on this subject. Of late, their denunciation of slavery as a sin, is loud and long.

I propose, therefore, to examine the sacred volume briefly, and if I am not greatly mistaken, I shall be able to make it appear that the institution of slavery has received, in the first place,

1st. The sanction of the Almighty in the Patriarchal age.

2d. That it was incorporated into the only National Constitution which ever emanated from God.

3d. That its legality was recognized, and its relative duties regulated, by Jesus Christ in his kingdom; and

4th. That it is full of mercy.

Before I proceed further, it is necessary that the terms used to designate the thing, be defined. It is not a name, but a thing, that is denounced as sinful; because it is supposed to be contrary to, and prohibited by, the Scriptures.

Our translators have used the term servant, to designate a state in which persons were serving, leaving us to gather the *relation*, between the party served and the party rendering the service, from other terms. The term slave, signifies with us, a definite state, condition, or relation, which is precisely that one which is denounced as sinful. This state, condition, or relation, is that in which one human being is held without his consent by another, as property, to be bo..ght, sold, and transferred, together with the increase, as property, forever. Now, this precise thing, is denounced by a portion of the people of these United States as the greatest individual and national sin that is among us, and is thought to be so hateful in the sight of God, as to subject the nation to ruinous judgments, if it be not removed. Now, I propose to show, from the Scriptures, that this state, condition, or

139

relation, did exist in the *patriarchal age*, and that the persons most extensively involved in the sin, if it be a sin, are the very persons who have been singled out by the Almighty as the objects of his special regard—whose character and conduct he has caused to be held up as *models* for future generations. Before we conclude slavery to be a thing hateful to God, and a great sin in his sight, it is proper that we should search the records he has given us with care, to see in what light he has looked upon it, and find the warrant, for concluding that we shall honor him by efforts to abolish it; which efforts, in their consequences, may involve the indiscriminate slaughter of the innocent and the guilty, the master and the servant. We all believe him to be a Being who is the same yesterday, to-day, and forever.

The first recorded language which was ever uttered in relation to slavery, is the inspired language of Noah. In God's stead he says, "Cursed be Canaan;" "a servant of servants shall he be to his brethren." "Blessed be the Lord God of Shem; and Canaan shall be his servant." "God shall enlarge Japheth, and he shall dwell in the tents of Shem; and Canaan shall be his servant." Gen. ix. 25, 26, 27. Here language is used, showing the *favor* which God would exercise to the posterity of Shem and Japheth, while they were holding the posterity of Ham in a state of *abject bondage*. May it not be said in truth, that God decreed this institution before it existed; and has he not connected its *existence*, with prophetic tokens of special favor, to those who should be slave owners or masters? He is the same God now, that he was when he gave these views of his moral character to the world; and unless the posterity of Shem and Japheth, from whom have sprung the Jews and all the nations of Europe and America, and a great part of Asia, (the African race that is in them excepted,)—I say, unless they are all dead, as well as the Canaanites or Africans, who descended from Ham, then it is quite possible that his favor may now be found with one class of men, who are holding another class in bondage. Be this as it may, God *decreed slavery*—and shows in that decree, tokens of good-will to the master. The sacred records occupy but a short space from this inspired ray on this subject, until they bring to our notice a man, that is held up as a model, in all that adorns human nature, and as one that God delighted to honor. This man is Abraham, honored in the sacred records with the appellation, "Father" of the "faithful." Abraham was a native of Ur of the Chaldees. From thence the Lord called him to go to a country which he would show him; and he obeyed, not knowing whither he went. He stopped for a time at Haran, where his father died. From thence he "took Sarai his wife, and Lot his brother's son, and all their substance, that they had gathered, and the souls they had gotten in Haran, and they went forth to go into the land of Canaan." Gen. xii. 5.

All the ancient Jewish writers of note, and Christian commentators agree, that by the "souls they had gotten in Haran," as our translators render it, are meant their slaves, or those persons they had bought with their money in Haran. In a few years after their arrival in Canaan, Lot with all he had was taken captive. So soon as Abraham heard it, he armed three hundred and eighteen slaves that were born in his house, and retook him. How great must have been the entire slave family, to produce at this period of Abraham's life, such a number of young slaves able to bear arms. Gen. xiv. 14.

Abraham is constantly held up in the sacred story as the subject of great distinction among the princes and sovereigns of the countries in which he sojourned. This distinction was on account of his great wealth. When he proposed to buy a burying-ground at Sarah's death of the children of Heth, he stood up and spoke with great humility of himself as "a stranger and sojourner among them," (Gen. xxiii. 4,) desirous to obtain a burying-ground. But in what light do they look upon him? "Hear us, my Lord, thou are a mighty prince among us." Gen. xxiii. 6. Such is the light in which they viewed him. What gave a man such distinction among such a people? Not moral qualities, but great wealth, and its inseparable concomitant, power. When the famine drove Abraham to Egypt, he received the highest honors of the reigning sovereign. This honor at Pharaoh's court was called forth by the visible tokens of immense wealth. In Genesis xii. 15, 16, we have the honor that was shown to him, mentioned, *with a list of his property*, which is given in these words, in the 16th verse: "He had sheep, and oxen, and he-asses, and men-servants, and maid-servants, and she-asses, and camels." The *amount* of his flocks may be inferred from the *number of slaves* employed in tending them. They were those he brought from Ur of the Chaldees, of whom the three hundred and eighteen were born; those gotten in Haran, where he dwelt for a short time; and those which he inherited from his father, who died in Haran. When Abraham *went up* from Egypt, it is stated in Genesis xiii. 2, that he was *"very rich,"* not only in *flocks* and *slaves*, but in *"silver* and *gold"* also.

After the destruction of Sodom, we see him sojourning in the kingdom of Gerar. Here he received from the sovereign of the country, the honors of equality; and Abimelech, the king, (as Pharaoh had done before him,) seeks Sarah for a wife, under the idea that she was Abraham's sister. When his mistake was discovered, he made Abraham a large present. Reason will tell us, that in selecting the items of this present, Abimelech was governed by the visible indications of Abraham's preference in articles of wealth—and that above all, he would present him with nothing which Abraham's sense of moral obligation would not allow him to own. Abimelech's present is thus described in Gen. xx. 14, 16: "And Abimelech took sheep, and oxen, and men-servants, and women-servants, and a thousand pieces of silver, and gave them unto Abraham." This present discloses to us what constituted the most highly-prized items of wealth, among these eastern sovereigns in Abraham's day.

God had promised Abraham's seed the land of Canaan, and that in his seed all the nations of the earth should be blessed. He reached the age of 85, and his wife the age of 75, while as yet, they had no child. At this period, Sarah's anxiety for the promised seed, in connection with her age, induced her to propose a female slave of the Egyptian stock, as a secondary wife, from which to obtain the promised seed. This alliance soon puffed the slaves with pride, and she became insolent to her mistress—the mistress complained to Abraham, the master. Abraham ordered Sarah to exercise her authority. Sarah did so, and pushed it to severity, and the slave absconded. The divine oracles inform us, that the angel of God found this runaway bondwoman in the wilderness; and if God had commissioned this angel to improve this opportunity of teaching the world how much he abhorred slavery, he took a bad plan to accomplish it. For, instead of repeating a homily upon doing to others as we "would they should do unto us," and heaping reproach upon Sarah, as a hypocrite, and Abraham as a tyrant, and giving Hagar direction how she might get into Egypt, from whence (according to Abolitionism) she had been unrighteously sold into bondage, the angel addressed her as "Hagar, Sarah's maid," Gen. xvi. 1–9; (thereby recognizing the relation of master and slave,) and asks her, "whither wilt thou go?" and she said "I flee from the face of my mistress." Quite a wonder she honored Sarah so much as to call her mistress; but she knew nothing of abolition, and God by his angel did not become her teacher.

We have now arrived at what may be called an *abuse* of the institution, in which one person is the property of another, and under their control, and subject to their authority without their consent; and if the Bible be the

142

book, which proposes to furnish the case which leaves it without doubt that God abhors the institution, here we are to look for it. What, therefore, is the doctrine in relation to slavery, in a case in which a rigid exercise of its arbitrary authority is called forth upon a helpless female; who might use a strong plea for protection, upon the ground of being the master's wife. In the face of this case, which is hedged around with aggravations as if God designed by it to awaken all the sympathy and all the abhorrence of that portion of mankind, who claim to have more mercy than God himself—but I say, in view of this strong case, what is the doctrine taught? Is it that God abhors the institution of slavery; that it is a reproach to good men; that the evils of the institution can no longer be winked at among saints; that Abraham's character must not be transmitted to posterity, with this stain upon it; that Sarah must no longer be allowed to live a stranger to the abhorrence God has for such conduct as she has been guilty of to this poor helpless female? I say, what is the doctrine taught? Is it so plain that it can be easily understood? and does God teach that she is a bond-woman or slave, and that she is to recognize Sarah as her mistress, and not her equal—that she must return and submit herself unreservedly to Sarah's authority? Judge for yourself, reader, by the angel's answer: "And the angel of the Lord said unto her, Return unto thy mistress, and submit thyself under her hands." Gen. xvi. 9.

But, says the spirit of abolition, with which the Bible has to contend, you are building your house upon the sand, for these were nothing but hired servants; and their servitude designates no such state, condition, or relation, as that, in which one person is made the property of another, to be bought, sold, or transferred forever. To this, we have two answers in reference to the subject, *before giving the law.* In the first place, the term, servant, in the schedules of property among the patriarchs, *does designate* the state, condition, or relation in which one person is the legal property of another, as in Gen. xxiv. 35, 36. Here Abraham's servant, who had been sent by his master to get a wife for his son Isaac, in order to prevail with the woman and her family, states, that the man for whom he sought a bride was the son of a man whom God had greatly blessed with riches; which he goes on to enumerate thus, in the 35th verse: "He hath given him flocks, and herds, and silver, and gold, and men-servants, and maid-servants, and camels, and asses;" then in verse 36th, he states the disposition his master had made of his estate: "My master's wife bare a son to my master when she was old, and unto him he hath given all that he hath." Here, servants are enumerated with silver and gold as part of the patrimony. And, reader, bear it in mind; as if to rebuke the doctrine of abolition, servants are not only inventoried as property, but as property which *God had given to Abraham*. After the death of Abraham, we have a view of Isaac at Gerar, when he had come into the possession of this estate; and this is the description given of him: "And the man waxed great, and went forward, and grew until he became very great; for he had possession of flocks, and possession of herds, and *great store of servants*." Gen. xxvi. 13, 14. This state, in which servants are made chattels, he received as an inheritance from his father, and passed to his son Jacob.

Again, in Gen. xvii., we are informed of a covenant God entered into with Abraham; in which he stipulates, to be a God to him and his *seed*, (not his servants,) and to give to his *seed* the land of Canaan for an everlasting possession. He expressly stipulates, that Abraham shall put the token of this covenant upon every servant born in his house, and upon every servant *bought with his money of any stranger*. Gen. xvii. 12, 13. Here again servants are *property*. Again, more than 400 years afterwards, we find the *seed* of Abraham, on leaving Egypt, directed to celebrate the rite, that was ordained as a memorial of their deliverance, viz: the Passover, at which time the same institution which makes *property of men and women*, is recognized, and the *servant bought with money*, is given the privilege of partaking, upon the ground of his being circumcised *by his master*, while the hired servant, over whom the master had no such control, is excluded until he *voluntarily* submits to circumcision; showing clearly that the institution of involuntary slavery then carried with it a right, on the part of a master *to choose* a religion *for the servant* who was his money, as Abraham did, by God's direction, when he imposed circumcision on those he had bought with his money,—when he was circumcised himself, with Ishmael his son, who was the only individual, beside himself, on whom he had a right to impose it, except the bond-servants bought of the stranger with his money, and their children born in his house. The next notice we have of servants as property, is from God himself, when clothed with all the visible tokens of his presence and glory on the top of Sinai, when he proclaimed his law to the millions that surrounded its base: "Thou shalt not covet thy neighbor's house, thou shalt not covet thy neighbor's wife, nor his man-servant, nor his maid-servant, nor his ox, nor his ass, nor anything that is thy neighbor's."

144

Ex. xx. 17. Here, is a patriarchal catalogue of property, having God for its author, the wife among the rest, who was then purchased, as Jacob purchased his two, by 14 years' service. Here, the term servant, as used by the Almighty, under the circumstances of the case could not be understood by these millions, as meaning anything but property, because the night they left Egypt, a few weeks before, Moses, by divine authority, recognized their servants as property, which they had bought with their money.

2d. In addition to the evidence from the context of these, and various other places, to prove the term servant to be identical in the import of its essential particulars with the term slave among us, there is unquestionable evidence, that, *in the patriarchal age*, there are two distinct states of servitude alluded to, and which are indicated by two distinct terms, or by the same term, and an adjective to explain.

These two terms, are first, servant or bond-servant; second, hireling or hired servant: the first, indicating involuntary servitude; the second, voluntary servitude for stipulated wages and a specified time. Although this admits of the clearest proof *under the law*, yet it admits of proof before the law was given. On the night the Israelites left Egypt, which was *before* the law was given, Moses, in designating the qualifications necessary for the passover, uses this language, Exod. xii. 44, 45: "Every man's servant that is bought for money, when thou hast circumcised him, then shall he eat thereof. A foreigner and an hired servant shall not eat thereof." This language carries to the human mind, with irresistible force, the idea of *two distinct states*—one a state of *freedom*, the other a state of *bondage*: in one of which, a person is serving with his *consent* for wages; in the other of which, a person is serving without his *consent*, according to his master's pleasure.

Again, in Job iii., Job expresses the strong desire he had been made by his afflictions to feel, that he had died in his infancy. "For now," says he, "should I have lain still and been quiet, I should have slept: then had I been at rest. There (meaning the grave) the wicked cease from troubling, and there the weary be at rest. There the prisoners rest together; they hear not the voice of the oppressor. The small and the great are there; and the servant is free from his master." Job iii. 11, 13, 17, 18, 19. Now, I ask any common-sense man to account for the expression in this connection, "there the servant is free from his master." Afflictions are referred to, arising out of *states* or *conditions* from which *ordinarily* nothing but *death* brings relief. *Death* puts an end to afflictions of body that are incurable, as he took his own to be, and therefore he desired it.

The troubles brought on good men by a wicked, persecuting world, last for life; but in *death* the wicked cease from troubling—*death* ends that *relation* or *state* out of which such troubles grow. The prisoners of the oppressors, in that age, stood in a *relation* to their *oppressor*, which led the oppressed to expect they would hear the voice of the *oppressor* until *death*. But *death* broke the *relation*, and was desired, because in the grave they would hear his voice no more.

All the distresses growing out of inequalities in human condition; as wealth and power on one side, and poverty and weakness on the other, were terminated by death; the grave brought both to a level: the small and the great are there, and there, (that is, in the grave,) he adds, the servant is free from his master; made so, evidently, by *death*. The *relation*, or *state*, out of which his oppression had arisen, being destroyed by *death*, he would be freed from them, because he would, by *death*, be freed from his master who inflicted them. This view of the case, and this only, will account for the use of such language. But upon a supposition that a *state* or *relation* among men is referred to, that is *voluntary*, such as that between a *hired servant* and his *employer*, that can be *dissolved* at the pleasure of the *servant*, the language is without meaning, and perfectly unwarranted; while such a *relation* as that of *involuntary* and *hereditary* servitude, where the master had *unlimited power* over his servant, and in an age when cruelty was common, there is the greatest propriety in making the servant, or slave, *a companion with himself, in affliction*, as well as the oppressed and afflicted, in every class, where *death alone* dissolved the *state*, or *condition* out of which their afflictions grew. Beyond all doubt, this language refers to a state of *hereditary bondage*, from the afflictions of which, *ordinarily*, nothing in that day brought relief but *death*.

Again, in chapter 7th, he goes on to defend himself in his eager desire for death, in an address to God. He says, it is natural for a servant to desire the shadow, and a hireling his wages: "As the servant earnestly desireth the shadow, and as the hireling looketh for the reward of his work," so it is with me, should be supplied. Job vii. 2. Now, with the previous light shed upon the use and meaning of these terms in the *patriarchal Scriptures*, can any man of candor bring himself to believe that two states or conditions are not

146

here referred to, in one of which, the highest reward after toil is mere *rest*; in the other of which, the reward was wages? And how appropriate is the language in reference to these two states.

The *slave* is represented as earnestly desiring the *shadow*, because his condition allowed him no prospect of anything more desirable; but the *hireling* is looking for the *reward of his work*, because *that* will be an equivalent for his fatigue.

So Job looked at *death*, as being to his *body* as the servant's *shade*, therefore he desired it; and like the *hireling's wages* because *beyond the grave*, he hoped to reap the fruit of his doings. Again, Job (xxxi.) finding himself the subject of suspicion (see from verse 1 to 30) as to the rectitude of his past life, clears himself of various sins, in the most solemn manner, as unchastity, injustice in his dealings, adultery, contempt of his servants, unkindness to the poor, covetousness, the pride of wealth, &c. And in the 13th, 14th, and 15th verses, he thus expresses himself: "If I did despise the cause of my man-servant or my maid-servant, when they contended with me, what then shall I do when God rises up? and when he visiteth, what shall I answer him? Did not he that made me in the womb, make him? And did not one fashion us in the womb?" Taking this language in connection with the language employed by Moses, in reference to the institution of involuntary servitude in *that age*, and especially in connection with the language which Moses employs *after the law was given*, and what else can be understood than a reference to a class of duties that slave owners felt themselves above stooping to notice or perform, but which, nevertheless, it was the duty of the righteous man to discharge; for, whatever proud and wicked men might think of a poor servant that stood in his estate, on an equality with brutes, yet, says Job, he that made me made them, and if I despise their reasonable causes of complaint, for injuries which they are made to suffer, and for the redress of which I only can be appealed to, then what shall I do, and how shall I fare, when I carry my causes of complaint to him who is my master, and to whom only I can go for relief? When he visiteth me for despising *their cause*, what shall I answer him for *despising mine*? He means that he would feel self-condemned, and would be forced to admit the justice of the retaliation. But on the supposition that allusion is had to *hired servants*, who were *voluntarily* working for *wages* agreed upon, and who were the *subjects of rights*, for the *protection of which* their appeal would be to "the judges in the gate," as much as any other class of men, then there is no point in the statement. For *doing that* which can be *demanded as a legal right*, gives us no claim to the character of *merciful benefactors*. Job himself was a great slaveholder, and, like Abraham, Isaac, and Jacob, won no small portion of his claims to character with God and men from the manner in which he discharged his duty to his slaves. Once more: the conduct of Joseph in Egypt, *as Pharaoh's counsellor*, under all the circumstances, proves him a friend to absolute slavery, as a form of government better adapted to the state of the world at that time, than the one which existed in Egypt; for certain it is, that he peaceably effected a change in the fundamental law, by which a *state, condition, or relation*, between Pharaoh and the Egyptians was established, which answers to the one now denounced as sinful in the sight of God. Being warned of God, he gathered up all the surplus grain in the years of plenty, and sold it out in the years of famine, until he gathered up all the money; and when money failed, the Egyptians came and said, "Give us bread;" and Joseph said, "Give your cattle, and I will give for your cattle, if money fail." When that year was ended, they came unto him the second year, and said, "There is not aught left in sight of my Lord, but our bodies and our lands. Buy us and our lands for bread." And Joseph bought all the land of Egypt for Pharaoh.

So the land became Pharaoh's, and as for the people, he removed them to cities, from one end of the borders of Egypt, even to the other end thereof. Then Joseph said unto the people, "Behold! I have bought you this day, and your land for Pharaoh;" and they said, "we will be Pharaoh's servants." See Gen. xlvii. 14, 16, 19, 20, 21, 23, 25. Having thus changed the fundamental law, and created a state of entire *dependence*, and *hereditary bondage*, he enacted in his sovereign pleasure, that they should give Pharaoh one part, and take the other four parts of the productions of the earth to themselves. How far the hand of God was in this overthrow of liberty, I will not decide; but from the fact that he has singled out the greatest slaveholders of that age, as the objects of his special favor, it would seem that the institution was one furnishing great opportunities to exercise grace and glorify God, as it still does, where its duties are faithfully discharged.

I have been tedious on this first proposition, but I hope the importance of the subject to Christians as well as to statesmen will be my apology. I have written it, not for victory over an adversary, or to support error or falsehood, but to gather up God's will in reference to holding men and women in *bondage, in the patriarchal age*. And it is clear, in the first place, that God decreed this state before it existed. Second. It is clear that the highest manifestations of good-will which he ever gave to mortal man, was given to Abraham, in that covenant in which he required him to circumcise all his *male servants, which he had bought with his money,* and that were *born of them* in his house. Third. It is certain that he gave *these servants* as *property* to Isaac. Fourth. It is certain that, as the owner of *these slaves,* Isaac received similar tokens of God's favor. Fifth. It is certain that Jacob, who inherited from Isaac his father, received like tokens of divine favor. Sixth. It is certain, from a fair construction of language, that Job, who is held up by God himself as a model of human perfection, was a great slaveholder. Seventh. It is certain, when God showed honor, and came down to bless Jacob's posterity, in taking them by the hand to lead them out of Egypt, *they were the owners of slaves that were bought with money, and treated* as *property; which slaves* were allowed of God to unite in celebrating the divine goodness to their *masters,* while *hired servants* were excluded. Eighth. It is certain that God interposed to give Joseph the power in Egypt, which he used, to create a state, or condition, among the Egyptians, which *substantially agrees* with *patriarchal* and *modern slavery.* Ninth. It is certain, that in reference to this institution in Abraham's family, and the surrounding nations, for five hundred years, it is never censured in any communication made from God to men. Tenth. It is certain, when God put a *period* to *that dispensation,* he *recognized slaves as property on Mount Sinai.* If, therefore, it has become sinful since, it cannot be from *the nature of the thing,* but from the *sovereign pleasure of God in its prohibition.* We will therefore proceed to our second proposition, which is—

Second. That it was incorporated in the only national constitution emanating from the Almighty. By common consent, that portion of time stretching from Noah, until the law was given to Abraham's posterity, at Mount Sinai, is called the patriarchal age; *this is the period we have reviewed,* in relation to this subject. From the giving of the law until the coming of Christ, is called the Mosaic or legal dispensation. From the coming of Christ to the end of time, is called the Gospel dispensation. The legal dispensation *is the period of time we propose now to examine,* in reference to the institution of involuntary and hereditary slavery; in order to ascertain, whether, during this period, *it existed at all,* and *if it did exist,* whether with the *divine sanction,* or *in violation of the divine will.* This dispensation is called the legal dispensation, because it was the pleasure of God to take

Abraham's posterity by miraculous power, then numbering near three millions of souls, and give them a written constitution of government, a country to dwell in, and a covenant of special protection and favor, for their obedience to his law until the coming of Christ. The laws which he gave them emanated from his sovereign pleasure, and were designed, in the first place, to make himself known in his essential perfections; second, in his moral character; third, in his relation to man; and fourth, to make known those principles of action by the exercise of which man attains his highest moral elevation, viz: supreme love to God, and love to others as to ourselves.

All the law is nothing but a preceptive exemplification of these two principles; consequently, the existence of a precept in the law, utterly irreconcilable with these principles, would destroy all claims upon us for an acknowledgment of its divine original. Jesus Christ himself has put his finger upon these two principles of human conduct, (Deut. vi. 5—Levit. xix. 18,) revealed in the law of Moses, and decided, that on them hang all the law and the prophets.

The Apostle Paul decides in reference to the relative duties of men, that whether written out in preceptive form in the law or not, they are all comprehended in this saying, viz: "thou shalt love thy neighbor as thyself." With these views to guide us, as to the acknowledged design of the law, viz: that of revealing the eternal principles of moral rectitude, by which human conduct is to be measured, so that sin may abound, or be made apparent, and righteousness be ascertained or known, we may safely conclude, that the institution of slavery, which legalizes the holding of one person in bondage as property forever by another, if it be morally wrong, or at war with the principle which requires us to love God supremely, and our neighbor as ourself, will, if noticed at all in the law, be noticed, for the purpose of being condemned as sinful. And if the modern views of abolitionists be correct, we may expect to find the institution marked with such tokens of divine displeasure, as will throw all other sins into the shade, as comparatively small, when laid by the side of this monster. What, then, is true? has God ingrafted hereditary slavery upon the constitution of government he condescended to give his chosen people—that people, among whom he promised to dwell, and that he required to be holy? I answer, he has. It is clear and explicit. He enacts, first, that his chosen people may take their money, go into the slave markets of the surrounding nations, (the seven devoted nations excepted,) and purchase men-servants and women-servants, and give

150

them, and their increase, to their children and their children's children, forever; and worse still for the refined humanity of our age—he guaranties to the foreign slaveholder perfect protection, while he comes in among the Israelites, for the purpose of dwelling, and raising and selling slaves, who should be acclimated and accustomed to the habits and institutions of the country. And worse still for the sublimated humanity of the present age, God passes with the right to buy and possess, the right to govern, by a severity which knows no bounds but the master's discretion. And if worse can be, for the morbid humanity we censure, he enacts that his own people may sell themselves and their families for limited periods, with the privilege of extending the time at the end of the 6th year to the 50th year or jubilee, if they prefer bondage to freedom. Such is the precise character of two institutions, found in the constitution of the Jewish commonwealth, emanating directly from Almighty God. For the 1,500 years, during which these laws were in force, God raised up a succession of prophets to reprove that people for the various sins into which they fell; yet there is not a reproof uttered against the institution of *involuntary slavery*, for any species of abuse that ever grew out of it. A severe judgment is pronounced by Jeremiah, (chapter xxxiv. see from the 8th to the 22d verse,) for an abuse or violation of the law, concerning the *voluntary* servitude of Hebrews; but the prophet pens it with caution, as if to show that it had no reference to any abuse that had taken place under the system of *involuntary slavery*, which existed by law among that people; the sin consisted in making hereditary bond-men and bond-women of Hebrews, which was positively forbidden by the law, and not for buying and holding one of another nation in hereditary bondage, which was as positively allowed by the law. And really, in view of what is passing in our country, and elsewhere, among men who profess to reverence the Bible, it would seem that these must be dreams of a distempered brain, and not the solemn truths of that sacred book.

Well, I will now proceed to make them good to the letter, see Lev. xxv. 44, 45, 46: "Thy bond-men and thy bond-maids which thou shalt have, shall be of the heathen that are round about you: of them shall ye buy bond-men and bond-maids. Moreover, of the children of the strangers that do sojourn among you, of them shall ye buy, and of their families that are with you, which they begat in your land. And they shall be your possession. And ye shall take them as an inheritance for your children after you, to inherit them for a possession, they shall be your bond-men forever." I ask any candid man, if the words of this institution could be more explicit? It is from God himself; it authorizes that people, to whom he had become *king and law-giver*, to purchase men and women as property; to hold them and their posterity in bondage; and to will them to their children as a possession for-ever; and more, it allows *foreign slaveholders* to *settle* and *live among them*; to *breed slaves* and *sell them*. Now, it is important to a correct under-standing of this subject, to connect with the right to *buy* and *possess*, as property, the amount of authority to *govern*, which is granted by the *law-giver*; this amount of authority is implied, in the first place, in the law which prohibits the exercise of rigid authority upon the Hebrews, who are al-lowed to sell themselves for limited times. "If thy brother be waxen poor, and be sold unto thee, thou shalt not *compel him* to serve as a *bond servant*, but as a *hired servant*, and as a *sojourner* he shall be with thee, and shall serve thee until the year of jubilee—*they shall not be sold as bond-men*; thou *shalt not rule over them with rigor*." Levit. xxv. 39, 40, 41, 42, 43. It will be evident to all, that here are *two states* of servitude; in reference to *one* of which, *rigid* or *compulsory* authority, is *prohibited*, and that its *ex-ercise is authorized in the other*.

Second. In the criminal code, that conduct is punished with death, when done to a *freeman*, which is not punishable at all, when done *by a master to a slave*; for the express reason, that the slave is the *master's money*. "He that smiteth a man, so that he die, shall surely be put to death." Exod. xxi. 11, 12. "If a man smite his servant or his maid, with a rod, and he die under his hand, he shall be surely punished; notwithstanding, if he continue a day or two, he shall not be punished, for he is his money." Exod. xxi. 20. Here is precisely the same crime: smiting a man so that he die; if it be a freeman, he shall surely be put to death, whether the man die under his hand or live a day or two after; but if it be a servant, and the master continued the rod until the servant died under his hand, then it must be evident that such a chastisement could not be necessary for any purpose of wholesome or rea-sonable authority, and therefore he may be punished, but not with death. But if the death did not take place for a day or two, then it is to be *presumed* that the master only aimed to use the rod, so far as was necessary to pro-duce subordination, and for this, the law which allowed him to lay out his money in the slave, would protect him against all punishment. This is the common-sense principle which has been adopted substantially in civilized countries, where involuntary slavery has been instituted, from that day until

152

this. Now, here are laws that authorize the holding of men and women in bondage, and chastising them with the rod, with a severity that terminates in death. And he who believes the Bible to be of divine authority, believes these laws were given by the Holy Ghost to Moses. I understand modern abolition sentiments to be sentiments of marked hatred against such laws; to be sentiments which would hold God himself in abhorrence, if he were to give such laws his sanction: but he has given them his sanction; therefore, they must be in harmony with his moral character. Again, the divine Lawgiver, in guarding the property right in slaves among his chosen people, sanctions principles which may work the separation of man and wife, father and children. Surely, my reader will conclude, if I make this good, I shall force a part of the saints of the present day to blaspheme the God of Israel. All I can say is, truth is mighty, and I hope it will bring us all to say, Let God be true, in settling the true principles of humanity, and every man a liar who says slavery was inconsistent with it, in the days of the Mosaic law. Now for the proof: "If thou buy a Hebrew servant, six years shall he serve thee, and in the seventh he shall go out free for nothing; if he came in by himself, he shall go out by himself; if he were married, then his wife shall go out with him; if his master have given him a wife (one of his bond-maids) and she have borne him sons and daughters, the wife and her children shall be her master's, and he shall go out by himself." Exodus, xxi. 2, 3, 4. Now, the God of Israel gives this man the option of being separated by the master, from his wife and children, or becoming himself a servant forever, with a mark of the fact, like our cattle, in the ear, that can be seen wherever he goes; for it is enacted, "If the servant shall plainly say, I love my master, my wife, and my children, I will not go out free, then his master shall bring him unto the judges, (in open court,) he shall also bring him unto the door, or unto the door post, (so that all in the courthouse, and those in the yard may be witnesses,) and his master shall bore his ear through with an awl; and he shall serve him forever." It is useless to spend more time in gathering up what is written in the Scriptures on this subject, from the giving of the law until the coming of Christ.

Here is the authority, from God himself, to hold men and women, and their increase, in slavery, and to transmit them as property forever; here is plenary power to govern them, whatever measure of severity it may require; provided only, that *to govern*, be the object in exercising it. Here is power given to the master, to separate man and wife, parent and child, by denying

153

ingress to his premises, sooner than compel him to free or sell the mother, that the marriage relation might be honored. The *preference* is given of God to *enslaving the father* rather than *freeing the mother and children.*

Under every view we are allowed to take of the subject, the conviction is forced upon the mind, that from Abraham's day, until the coming of Christ, (a period of two thousand years,) this institution found favor with God. No marks of his displeasure are found resting upon it. It must, therefore, in its moral nature, be in harmony with those moral principles which he requires to be exercised by the law of Moses, and which are the principles that secure harmony and happiness to the universe, viz: supreme love to God and the love of our neighbor as ourself. Deut. vi. 6—Levit. xix. 18. To suppose that God has laid down these fundamental principles of moral rectitude in his law, as the soul that must inhabit every preceptive requirement of that law, and yet to suppose he created relations among the Israelites, and prescribed relative duties growing out of these relations, that are hostile to the spirit of the law, is to suppose what will never bring great honor or glory to our Maker. But if I understand that spirit which is now warring against slavery, this is the position which the spirit of God forces it to occupy, viz: that God has ordained slavery, and yet slavery is the greatest of sins. Such was the state of the case when Jesus Christ made his appearance. We propose—

Third. To show that Jesus Christ recognized this institution as one that was lawful among men, and regulated its relative duties.

Having shown from the Scriptures, that slavery existed with Abraham and the patriarchs, with divine approbation, and having shown from the same source, that the Almighty incorporated it in the law, as an institution among Abraham's seed, until the coming of Christ, our precise object now is, to ascertain whether *Jesus Christ has abolished it*, or *recognized it* as a *lawful relation*, existing among men, and prescribed duties which belong to it, as he has other *relative* duties; such as those between husband and wife, parent and child, magistrate and subject.

And first, I may take it for granted, without proof, that he has not abolished it by commandment, for none pretend to this. This, by the way, is a singular circumstance, that Jesus Christ should put a system of measures into operation, which have for their object the subjugation of all men to him as a law-giver—kings, legislators, and private citizens in all nations; at

154

a time, too, when hereditary slavery existed in all; and after it had been incorporated for fifteen hundred years into the Jewish constitution, immediately given by God himself. I say, it is passing strange, that under such circumstances, Jesus should fail to prohibit its further existence, if it was his intention to abolish it. Such an omission or oversight cannot be charged upon any other legislator the world has ever seen. But, says the Abolitionist, he has introduced new moral principles, which will extinguish it as an unavoidable consequence, without a direct prohibitory command. What are they? "Do to others as you would they should do to you." Taking these words of Christ to be a body, inclosing a moral soul in them, what soul, I ask, is it?

The same embodied in these words of Moses, Levit. xix. 18: "thou shalt love thy neighbor as thyself;" or is it another? It cannot be another, but it must be the very same, because Jesus says, there are but two principles in being, in God's moral government, *one* including all that is *due to God*, the *other* all that is *due to men*.

If, therefore, doing to others as we would they should do to us, means precisely what loving our neighbor as ourself means, then Jesus has added no new moral principle above those in the law of Moses, to prohibit slavery, for in his law is found this principle, and slavery also.

The very God that said to them, they should love him supremely, and their neighbors as themselves, said to them also, "of the heathen that are round about you, thou shalt buy bond-men and bond-women, and they shall be your possession, and ye shall take them as an inheritance for your children after you, to inherit them as a possession; they shall be your bond-men forever." Now, to suppose that Jesus Christ left his disciples to find out, without a revelation, that slavery must be abolished, as a natural consequence from the fact, that when God established the relation of master and servant under the law, he said to the master and servant, each of you must love the other as yourself, is, to say the least, making Jesus to presume largely upon the intensity of their intellect, that they would be able to spy out a discrepancy in the law of Moses, which God himself never saw. Again: if "do to others as ye would they should do to you," is to abolish slavery, it will for the same reason, level all inequalities in human condition. It is not to be admitted, then, that Jesus Christ introduced any new moral principle that must, of necessity, abolish slavery. The principle relied on to prove it, stands boldly out to view in the code of Moses, as the *soul*, that must *regulate*, and *control*, the *relation of master* and *servant*, and therefore cannot abolish it.

Why a master cannot do to a servant, or a servant to a master, as he would have them do to him, as soon a wife to a husband or a husband to a wife, I am utterly at a loss to know. The wife is "subject to her husband in all things" by divine precept. He is her "head," and God "suffers her not to usurp authority over him." Now, why in such a relation as this, we can do to others as we would they should do to us, any sooner than in a relation, securing to us what is just and equal as servants, and due respect and faithful service rendered with good will to us as masters, I am at a loss to conceive. I affirm then, first, (and no man denies,) that Jesus Christ has not abolished slavery by a prohibitory command: and second, I affirm, he has introduced no new moral principle which can work its destruction under the gospel dispensation; and that the principle relied on for this purpose, is a fundamental principle of the Mosaic law, under which slavery was instituted by Jehovah himself: and third, with this absence of positive prohibition, and this absence of principle, to work its ruin, I affirm, that in all the Roman provinces, where churches were planted by the Apostles, hereditary slavery existed, as it did among the Jews, and as it does now among us, (which admits of proof from history that no man will dispute who knows anything of the matter,) and that in instructing such churches, the Holy Ghost by the Apostles, has recognized the institution, as one *legally existing* among them, to be perpetuated in the church, and that its duties are prescribed.

Now for the proof: To the church planted at Ephesus, the capital of the lesser Asia, Paul ordains by letter, subordination in the fear of God,—first between wife and husband; second, child and parent; third, servant and master; *all, as states, or conditions, existing among the members.*

The relative duties of each state, are pointed out; those between the servant and master in these words: "Servants be obedient to them who are your masters, according to the flesh, with fear and trembling, in singleness of your heart as unto Christ; not with eye service as men pleasers, but as the servants of Christ, doing the will of God from the heart, with good will, doing service, as to the Lord and not to men, knowing that whatsoever good thing any man doeth, the same shall he receive of the Lord, whether he be bond or free. And ye masters do the same things to them, forbearing threatening, knowing that your master is also in heaven, neither is there respect of persons with him." Here, by the Roman law, the servant was property, and the control of the master unlimited, as we shall presently prove.

To the church at Colosse, a city of Phrygia, in the lesser Asia,—Paul in his letter to them, recognizes the three relations of wives and husbands, parents and children, servants and masters, as relations existing among the members; (here the Roman law was the same;) and to the servants and masters he thus writes: "Servants obey in all things your masters, according to the flesh: not with eye service, as men pleasers, but in singleness of heart, fearing God: and whatsoever you do, do it heartily, as to the Lord and not unto men; knowing that of the Lord ye shall receive the reward of the inheritance, for ye serve the Lord Christ. But he that doeth wrong shall receive for the wrong he has done; and there is no respect of persons with God. Masters give unto your servants that which is just and equal, knowing that you also have a master in heaven."

The same Apostle writes a letter to the church at Corinth;—a very important city, formerly called the eye of Greece, either from its location, or intelligence, or both, and consequently, an important point, for radiating light in all directions, in reference to subjects connected with the cause of Jesus Christ; and particularly, in the bearing of its practical precepts on civil society, and the political structure of nations. Under the direction of the Holy Ghost, he instructs the church, that, on this particular subject, *one general principle* was ordained of God, applicable alike in all countries and at all stages of the church's future history, and that it was this: "*as the Lord has called every one, so let him walk.*" "Let every man abide in the same calling wherein he is called." "Let every man wherein he is called, therein abide with God." 1 Cor. vii. 17, 20, 24. "*And so ordain I in all churches;*" vii. 17. The Apostle thus explains his meaning:

"Is any man called being circumcised? Let him not become uncircumcised.

"Is any called in uncircumcision? Let him not be circumcised.

"Art thou called, being a servant? Care not for it, but if thou mayst be made free, use it rather;" vii. 18, 21. Here, by the Roman law, slaves were property,—yet Paul ordains, in this and all other churches, that Christianity gave them no title to freedom, but on the contrary, required them not to care for being slaves, or in other words, to be contented with their *state*, or *relation*, unless they could be *made free*, in a lawful way.

Again, we have a letter by Peter, who is the Apostle of the circumcision—addressed especially to the Jews, who were scattered through various provinces of the Roman empire; comprising those provinces especially, which were the theatre of their dispersion, under the Assyrians and Babylonians. Here, for the space of 750 years, they had resided, during which time those revolutions were in progress which terminated the Babylonian, Medo-Persian, and Macedonian empires, and transferred imperial power to Rome. These revolutionary scenes of violence left one half the human race (within the range of their influence,) in abject bondage to the one half. This was the state of things in these provinces addressed by Peter, when he wrote. The chances of war, we may reasonably conclude, had assigned a full share of bondage to this people, who were despised of all nations. In view of their enslaved condition to the Gentiles; knowing, as Peter did, their seditious character; foreseeing, from the prediction of the Saviour, the destined bondage of those who were then free in Israel, which was soon to take place, as it did, in the fall of Jerusalem, when all the males over seventeen, were sent to work in the mines of Egypt, as slaves to the State, and all the males under, amounting to upwards of ninety-seven thousand, were sold into domestic bondage;—I say, in view of these things, Peter was moved by the Holy Ghost to write to them, and his solicitude for such of them as were in slavery, is very conspicuous in his letter; (read carefully from 1st Peter, 2d chapter, from the 13th verse to the end;) but it is not the solicitude of an abolitionist. He thus addresses them: "Dearly beloved, I beseech you." He thus instructs them: "Submit yourselves to every ordinance of man for the Lord's sake." "For so is the will of God." "Servants, be subject to your masters with all fear, not only to the good and gentle, but also to the froward." 1st Peter ii. 11, 13, 15, 18. What an important document is this!—enjoining political subjection to *governments of every form*, and Christian subjection on the part of servants to their masters, whether good or bad; for the purpose of showing forth to advantage, the *glory of the Gospel*, and putting to silence the ignorance of foolish men, who might think it seditious.

By "every ordinance of man," as the context will show, is meant governmental regulations or laws, as was that of the Romans for enslaving their prisoners taken in war, instead of destroying their lives.

When such enslaved persons came into the church of Christ let them (says Peter) "be subject to their masters with all fear," whether such masters be good or bad. It is worthy of remark, that he says much to secure civil subordination to the State, and hearty and cheerful obedience to the masters, on the part of servants; yet he says nothing to masters in the whole letter. It would seem from this, that danger to the cause of Christ was on the side of *insubordination among the servants*, and *a want of humility with inferiors*, rather than *haughtiness among superiors* in the church.

Gibbon, in his Rome, vol. 1, pages 25, 26, 27, shows, from standard authorities, that Rome at this time swayed its sceptre over one hundred and twenty millions of souls; that in every province, and in every family, *absolute slavery existed*; that it was at least fifty years later than the date of Peter's letters, before the absolute power of life and death over the slave was *taken from the master*, and *committed to the magistrate*; that about sixty millions of souls were held as property in this abject condition; that the price of a slave was four times that of an ox; that their punishments were very sanguinary; that in the second century, when their condition began to improve a little, emancipation was prohibited, except for great personal merit, or some public service rendered to the State; and that it was not until the third or fourth generation after freedom was obtained, that the descendants of a slave could share in the honors of the State. This is the *state, condition*, or *relation* among the *members of all the apostolic churches*, whether among *Gentiles* or *Jews*; which the Holy Ghost, by Paul for the Gentiles, and Peter for the Jews, recognizes as lawful; the mutual duties of which he prescribes in the language above. Now, I ask, can any man in his proper senses, from these premises, bring himself to conclude that slavery is *abolished by Jesus Christ*, or that obligations are imposed by him upon his disciples that are subversive of the institution? Knowing as we do from contemporary historians, that the institution of slavery existed at the time and to the extent stated by Gibbon—what sort of a soul must a man have, who, with these facts before him, will conceal the truth on this subject, and hold Jesus Christ responsible for a scheme of treason that would, if carried out, have brought the life of every human being on earth at the time, into the most imminent peril, and that must have worked the destruction of half the human race?

At Rome, the authoritative centre of that vast theatre upon which the glories of the cross were to be won, a church was planted. Paul wrote a long letter to them. On this subject it is full of instruction.

Abolition sentiments had not dared to show themselves so near the imperial sword. To warn the church against their treasonable tendency, was therefore unnecessary. Instead, therefore, of special precepts upon the subject of relative duties between master and servant, he lays down a system of practical morality, in the 12th chapter of his letter, which must commend itself equally to the king on his throne, and the slave in his hovel; for while its practical operation leaves the subject of earthly government to the discretion of man, it secures the exercise of sentiments and feelings that must exterminate everything inconsistent with doing to others as we would they should do unto us: a system of principles that will give moral strength to governments; peace, security, and good will to individuals; and glory to God in the highest. And in the 13th chapter, from the 1st to the end of the 7th verse, he recognizes human government as an ordinance of God, which the followers of Christ are to obey, honor, and support; not only from dread of punishment, but *for conscience sake*; which I believe abolitionism refuses most positively to do to such governments as *from the force of circumstances* even *permit* slavery.

Again. But we are furnished with additional light, and if we are not greatly mistaken, with light which arose out of circumstances analogous to those which are threatening at the present moment to overthrow the peace of society, and deluge this nation with blood. To Titus whom Paul left in Crete, to set in order the things that were wanting, he writes a letter, in which he warns him of false teachers, that were to be dreaded on account of their doctrine. While they professed "to know God," that is, to know his will under the gospel dispensation, "in works they denied him;" that is, they did, and required others to do, what was contrary to his will under the gospel dispensation. "They were abominable," that is, to the church and state, "and disobedient," that is, to the authority of the Apostles, and the civil authority of the land. Titus, he then exhorts, "to speak the things that become sound doctrine;" that is, that the members of the church observe the law of the land, and obey the civil magistrate; that "servants be obedient to their own masters, and please them well in all things," not "answering again, not purloining, but showing all good fidelity that they may adorn the doctrine of God our Saviour in all things," *in that which subjects the ecclesiastical to the civil authority in particular.* "These things speak, and exhort and rebuke with all authority; let no man despise thee. Put them in mind to be subject to principalities and powers, to obey magistrates." Titus i. 16, and ii. from 1 to 10, and iii. 1. The context shows that a doctrine was taught by these wicked men, which tended in its influence on servants, to bring the Gospel of Christ into contempt, in church and state, because of its seditious and insubordinate nature.

But at Ephesus, the capital of the lesser Asia, where Paul had labored with great success for three years—a point of great importance to the Gospel cause—the Apostle left Timothy for the purpose of watching against the false teachers, and particularly against the abolitionists. In addition to a letter which he had addressed to this church previously, in which the mutual duty of master and servant is taught, and which has already been referred to, he further instructs Timothy by letter on the same subject: "Let as many servants as are under the yoke count their masters worthy of all honor, that the name of God and his doctrine be not blasphemed." 1 Tim. vi. 1. These were unbelieving masters, as the next verse will show. In this church at Ephesus, the circumstances existed, which are brought to light by Paul's letter to Timothy, that must silence every cavil, which men, who do not know God's will on this subject, may start until time ends. In an age filled with literary men, who are employed in transmitting historically, to future generations, the structure of society in the Roman Empire; that would put it in our power at this distant day, to know the state or condition of a slave in the Roman Empire, as well as if we had lived at the time, and to know beyond question, that his condition was precisely that one, which is now denounced as sinful: in such an age, and in such circumstances, Jesus Christ causes his will to be published to the world; and it is this, that if a Christian slave have an unbelieving master, who acknowledges no allegiance to Christ, this believing slave must count his master worthy of all honor, according to what the Apostle teaches the Romans, "Render, therefore, to all their dues, tribute to whom tribute is due, custom to whom custom is due, fear to whom fear, honor to whom honor." Rom. xiii. 7. Now, honor is enjoined of God in the Scriptures, from children to parents—from husbands to wives—from subjects to magistrates and rulers, and here by Jesus Christ, from Christian slaves to unbelieving masters, who held them as property by law, with power over their very lives. And the command is remarkable. While we are commanded to honor father and mother, without adding to the precept "all honor," here a Christian servant is bound to render to his unbelieving master "all honor." Why is this? Because in the one case nature moves in the direction of the command; but in the other, against it. Nature being subjected to the law of grace, might be disposed to obey reluctantly; hence the amplitude of the command. But what purpose was to be answered by this devotion of the slave? The Apostle answers, "that the name of God and his doctrine (of subordination to the law-making power) be not blasphemed,"

161

as they certainly would by a contrary course on the part of the servant for the most obvious reason in the world; while the sword would have been drawn against the Gospel, and a war of extermination waged against its propagators, in every province of the Roman Empire, for there was slavery in all; and so it would be now.

But, say the caviler, these directions are given to Christian slaves whose masters did not acknowledge the authority of Christ to govern them; and are therefore defective as proof, that he approves of one Christian man holding another in bondage. Very well, we will see. In the next verse, (1 Timothy vi. 2,) he says, "and they that have believing masters, let them not despise them, because they are brethren, but rather do them service, because they are faithful and beloved, partakers of the benefit." Here is a great change; instead of a command to a believing slave to render to a believing master *all honor*, and thereby making that believing master in *honor* equal to an unbelieving master, here is rather an exhortation to the slave *not to despise him, because he is a believer.* Now, I ask, why the circumstance of a master becoming a believer in Christ, should become the cause of his believing slave despising him, while that slave was supposed to acquiesce in the duty of rendering all honor to that master before he became a believer? I answer, *precisely*, and *only, because* there were *abolition teachers* among them, who *taught otherwise*, and consented not to wholesome words, *even the words of our Lord Jesus Christ.* 1 Timothy vii. 3: and "to the doctrine which is according to godliness," taught in the 8th verse, viz: having food and raiment, servants should therewith be content; for the pronoun us, in the 8th verse of this connection, means *especially* the *servants he was instructing*, as well as Christians in general. These men taught, that godliness abolished slavery, that it gave the title of freedom to the slave, and that so soon as a man professed to be subject to Christ, and refused to liberate his slaves, he was a hypocrite, and deserved not the countenance of any who bore the Christian name. Such men, the Apostle says, are "proud, (just as they are now,) knowing nothing," (that is, on this subject,) but "doating about questions, and strifes of words, whereof cometh envy, strife, railings, evil surmisings, perverse disputings of men of corrupt minds, and destitute of the truth, supposing that gain is godliness: from such withdraw thyself." 1 Tim. vi. 4, 5.

Such were the bitter fruits which abolition sentiments produced in the Apostolic day, and such precisely are the fruits they produce now.

162

Now, I say, here is the case made out, which certainly would call forth the command from Christ, to abolish slavery, if he ever intended to abolish it. Both the servant and the master were one in Christ Jesus. Both were members of the same church, both were under unlimited and voluntary obedience to the same divine lawgiver.

No political objection existed at the time against their obedience to him on the subject of slavery; and what is the will, not of Paul, but of the Lord Jesus Christ, immediately in person, upon the case thus made out? Does he say to the master, having put yourself under my government, you must no longer hold your brother in bondage? Does he say to the slave, if your master does not release you, you must go and talk to him privately, about this trespass upon your rights under the law of my kingdom; and if he does not hear you, you must take two or three with you; and if he does not hear them then you must tell it to the church, and have him expelled from my flock, as a wolf in sheep's clothing? I say, what does the Lord Jesus say to this poor believing slave, concerning a master who held unlimited power over his person and life, under the Roman law? He tells him that the very circumstance of his master's being a brother, constitutes the reason why he should be more ready to do him service; for, in addition to the circumstance of his being a brother who would be benefited by his service, he would as a brother give him what was just and equal in return, and "forbear threatening," much less abusing his authority over him, for that he (the master) also had a master in heaven, who was no respecter of persons. It is taken for granted, on all hands pretty generally, that Jesus Christ has at least been silent, or that he has not personally spoken on the subject of slavery. Once for all, I deny it. Paul, after stating that a slave was to honor an unbelieving master, in the 1st verse of the 6th chapter, says in the 2d verse, that to a believing master, he is the rather to do service, because he who partakes of the benefit is his brother. He then says, if any man teach otherwise, (as all Abolitionists then did, and now do,) and consent not to wholesome words, "even the words of our Lord Jesus Christ." Now, if our Lord Jesus Christ uttered such words, how dare we say he has been silent? If he has been silent, how dare the Apostle say these are the words of our Lord Jesus Christ, if the Lord Jesus Christ never spoke them? Where or when, or on what occasion he spoke them, we are not informed; but certain it is, that Paul has borne false witness, or that Jesus Christ has uttered the words that impose an obligation on servants, who are abject slaves, to render service with good will from the heart, to believing masters, and to account their unbelieving masters, as worthy of all honor, that the name of God and his doctrine be not blasphemed. Jesus Christ revealed to Paul the doctrine which Paul has settled throughout the Gentile world, (and by consequence, the Jewish world also,) on the subject of slavery, so far as it affects his kingdom. As we have seen, it is clear and full.

From the great importance of the subject, involving the personal liberty of half the human race at that time, and a large portion of them at all times since, it is not to be wondered at, that Paul would carry the question to the Savior, and plead for a decisive expression of his will, that would forever do away the necessity of inferring anything by reasoning from the premises laid down in the former dispensation; or in the Patriarchal age; and at Ephesus, if not at Crete, the issue is fairly made, between Paul on the one side, and certain abolition teachers on the other, when, in addition to the official intelligence ordinarily given to the Apostles by the Holy Ghost, to guide them into all truth, he affirms, that the doctrine of perfect civil subordination, on the part of hereditary slaves to their masters, whether believers or unbelievers, was one which he, Paul, taught in the words of the Lord Jesus Christ himself.

The Scriptures we have adduced from the New Testament, to prove the recognition of hereditary slavery by the Savior, as a lawful relation in the sight of God, lose much of their force from the use of a word by the translators, which by time, has lost much of its original meaning; that is, the word *servant*. Dr. Johnson, in his Dictionary, says: "Servant is one of the few words, which by time has acquired a softer signification than its original, knave, degenerated into cheat. While *servant*, which signified originally, a person preserved from death by the conqueror, and reserved for slavery, signifies only an obedient attendant." Now, all history will prove that the servants of the New Testament addressed by the Apostles, in their letters to the several churches throughout the Roman Empire, were such as were preserved from death by the conqueror, and taken into slavery. This was their condition, and it a fact well known to all men acquainted with history. Had the word which designates their condition, in our translation, lost none of its original meaning, a common man could not have fallen into a mistake as to the condition indicated. But to waive this fact, we are furnished with all the evidence that can be desired. The Savior appeared in an age of learning—the enslaved condition of half the Roman Empire, at the time, is a fact embodied with all the historical records—the constitution God gave the Jews, was in harmony with the Roman regulation on the subject of slavery. In this state of things, Jesus ordered his Gospel to be preached in all the world, and to every creature. It was done as directed; and masters and servants, and persons in all conditions, were brought by the Gospel to obey the Savior. Churches were constituted. We have examined the letters written to the churches, composed of these materials. The result is, that each member is furnished with a law to regulate the duties of his civil station—from the highest to the lowest.

We will remark, in closing under this head, that we have shown from the text of the sacred volume, that when God entered into covenant with Abraham, it was with him as a slaveholder; that when he took his posterity by the hand in Egypt, five hundred years afterwards to confirm the promise made to Abraham, it was done with them as slaveholders; that when he gave them a constitution of government, he gave them the right to perpetuate hereditary slavery; and that he did not for the fifteen hundred years of their national existence, express disapprobation towards the institution.

We have also shown from authentic history that the institution of slavery existed in every family, and in every province of the Roman Empire, at the time the gospel was published to them.

We have also shown from the New Testament, that all the churches are recognized as composed of masters and servants; and that they are instructed by Christ how to discharge their relative duties; and finally, that in reference to the question which was then started, whether Christianity did not abolish the institution, or the right of one Christian to hold another Christian in bondage, we have shown, that "the words of our Lord Jesus Christ" are, that so far from this being the case, it adds to the obligation of the servant to render service with good will to his master, and that gospel fellowship is not to be entertained with persons who will not consent to it!

I propose, in the fourth place, to show that the institution of slavery is full of mercy. I shall say but a few words on this subject. Authentic history warrants this conclusion, that for a long period of time, it was this institution alone which furnished a motive for sparing the prisoner's life. The chances of war, when the earth was filled with small tribes of men, who had a passion for it, brought to decision, almost daily, conflicts, where nothing

165

but this institution interposed an inducement to save the vanquished. The same was true in the enlarged schemes of conquest, which brought the four great universal empires of the Scriptures to the zenith of their power.

The same is true in the history of Africa, as far back as we can trace it. It is only sober truth to say, that the institution of slavery has saved from the sword more lives, including their increase, than all the souls who now inhabit this globe.

The souls thus conquered and subjected to masters, who feared not God nor regarded men, in the days of Abraham, Job, and the Patriarchs, were surely brought under great obligations to the mercy of God, in allowing such men as these to purchase them, and keep them in their families.

The institution when ingrafted on the Jewish constitution, was designed principally, not to enlarge the number, but to ameliorate the condition of the slaves in the neighboring nations.

Under the Gospel, it has brought within the range of Gospel influence, millions of Ham's descendants among ourselves, who, but for this institution, would have sunk down to eternal ruin; knowing not God, and strangers to the Gospel. In their bondage here on earth, they have been much better provided for, and great multitudes of them have been made the freemen of the Lord Jesus Christ, and left this world rejoicing in hope of the glory of God. The elements of an empire, which I hope will lead Ethiopia very soon to stretch out her hands to God, is the fruit of the institution here. An officious meddling with the institution, from feelings and sentiments unknown to the Bible, may lead to the extermination of the slave race among us, who, taken as a whole, are utterly unprepared for a higher civil state; but benefit them, it cannot. Their condition, *as a class*, is now better than that of any other equal number of laborers on earth, and is daily improving.

If the Bible is allowed to awaken the spirit, and control the philanthropy which works their good, the day is not far distant when the highest wishes of saints will be gratified, in having conferred on them all that the spirit of good-will can bestow. This spirit which was kindling into life, has received a great check among us of late, by that trait which the Apostle Peter reproves and shames in his officious countrymen, when he says: "But let none of you suffer as a murderer, or as a thief, or as an evil doer, or as a busy-body in other men's matters." Our citizens have been murdered—our property has been stolen, (if the receiver is as bad as the thief,)—our lives have been put in jeopardy—our characters traduced—and attempts made to force politi-

166

cal slavery upon us in the place of domestic, by strangers who have no right to meddle with our matters. Instead of meditating generous things to our slaves, as a return for Gospel subordination, we have to put on our armor to suppress a rebellious spirit, engendered by "false doctrine," propagated by men "of corrupt minds, and destitute of the truth," who teach them that the gain of freedom to the slave, is the only proof of godliness in the master. From such, Paul says we must withdraw ourselves; and if we fail to do it, and to rebuke them with all the authority which "the words of our Lord Jesus Christ" confer, we shall be wanting in duty to him, to ourselves, and to the world.

THORNTON STRINGFELLOW

IV. JAMES HENRY HAMMOND
Letter to an English Abolitionist

"Into . . . Eden is coming Satan in the guise of an Abolitionist."

James Henry Hammond was born in South Carolina in 1807. Son of a schoolmaster who had moved South at the turn of the century, young Hammond graduated from South Carolina College in 1825. After several years teaching while he prepared for the bar, Hammond began the practice of law in Columbia. Caught up in the excitement of the Nullification controversy, Hammond gained prominence as a strongly sectionalist newspaper editor. After a fortunate marriage to a Charleston heiress, Hammond left public life to manage the ten-thousand-acre plantation and 147 slaves he had acquired as a result of the union. Elected to Congress, Hammond moved to Washington in 1835. But after a stunning debut attacking the reception of abolitionist petitions by the House of Representatives, he was stricken with a nervous ailment and resigned his seat to travel in Europe. In 1842 he reentered politics as governor of his native state and gained national attention during the next few years with his proslavery and anti-tariff publications. At the end of his term, Hammond returned once again to his plantation, where he continued to write on agricultural and political topics until he was chosen for the U.S. Senate in 1857. Upon Lincoln's election, Hammond resigned and returned home once again. His health declined throughout the war years, and he died in November, 1864, just before Sherman began his march through South Carolina.[1]

The selection below is the first of two letters that Hammond published in

1. On Hammond's life there are two major collections of papers: the James Henry Hammond Papers, Library of Congress, and James Henry Hammond Papers, South Caroliniana Library, University of South Carolina, Columbia. The only published biography is Elizabeth Merritt, *James Henry Hammond, 1807–1864* (Baltimore: Johns Hopkins University Press, 1923), although Robert Tucker's unpublished dissertation is more useful: "James Henry Hammond: South Carolinian" (Ph.D. dissertation, University of North Carolina, 1958). See also Drew Gilpin Faust, *A Sacred Circle: The Dilemma of the Intellectual in the Old South, 1840–1860* (Baltimore: Johns Hopkins University Press, 1977).

the Columbia *South Carolinian* in 1845. Within the next year, the work was twice reissued in pamphlet form as *Two Letters on Slavery in the United States, Addressed to Thomas Clarkson, Esq.* Hammond had made his proslavery debut the preceding year with *Letter of His Excellency Governor Hammond to the Free Church of Glasgow on the Subject of Slavery*, but the Clarkson letters gained him a prominence throughout the South that he had not before attained, and he was deluged with congratulatory letters from admiring fellow southerners. The Clarkson letters were reprinted in both *The Pro-Slavery Argument as Maintained by the Most Distinguished Writers of the Southern States* and in *Cotton is King and Pro-Slavery Arguments*, the two major anthologies of defenses of human bondage.[2]

In his appeal to Thomas Clarkson, noted British opponent of slavery and the slave trade, Hammond touched upon the various types of justification that formed the core of the proslavery argument. He summarized biblical defenses, then offered social, political, and moral rationalizations. Hammond regared slavery as the "corner-stone" of republican institutions and specifically noted that it bestowed advantages on nonslaveholding whites, as well as on masters and slaves. Comparing the South's system of labor with that of England, Hammond concluded that southern slaves were far better off than British operatives and vigorously defended his region against the allegations of cruelty leveled by abolitionists. Every society, he admitted, contained evil and suffering, but in the South, he asserted, these were minimized by the social arrangements of slavery. Indeed, many of the harsh aspects of the existing system, Hammond insisted, were the direct result of abolitionist meddling, which had compelled masters to be more rigorous in the management of their slaves.[3]

2. James Henry Hammond, *Two Letters on Slavery in the United States, Addressed to Thomas Clarkson, Esq.* (Columbia: Allen, McCarter & Co., 1845) and *Gov. Hammond's Letters on Southern Slavery: Addressed to Thomas Clarkson, the English Abolitionist* (Charleston: Walker and Burke, 1845); James Henry Hammond, *Letter of His Excellency Governor Hammond to the Free Church of Glasgow on the Subject of Slavery* (Columbia: A. H. Pemberton, 1844); James Henry Hammond, "Hammond's Letters on Slavery," *The Pro-Slavery Argument as Maintained by the Most Distinguised Authors of the Southern States* (Charleston: Walker, Richards & Co., 1852), 99–174.

3. On Hammond's proslavery thought, see Drew Gilpin Faust, *A Sacred Circle*, vi; on the origins of his ideas about British wage slavery, see Drew Gilpin Faust, "A Slaveowner in a Free Society: James Henry Hammond on the Grand Tour, 1836–1837," *South Carolina Historical Magazine*, LXXXI (July, 1980), 189–206; and on Hammond as slave master, see Drew Gilpin Faust, "Culture, Conflict, and Community: The Meaning of Power on an Ante-Bellum Plantation," *Journal of Social History*, XIV (September, 1980), 83–97.

Letter to an English Abolitionist

SILVER BLUFF, (So. Ca.,) January 28, 1845.

Sir: I received, a short time ago, a letter from the Rev. Willoughby M. Dickinson, dated at your residence, "Playford Hall, near Ipswich, 26th November, 1844," in which was enclosed a copy of your Circular Letter, addressed to professing Christians in our Northern States, having no concern with Slavery, and to others there. I presume that Mr. Dickinson's letter was written with your knowledge, and the document enclosed with your consent and approbation. I therefore feel that there is no impropriety in my addressing my reply directly to yourself, especially as there is nothing in Mr. Dickinson's communication requiring serious notice. Having abundant leisure, it will be a recreation to devote a portion of it to an examination and free discussion of the question of Slavery as it exists in our Southern States: and since you have thrown down the gauntlet to me, I do not hesitate to take it up.

Familiar as you have been with the discussions of this subject in all its aspects, and under all the excitements it has occasioned for sixty years past, I may not be able to present much that will be new to you. Nor ought I to indulge the hope of materially affecting the opinions you have so long cherished, and so zealously promulgated. Still, time and experience have developed facts, constantly furnishing fresh tests to opinions formed sixty years since, and continually placing this great question in points of view, which could scarcely occur to the most consummate intellect even a quarter of a century ago: and which may not have occurred yet to those whose previous convictions, prejudices, and habits of thought, have thoroughly and permanently biased them to one fixed way of looking at the matter: while there are peculiarities in the operation of every social system, and special local as well as moral causes materially affecting it, which no one, placed at the distance you are from us, can fully comprehend or properly appreciate. Besides, it may be possibly, a novelty to you to encounter one who conscientiously believes the domestic Slavery of these States to be not only an inexorable necessity for the present, but a moral and humane institution, productive of the greatest political and social advantages, and who is disposed, as I am, to defend it on these grounds.

I do not propose, however, to defend the African slave trade. That is no longer a question. Doubtless great evils arise from it as it has been, and is

170

now conducted: unnecessary wars and cruel kidnapping in Africa: the most shocking barbarities in the middle passage: and perhaps a less humane system of Slavery in countries continually supplied with fresh laborers at a cheap rate. The evils of it, however, it may be fairly presumed, are greatly exaggerated. And if I might judge of the truth of transactions stated as occurring in this trade, by that of those reported as transpiring among us, I should not hesitate to say, that a large proportion of the stories in circulation are unfounded, and most of the remainder highly colored.

On the passage of the Act of Parliament prohibiting this trade to British subjects rests, what you esteem, the glory of your life. It required twenty years of arduous agitation, and the intervening extraordinary political events, to convince your countrymen, and among the rest your pious king, of the expediency of the measure: and it is but just to say, that no one individual rendered more essential service to the cause than you did. In reflecting on the subject, you cannot but often ask yourself: What, after all, has been accomplished; how much human suffering has been averted; how many human beings have been rescued from transatlantic Slavery? And on the answers you can give these questions, must in a great measure, I presume, depend on the happiness of your life. In framing them, how frequently must you be reminded of the remark Mr. Grosvenor, in one of the early debates upon the subject, which I believe you have yourself recorded, "that he had twenty objections to the abolition of the slave trade: the first was, *that it was impossible*—the rest he need not give." . . .

Experience having settled the point, that this trade *cannot be abolished by the use of force*, and that blockading squadrons serve only to make it more profitable and more cruel, I am surprised that the attempt is persisted in, unless it serves as a cloak to other purposes. It would be far better than it now is, for the African, if the trade was free from all restrictions, and left to the mitigation and decay which time and competition would surely bring about. If kidnapping, both secretly and by war made for the purpose, could be by any means prevented in Africa, the next greatest blessing you could bestow upon that country would be to transport its actual slaves in comfortable vessels across the Atlantic. Though they might be perpetual bondsmen, still they would emerge from darkness to light—from barbarism into civilization—from idolatry to Christianity—in short from death to life.

But let us leave the African slave-trade, which has so signally defeated the *philanthropy* of the world, and turn to American Slavery, to which you

171

have now directed your attention, and against which a crusade has been preached as enthusiastic and ferocious as that of Peter the Hermit—destined, I believe, to be about as successful. And here let me say, there is a vast difference between the two, though you may not acknowledge it. The wisdom of ages has concurred in the justice and expediency of establishing rights by prescriptive use, however tortious in their origin they may have been. You would deem a man insane, whose keen sense of equity would lead him to denounce your right to the lands you hold, and which perhaps you inherited from a long line of ancestry, because your title was derived from a Saxon or Norman conqueror, and your lands were originally wrested by violence from the vanquished Britons. And so would the New-England abolitionist regard any one who would insist that he should restore his farm to the descendants of the slaughtered red men, to whom God had as clearly given it as he gave life and freedom to the kidnapped African. That time does not consecrate wrong, is a fallacy which all history exposes; and which the best and wisest men of all ages and professions of religious faith have practically denied. The means, therefore, whatever they may have been, by which the African race now in this country have been reduced to Slavery, cannot affect us, since they are our property, as your land is yours, by inheritance or purchase and prescriptive right. You will say that man cannot hold *property in man.* The answer is, that he can and *actually does* hold property in his fellow all the world over, in a variety of forms, and *has always done so.* I will show presently his authority for doing it.

If you were to ask me whether I am an advocate of Slavery in the abstract, I should probably answer, that I am not, according to my understanding of the question. I do not like to deal in abstractions. It seldom leads to any useful ends. There are few universal truths. I do not now remember any single moral truth universally acknowledged. We have no assurance that it is given to our finite understanding to comprehend abstract moral truth. Apart from revelation and the inspired writings, what ideas should we have even of God, salvation and immortality? Let the heathen answer. Justice itself is impalpable as an abstraction, and abstract liberty the merest phantasy that ever amused the imagination. This world was made for man, and man for the world as it is. We ourselves, our relations with one another and with all matter, are real, not ideal. I might say that I am no more in favor of Slavery in the abstract, than I am of poverty, disease, deformity, idiocy, or any other inequality in the condition of the human family; that I love per-

172

fection, and think I should enjoy a millennium such as God has promised. But what would that amount to? A pledge that I would join you to set about eradicating those apparently inevitable evils of our nature, in equalizing the condition of all mankind, consummating the perfection of our race, and introducing the millennium? By no means. To effect these things, belongs exclusively to a higher power. And it would be well for us to leave the Almighty to perfect his own works and fulfil his own covenants. Especially, as the history of the past shows how entirely futile all human efforts have proved, when made for the purpose of aiding Him in carrying out even his revealed designs, and how invariably he has accomplished them by unconscious instruments, and in the face of human expectation. Nay more, that every attempt which has been made by fallible man to extort from the world obedience to his "abstract" notions of right and wrong, has been invariably attended with calamities dire, and extended just in proportion to the breadth and vigor of the movement. On Slavery in the abstract, then, it would not be amiss to have as little as possible to say. Let us contemplate it as it is. And thus contemplating it, the first question we have to ask ourselves is, whether it is contrary to the will of God, as revealed to us in his Holy Scriptures—the only certain means given us to ascertain his will. If it is, then Slavery is a sin. And I admit at once that every man is bound to set his face against it, and to emancipate his slaves, should he hold any.

Let us open these Holy Scriptures. In the twentieth chapter of Exodus, seventeenth verse, I find the following words: "Thou shalt not covet thy neighbor's house, thou shalt not covet thy neighbor's wife, nor his man-servant, nor his maid-servant, nor his ox, nor his ass, nor anything that is thy neighbor's"—which is the tenth of those commandments that declare the essential principles of the great moral law delivered to Moses by God himself. Now, discarding all technical and verbal quibbling as wholly unworthy to be used in interpreting the Word of God, what is the plain meaning, undoubted intent, and true spirit of this commandment? Does it not emphatically and explicitly forbid you to disturb your neighbor in the enjoyment of his property; and more especially of that which is here specifically mentioned as being lawfully, and by this commandment made sacredly his? Prominent in the catalogue stands his "man-servant and his maid-servant," who are thus distinctly *consecrated as his property*, and guaranteed to him for his exclusive benefit, in the most solemn manner. You attempt to avert the otherwise irresistible conclusion, that Slavery was thus ordained by God, by declaring that the word "slave" is not used here, and is not to be found in the Bible. And I have seen many learned dissertations on this point from abolition pens. It is well known that both the Hebrew and Greek words translated "servant" in the Scriptures, mean also, and most usually, "slave." The use of the one word, instead of the other, was a mere matter of taste with the translators of the Bible, as it has been with all the commentators and religious writers, the latter of whom have, I believe, for the most part, adopted the term "slave," or use both terms indiscriminately. If, then, these Hebrew and Greek words include the idea of both systems of servitude, the conditional and unconditional, they should, as the major includes the minor proposition, be always translated "slaves," unless the sense of the whole text forbids it. The real question, then is, what idea is intended to be conveyed by the words used in the commandment quoted? And it is clear to my mind, that as no limitation is affixed to them, and the express intention was to secure to mankind the peaceful enjoyment of every species of property, that the terms "men-servants and maid-servants" include all classes of servants, and establish a lawful, exclusive, and indefeasible interest equally in the "Hebrew brother who shall go out in the seventh year," and "the yearly hired servant," and "those purchased from the heathen round about," who were to be "bondmen forever," *as the property of their fellow-man.*

You cannot deny that there were among the Hebrews "bondmen forever." You cannot deny that God especially authorized his chosen people to purchase "bondmen forever" from the heathen, as recorded in the twenty-fifth chapter of Leviticus, and that they are there designated by the very Hebrew word used in the tenth commandment. Nor can you deny that a "BONDMAN FOREVER" is a "SLAVE;" yet you endeavor to hang an argument of immortal consequence upon the wretched subterfuge, that the precise word "slave" is not to be found in the *translation* of the Bible. As if the translators were canonical expounders of the Holy Scriptures, and *their words,* not *God's meaning,* must be regarded as his revelation.

It is vain to look to Christ or any of his Apostles to justify such blasphemous perversions of the word of God. Although Slavery in its most revolting form was everywhere visible around them, no visionary notions of piety or philanthropy ever tempted them to gainsay the LAW, even to mitigate the cruel severity of the existing system. On the contrary, regarding Slavery as an *established,* as well as *inevitable condition of the human society,* they never hinted at such a thing as its termination on earth, any more than that

174

"the poor may cease out of the land," which God affirms to Moses shall never be: and they exhort "all servants under the yoke" to "count their masters as worthy of all honor:" "to obey them in all things according to the flesh; not with eye-service as men-pleasers, but in singleness of heart, fearing God;" "not only the good and gentle, but also the froward:" "for what glory is it if when ye are buffetted for your faults ye shall take it patiently? but if when ye do well and suffer for it ye take it patiently, this is acceptable of God." St. Paul actually apprehended a runaway slave, and sent him to his master! Instead of deriving from the Gospel any sanction for the work you have undertaken, it would be difficult to imagine sentiments and conduct more strikingly in contrast, than those of the Apostles and the abolitionists.

It is impossible, therefore, to suppose that Slavery is contrary to the will of God. It is equally absurd to say that American Slavery differs in form or principle from that of the chosen people. *We accept the Bible terms as the definition of our Slavery, and its precepts as the guide of our conduct.* We desire nothing more. Even the right to "buffet," which is esteemed so shocking, finds its express license in the gospel. 1 Peter ii. 20. Nay, what is more, God directs the Hebrews to "bore holes in the ears of their brothers" to *mark* them, when under certain circumstances they become *perpetual slaves.* Exodus xxi. 6.

I think, then, I may safely conclude, and I firmly believe, that American Slavery is not only not a sin, but especially commanded by God through Moses, and approved by Christ through his apostles. And here I might close its defence; for what God ordains, and Christ sanctifies, should surely command the respect and toleration of man. But I fear there has grown up in our time a transcendental religion, which is throwing even transcendental philosophy into the shade—a religion too pure and elevated for the Bible; which seeks to erect among men a higher standard of morals than the Almighty has revealed, or our Saviour preached; and which is probably destined to do more to impede the extension of God's kingdom on earth than all the infidels who have ever lived. Error is error. It is as dangerous to deviate to the right hand as the left. And when men, professing to be holy men, and who are by numbers so regarded, declare those things to be sinful which our Creator has expressly authorized and instituted, they do more to destroy his authority among mankind than the most wicked can effect, by proclaiming that to be innocent which he has forbidden. To this self-righteous and self-exalted class belong all the abolitionists whose writings I

have read. With them it is no end of the argument to prove your propositions by the text of the Bible, interpreted according to its plain and palpable
meaning, and as understood by all mankind for three thousand years before
their time. They are more ingenious at construing and interpolating to ac-
commodate it to their new-fangled and etherial code of morals, than ever
were Voltaire and Hume in picking it to pieces, to free the world from what
they considered a delusion. When the abolitionists proclaim "man-stealing"
to be a sin, and show me that it is so written down by God, I admit them to
be right, and shudder at the idea of such a crime. But when I show them that
to hold "bondmen forever" is ordained by God, *they deny the Bible, and set
up in its place a law of their own making.* I must then cease to reason with
them on this branch of the question. Our religion differs as widely as our
manners. The great judge in our day of final account must decide between us.

Turning from the consideration of slaveholding in its relations to man as
an accountable being, let us examine it in its influence on his political and
social state. Though, being foreigners to us, you are in no wise entitled to
interfere with the civil institutions of this country, it has become quite common for your countrymen to decry Slavery as an enormous political evil to
us, and even to declare that our Northern States ought to withdraw from
the Confederacy rather than continue to be contaminated by it. The American abolitionists appear to concur fully in these sentiments, and a portion,
at least, of them are incessantly threatening to dissolve the Union. Nor
should I be at all surprised if they succeed. It would not be difficult, in my
opinion, to conjecture which region, the North or South, would suffer most
by such an event. For one, I should not object, by any means, to cast my lot
in a confederacy of States whose citizens might all be slaveholders.

I endorse without reserve the much abused sentiment of Governor
M'Duffie, that "Slavery is the corner-stone of our republican edifice;" while
I repudiate, as ridiculously absurd, that much lauded but nowhere accredited dogma of Mr. Jefferson, that "all men are born equal." No society has
ever yet existed, and I have already incidentally quoted the highest authority
to show that none ever will exist, without a natural variety of classes. The
most marked of these must, in a country like ours, be the rich and the poor,
the educated and the ignorant. It will scarcely be disputed that the very poor
have less leisure to prepare themselves for the proper discharge of public
duties than the rich; and that the ignorant are wholly unfit for them at all.
In all countries save ours, these two classes, or the poor rather, who are pre-

176

sumed to be necessarily ignorant, are by law expressly excluded from all participation in the management of public affairs. In a Republican Government this cannot be done. Universal suffrage, though not essential in theory, seems to be in fact a necessary appendage to a republican system. Where universal suffrage obtains, it is obvious that the government is in the hands of a numerical majority; and it is hardly necessary to say that in every part of the world more than half the people are ignorant and poor. Though no one can look upon poverty as a crime, and we do not here generally regard it as any objection to a man in his individual capacity, still it must be admitted that it is a wretched and insecure government which is administered by its most ignorant citizens, and those who have the least at stake under it. Though intelligence and wealth have great influence here, as everywhere, in keeping in check reckless and unenlightened numbers, yet it is evident to close observers, if not to all, that these are rapidly usurping all power in the non-slaveholding States, and threaten a fearful crisis in republican institutions there at no remote period. In the slaveholding States, however, nearly one-half of the whole population, and those the poorest and most ignorant, have no political influence whatever, because they are slaves. Of the other half, a large proportion are both educated and independent in their circumstances, while those who unfortunately are not so, being still elevated far above the mass, are higher toned and more deeply interested in preserving a stable and well ordered government, than the same class in any other country. Hence, Slavery is truly the "corner-stone" and foundation of every well-designed and durable "republican edifice."

With us every citizen is concerned in the maintenance of order, and in promoting honesty and industry among those of the lowest class who are our slaves; and our habitual vigilance renders standing armies, whether of soldiers or policemen, entirely unnecessary. Small guards in our cities, and occasional patrols in the country, ensure us a repose and security known no where else. You cannot be ignorant that, excepting the United States, there is no country in the world whose existing government would not be overturned in a month, but for its standing armies, maintained at an enormous and destructive cost to those whom they are destined to over-awe—so rampant and combative is the spirit of discontent wherever nominal free labor prevails, with its ostensive privileges and its dismal servitude. Nor will it be long before the "*free States*" of this Union will be compelled to introduce the same expensive machinery, to preserve order among their "free and equal" citizens. Already has Philadelphia organized a permanent battalion for this purpose; New-York, Boston and Cincinnati will soon follow her example; and then the smaller towns and densely populated counties. The intervention of their militia to repress violations of the peace is becoming a daily affair. A strong government, after some of the old fashions—though probably with a new name—sustained by the force of armed mercenaries, is the ultimate destiny of the non-slave-holding section of this confederacy, and one which may not be very distant.

It is a great mistake to suppose, as is generally done abroad, that in case of war slavery would be a source of weakness. It did not weaken Rome, nor Athens, nor Sparta, though their slaves were comparatively far more numerous than ours, of the same color for the most part with themselves, and large numbers of them familiar with the use of arms. I have no apprehension that our slaves would seize such an opportunity to revolt. The present generation of them, born among us, would never think of such a thing at any time, unless instigated to it by others. Against such instigations we are always on our guard. In time of war we should be more watchful and better prepared to put down insurrections than at any other periods. Should any foreign nation be so lost to every sentiment of civilized humanity, as to attempt to erect among us the standard of revolt, or to invade us with black troops, for the base and barbarous purpose of stirring up servile war, their efforts would be signally rebuked. Our slaves could not be easily seduced, nor would any thing delight them more than to assist in stripping Cuffee of his regimentals to put him in the cotton-field, which would be the fate of most black invaders, without any very prolix form of "apprenticeship." If, as I am satisfied would be the case, our slaves remained peaceful on our plantations, and cultivated them in time of war under the superintendence of a limited number of our citizens, it is obvious that we could put forth more strength in such an emergency, at less sacrifice, than any other people of the same numbers. And thus we should in every point of view, "out of this nettle danger, pluck the flower safety."

How far Slavery may be an advantage or disadvantage to those not owning slaves, yet united with us in political association, is a question for their sole consideration. It is true that our representation in Congress is increased by it. But so are our taxes; and the non slave-holding States, being the majority, divide among themselves far the greater portion of the amount levied by the Federal Government. And I doubt not that, when it comes to a close calculation, they will not be slow in finding out that the balance of profit arising from the connection is vastly in their favor.

In a social point of view the abolitionists pronounce Slavery to be a monstrous evil. If it was so, it would be our own peculiar concern, and superfluous benevolence in them to lament over it. Seeing their bitter hostility to us, they might leave us to cope with our own calamities. But they make war upon us out of excess of charity, and attempt to purify by covering us with calumny. You have read and assisted to circulate a great deal about affrays, duels and murders, occurring here, and all attributed to the terrible demoralization of Slavery. Not a single event of this sort takes place among us, but it is caught up by the abolitionists, and paraded over the world, with endless comments, variations and exaggerations. You should not take what reaches you as a mere sample, and infer that there is a vast deal more you never hear. You hear all, and more than all, the truth.

It is true that the point of honor is recognized throughout the slave region, and that disputes of certain classes are frequently referred for adjustment, to the "trial by combat." It would not be appropriate for me to enter, in this letter, into a defence of the practice of duelling, nor to maintain at length, that it does not tarnish the character of a people to acknowledge a standard of honor. Whatever evils may arise from it, however, they cannot be attributed to Slavery, since the same custom prevails both in France and England. . . . Slavery has nothing to do with these things. Stability and peace are the first desires of every slave-holder, and the true tendency of the system. It could not possibly exist amid the eternal anarchy and civil broils of the ancient Spanish dominions in America. And for this very reason, domestic Slavery has ceased there. So far from encouraging strife, such scenes of riot and bloodshed, as have within the last few years disgraced our Northern cities, and as you have lately witnessed in Birmingham and Bristol and Wales, not only never have occurred, but I will venture to say, never will occur in our slave-holding States. The only thing that can create a mob (as you might call it) here, is the appearance of an abolitionist, whom the people assemble to chastise. And this is no more of a mob, than a rally of shepherds to chase a wolf out of their pastures would be one. . . .

It is roundly asserted, that we are not so well educated nor so religious here as elsewhere. I will not go into tedious statistical statements on these subjects. Nor have I, to tell the truth, much confidence in the details of what are commonly set forth as statistics. As to education, you will probably admit that slave-holders should have more leisure for mental culture than most people. And I believe it is charged against them, that they are peculiarly fond of power, and ambitious of honors. If this be so, as all the power and honors of this country are won mainly by intellectual superiority, it might be fairly presumed, that slave-holders would not be neglectful of education. In proof of the accuracy of this presumption, I point you to the facts, that our Presidential chair has been occupied for forty-four out of fifty-six years, by slave-holders; that another has been recently elected to fill it for four more, over an opponent who was a slave-holder also; and that in the Federal Offices and both Houses of Congress, considerably more than a due proportion of those acknowledged to stand in the first rank are from the South. In this arena, the intellects of the free and slave States meet in full and fair competition. Nature must have been unusually bountiful to us, or we have been at least reasonably assiduous in the cultivation of such gifts as she has bestowed—unless indeed you refer our superiority to moral qualities, which I am sure *you* will not. More wealthy we are not; nor would mere wealth avail in such rivalry.

The piety of the South is unobtrusive. We think it proves but little, though it is a confident thing for a man to claim that he stands higher in the estimation of his Creator, and is less a sinner than his neighbor. If vociferation is to carry the question of religion, the North, and probably the Scotch, have it. Our sects are few, harmonious, pretty much united among themselves, and pursue their avocations in humble peace. In fact, our professors of religion seem to think—whether correctly or not—that it is their duty "to do good in secret," and to carry their holy comforts to the heart of each individual, without reference to class *or color*, for his special enjoyment, and not with a view to exhibit their zeal before the world. So far as numbers are concerned, I believe our clergymen, when called on to make a showing, have never had occasion to blush, if comparisons were drawn between the free and slave States. And although our presses do not teem with controversial pamphlets, nor our pulpits shake with excommunicating thunders, the daily walk of our religious communicants furnishes, apparently, as little food for gossip as is to be found in most other regions. It may be regarded as a mark of our want of excitability—though that is a quality accredited to us in an eminent degree—that few of the remarkable religious *Isms* of the present day have taken root among us. We have been so irreverent as to laugh at Mormonism and Millerism, which have created such commotions farther North; and modern prophets have no honor in our country. Shakers, Rappists, Dunkers, Socialists, Fourrierists and the like, keep themselves afar off. Even Puseyism has not yet moved us. You may attribute this to our domestic Slavery if you choose. I believe you would do so justly. There is no material here for such characters to operate upon.

But your grand charge is, that licentiousness in intercourse between the sexes, is a prominent trial of our social system, and that it necessarily arises from Slavery. This is a favorite theme with the abolitionists, male and female. Folios have been written on it. It is a common observation, that there is no subject on which ladies of eminent virtue so much delight to dwell, and on which in especial learned old maids, like Miss Martineau, linger with such an insatiable relish. They expose it in the slave States with the most minute observance and endless iteration. Miss Martineau, with peculiar gusto, relates a series of scandalous stories, which would have made Boccacio jealous of her pen, but which are so ridiculously false as to leave no doubt, that some wicked wag, knowing she would write a book, has furnished her materials—a game too often played on tourists in this country. The constant recurrence of the female abolitionists to this topic, and their bitterness in regard to it, cannot fail to suggest to even the most charitable mind, that

"Such rage without betrays the fires within."

Nor are their immaculate coadjutors of the other sex, though perhaps less specific in their charges, less violent in their denunciations. But recently in your Island, a clergyman has, at a public meeting, stigmatized the whole slave region as a "brothel." Do these people thus cast stones, being "without sin?" Or do they only

"Compound for sins they are inclined to
By damning those they have no mind to."

Alas that David and Solomon should be allowed to repose in peace—that Leo should be almost canonized, and Luther more than sainted—that in our own day courtezans should be formally licensed in Paris, and tenements in London rented for years to women of the town for the benefit of the Church, with the knowledge of the Bishop—and the poor slave States of

America alone pounced upon, and offered up as a holocaust on the altar of immaculateness, to atone for the abuse of natural instinct by all mankind; and if not actually consumed, at least exposed, anathematized and held up to scorn, by those who

> "Write,
> Or with a rival's or an eunuch's spite."

But I do not intend to admit that this charge is just or true. Without meaning to profess uncommon modesty, I will say that I wish the topic could be avoided. I am of opinion, and I doubt not every right-minded man will concur, that the public exposure and discussion of this vice, even to rebuke, invariably does more harm than good; and that if it cannot be checked by instilling pure and virtuous sentiments, it is far worse than useless to attempt to do it, by exhibiting its deformities. I may not, however, pass it over; nor ought I to feel any delicacy in examining a question, to which the slave-holder is invited and challenged by clergymen and virgins. So far from allowing, then, that licentiousness pervades this region, I broadly assert, and I refer to the records of our courts, to the public press, and to the knowledge of all who have ever lived here, that among our white population there are fewer cases of divorce, separation, crim. con., seduction, rape and bastardy, than among any other five millions of people on the civilized earth. And this fact I believe will be conceded by the abolitionists of this country themselves. I am almost willing to refer it to them and submit to their decision on it. I would not hesitate to do so, if I thought them capable of an impartial judgment on any matter where Slavery is in question. But it is said, that the licentiousness consists in the constant intercourse between white males and colored females. One of your heavy charges against us has been, that we regard and treat these people as brutes; you now charge us with habitually taking them to our bosoms. I will not comment on the inconsistency of these accusations. I will not deny that some intercourse of the sort does take place. Its character and extent, however, are grossly and atrociously exaggerated. No authority, divine or human, has yet been found sufficient to arrest all such irregularities among men. But it is a known fact, that they are perpetrated here, for the most part, in the cities. Very few mulattoes are reared on our plantations. In the cities, a large proportion of the inhabitants do not own slaves. A still larger proportion are natives of the North, or foreigners. They should share, and justly, too, an equal part in this sin with the slave-holders. Facts cannot be ascertained, or I doubt not, it would appear that they are the chief offenders. If the truth be otherwise, then persons from abroad have stronger prejudices against the African race than we have. Be this as it may, it is well known, that this intercourse is regarded in our society as highly disreputable. If carried on habitually, it seriously affects a man's standing, so far as it is known; and he who takes a colored mistress—with rare and extraordinary exceptions—loses caste at once. You will say that *one* exception should damn our whole country. How much less criminal is it to take a white mistress? In your eyes it should be at least an equal offence. Yet look around you at home, from the cottage to the throne, and count how many mistresses are kept in unblushing notoriety, without loss of caste. Such cases are nearly unknown here, and down even to the lowest walks of life, it is almost invariably fatal to a man's position and prospects to keep a mistress openly, whether white or black. What Miss Martineau relates of a young man's purchasing a colored concubine from a lady, and avowing his designs, is too absurd even for contradiction. No person would dare to allude to such a subject, in such a manner, to any decent female in this country.

After all, however, the number of the mixed breed, in proportion to that of the black, is infinitely small, and out of the towns next to nothing. And when it is considered that the African race has been among us for two hundred years, and that those of the mixed breed continually intermarry—often rearing large families—it is a decided proof of our continence, that so few comparatively are to be found. Our misfortunes are two-fold. From the prolific propagation of these mongrels among themselves, we are liable to be charged by tourists with delinquencies where none have been committed, while, where one has been, it cannot be concealed. Color marks indelibly the offence, and reveals it to every eye. Conceive that, even in your virtuous and polished country, if every bastard, through all the circles of your social system, was thus branded by nature and known to all, what shocking developments might there not be! How little indignation might your saints have to spare for the licentiousness of the slave region. But I have done with this disgusting topic. And I think I may justly conclude, after all the scandalous charges which tea-table gossip, and long-gowned hypocrisy have brought against the slave-holders, that a people whose men are proverbially brave, intellectual and hospitable, and whose women are unaffectedly chaste, devoted to domestic life, and happy in it, can neither be degraded nor demor-

183

alized, whatever their institutions may be. My decided opinion is, that our system of Slavery contributes largely to the development and culture of these high and noble qualities.

In an economical point of view—which I will not omit—Slavery presents some difficulties. As a general rule, I agree it must be admitted, that free labor is cheaper than slave labor. It is a fallacy to suppose that ours is *unpaid labor*. The slave himself must be paid for, and thus his labor is all purchased at once, and for no trifling sum. His price was, in the first place, paid mostly to your countrymen, and assisted in building up some of those colossal English fortunes, since illustrated by patents of nobility, and splendid piles of architecture, stained and cemented, if you like the expression, with the blood of kidnapped innocents; but loaded with no heavier curses than abolition and its begotten fanaticisms have brought upon your land—some of them fulfilled, some yet to be. But besides the first cost of the slave, he must be fed and clothed, well fed and well clothed, if not for humanity's sake, that he may do good work, retain health and life, and rear a family to supply his place. When old or sick, he is a clear expense, and so is the helpless portion of his family. No poor law provides for him when unable to work, or brings up his children for our service when we need them. These are all heavy charges on slave labor. Hence, in all countries where the denseness of the population has reduced it to a matter of perfect certainty, that labor can be obtained, whenever wanted, and the laborer be forced, by sheer necessity, to hire for the smallest pittance that will keep soul and body together, and rags upon his back while in actual employment—dependent at all other times on alms or poor rates—in all such countries it is found cheaper to pay this pittance, than to clothe, feed, nurse, support through childhood, and pension in old age, a race of slaves. Indeed, the advantage is so great as speedily to compensate for the loss of the value of the slave. And I have no hesitation in saying, that if I could cultivate my lands on these terms, I would, without a word, resign my slaves, provided they could be properly disposed of. But the question is, whether free or slave labor is cheapest to us in this country, at this time, situated as we are. And it is decided at once by the fact that we cannot avail ourselves of any other than slave labor. We neither have, nor can we procure, other labor to any extent, or on anything like the terms mentioned. We must, therefore, content ourselves with our dear labor, under the consoling reflection that what is lost to us, is gained to humanity; and that, inasmuch as our slave costs us more

184

than your free man costs you, by so much is he better off. You will promptly say, emancipate your slaves, and then you will have free labor on suitable terms. That might be if there were five hundred where there now is one, and the continent, from the Atlantic to the Pacific, was as densely populated as your Island. But until that comes to pass, no labor can be procured in America on the terms you have it.

While I thus freely admit that to the individual proprietor slave labor is dearer than free, I do not mean to admit as equally clear that it is dearer to the community and to the State. Though it is certain that the slave is a far greater consumer than your laborer, the year round, yet your pauper system is costly and wasteful. Supported by your community at large, it is not administered by your hired agents with that interested care and economy—not to speak of humanity—which mark the management of ours, by each proprietor, for his own non-effectives; and is both more expensive to those who pay, and less beneficial to those who receive its bounties. Besides this, Slavery is rapidly filling up our country with a hardy and healthy race, peculiarly adapted to our climate and productions, and conferring signal political and social advantages on us as a people, to which I have already referred.

I have yet to reply to the main ground on which you and your coadjutors rely for the overthrow of our system of Slavery. Failing in all your attempts to prove that it is sinful in its nature, immoral in its effects, a political evil, and profitless to those who maintain it, you appeal to the sympathies of mankind, and attempt to arouse the world against us by the most shocking charges of tyranny and cruelty. You begin by a vehement denunciation of "the irresponsible power of one man over his fellow men." The question of the responsibility of power is a vast one. It is the great political question of modern times. Whole nations divide off upon it and establish different fundamental systems of government. That "responsibility," which to one set of millions seems amply sufficient to check the government, to the support of which they devote their lives and fortunes, appears to another set of millions a mere mockery of restraint. And accordingly as the opinions of these millions differ, they honor each other with the epithets of "serfs" or "anarchists." It is ridiculous to introduce such an idea as this into the discussion of a mere domestic institution; but since you have introduced it, I deny that the power of the slave-holder in America is "irresponsible." He is responsible to God. He is responsible to the world—a responsibility which abolitionists do not intend to allow him to evade—and in acknowledgment of

185

which, I write you this letter. He is responsible to the community in which he lives, and to the laws under which he enjoys his civil rights. Those laws do not permit him to kill, to maim, or to punish beyond certain limits, or to overtask, or to refuse to feed and clothe his slave. In short, they forbid him to be tyrannical or cruel. If any of these laws have grown obsolete, it is because they are so seldom violated, that they are forgotten. You have disinterred one of them, from a compilation by some Judge Stroud of Philadelphia, to stigmatize its inadequate penalties for killing, maiming, &c. Your object appears to be—you can have no other—to produce the impression, that it must be often violated on account of its insufficiency. You say as much, and that it marks our estimate of the slave. You forget to state that this law was enacted by *Englishmen*, and only indicates *their* opinion of the reparation due for these offences. Ours is proved by the fact, though perhaps unknown to Judge Stroud or yourself, that we have essentially altered this law; and the murder of a slave has for many years been punishable with death in this State. And so it is, I believe, in most or all the slave States. You seem well aware, however, that laws have been recently passed in all these States, making it penal to teach slaves to read. Do you know what occasioned their passage, and renders their stringent enforcement necessary? I can tell you. It was the abolition agitation. If the slave is not allowed to read his bible, the sin rests upon the abolitionists; for they stand prepared to furnish him with a key to it, which would make it, not a book of hope, and love, and peace, but of despair, hatred and blood; which would convert the reader, not into a Christian, but a demon. To preserve him from such a horrid destiny, it is a sacred duty which we owe to our slaves, not less than to ourselves, to interpose the most decisive means. If the Catholics deem it wrong to trust the bible to the hands of ignorance, shall we be excommunicated because we will not give it, and with it the corrupt and fatal commentaries of the abolitionists, to our slaves? Allow our slaves to read your writings, stimulating them to cut our throats! Can you believe us to be such unspeakable fools? . . .

Still, though a slaveholder, I freely acknowledge my obligations as a man; and that I am bound to treat humanely the fellow-creatures whom God has entrusted to my charge. I feel, therefore, somewhat sensitive under the accusation of cruelty, and disposed to defend myself and fellow-slaveholders against it. It is certainly the interest of all, and I am convinced that it is also the desire of every one of us, to treat our slaves with proper kindness. It is necessary to our deriving the greatest amount of profit from them. Of this we are all satisfied. And you snatch from us the only consolation we Americans could derive from the opprobrious imputation of being wholly devoted to making money, which your disinterested and gold-despising countrymen delight to cast upon us, when you nevertheless declare that we are ready to sacrifice it for the pleasure of being inhuman. You remember that Mr. Pitt could not get over the idea that self-interest would ensure kind treatment to slaves, until you told him your woful stories of the middle passage. Mr. Pitt was right in the first instance, and erred, under your tuition, in not perceiving the difference between a temporary and permanent ownership of them. Slaveholders are no more perfect than other men. They have passions. Some of them, as you may suppose, do not at all times restrain them. Neither do husbands, parents and friends. And in each of these relations, as serious suffering as frequently arises from uncontrolled passions, as ever does in that of master and slave, and with as little chance of indemnity. Yet you would not on that account break them up. I have no hesitation in saying that our slaveholders are kind masters, as men usually are kind husbands, parents and friends—as a general rule, kinder. A bad master—he who overworks his slaves, provides ill for them, or treats them with undue severity—loses the esteem and respect of his fellow-citizens to as great an extent as he would for the violation of any of his social and most of his moral obligations. What the most perfect plan of management would be, is a problem hard to solve. From the commencement of Slavery in this country, this subject has occupied the minds of all slaveholders, as much as the improvement of the general condition of mankind has those of the most ardent philanthropists; and the greatest progressive amelioration of the system has been effected. You yourself acknowledge that in the early part of your career you were exceedingly anxious for the *immediate* abolition of the slave trade, lest those engaged in it should so mitigate its evils as to destroy the force of your arguments and facts. The improvement you then *dreaded* has gone on steadily here, and would doubtless have taken place in the slave trade, but for the measures adopted to suppress it.

Of late years we have been not only annoyed, but greatly embarrassed in this matter, by the abolitionists. We have been compelled to curtail some privileges; we have been debarred from granting new ones. In the face of discussions which aim at loosening all ties between master and slave, we have in some measure to abandon our efforts to attach them to us, and con-

187

trol them through their affections and pride. We have to rely more and more on the power of fear. We must, in all our intercourse with them, assert and maintain strict mastery, and impress it on them that they are slaves. This is painful to us, and certainly no present advantage to them. But it is the direct consequence of the abolition agitation. We are determined to continue masters, and to do so we have to draw the rein tighter and tighter day by day to be assured that we hold them in complete check. How far this process will go on, depends wholly and solely on the abolitionists. When they desist, we can relax. We may not before. I do not mean by all this to say that we are in a state of actual alarm and fear of our slaves; but under existing circumstances we should be ineffably stupid not to increase our vigilance and strengthen our hands. You see some of the fruits of your labors. I speak freely and candidly—not as a colonist, who, though a slaveholder, has a master; but as a free white man, holding, under God, and resolved to hold, my fate in my own hands; and I assure you that my sentiments, and feelings, and determinations, are those of every slaveholder in this country.

The research and ingenuity of the abolitionists, aided by the invention of runaway slaves—in which faculty, so far as improvising falsehood goes, the African race is without a rival—have succeeded in shocking the world with a small number of pretended instances of our barbarity. The only wonder is, that considering the extent of our country, the variety of our population, its fluctuating character, and the publicity of all our transactions, the number of cases is so small. It speaks well for us. Yet of these, many are false, all highly colored, some occurring half a century, most of them many years ago; and no doubt a large proportion of them perpetrated by foreigners. With a few rare exceptions, the emigrant Scotch and English are the worst masters among us, and next to them our Northern fellow-citizens. Slaveholders born and bred here are always more humane to slaves, and those who have grown up to a large inheritance of them, the most so of any—showing clearly that the effect of the system is to foster kindly feelings. I do not mean so much to impute innate inhumanity to foreigners, as to show that they come here with false notions of the treatment usual and necessary for slaves, and that newly acquired power here, as everywhere else, is apt to be abused. I cannot enter into a detailed examination of the cases stated by the abolitionists. It would be disgusting, and of little avail. I know nothing of them. I have seen nothing like them, though born and bred here, and have rarely heard of anything at all to be compared to them. Permit me to

188

say that I think most of *your* facts must have been drawn from the West Indies, where undoubtedly slaves were treated much more harshly than with us. This was owing to a variety of causes, which might, if necessary, be stated. One was, that they had at first to deal more extensively with barbarians fresh from the wilds of Africa; another, and a leading one, the absenteeism of proprietors. Agents are always more unfeeling than owners, whether placed over West Indian or American slaves, or Irish tenantry. We feel this evil greatly even here. You describe the use of *thumb screws*, as one mode of punishment among us. I doubt if a thumb screw can be found in America. I never saw or heard of one in this country. Stocks are rarely used by private individuals, and confinement still more seldom, though both are common punishments for whites, all the world over. I think they should be more frequently resorted to with slaves, as substitutes for flogging, which I consider the most injurious and least efficacious mode of punishing them for serious offences. It is not degrading, and unless excessive, occasions little pain. You may be a little astonished, after all the flourishes that have been made about "cart whips," &c., when I say flogging is not the most degrading punishment in the world. It may be so to a white man in most countries, but how is it to the white boy? That necessary coadjutor of the schoolmaster, the "birch," is never thought to have rendered infamous the unfortunate victim of pedagogue ire; nor did Solomon in his wisdom dream that he was counselling parents to debase their offspring, when he exhorted them not to spoil the child by sparing the rod. Pardon me for recurring to the now exploded ethics of the Bible. Custom, which, you will perhaps agree, makes most things in this world good or evil, has removed all infamy from the punishment of the lash to the slave. Your blood boils at the recital of stripes inflicted on a man; and you think you should be frenzied to see your own child flogged. Yet see how completely this is ideal, arising from the fashions of society. You doubtless submitted to the rod yourself, in other years, when the smart was perhaps as severe as it would be now; and you have never been guilty of the folly of revenging yourself on the Preceptor, who, in the plenitude of his "irresponsible power," thought proper to chastise your son. So it is with the negro, and the negro father.

As to chains and irons, they are rarely used; never, I believe, except in cases of running away. You will admit that if we pretend to own slaves, they must not be permitted to abscond whenever they see fit; and that if nothing else will prevent it, these means must be resorted to. See the inhumanity

189

necessarily arising from Slavery, you will exclaim. Are such restraints imposed on no other class of people, giving no more offence? Look to your army and navy. If your seamen, impressed from their peaceful occupations, and your soldiers, recruited at the gin-shops—both of them as much kidnapped as the most unsuspecting victim of the slave trade, and doomed to a far more wretched fate—if these men manifest a propensity to desert, the heaviest manacles are their mildest punishment. It is most commonly death, after summary trial. But armies and navies, you say, are indispensable, and must be kept up at every sacrifice. I answer, that they are no more indispensable than Slavery is to us—and to *you*; for you have enough of it in your country, though the form and name differ from ours.

Depend upon it that many things, and in regard to our slaves, most things which appear revolting at a distance, and to slight reflection, would, on a nearer view and impartial comparison with the customs and conduct of the rest of mankind, strike you in a very different light. Remember that on our estates we dispense with the whole machinery of public police and public courts of justice. Thus we try, decide, and execute the sentences, in thousands of cases, which in other countries would go into the courts. Hence, most of the acts of our alleged cruelty, which have any foundation in truth. Whether our patriarchal mode of administering justice is less humane than the Assizes, can only be determined by careful enquiry and comparison. But this is never done by the abolitionists. All our punishments are the outrages of "irresponsible power." If a man steals a pig in England, he is transported—torn from wife, children, parents, and sent to the antipodes, infamous, and an outcast forever, though probably he took from the superabundance of his neighbor to save the lives of his famishing little ones. If one of our well-fed negroes, merely for the sake of fresh meat, steals a pig, he gets perhaps forty stripes. If one of your cottagers breaks into another's house, he is hung for burglary. If a slave does the same here, a few lashes, or it may be, a few hours in the stocks, settles the matter. Are our courts or yours the most humane? If Slavery were not in question, you would doubtless say ours is mistaken lenity. Perhaps it often is; and slaves too lightly dealt with sometimes grow daring. Occasionally, though rarely, and almost always in consequence of excessive indulgence, an individual rebels. This is the highest crime he can commit. It is treason. It strikes at the root of our whole system. His life is justly forfeited, though it is never intentionally taken, unless after trial in our public courts. Sometimes, however, in captur-

190

ing, or in self-defence, he is unfortunately killed. A legal investigation always follows. But, terminate as it may, the abolitionists raise a hue and cry, and another "shocking case" is held up to the indignation of the world by tender-hearted male and female philanthropists, who would have thought all right had the master's throat been cut, and would have triumphed in it.

I cannot go into a detailed comparison between the penalties inflicted on a slave in our patriarchal courts, and those of the Courts of Sessions, to which freemen are sentenced in all civilized nations; but I know well that if there is any fault in our criminal code, it is that of excessive mildness.

Perhaps a few general facts will best illustrate the treatment this race receives at our hands. It is acknowledged that it increases at least as rapidly as the white. I believe it is an established law, that population thrives in proportion to its comforts. But when it is considered that these people are not recruited by immigration from abroad, as the whites are, and that they are usually settled on our richest and least healthy lands, the fact of their equal comparative increase and greater longevity, outweighs a thousand abolition falsehoods, in favor of the leniency and providence of our management of them. It is also admitted that there are incomparably fewer cases of insanity and suicide among them than among the whites. The fact is, that among the slaves of the African race these things are almost wholly unknown. However, frequent suicide may have been among those brought from Africa, I can say that in my time I cannot remember to have known or heard of a single instance of deliberate self-destruction, and but of one of suicide at all. As to insanity, I have seen but one permanent case of it, and that twenty years ago. It cannot be doubted that among three millions of people there must be some insane and some suicides; but I will venture to say that more cases of both occur annually among every hundred thousand of the population of Great Britain, than among all our slaves. Can it be possible, then, that they exist in that state of abject misery, goaded by constant injuries, outraged in their affections, and worn down with hardships, which the abolitionists depict, and so many ignorant and thoughtless persons religiously believe?

With regard to the separation of husbands and wives, parents and children, nothing can be more untrue than the inferences drawn from what is so constantly harped on by abolitionists. Some painful instances perhaps may occur. Very few that can be prevented. It is, and it always has been, an object of prime consideration with our slaveholders, to keep families together.

Negroes are themselves both perverse and comparatively indifferent about this matter. It is a singular trait, that they almost invariably prefer forming connexions with slaves belonging to other masters, and at some distance. It is, therefore, impossible to prevent separations sometimes, by the removal of one owner, his death, or failure, and dispersion of his property. In all such cases, however, every reasonable effort is made to keep the parties together, if they desire it. And the negroes forming these connexions, knowing the chances of their premature dissolution, rarely complain more than we all do of the inevitable strokes of fate. Sometimes it happens that a negro prefers to give up his family rather than separate from his master. I have known such instances. As to wilfully selling off a husband, or wife, or child, I believe it is rarely, very rarely done, except when some offence has been committed demanding "transportation." At sales of estates, and even at Sheriff's sales, they are always, if possible, sold in families. On the whole, notwithstanding the migratory character of our population, I believe there are more families among our slaves, who have lived and died together without losing a single member from their circle, except by the process of nature, and in the enjoyment of constant, uninterrupted communion, than have flourished in the same space of time, and among the same number of civilized people in modern times. And to sum up all, if pleasure is correctly defined to be the absence of pain—which, so far as the great body of mankind is concerned, is undoubtedly its true definition—I believe our slaves are the happiest three millions of human beings on whom the sun shines. Into their Eden is coming Satan in the guise of an abolitionist.

As regards their religious condition, it is well known that a majority of the communicants of the Methodist and Baptist churches of the South are colored. Almost everywhere they have precisely the same opportunities of attending worship that the whites have, and, besides special occasions for themselves exclusively, which they prefer. In many places not so accessible to clergymen in ordinary, missionaries are sent, and mainly supported by their masters, for the particular benefit of the slaves. There are none I imagine who may not, if they like, hear the gospel preached at least once a month—most of them twice a month, and very many every week. In our thinly settled country the whites fare no better. But in addition to this, on plantations of any size, the slaves who have joined the church are formed into a class, at the head of which is placed one of their number, acting as deacon or leader, who is also sometimes a licensed preacher. This class assembles for religious exercises weekly, semi-weekly, or oftener, if the members choose. In some parts, also, Sunday schools for blacks are established, and Bible classes are orally instructed by discreet and pious persons. Now where will you find a laboring population possessed of greater religious advantages than these? Not in London, I am sure, where it is known that your churches, chapels, and religious meetinghouses, of all sorts, cannot contain one-half of the inhabitants.

I have admitted, without hesitation, what it would be untrue and profitless to deny, that slaveholders are responsible to the world for the humane treatment of the fellow-beings whom God has placed in their hands. I think it would be only fair for you to admit, what is equally undeniable, that every man in independent circumstances, all the world over, and every government, is to the same extent responsible to the whole human family, for the condition of the poor and laboring classes in their own country, and around them, wherever they may be placed, to whom God has denied the advantages he has given themselves. If so, it would naturally seem the duty of true humanity and rational philanthropy to devote their time and labor, their thoughts, writings and charity, first to the objects placed as it were under their own immediate charge. And it must be regarded as a clear evasion and skilful neglect of this cardinal duty, to pass from those whose destitute situation they can plainly see, minutely examine and efficiently relieve, to enquire after the condition of others in no way entrusted to their care, to exaggerate evils of which they cannot be cognizant, to expend all their sympathies and exhaust all their energies on these remote objects of their unnatural, not to say dangerous, benevolence; and finally, to calumniate, denounce, and endeavor to excite the indignation of the world against their unoffending fellow-creatures for not hastening, under their dictation, to redress wrongs which are stoutly and truthfully denied, while they themselves go but little farther in alleviating those chargeable on them than openly and unblushingly to acknowledge them. There may be indeed a sort of merit in doing so much as to make such an acknowledgment, but it must be very modest if it expects appreciation.

Now I affirm, that in Great Britain the poor and laboring classes of your own race and color, not only your fellow-beings, but your *fellow-citizens*, are more miserable and degraded, morally and physically, than our slaves; to be elevated to the actual condition of whom, would be to these, *your fellow-citizens*, a most glorious act of *emancipation*. And I also affirm, that the poor and laboring classes of our older free States would not be in a much more enviable condition, but for our Slavery. One of their own Senators has declared in the U.S. Senate, "that the repeal of the Tariff would reduce New-England to a howling wilderness." And the American Tariff is neither more nor less than a system by which the slave States are plundered for the benefit of those States which do not tolerate Slavery.

To prove what I say of Great Britain to be true, I make the following extracts from the Reports of Commissioners appointed by Parliament, and published by order of the House of Commons. I can make but few and short ones. But similar quotations might be made to any extent, and I defy you to deny that these specimens exhibit the real condition of your operatives in every branch of your industry. There is of course a variety in their sufferings. But the same incredible amount of toil, frightful destitution, and utter want of morals, characterize the lot of every class of them.

Collieries.—"I wish to call the attention of the Board to the pits about Brampton. The seams are so thin that several of them have only two feet headway to all the working. They are worked altogether by boys from eight to twelve years of age, on all-fours, with a dog belt and chain. The passages being neither ironed nor wooded, and often an inch or two thick with mud. In Mr. Barnes' pit these poor boys have to drag the barrows with one hundred weight of coal or slack sixty times a day sixty yards, and the empty barrows back, without once straightening their backs, unless they choose to stand under the shaft, and run the risk of having their heads broken by a falling coal."—*Report on Mines*, 1842, p. 71. "In Shropshire the seams are no more than eighteen or twenty inches."—*Ibid.*, p. 67. "At the Booth pit," says Mr. Scriven, "I walked, rode, and crept eighteen hundred yards to one of the nearest faces."—*Ibid.* "Chokedamp, firedamp, wild fire, sulphur, and water, at all times menace instant death to the laborers in these mines." "Robert North, aged 16: Went into the pit at seven years of age, to fill up skips. I drew about twelve months. When I drew by the girdle and chain my skin was broken, and the blood ran down. I durst not say anything. If we said anything, the butty, and the reeve, who works under him, would take a stick and beat us."—*Ibid.* "The usual punishment for theft is to place the culprit's head between the legs of one of the biggest boys, and each boy in the pit—sometimes there are twenty—inflicts twelve lashes on the back and rump with a cat."—*Ibid.* "Instances occur in which children are taken into these mines to work as early as four years of age, sometimes at five, not unfrequently at six and seven, while from eight to nine is the ordinary age at which these employments commence."—*Ibid.* "The wages paid at these mines is from two dollars fifty cents to seven dollars fifty cents per month for laborers, according to age and ability, and out of this they must support themselves. They work twelve hours a day."—*Ibid.*

In Calico Printing.—"It is by no means uncommon in all the districts for children five or six years old to be kept at work fourteen to sixteen hours consecutively."—*Report on Children*, 1842, p. 59.

I could furnish extracts similar to these in regard to every branch of your manufactures, but I will not multiply them. Everybody knows that your operatives habitually labor from twelve to sixteen hours, men, women, and children, and the men occasionally twenty hours per day. In lace-making, says the last quoted report, children sometimes commence work at two years of age.

Destitution.—It is stated by your Commissioners that forty thousand persons in Liverpool, and fifteen thousand in Manchester, live in cellars; while twenty-two thousand in England pass the night in barns, tents, or the open air. "There have been found such occurrences as seven, eight, and ten persons in one cottage, I cannot say for one day, but for whole days, without a morsel of food. They have remained on their beds of straw for two successive days, under the impression that in a recumbent posture the pangs of hunger were less felt."—*Lord Brougham's Speech*, 11th July, 1842. A volume of frightful scenes might be quoted to corroborate the inferences to be necessarily drawn from the facts here stated. I will not add more, but pass on to the important enquiry as to

Morals and Education. "Elizabeth Barrett, aged 14: I always work without stockings, shoes, or trowsers. I wear nothing but a shift. I have to go up to the headings with the men. *They are all naked* there. I am got used to that." *Report on Mines.* "As to illicit sexual intercourse it seems to prevail universally, and from an early period of life." "The evidence might have been doubled, which attest the early commencement of sexual and promiscuous intercourse among boys and girls." "A lower condition of morals, in the fullest sense of the term, could not, I think, be found. I do not mean by this that there are many more prominent vices among them, but that moral feelings and sentiments do not exist. *They have no morals.*" "Their appearance, manners, and moral natures—so far as the word *moral* can be applied to them—are in accordance with their half-civilized condition."— *Report on Children*. "More than half a dozen instances occurred in Manchester, where a man, his wife, and his wife's grown-up sister, habitually occupied the same bed."—*Report on Sanitary Condition*. "Robert Crucilow, aged 16: I don't know anything of Moses—never heard of France. I don't know what America is. Never heard of Scotland or Ireland. Can't tell how many weeks there are in a year. There are twelve pence in a shilling, and twenty shillings in a pound. There are eight pints in a gallon of ale."— *Report on Mines*. "Ann Eggly, aged 18: I walk about and get fresh air on Sundays. I never go to church or chapel. I never heard of Christ at all."— *Ibid*. Others: "The Lord sent Adam and Eve on earth to save sinners." "I don't know who made the world; I never heard about God." "I don't know Jesus Christ—I never saw him—but I have seen Foster who prays about him." "Employer: You have expressed surprise at Thomas Mitchel's not hearing of God. I judge there are few colliers here about that have."—*Ibid*. I will quote no more. It is shocking beyond endurance to turn over your records, in which the condition of your laboring classes is but too faithfully depicted. Could our slaves but see it, they would join us in lynching the abolitionists, which, by the by, they would not now be loth to do. We never think of imposing on them such labor, either in amount or kind. We never put them to *any work*, under ten, more generally at twelve years of age, and then the very lightest. Destitution is absolutely unknown—never did a slave starve in America; while in moral sentiments and feelings, in religious information, and even in general intelligence, they are infinitely the superiors of your operatives. When you look around you, how dare you talk to us before the world of Slavery? For the condition of your wretched laborers, you, and every Briton who is not one of them, are responsible before God and man. If you are really humane, philanthropic, and charitable, here are objects for you. Relieve them. Emancipate them. Raise them from the condition of brutes, to the level of human beings—of American slaves, at least. Do not for an instant suppose that the *name* of being freemen is the slightest comfort to them, situated as they are, or that the bombastic boast that "whoever touches British soil stands redeemed, regenerated, and disenthralled," can meet with anything but the ridicule and contempt of mankind, while that soil swarms, both on and under its surface, with the most abject and degraded wretches that ever bowed beneath the oppressor's yoke.

196

I have said that Slavery is an established and inevitable condition to human society. I do not speak of the *name*, but the *fact*. The Marquis of Normanby has lately declared your operatives to be "*in effect slaves*." Can it be denied? Probably, for such philanthropists as your abolitionists care nothing for facts. They deal in terms and fictions. It is the *word* "slavery" which shocks their tender sensibilities; and their imaginations associate it with "hydras and chimeras dire." The thing itself, in its most hideous reality, passes daily under their view unheeded—a familiar face, touching no chord of shame, sympathy or indignation. Yet so brutalizing is your iron bondage that the English operative is a bye-word through the world. When favoring fortune enables him to escape his prison house, both in Europe and America he is shunned. With all the skill which fourteen hours of daily labor from the tenderest age has ground into him, his discontent, which habit has made second nature, and his depraved propensities, running riot when freed from his wonted fetters prevent his employment whenever it is not a matter of necessity. If we derived no other benefit from African Slavery in the Southern States than that it deterred your *freedmen* from coming hither, I should regard it as an inestimable blessing.

And how unaccountable is that philanthropy, which closes its eyes upon such a state of things as you have at home, and turns its blurred vision to our affairs beyond the Atlantic, meddling with matters which no way concern them—presiding, as you have lately done, at meetings to denounce the "iniquity of our laws" and "the atrocity of our practices," and to sympathize with infamous wretches imprisoned here for violating decrees promulgated both by God and man? Is this doing the work of "your Father which is in heaven," or is it seeking only "that you may have glory of man?" Do you remember the denunciation of our Saviour, "Woe unto you, Scribes and Pharisees; hypocrites! for ye make clean the outside of the cup and platter, but within they are full of extortion and excess."

But after all, supposing that every thing you say of Slavery be true, and its abolition a matter of the last necessity, how do you expect to effect emancipation, and what do you calculate will be the result of its accomplishment? As to the means to be used, the abolitionists, I believe, affect to differ, a large proportion of them pretending that their sole purpose is to apply "moral suasion" to the slaveholders themselves. As a matter of curiosity, I should like to know what their idea of this "moral suasion" is. Their discourses—yours is no exception—are all tirades, the exordium, argument and peroration, turning on the epithets "tyrants," "thieves," "murderers," addressed to us. They revile us as "atrocious monsters," "violators of the laws of nature, God and man," our homes the abode of every iniquity, our land a "brothel." We retort, that they are "incendiaries" and "assassins." Delightful argument! Sweet, potent "moral suasion!" What slave has it freed—what proselyte can it ever make? But if your course was wholly different—if you distilled nectar from your lips, and discoursed sweetest music, could you reasonably indulge the hope of accomplishing your object by such means? Nay, supposing that we were all convinced, and thought of Slavery precisely as you do, at what era of "moral suasion" do you imagine you could prevail on us to give up a thousand millions of dollars in the value of our slaves, and a thousand millions of dollars more in the depreciation of our lands, in consequence of the want of laborers to cultivate them? Consider: were ever any people civilized or savage, persuaded by any argument, human or divine, to surrender voluntarily two thousand millions of dollars? Would you think of asking five millions of Englishmen to contribute, either at once or gradually, four hundred and fifty millions of pounds of sterling to the cause of philanthropy, even if the purpose to be accomplished was not of doubtful goodness? If you are prepared to undertake such a scheme, try it at home. Collect your fund—return us the money for our slaves, and do with them as you like. Be all the glory yours, fairly and honestly won. But you see the absurdity of such an idea. Away, then, with your pretended "moral suasion." You know it is mere nonsense. The abolitionists have no faith in it themselves. Those who expect to accomplish any thing count on means altogether different. They aim, first, to alarm us: that failing, to compel us by force to emancipate our slaves, at our own risk and cost. To these purposes they obviously direct all their energies. Our Northern liberty men endeavored to disseminate their destructive doctrine among our slaves, and excite them to insurrection. But we have put an end to that, and stricken terror into them. They dare not show their faces here. Then they declared they would dissolve the Union. Let them do it. The North would repent it far more than the South. We are not alarmed at the idea. We are well content to give up the Union sooner than sacrifice two thousand millions of dollars, and with them all the rights we prize. You may take it for granted that it is impossible to persuade or alarm us into emancipation, or to making the first step towards it. Nothing, then, is left to try, but sheer force. If the abolitionists are prepared to expend their own treasure and shed their own blood as freely as they ask us to do ours, let them come. We do not court the conflict; but we will not and we cannot shrink from it. If they are not ready to go so far; if, as I expect, their philanthropy recoils from it; if they are looking only for *cheap* glory, let them turn their thoughts elsewhere, and leave us in peace. Be the sin, the danger and the evils of Slavery all our own. We compel, we ask none to share them with us. . . .

But what do you calculate will be the result of emancipation, by whatever means accomplished? You will probably point me, by way of answer, to the West Indies—doubtless to Antigua, the great boast of abolition. Admitting that it has succeeded there—which I will do for the sake of the argument—do you know the reason of it? The true and only causes of whatever success has attended it in Antigua are, that the population was before crowded, and all or nearly all the arable land in cultivation. The emancipated negroes could not, many of them, get away if they desired; and knew not where to go, in case they did. They had, practically, no alternative but to remain on the spot; and remaining, they must work on the terms of the proprietors, or perish—the strong arm of the mother country forbidding all hope of seizing the land for themselves. The proprietors, well knowing that they could thus command labor for the merest necessities of life, which was much cheaper than maintaining the non-effective as well as effective slaves in a style which decency and interest, if not humanity, required, willingly accepted half their value, and at once realized far more than the interest on the other half in the diminution of their expenses, and the reduced comforts of the *freemen*. One of your most illustrious judges, who was also a profound and philosophical historian, has said "that villeinage was not abolished, but went into decay in England." This was the process. This has been the process wherever (the name of) villeinage or slavery has been successfully abandoned. Slavery, in fact, "went into decay" in Antigua. I have admitted that, under similar circumstances, it might profitably cease here—that is, profitably to the individual proprietors. Give me half the value of my slaves, and compel them to remain and labor on my plantation, at ten to eleven cents a day, as they do in Antigua, supporting themselves and families, and you shall have them to-morrow, and if you like dub them "free." Not to stickle, I would surrender them without price. No—I recall my words: My humanity revolts at the idea. I am attached to my slaves, and would not have act or part in reducing

199

them to such a condition. I deny, however, that Antigua, as a community, is, or ever will be, as *prosperous* under present circumstances, as she was before abolition, though fully ripe for it. The fact is well known. The reason is that the African, if not a distinct, is an inferior race, and never will effect, as it never has effected, as much in any other condition as in that of Slavery.

I know of no *slaveholder* who has visited the West Indies since Slavery was abolished, and published *his* views of it. All our facts and opinions come through the friends of the experiment, or at least those not opposed to it. Taking these, even without allowance, to be true as stated, I do not see where the abolitionists find cause for exultation. The tables of exports, which are the best evidences of the condition of a people, exhibit a woful falling off—excused, it is true, by unprecedented droughts and hurricanes, to which their free labor seems unaccountably more subject than slave labor used to be. I will not go into detail. It is well known that a large proportion of British legislation and expenditure, and that proportion still constantly increasing, is most anxiously devoted to repairing the monstrous error of emancipation. You are actually galvanizing your expiring colonies. The truth, deduced from all the facts, was thus pithily stated by the London Quarterly Review, as long ago as 1840: "None of the benefits anticipated by mistaken good intentions have been realized, while every evil wished for by knaves and foreseen by the wise has been painfully verified. The wild rashness of fanaticism has made the emancipation of the slaves equivalent to the loss of one-half of the West Indies, and yet put back the chance of negro civilization." . . . Such are the *real fruits* of your never-to-be-too-much-glorified abolition, and the valuable dividend of your twenty millions of pounds sterling invested therein.

If any farther proof was wanted of the utter and well-known, though not yet openly avowed, failure of West Indian emancipation, it would be furnished by the startling fact, that THE AFRICAN SLAVE TRADE HAS BEEN ACTUALLY REVIVED UNDER THE AUSPICES AND PROTECTION OF THE BRITISH GOVERNMENT. Under the specious guise of "immigration," they are replenishing those Islands with slaves from the coast of Africa. Your colony of Sierra Leone, founded on that coast to prevent the slave trade, and peopled, by the bye, in the first instance, by negroes stolen from these States during the Revolutionary War, is the depot to which captives taken from slavers by your armed vessels are transported. I might say returned, since nearly half the

Africans carried across the Atlantic are understood to be embarked in this vicinity. The wretched survivors, who are there set at liberty, are immediately seduced to "immigrate" to the West Indies. The business is systematically carried on by black "delegates," sent expressly from the West Indies, where, on arrival, the "immigrants" are *sold into Slavery* for twenty-one years, under conditions ridiculously trivial and wickedly void, since few or none will ever be able to derive any advantage from them. The whole prime of life thus passed in bondage, it is contemplated, and doubtless it will be carried into effect, to turn them out in their old age to shift for themselves, and to supply their places with fresh and vigorous "immigrants." Was ever a system of Slavery so barbarous devised before? Can you think of comparing it with ours? Even your own religious missionaries at Sierra Leone denounce it "as worse than the slave state in Africa." And your black delegates, fearful of the influence of these missionaries, as well as on account of the inadequate supply of captives, are now preparing to procure the able-bodied and comparatively industrious Kroomen of the interior, by *purchasing from their head-men* the privilege of inveigling them to the West India market! So ends the magnificent farce—perhaps I should say tragedy, of West India abolition! I will not harrow your feelings by asking you to review the labors of your life and tell me what you and your brother enthusiasts have accomplished for "injured Africa," but while agreeing with Lord Stowell, that "villeinage decayed," and admitting that Slavery might do so also, I think I am fully justified by passed and passing events in saying, as Mr. Grosvenor said of the slave trade, that its *abolition* is "impossible."

You are greatly mistaken, however, if you think that the consequences of emancipation here would be similar and no more injurious than those which followed from it in your little sea-girt West India Islands, where nearly all were blacks. The system of Slavery is not in "decay" with us. It flourishes in full and growing vigor. Our country is boundless in extent. Dotted here and there with villages and fields, it is, for the most part, covered with immense forests and swamps of almost unknown size. In such a country, with a people so restless as ours, communicating of course some of that spirit to their domestics, can you conceive that any thing short of the power of the master over the slave, could confine the African race, notoriously idle and improvident, to labor on our plantations? Break this bond, but for a day, and these plantations will be solitudes. The negro loves change, novelty

201

and sensual excitements of all kinds, *when awake.* "Reason and order," of which Mr. Wilberforce said "liberty was the child," do not characterize him. Released from his present obligations, his first impulse would be to go somewhere. And here no natural boundaries would restrain him. At first they would all seek the towns, and rapidly accumulate in squalid groups upon their outskirts. Driven thence by the "armed police," which would immediately spring into existence, they would scatter in all directions. Some bodies of them might wander towards the "free" States, or to the Western wilderness, marking their tracks by their depredations and their corpses. Many would roam wild in our "big woods." Many more would seek the recesses of our swamps for secure covert. Few, very few of them, could be prevailed on to do a stroke of work, none to labor continuously, while a head of cattle, sheep or swine could be found in our ranges, or an ear of corn nodded in our abandoned fields. These exhausted, our folds and poultry yards, barns and store houses, would become their prey. Finally, our scattered dwellings would be plundered, perhaps fired, and the inmates murdered. How long do you suppose that we could bear these things? How long would it be before we should sleep with rifles at our bedsides, and never move without one in our hands? This work once begun, let the story of our British ancestors and the aborigines of this country tell the sequel. Far more rapid, however, would be the catastrophe. "Ere many moons went by," the African race would be exterminated, or reduced again to Slavery, their ranks recruited, after your example, by fresh "emigrants" from their fatherland.

Is timely preparation and gradual emancipation suggested to avert these horrible consequences? I thought your experience in the West Indies had, at least, done so much as to explode that idea. If it failed there, much more would it fail here, where the two races, approximating to equality in numbers, are daily and hourly in the closest contact. Give room for but a single spark of real jealousy to be kindled between them, and the explosion would be instantaneous and universal. It is the most fatal of all fallacies, to suppose that these two races can exist together, after any length of time, or any process of preparation, on terms at all approaching to equality. Of this, both of them are finally and fixedly convinced. They differ essentially, in all the leading traits which characterize the varieties of the human species, and color draws an indelible and insuperable line of separation between them.

202

Every scheme founded upon the idea that they can remain together on the same soil, beyond the briefest period, in any other relation than precisely that which now subsists between them, is not only preposterous, but fraught with deepest danger. If there was no alternative but to try the "experiment" here, reason and humanity dictate that the sufferings of "gradualism" should be saved, and the catastrophe of "immediate abolition" enacted as rapidly as possible. Are you impatient for the performance to commence? Do you long to gloat over the scenes I have suggested, but could not hold the pen to portray? In your long life many such have passed under your review. You know that *they* are not *"impossible."* Can they be to your taste? Do you believe that in laboring to bring them about, the abolitionists are doing the will of God? No! God is not there. It is the work of Satan. The arch-fiend, under specious guises, has found his way into their souls, and with false appeals to philanthropy, and foul insinuations to ambition, instigates them to rush headlong to the accomplishment of his diabolical designs.

We live in a wonderful age. The events of the last three quarters of a century appear to have revolutionized the human mind. Enterprise and ambition are only limited in their purposes by the horizon of the imagination. It is the transcendental era. In philosophy, religion, government, science, arts, commerce, nothing that has been is to be allowed to be. Conservatism, in any form, is scoffed at. The slightest taint of it is fatal. Where will all this end? If you can tolerate one ancient maxim, let it be that the best criterion of the future is the past. That, if anything, will give a clue. And, looking back only through your time, what was the earliest feat of this same transcendentalism? The rays of the new moral Drummond Light were first concentrated to a focus at Paris, to illuminate the universe. In a twinkling it consumed the political, religious and social systems of France. It could not be extinguished there until literally drowned in blood. And then, from its ashes arose that supernatural man, who, for twenty years, kept affrighted Europe in convulsions. Since that time, its scattered beams, refracted by broader surfaces, have, nevertheless, continued to scathe wherever they have fallen. What political structure, what religious creed, but has felt the galvanic shock, and even now trembles to its foundations? Mankind, still horror-stricken by the catastrophe of France, have shrunk from rash experiments upon social systems. But they have been practicing in the East, around the Mediterranean, and through the West India Islands. And growing confident, a portion of them seem desperately bent on kindling the all-devouring flame in the bosom of our land. Let it once again blaze up to heaven, and another cycle of blood and devastation will dawn upon the world. For our own sake, and for the sake of those infatuated men who are madly driving on the conflagration; for the sake of human nature, we are called on to strain every nerve to arrest it. And be assured our efforts will be bounded only with our being. Nor do I doubt that five millions of people, brave, intelligent, united, and prepared to hazard every thing, will, in such a cause, with the blessing of God, sustain themselves. At all events, come what may, it is ours to meet it.

We are well aware of the light estimation in which the abolitionists, and those who are taught by them, profess to hold us. We have seen the attempt of a portion of the Free Church of Scotland to reject our alms, on the ground that we are "slave-drivers," after sending missionaries to solicit them. . . . These people may exhaust their slang, and make black-guards of themselves, but they cannot defile us. And as for the suggestion to exclude slaveholders from your London clubs, we scout it. Many of us, indeed, do go to London, and we have seen your breed of gawky lords, both there and here, but it never entered into our conceptions to look on them as better than ourselves. The American slaveholders, collectively or individually, ask no favors of any man or race who tread the earth. In none of the attributes of men, mental or physical, do they acknowledge or fear superiority elsewhere. They stand in the broadest light of the knowledge, civilization and improvement of the age, as much favored of heaven as any of the sons of Adam. Exacting nothing undue, they yield nothing but justice and courtesy, even to royal blood. They cannot be flattered, duped, nor bullied out of their rights or their propriety. They smile with contempt at scurrility and vaporing beyond the seas, and they turn their backs upon it where it is "irresponsible;" but insolence that ventures to look them in the face, will never fail to be chastised.

I think I may trust you will not regard this letter as intrusive. I should never have entertained an idea of writing it, had you not opened the correspondence. If you think anything in it harsh, review your own—which I regret that I lost soon after it was received—and you will probably find that you have taken your revenge before hand. If you have not, transfer an equitable share of what you deem severe, to the account of the abolitionists at large. They have accumulated against the slaveholders a balance of invective, which, with all our efforts, we shall not be able to liquidate much short of the era in which your national debt will be paid. At all events, I have no desire to offend you personally, and, with the best wishes for your continued health, I have the honor to be,

Your obedient servant,
J. H. HAMMOND.

Thos. Clarkson, Esq.

V. JOSIAH C. NOTT
Two Lectures on the Natural History
of the Caucasian and Negro Races

"There is a marked difference between the heads of the Caucasian and the Negro, and there is a corresponding difference no less marked in their intellectual and moral qualities."

Josiah Nott was born in 1804 to a prominent South Carolina family. At the age of twenty, he graduated from South Carolina College, where he was a close friend of James Henry Hammond. Nott studied at the College of Physicians and Surgeons in New York City and received a medical degree from the University of Pennsylvania in 1827. After two years as a lecturer in anatomy at Pennsylvania, Nott returned to Columbia, South Carolina, to practice. In 1835 he traveled to Paris for further medical study and opened a practice in Mobile, Alabama, upon his return. A leading surgeon of his region, Nott was appointed a visiting professor of anatomy at the University of Louisiana in 1857 and played a leading role in the founding of the Medical College of Alabama the following year. An active scholar and clinician, Nott published on yellow fever, hypnotism, bone and joint injuries, surgical techniques, and ethnology. During the Civil War, Nott served in the Confederate Army, but after Appomattox he moved North, first to Baltimore, then to New York City, where he continued his medical practice and research. In 1872 he retired to the South and died in Mobile a year later.[1]

Nott was the most prominent southern exponent of the doctrines of ethnology, a science of racial differences that gained increasing recognition and legitimacy in the eyes of Americans in the late antebellum period.[2] Because

1. On Nott's life, see William Stanton, *The Leopard's Spots: Scientific Attitudes Toward Race in America, 1815–1859* (Chicago: University of Chicago Press, 1960).
2. Nott was closely associated with ethnology's foremost national proponents and even published joint works with George Gliddon, a leader of the American School of Ethnology. See Josiah C. Nott and George Gliddon, *Types of Mankind: or Ethnological Researches, Based*

he believed that scientific realities should prescribe social and moral relationships, Nott thought that ethnology offered unimpeachable support for southern slavery. The truths of science, he argued, had "deep Political, Moral and Religious import."

The selection that follows is from Nott's *Two Lectures on the Natural History of the Caucasian and Negro Races*, which were originally delivered as popular addresses in Mobile, then published there as a pamphlet in 1844. Nott sought in these orations to prove that blacks and whites were two permanently distinct and unequal species, created separately from the beginning of time. Although Nott protested his loyalty to the truths of Christianity, his polygenist assertions challenged prevailing religious doctrines, especially biblical accounts of Creation and of world chronology. Recognizing that such an assault would hardly win him popularity in the religiously orthodox South, Nott endeavored to portray his scientific inquiries as but a new form of "Christian's duty"—an exploration in "Natural Theology." Nevertheless, his arguments were to incite considerable conflict in the South and to arouse the ire of southern clergymen in particular. As a result, many proslavery advocates sought to avoid Nott's extreme position and to evade the controversy over the origin of races altogether.[3]

Nott's *Lectures* employed a variety of empirical evidence to support their argument for distinct species among men. Cranial measurements, census data—which were in fact wholly inaccurate because of the errors of the 1840 U.S. Census—and a highly dubious style of analogical reasoning served as justifications for his hypotheses. Nott assumed throughout, as he stated explicitly in the quotation from poet Alexander Pope that closed the

---

upon the Ancient Monuments, Paintings, Sculptures, and Crania of Races, and upon Their Natural, Geographical, Philological and Biblical History (Philadelphia: Lippincott, Grambo and Co., 1854), and *Indigenous Races of the Earth: or New Chapters of Ethnological Inquiry* (Philadelphia: J. B. Lippincott and Co., 1857). Nott's other significant publications on ethnology were *Two Lectures on the Connection Between the Biblical and Physical History of Man. Delivered by Invitation, from the Chair of Political Economy etc. of the Louisiana University, in December 1848* (New York: Bartlett and Welford, 1849); *The Negro Race: Its Ethnology and History. By the Author of 'Types of Mankind'. To Major-General O. O. Howard, Superintendant of Freedman's Bureau, etc.* (Mobile: n.p., 1866); *The Physical History of the Jewish Race* (Charleston: Walker and James, 1850).

3. Josiah C. Nott, M.D., *Two Lectures on the Natural History of the Caucasian and Negro Races* (Mobile: Dade and Thompson, 1844). See also Nott's angry reply to an attack in the *Southern Presbyterian Review*: Josiah C. Nott, *Chronology Ancient and Scriptural* (Charleston: Walker and James, 1850). Another prominent southern supporter of ethnology, Samuel Cartwright, sought to avoid the polygenist controversy; nevertheless, he was attacked as bitterly as Nott.

piece, "WHATEVER IS, IS RIGHT." To describe nature, he believed, was to present God's design for man in the social and moral, as well as the physical, dimension of his existence. Such an emphasis fit neatly with fundamental assumptions of the conservative organic outlook characteristic of so much of southern social thought and of the proslavery argument particularly. But Nott coupled this remonstrance against change with a challenge to traditional biblical literalism that could not but alienate large numbers of his fellow southerners.

Two Lectures on the Natural History of the Caucasian and Negro Races

The question of the unity of the Human Race is a grave one—it has elicited a vast deal of talent and research, and is deserving of the profoundest study—most candid men have acknowledged its difficulty, and that all past time has afforded no data, by which it can be definitively settled. My object is to place before the world *new facts*, which may assist in forming a rational conclusion on this vexed question.

When we look around us and see the various complexions, and various physical conformations which exist in the human race, as the Caucasian, Mongol, Malay, Indian and Negro, we have naturally forced upon our minds the inquiry, *are all these derived from one pair, or are they of distinct origins?*

This subject is attended by the same difficulty which has impeded the advancement of other departments of Natural History, as well as the Sciences of Astronomy and Geology. In their infancy, discoveries in these sciences, were regarded as inconsistent with the Mosaic account of the creation, and they have encountered determined opposition from well meaning and other religious persons. The scientific men who have been bold enough to speak truth, and to uphold the works of God, have been persecuted by those who mistake their own intellects for a measure of wisdom, and their own passions and prejudices for the will of heaven.

When Gallileo promulgated the great truth that the sun stands still, and the earth moves round it, he was attacked and persecuted by the whole priesthood—he was twice brought before the Inquisition and forced to renounce his doctrines.— Time, however, has served to show that Gallileo was right, and the Bible still stands "the rock of ages."

The Unity of the Human Race is a question appertaining to Natural History, which should be left open to fair and honest investigation, and made to stand or fall according to the facts.

I should therefore, have much preferred, not to involve theological points, but I know that *others* will do it—that I shall have anathamas heaped on my head, and wrong motives imputed to me—false issues will be made and the true points for discussion evaded.

I am prepared for all this—those who know me well, I have the vanity to believe, will do me justice; and I am quite indifferent to the censure of those who hold up Christ as their model, while they are pouring out phials of wrath.

My object is truth, and I care not which way the question is decided, provided the decision is a correct one. I have accumulated a number of curious and interesting facts, some of which are new, and I have interpreted them dispassionately. My conclusions may be disputed, but they cannot be disproved in the present state of the science of Natural History.— *New facts* must be brought to light before *certain* conclusions to the contrary are arrived at.

The Mosaic account . . . sheds no satisfactory light on this question. The book of Genesis has proved to be a field of endless and angry discussion amongst Doctors of Divinity, and they are now no nearer agreeing than they were 2000 years ago. *All that they have proved is, that they know nothing about it.* The world was made for us all, and there is no reason why I am not as much entitled to an opinion as any Protestant, Jew or Catholic.

Luther, speaking of the Book of Genesis, says: "There has not hitherto, been any one in the church, that has with sufficient propriety and exactness, expounded the whole of these subjects; for expositors have so mixed them up with various, diversified and never ending inquiries, as to make it apparent *that God has reserved to himself alone this majesty of wisdom, and the sound understanding of this chapter*; leaving to us the general knowledge that the world had a beginning, and was created out of nothing by God. This general knowledge is clearly derived from the text. But with respect to the particular things, there is very much that is involved in difficulty and doubt, and about which questions without end are agitated."

209

Calvin says: "Two opposite errors are common—some persons finding that themselves or the bulk of men have been imposed upon, reject in the mass all religious doctrines; others with weak credulity, indiscriminately embrace whatsoever is proposed to them in the name of God. Each extreme is wrong. The former class filled with proud prejudice, bar themselves out from the way of improvement; the others rashly expose themselves to every wind of error. From these two extremes, Paul recalls the Thesalonians to the middle path; *forbidding the condemnation of any sentiment till it be first examined*: and admonishing that we should exercise a just judgment before we receive as certain, that which is proposed to us. *Nothing is more hurtful than the petulent and conceited disposition, by which we take up a dislike to any sentiment, without taking the trouble of a fair examination.*"

When the Doctors differ, who is to decide? My reply is, God himself. We are to appeal to Analogies, facts, induction and to the universal and undeviating laws of Nature. *The plurality of species in the human race does no more violence to the Bible, than do the admitted facts of Astronomy and Geology.*

Astronomy has struggled through all opposition. Geology and Natural History, though still under the ban of the inquisition, are rapidly progressing towards perfection. The religion of Christ too, is advancing as the world becomes more enlightened, and they can and will march on together, receiving light from each other, and upholding the wisdom, goodness and glory of God.

The study of Natural Theology is receiving more and more attention every year, and my firm conviction is, that great injury has been done to revealed religion by forbidding the study of God in the vastness and majesty of his works. This is the study by which the existence of a God is demonstrated, and when this first step is gained, the next which the enquirer takes, is to ask if God has spoken to man? If so, when and where?

"How do you know," said a traveller to a poor Arab of the desert, "that there is a God?" "In the same manner," he replied, "that I trace the footsteps of an animal by the prints which it leaves upon the sand."

The words and works of God, if *properly understood*, can never be opposed to each other—they are two streams which flow from the same pure fountain, and must at last mingle in the great sea of truth.

In my lectures I distinctly and honestly disclaimed any wish or intention of throwing doubts over the divine origin of either the New or Old Testa-

210

ments, and went on to say, "Take away even the Divinity of the Bible, and he is no friend to man who would wish to pull the fabric down—it is necessary for our welfare in this world, that good morals should be taught, and where, I would ask, can we find a system so pure and so conducive to our happiness as that of Christ?"

It should be born in mind, that we are now in the 19th century, which is marked by an advanced state of the sciences hitherto unknown, and that Biblical commentators have been *forced to make large concessions to Astronomy, Natural History and Geology.* . . .

The unity of the human race is spoken of so seldom in the New Testament, and in such a passing way as to leave room for rational doubts on the subject; we are therefore at liberty to appeal to facts.

I will here lay down a chain of propositions for examination, and I would appeal to every candid man who has studied Geology and Natural History, to say whether they are not true.

1st. Have there not been *several* creations and destructions in the Animal and Vegetable kingdoms, *previous* to the creation spoken of by Moses?

2nd. Is it not admitted by Naturalists, that many of the animals *now* upon the earth are entirely different from those which existed *before* the flood, and that if the flood was universal these animals *have been created since?*

3d. Is it not admitted by Naturalists that the Ark only contained the animals which *inhabited the part of the earth in which Noah dwelt*, and that it is a Zoological and physical impossibility that the Ark could have contained pairs and septuples of *all* the animals now on the earth?

4th. Is it not a fact, that Islands newly emerged from the ocean, become covered with plants, *differing from all others* in other parts of the globe—thus showing that the creative power of the Almighty is *still* exercised, whenever circumstances are ready for it?

5th. Does not all this prove that the account given by Moses is *imperfect*, and that much has been *omitted* of the infinite works of the creator, both *before* and *after* the creation of which he speaks?

6th. Has God anywhere said that he never intended to create another man, or that other races were not created in distant parts of the globe. I would ask, after all these admitted truths, is there any thing so revolting in the idea that a Negro, Indian, or Malay, may have been created since the flood of Noah, or (if the flood was not universal) before this epoch?

I know it will be said that Negroes existed at the time that Moses wrote, but to this I will reply that Moses must have known equally well of a vast number of animals which did not descend from the Ark, and which were not included in his account.

I set out then with the proposition, that there is a Genus, Man, comprising two or more species—that physical causes cannot change a White man into a Negro, and that to say this change has been effected by a direct act of providence, is an assumption which *cannot be proven, and is contrary to the great chain of Nature's laws.*

Lecture 1.

Before entering upon the Natural History of the human race, it is indispensably necessary, as a preliminary step, to examine some points in chronology, and to take a glance at the early history of Egypt. I must show that the Caucasian or White, and the Negro races were distinct at a very remote date, and *that the Egyptians were Caucasians.* Unless this point can be established the contest must be abandoned.

In order to show how completely we are left in the dark on this subject by the Old Testament, it will be necessary to make some allusion to the *diversity* of chronological computations.

The commonly received opinion is that our globe was created 4004 years before Christ, and that the Deluge took place 2348 B.C.

These computations let it be remembered, were made by *Arch Bishop Usher*, were adopted by an Act of the British Parliament and are the dates annexed to our Bibles. . . . These dates then, are entitled to no more respect than any other *human opinions.*

Some may be surprised to learn that there are, besides that of Bishop Usher, *more than 300 computations* for the creation and deluge—these computations too are made by learned divines, and differ at least 1500 years. I will cite a few only of the most prominent, as I am desirous of avoiding prolixity.

Creation		*Deluge*	*Exodus*	
Septuagint,	5586 B.C.	3246 B.C.	Josephus,	1648 B.C.
Hebrew text,	4161	2228	Eng Bible	1491
English Bible	4004	2348		

212

These are sufficient to show how widely the highest and most competent authorities differ on these points.

There is even a difference of 10 years in the dates given for the birth of Christ and Moses has left no data, nor is there anything in the History of Egypt, by which *His* time can be determined.

Modern science establishes beyond the possibility of a doubt, the fact, that these dates, for the creation at least, are too short, and probably by many thousand years. I presume there are few if any divines of the present day, conversant with Geology and Natural History, who do not concur in this opinion, and who do not believe there have been other floods besides the one spoken of by Moses.

In writing the Natural History of the human race, we must commence with the subsidence of *the* Deluge; this as I have stated, is placed by Usher, 2348 B.C. Now I propose to show by positive proofs from recent examination of Egyptian monuments that this date is erroneous—that Negroes existed in Africa before this date of the flood, and that there is reason to believe they did not descend from Noah's family.

Moses dwelt in Egypt some 1500 years B.C., and is said to have been "learned in all the wisdom" of this singular and interesting country. We have all heard from our childhood of her Pyramids, her magnificent temples, her obelisks and other monuments of her surprising greatness. . . .

Historians have assigned to Egypt 31 Dynasties, comprising 378 Kings, previous to the conquest by Alexander the great, which took place 332 B.C., and a large proportion of these dynasties have been *verified* by the hieroglyphic inscriptions. The obelisks, tombs and other monuments had inscribed on them the name of each monarch, the number of years he reigned, the principal events of his reign, &c., and by putting together these reigns in their proper order, we get at positive dates.

The *positive* monumental data go back to the year B.C. 2272, which is *within 72 years* of Usher's date of the flood.

The list of monuments are not *perfect* beyond that date—many have been destroyed, in consequence of which, the date of some of the Kings cannot be determined with precision.

Besides Manetho, the Egyptian historian, we have the authority of Herodotus, Eratosthenes, Diodorus, Josephus, the old Egyptian Chronicle, as well as the hieroglyphics, to prove that Menes was the first King of Egypt—

213

it is certain that he reigned *long previous* to the positive date above given, and Champollion and Rosellini place him about 2750 years B.C. *which is 400 years before our date of the deluge.*

The Pyramids were built between the time of Menes, the 1st King, and 2272 B.C., and hieroglyphic writing was common at the time of the Pyramids.

Now all these statements are not mere conjectures, but positive facts, engraven upon stone at the time the events recorded transpired; they are just as much to be relied on as the inscriptions on the Bunker Hill, or Battle Monument at Baltimore.

Another proof of the remote date of the flood, or of its limited extent, is seen in the great age of certain trees in Africa and Central America—distinguished Botanists assert that some of these trees are 6000 years old—full grown trees may have been created when Adam was, but we have no reason to believe they have been since—this fact then, which no Botanists doubts, proves that the flood took place at least 6000 years ago, or it was not universal.

It is recorded that the largest Pyramid took 100,000 men 20 years to build it; the immense masses of stone of which it is built, were brought from a great distance and transported across the Nile. And it is recorded in hieroglyphics, that it took 10 years to prepare the materials before the construction commenced.

Now let me ask, if several hundred of these pyramids existed, with a vast number of other stupendous monuments—if Memphis and Thebes were built and contained with the country around, a population which could execute all these wonderful things—if all the useful arts and sciences, together with Astronomy, existed at this remote date; how many centuries previous must this country have been populated? It is difficult for the mind to reach it. Reflect for a moment on the slow progress which a nation must make from infancy to such perfection. . . .

Egypt is the earliest point of civilization of which we have any records: the history of this country is doubly interesting to us as it has been asserted by most historians, it was originally inhabited by negroes, and that from this race all the Arts and Sciences have been derived.

I shall however be able to show satisfactorily, that recent investigations have overthrown all previously received opinions on the subject, and that the Egyptians were a Caucasian race.

214

In the allotment of territories to the offspring of Noah, Egypt was given as an inheritance to Mizraim, the son of Ham. He must have proceded with his companions from the banks of the Euphrates, along the borders of the Mediterranean, and across the Isthmus of Suez, to his point of destination—as lower Egypt, near the mouth of the Nile was most easy of access, and the most fertile country, it is reasonable to suppose that here their first settlement was made. Mizraim being a descendant of Noah, was of course a Caucasian.

Shem and Ham were twin brothers—the word Shem, means white, and Ham, means dark, or swarthy, but not black. It is probably therefore, that there was the same difference between them, that we often see between brothers here. Many have supposed Ham to be the progenitor of the negro race. There was no curse upon him, and there is nothing in the Bible which induces such a belief; but this point is settled by the fact which I shall prove, that the Egyptians were not Negroes.

The curse of heaven fell upon Canaan, but we have no reason to believe that the curse was a physical one. Canaan too took possession of Palestine, and not any part of Africa; and his descendants were Caucasians.

Mr. J. S. Gliddon asserts that it can be proven by paintings and sculptures, of a date earlier than 1500 years B.C.—that the Canaanites and Negroes were as different as the whites and negroes are of the present age, and that the negroes then presented the same physical characteristics which they do now, after a lapse of 3,500 years.

The drawings and sculptures of this early date, often represent negroes as slaves and captives; and as an evidence of the estimation in which this black race was held, even at this remote date, the inscriptions designated their country as "*barbarian, and their race as perverse.*"

You will remember that the Nile runs north and empties into the Mediterranean, and that it takes its rise towards the center of Africa, far into the country which is now, and has been, as far back as history can trace, inhabited by Negroes.

According to most historians, civilization commenced high up the Nile in Ethopia, and was thence brought down towards its mouth into Egypt. Late investigations, however, have disproved this assertion, and shown by positive facts, that the oldest monuments are found in Egypt, particularly at Memphis.

It is now proven that time and circumstances did not effect any material

215

change in Ham's progeny, and that his lineal descendants were pure Caucasians. They very naturally were modified in upper Egypt, by admixture with the Ethiopians, Arabs and others, who bordered on their territory. To this day, Mr. Gliddon says, the Fellahs, or people of lower Egypt, are but little mixed.

Now I would ask with Mr. Gliddon, how long must it have taken for the descendants of Ham to have gone from the banks of the Euphrates in Asia, into Africa and up the Nile 1500 miles—there grow into a powerful nation—carry the Arts and Sciences to the highest state of perfection, and next, as an additional evidence of civilization, turn perfectly black—afterwards come down the Nile again 1500 miles to its mouth, and to cap the climax, turn white again; this too, in a climate where no one's skin has changed in the last 4000 years? Now if there is any miracle in the Bible more wonderful than this, I should like to know what it is. All these events too, according to the Hebrew version, happen in 100 years, and according to the Septuagint 500.

Besides the proofs drawn from the hieroglyphics, paintings, sculptures, &c., there are others which not only strongly corroborate, but amount to perfect demonstration of the fact, that the Ancient Egyptians were Caucasians.

The great Naturalist, Cuvier, has spent much time and labor on this point, and after a careful examination of 50 Mummies, asserts that they are Caucasian, and have no resemblance whatever to the Negro; the head, the whole skeleton and the hair are Caucasian. In this opinion all distinguished naturalists concur.

Dr. Morton, of Philadelphia, who has devoted much attention to these subjects, and who has acquired a distinguished reputation, not only in this country, but throughout the Scientific world, has thrown very important light on this point.

Dr. Morton's facts are drawn from an examination of 100 Egyptian heads taken from 7 different repositories of the dead, particularly Memphis and Thebes. These heads were collected and presented to him by Mr. Gliddon, who was Consul at Cairo, for 23 years.

In a paper read by Dr. Morton, before the American Philosophical Society, he first took a view of those nations with whom the Egyptians appear to have held intercourse, either for war or commerce, in the early epochs of their history; and amongst those whom he has been able to identify, from a comparison of the heads figured in the work of Rossellini [sic], are the

216

Celts, the Scythians, the Pelasgic and Semetic nations, the Hindoos, Arabs and Negroes. He has classed the whole series of heads in the following manner:

1st Arcto-Egyptians—Under which designation are embraced the purer Caucasian nations, as seen in the Semetic tribes of Western Asia, and the Pelasgic communities of Southern Europe.

2d Austro-Egyptians—In which the cranium blends the characters of the Hindoo and Southern Arab; which people, in the opinion of the author, were engrafted on the aboriginal population of Ethopia, and thus gave rise to the celebrated Meroite nations of antiquity.

3d Negroloid crainia, in which the osteological development corresponds to that of the Negro, while the hair, though harsh and sometimes wirey, is long and not wooly: thus presenting the combination of features which are familiar in the Mulatto grades of the present day.

4th Negro.

In many crania, the Arcto-Egyptian, Austro-Egyptians, and Semetic characters are variously blended; while a few also present traces of Negro lineage, modifying the feaures of the preceding types.

The Caucasian Crania, in the whole, constitute 9 in 10; the Negroloid, about 1 in 14—and out of the whole 100 skulls, there is but one unmixed Negro.

A very striking fact too, is, that the pure Caucasian heads are found at Memphis, near the mouth of the Nile, and as you ascend the river into the interior of Africa and approach Nubia, the Caucasian character is gradually lost—they become mingled with Negro and other tribes.

The author refers the blending of Arcto-Egyptian and Austral-Egyptian and other communities, to three principal periods of Egyptian history, viz:

1st The Conquest by the Hykshos or Shepherd Kings, 2082 B.C., when the Egyptians of all ranks were driven into Ethiopia for a period of 260 years.

2d. The Ethiopian Dynasty of 3 Kings which lasted 40 years, beginning 719 years B.C.

3d. The conquest by Cambyses B.C. 525, when the distinctions of caste and nation were comparatively disregarded for upwards of two centuries, during which period the people of Asia, Europe and Nigritia, were freely admitted into Egypt.

Dr. Morton's ethnographical researches, conjoined with the evidence of history and the monuments, have led him to draw the following conclusions:

217

1st. That Egypt was originally peopled by the Caucasian race.

2d. That the great preponderance of heads, conforming in all their characters to those of the purer Caucasian nations, as seen in the Pelasgic and Semetic tribes, suggests the inference that the valley of the Nile, derived its primitive civilized inhabitants from one of these sources; and that the greater proportion of this series of crania in Lower Egypt may, perhaps, serve to indicate the seats of early colonization.

3d. That the Austral-Egyptian, or Meroite communities, were in a great measure derived from the Indo-Arabian stock: thus pointing to a triple Caucasian source for the origin of the Egyptians, when regarded as one people extending from Meroe to the Delta.

4th. That the Negro race exists in the catacombs in the mixed or Negroloid character; that even in this modified type their presence is comparatively unfrequent, and that if Negroes, as is more than probable, were numerous in Egypt, their social position was chiefly in ancient times what it yet is—that of Plebians, Servants and Slaves.

Independant of the bearing of many of these interesting facts, the conclusion to my mind, is irresistable, that the civilization of Egypt is attributable to these Caucasian heads; because civilization does not now and never has as far as we know from history, been carried to this perfection by any other race than the Caucasian—how can any reasoning mind come to any other conclusion?

It is clear then that history, the Egyptian Monuments, her paintings and sculptures, the examination of skulls by Cuvier, Morton and others, Analogy, and every thing else connected with this country, combine to prove beyond the possibility of a doubt, that the Ancient Egyptian race were Caucasians.

Positive historical facts prove too, that Egypt has been conquered in early times by various inferior tribes, and the blood of her people adulterated. Besides the conquest of the Hykshos, the Ethiopians, Persians and others, she has more recently been conquered by the Greeks, the Romans and the Turks.

But even the pure blood of Greece and Rome could not wash out the black stain, both moral and physical, which she has received.

Naturalists have strangely overlooked the effects of mixing races, when the illustrations drawn from the crossing of animals speak so plainly—man

218

physically is, but an animal at last, with the same physiological laws which govern others.

This adulteration of blood is the reason why Egypt and the Barbary States never can again rise, until the present races are exterminated, and the Caucasian substituted.

Wherever in the history of the world the inferior races have conquered and mixed in with the Caucasian, the latter have sunk into barbarism.

Greece and Rome have been conquered and crushed to the earth by oppression, but the blood of the Greeks and Romans is still comparatively pure, and the genius of those nations still lives.

Every now and then some one rises up, breaks through all tramels and shows that the Caucasian head is still there. They have not the physical force to break the fetters which bind them, but they still have their Poets, Painters, Sculptors and Philosophers.

We have no evidence that civilization has ever eminated from Africa beyond Egypt, and we know that all modern attempts to carry civilization into it have failed.

When I was in Paris I attended the Hospitals every day in company with about a dozen young Egyptians, who were sent over by Mehamet Ali— nothing could be more evident than their mixed blood—some looked like mulattoes, others like the cross of Indian and white races. When I looked upon them and saw the material with which Mehamet Ali had to work, I was convinced that Egypt's sun of glory was set, never again to rise.

Analogy.—When we cast our eyes over the whole range of natural history, we find a surprising simplicity and uniformity in the laws of nature—a wonderful adaptation of things to the circumstances in which they are placed. This uniformity of laws often assists us immensely when we are wanting in facts in one branch—analogies drawn from others shed important light.

In illustration of the natural history of man for instance, analogies have been drawn from the whole animal and vegitable kingdoms; many of these analogies are curious and interesting, and they are so numerous and varied as to afford strong arguments, both for and against the unity of the human race.

Both animal and vegitable kingdoms are divided and subdivided into genera, species and varieties.

As we shall have frequent use for the term species, it will be well to define it before we proceed farther.

We mean then by the term Species, a race of Animals or Plants, marked by peculiarities of structure, which have always been constant and undeviating—two races are considered specifically different, if they are distinguished from each other by some peculiarities which one cannot be supposed to have acquired, or the other lost, through any known operation of physical causes.

The Horse and Ass, for example, are the same genus, but different species, because no physical causes could have produced such dissimilarity.

Genus, is a more comprehensive term, it includes all the species of a class; for example, the Ourang Outang, Apes, Baboons, &c., are all of one genus though different species.

My belief too, is, that there is a Genus *Homo*, with its species and varieties.

It would be almost an anomaly in nature if man should be restricted to one species. . . .

The whole range of natural history proves another law, viz: that particular species of both plants and animals, are suited to certain climates and soils and no other.

Islands newly emerged from the ocean, without a sprig of vegetation, soon become covered with plants, different from plants in any other part of the world, but showing a family likeness to those of the nearest mainland.

Terra Australis, which is very remotely situated, has a stock of plants and animals altogether peculiar. It contains entire genera of Animals, which have not been discovered elsewhere—animals too, which are very curious in their anatomical and physiological characters—the different species of the Kangaroo, and many others.

The Elephant, Rhinoceros, Hippopotamus, Giraffe, Camel, Horse—most of the Ox kind belong to the old continent exclusively. Lions, Tigers, Hyenas, &c., to Asia and Africa; the Quagga and Zebra to Southern Africa. . . .

Now I would ask, if this be a general law, by which nature is governed throughout all creation, is it reasonable that man alone should form an exception.

None of these plants and animals can be propagated out of the climate to which they are adapted by nature—and man forms no exception to the general law. The white man cannot live in tropical Africa, or the African in the frigid zone.

Wherever colonies of Europeans have been formed, in temperate countries, they have soon flourished, and the white population has multiplied so fast, as to encroach upon the native, and in many instances, entirely supersede them. But in Africa, colonies of Europeans and Asiatics have dwindled away and become extinct. The coast of Zanguebar was colonized many centuries ago by Arabians, and afterwards by Portuguese—at a still earlier period by Phenicians. Other colonies have been formed in Mozambique, Quiola, Kongo, &c., but the climate has prevented population from flourishing and multiplying. Were it not for these facts we should certainly see white colonies there like every where else, where fortune is to be gained.

On the other hand, the proofs are quite as positive to show that the negro is equally unsuited to a cold climate.

Though a constant influx of negro slaves takes place from Soudan into Turkey, it is without effect or impression.

Herodotus tells us that there was once a colony of Black wooly headed Africans at Colchis, but they are extinct.

No black race in short has been, or can be established at any great distance from the equator.

Look at the bills of mortality in our northern cities, and you will see the proportion of deaths amongst the blacks, increasing as you go north, until you get to Boston, where the proportion is three to one compared to whites.

This has been attributed to their habits and condition, but if I had time I could prove positively, that climate there has its influence.

I have in another place mentioned the fact that a cold climate so freezes their brains as to make them insane or idiotical. . . .

Some very curious and striking analogies have been brought forward from the animal kingdom to prove, that physical causes, have produced changes in color, hair, form and instincts, quite as great as those which are seen in the human race—the varieties in Rabbits, Cats, Dogs, Oxen, Foxes, Fowls, &c. &c. have been cited.

All the swine in Piedmont, are black; in Normandy white; in Bavaria brown. The Oxen in Hungary are gray; in Franconia red. Horses and dogs in Corsica are spotted: the Turkies of Normandy are black, those of Hanover white, &c.—The dray horse of London and the Shetland Poney, are the same species. The Wild Boar and Berkshire; the large cock and the Bantom; the long legged Ox of the Cape of Good Hope, and the Durham, &c.

One of the most striking instances is the variety of Dogs, which are *supposed* to be of but one species. The New Foundland, the Bull, the Grey Hound, the Pointer, the Terrier, Poodle, &c., certainly differ in their heads, form, size, color, hair, instincts, &c., as much as the different varieties of men—a more striking illustration of the effects of physical causes, could not be given.

Now all these changes we freely admit, but does this prove that physical causes have the same power to change man? If climate, food and other physical causes can thus change man, why, I would ask, have they not done it? And why cannot the written history of the world for two thousand years adduce instances?

The human race have been living in the same places where these mighty changes have been effected in animals, and still man is comparatively unchanged. Why in these countries are men so much alike and animals so different? The answer is that human constitutions are less mutable, and men have the power and means of protecting themselves by houses, clothing, fires, &c., against the action of such causes.

Why should all the asserted changes in the human race have taken place in ages beyond the reach of history. Will any one pretend that human nature is not the same now that it was 5,000 years ago? And that the same physical causes have not been at work?

Tradition speaks of migrations, floods, wars and great convulsions in nature—it tells of fiery dragons, hydras, giants and other monsters, but no where are we told that the Ethiopian has changed his skin—even poetry and fable are silent on this point.

Lecture 2.

PHYSICAL DIFFERENCES.—The Anatomical and Physiological differences, between the Caucasian, the Malay, Mongol, Indian and Negro races, have elicited a great deal of scientific research, and I might very well write an octavo on these points alone. Time, however compels me to restrict my lecture to a parallel between the Caucasian and Negro races. I wish it farther to be understood, that my parallel will be limited to the race of Negroes

222

which we see in this country, and which I shall presently describe. There are many other tribes in Africa, which differ widely in color, physical and intellectual characters.

When the Caucasian and Negro are compared, one of the most striking and important points of difference is seen in the conformation of the head.

The head of the Negro is smaller by a full tenth—the forehead is narrower and more receding, in consequence of which the anterior or intellectual portion of the brain is defective.—The upper jaw is broader and more projecting—the under jaw inclines out, and is deficient in chin; the lips are larger and correspond with the bony structure; the teeth point obliquely forward and resemble in shape those of Carnivorous animals; the bones of the head are thicker, more dense and heavy, and the same fact exists with regard to the other bones of the skeleton.

Dr. Gall, in his laborious researches, has established the important fact, which is now conceded, that there is in the animal kingdom, a regular gradation in the form of the brain, from the Caucasian down to the lowest order of animals, and that the intellectual faculties and instincts are commensurate with the size and form.* [* Note.—I beg leave here, once for all, to state that I have never studied and do not advocate the details of Phrenology, but no one doubts that the brain is the organ of intellect and instinct, and that the *general* facts of Phrenology are true.]

In animals where the senses and sensual faculties predominate, the nerves coming off from the brain are large, and we find the nerves of the Negro larger than those of the Caucasian.

In other portions of the skeleton, differences not less marked, are presented. The arm of the African is much longer than in the Caucasian—a Negro of 5 feet 6 has an arm as long as a white man of 6 feet. The arm from the elbow to the hand is much longer in proportion, than in the white man—his hand is longer, more bony and tendinous—the nails more projecting and stronger.

The chest of the negro is more compressed laterally, and deeper through from before backwards—the bones of the pelvis in the male are more slender and narrow; the muscle on the sides of the pelvis are less full, but more full posteriorly.

In the two races the lower limbs are in their relative proportion reversed —in their *entire* measurement, the legs of the African are shorter, but the thigh longer and flatter—the bones at the knee joint instead of being straight, are joined at an obtuse angle, pointing forward. The shape of the shin bone, calf, foot and heel, are familiar to you all.

Now it will be seen from this hasty sketch, how many points of resemblance Anatomists have established between the Negro and Ape. It is seen in the head and face, the arms and hands, the compressed chest, the bones and muscles of the pelvis, the flat long thighs, the forward bend of the knee, in the leg, foot and toes. In short, place beside each other average specimens of the Caucasian, Negro and Ourang Outang, and you will perceive a regular and striking gradation—substitute for the Negro a Bushman or Hottentot from the Cape of Good Hope, and the contrast is still stronger. . . .

The difference to an Anatomist, between the Bushman or Negro and the Caucasian, is greater than the difference in the skeletons of the Wolf, Dog and Hyena, which are allowed to be distinct species; or the Tiger and Panther.

Now can all these deep, radical and enduring differences be produced by climate and other causes assigned? It is incumbent on those who contend for such an opinion, to show that such changes either *have* taken place, or that similar changes in the *human race* are *now in progress*.

It is now 1,700 years since the Jews were banished from their native country, and soon after this event a colony of them settled on the coast of Malabar, amongst a people whose color was black; they were visited a few years ago by Dr. Claudius Buchanan, who states in his travels, that in complexion, form and features, they still preserve the characteristics of the Jews of Europe—the natives too, are still unchanged. . . .

The same facts are observed in the Portuguese colonies in Mozambique and Zanguebar, on the Eastern Coast of Tropical Africa.

The Spanish settlements in Tropical America, and the English settlements in the West Indies, present the same facts—great numbers have died from the effect of climate—the complexion has lost its rudiness, and their skins have become swarthy and bilious—their frames have become attenuated, because nature never intended them for this climate; but their features are still the same. Their children are born fair, and if carried to a temperate climate, would remain so. Every thing goes to prove that there is a limit to the effect of climate. The Caucasian though effected to a certain extent by climate, cannot be transformed into a negro, or a negro into an Ourang Outang.

224

The Moors have inhabited some parts of Tropical Africa from time imme-morial, yet neither in complexion, feature, form, hair, or in any thing else, have they made any approximation towards the Negro. . . .

It is about two centuries since the Africans were introduced into this country, the 8th or 9th generation is now amongst us, and the race is un-changed. The Negroes have been improved by comforts and good feeding which they have been unaccustomed to; but they are Negroes still. . . .

What too are the facts with regard to the aborigines of America? I will here give some facts from Dr. Morton's Cranica Americana.

Although, says he, the Americans possess a pervading and characteristic complexion, there are occasional and very remarkable deviations, including all the tints from a decided white to an unequivocally black skin. He shows also, by numerous authorities, that climate exerts a *subordinate* agency in producing these diversified hues. The tribes which wander along the burn-ing plains of the equinoctial region, have no darker skins than the moun-taineers of the temperate zone.—Again, the Puelches and other inhabitants of the Megallanic region, beyond the 55th degree of South Latitude, are ab-solutely darker than the Abipones, Macobios and Tobas, who are many de-grees nearer the Equator. While the Botocudys are of a clear brown color, and sometimes nearly white at no great distance from the Tropic; and more-over, while the Guyacas, under the line are characterised by a fair complex-ion, the Charruas, who are almost black, inhabit the 50th degree of South Latitude; and yet blacker Californians are 25 degrees north of the Equator. *After all*, he adds, these differences in complexion are *extremely partial*, forming mere *exceptions* to the primitive and national tint, that charac-terises these people from Cape Horn to the Canadas.

The cause of the anomalies is not readily explained; that it is not climate, is sufficiently obvious; and whether it arises from partial immigrations from other countries, remains yet to be decided." . . .

The Tartars are brown and the Europeans white in the same latitude.

It is well known to the naturalist, that the skins of the white and black races differ widely in their anatomical and physiological characters; but de-tails on this point would here be out of place. The skin in all the races is composed of several lamina—the outer is called the cuticle, and is thin and transparent—the second is a vascular net work, called the Rete Mocusum, and it is on this that the color of the skin depends—it secretes a black pig-ment or paint, which gives the black skin to the negro, and it will from this

225

be seen that the blackness cannot be caused by the rays of the sun producing a change in its color. In a sailor or out door laborer, who is exposed to the sun, the skin is, as we express it, tanned or burnt—becomes dark, but there is none of this pigment secreted, and the change in the father is not transmitted to the child.

Another striking fact is seen in negro children—when born they are almost as fair as a white child, but in a very short time and without any exposure to the sun, this black pigment is secreted, and the skin becomes black—here is a function different from any in the whites.

The skin of the African too, is known to generate less heat, and he therefore stands a hot climate better, and a cold worse than the white man.

We are all familiar also, with the *bouquet odour* of a negro's skin, which cannot be accounted for by accidental causes.

In this discussion great weight has been given to the admitted fact, that the color of the skin in the old world, is generally found to accord with climate. The white man is found in the cold and temperate regions, the black in the torrid zone, and the intermediate complexions between the two.

There are however, as we have seen, so many exceptions to the rule as to destroy it.

Moreover, if different pairs of the human race, of different complexions and physical conformations, were placed by the creator in the positions best suited to their organization, they would naturally multiply and spread—after a time the different races would come in contact, mingle together and form intermediate varieties. In fact this is a picture of what is now going on all over the world. I have been often struck by the resemblance of the colored creoles in New Orleans, to the Mongol race—many of them have the high cheek bones, oblique eyes and other characteristics.

If the position I take be true, that the human race is descended from *several or many* original pairs, it is reasonable to suppose that there is not at present a single unmixed race on the face of the earth.* [* Note—It has been *supposed* that the varieties of the human race were produced at the Tower of Babel, when the confusion of tongues occurred; but so remarkable an occurrence would have been mentioned. We might just as well *suppose* that some were changed into Monkeys, while others were changed into negroes. In arguing a question of this kind we want *facts*.]

Look at the population of the United States. From how many nations have we received crosses? Read the early history of Great Britain, France,

Germany, Egypt, in short the whole world as far as we have records—who now can tell what blood predominates in each nation?

Much stress has been laid upon the variety of complexions, hair and conformation, seen in what is *supposed to be* the same race. Take England for example, where you find people of very different features and forms—the complexions vary from fair to tawney, and the hair from blond to black.

These facts have been cited to show that varieties spring up in the same race, which if separated and allowed to multiply alone, would make permanent varieties as distinct as the Caucasian, Mongol and Negro. But I would ask, how much of this may not be attributable to mingling of races originally different?

Every man conversant with the breeding of Horses, Cattle, Dogs and sheep, is aware of the effect of the slightest taint of impure blood—there are no data by which we can determine the length of time which it will endure. An English turfman will not own a horse whose pedigree cannot be traced back to the remotest records of pure blood, and what is remarkable, no horse has ever been the progenitor of successful runners, who has been *known to have one drop* of impure blood in his veins. The celebrated race horse Plenipo, is a facsimile of one of his ancesters 8 generations back, and unlike the intermediate links. A strong likeness is sometimes remarked in race horses, to the Godolphin Arabian, who was brought to England, over a hundred years ago. Look at the family portraits of the Bourbon family, and many others in Europe—though they have been intermarrying with other families for generations, the likeness is still preserved. . . .

Man and animals are doubtless governed by the same general physiological laws, and no one can calculate the results which may arise from crossing races. My belief is that the human race are descended from original stocks, which were essentially different—that these original stocks were placed by an Allwise Creator in the climate and situation best suited to their organization.

The black man was placed in Tropical Africa, because he was suited to this climate and no other. The white man was placed in Europe and Asia, for the same reason. I have elsewhere given facts to prove this. The statistics of our northern cities show that the proportion of deaths amongst the blacks, compared to the whites, is nearly three to one. Facts of a different nature and not less astounding, have recently been published in the Southern Literary Messenger, taken from authentic statistics.

Among the slave population of Louisiana, the insane and idiots number 1 in 4,310; in South Carolina 1 in 2,477; in Virginia 1 in 1,299; but what a different picture is presented at the North—in Massachusetts there is in that class of population, 1 insane or idiot, in 43; and in Maine, 1 in 14!

Now much of this is attributable to climate, but not all as I shall show hereafter. In the Northern cities there is a large proportion of Mulattoes, who I regard and shall attempt to prove, are *Hybrids*. These Hybrids we *know* to be shorter lived than the whites or blacks, and probably more prone to insanity—but the *facts* stand, and construe them as you please, they go strongly to prove the existence of distinct species in the human race.

QUESTION OF HYBRIDS.—A *hybrid* offspring is the strongest and most unequivocal proof of the distinctness of species. The mule for instance, is the hybrid offspring of the horse and ass; its inability to produce offspring, and other peculiarities, leave no doubt that the parent stocks are distinct species.

In an article which I published in the July number of the American Medical Journal, I brought forward a number of facts to prove that the *Mulatto was a hybrid*, and as a necessary inference, that the white and negro races were now, if not always, distinct species. As these facts are very intimately connected with the subject of the present lecture, I will here recapitulate them with some additions, and will first give an extract from a very sensible article published in the spring of '43, in the Boston Medical and Surgical Journal, under signature of "philanthropist."

The writer says: From authentic statistics and extensive corroborating information, obtained from sources to me of *unquestionable authority*, together with my own observations, I am led to believe that the following statements are substantially correct:

1st. That the longevity of the Africans is greater than that of the inhabitants of any other part of the Globe.

2d. That *Mulattoes* (i.e.) those born of parents one being African and the other white or Caucasian, are the *shortest lived of any class of the human race*.

3d. That the Mulattoes are not more liable to die under the age of 25, than the whites or blacks; *but from 25 to 40, their deaths are as 10 to 1, of either the whites or blacks between those ages—from 40 to 55 the deaths are 50 to 1, and from 55 to 70, 100 to 1.*

4th. That the mortality of the free people of color is more than 100 per cent greater than that of slaves.

5th. That those of unmixed extraction in the free states, are not more liable to sickness, or premature death, than the whites of their rank and condition in society; but that the striking mortality, so manifest amongst the free people of color, is in every community and section of the country, *invariably confined to the Mulattoes.*

"It was remarked by a gentleman from the south, eminent for his intellectual attainments, and distinguished for his correct observation, and who has lived many years in the Southern States, that he did not believe that he had ever seen a mulatto of 70 years of age."

From a correspondence published in the Boston statesman, in April last, are taken the following statistics:

In a colored population of 2.634.348 including free blacks, there are 1.980 over 100 years of age; whereas there are but 647 whites over 100, in a population of 14.581.000.

Dr. Niles in a pamphlet published in 1827, gave a comparative statement of mortality in the cities of Philadelphia, New York and Baltimore, deduced from official reports of the Boards of Health of the respective cities, from which it appears that in the years 1823−4−5 and 6, the deaths were as follows:

	New York	*Philadelphia*	*Baltimore*
Whites	1 in 40	1 in 31.82	1 in 44.29
Free blacks	1 in 18	1 in 19.91	1 in 32
Slaves			1 in 77

In Boston the number of deaths annually, among the colored population, is about 1 in 15, and there are fewer pure blacks in this city than any other. "The same comparative mortality between mulattoes and blacks exists in the West Indies and Guaiana, where unfavorable social causes do not operate against the Mulattoes, as in the United States."

Fifteen years professional intercourse and observation have led me to conclusions which correspond very closely with those of Philanthropist. I would add:

1st. That the mulattoes are intermediate in intelligence between the blacks and whites.

2d. That they are less capable of undergoing fatigue and hardships, than the blacks or whites.

3d. That the mulatto women are particularly delicate, and subject to a variety of chronic diseases.

4th. That the women are bad breeders and bad nurses—many do not conceive—most are subject to abortions, and a large portion of the children die young in the southern States.

5th. That the two sexes when they intermarry, are less prolific than when crossed on one of the parent stocks.

6th That Negroes and mulattoes are exempt in a surprising degree from yellow fever.

The subject of hybrids, is a very curious one, on which much might be said, but we have space only for a few general remarks.

There are a great variety of hybrids, running through the whole chain of animated nature, in both animal and vegetable kingdoms. Some hybrids do not breed—as the Mule for example. There are rare instances of their having propagated when crossed back, on one of the parent stocks. There are other hybrids, which do propagate perfectly—as the offspring of the Goat and Ewe—the Goldfinch and Canary bird—the Cygnoides (Chinese Goose) and the common Goose, &c. &c.

Those hybrids, (which do breed) when bred together, have a tendency to run out, and change back to one of the parent stocks—the hybrid geese for instance, if kept alone, degenerate into common geese in a very few generations. This has been remarked too, in the mulattoes of the West Indies, and there are now families in Mobile from the same parents, some of whom are nearly black, and others nearly white; where there is every reason to believe that the mothers have been faithful to their husbands.

Another general law laid down by naturalists, is, that the hybrid derives its size and internal structure principally from the mother; a striking example of which is given in the mule.

The mule or offspring of the Mare and Ass, is a large and powerful animal, having the internal organization of the mother. The Bardeau, or hinny, on the contrary, (the offspring of the Horse and Jenny) is a small and comparatively worthless animal.

Buffon and other Naturalists assert also, that in hybrids the head resembles the father. A familiar illustration may be again seen in the Mule. The

230

offspring of the Ass and Mare, has the long ears, large coarse head, expression and other peculiarities of his dignified progenitor. In the Bardeau, on the contrary the head of the horse is preserved—it is long and lean, with short ears. This law has an important bearing on the subject now before us.

It is well settled by naturalists, that the brain of the Negro, when compared with the Caucasian, is smaller by a tenth, and is particularly defective in the anterior or intellectual lobes, and that the intellect is wanting in the same proportion. In the white race the fact is notorious, that the child derives its intellect much more from the mother than the father.—it is an old remark that a stupid mother never produces an intelligent family of children. Look the world over and ask who are the mothers of the eminent men, and it will be found that there are few exceptions to the rule that the mothers are above, and most of them far above mediocrity.

But this important law of nature is reversed when the white man is crossed upon the Negresse or Indian woman—the law of hybrids is shown at once—in the offspring the brain is enlarged, the facial angle increased, and the intellect improved in a marked degree. Every one at the south is familiar with the fact that the mulattoes have more intelligence than negroes, make bad slaves, and are always leaders in insurrections. . . .

I have called attention in another part of my lecture, to some interesting statistics to show the effect of cold climate and social condition combined in producing idiocy and insanity in the free blacks of the northern States. I have no facts yet to ground an opinion upon, but I have little doubt that it will be found that these effects, like disease and early deaths, are confined mostly to the mulattoes. I have shown that in Maine, 1 in 14, and in Massachusetts 1 in 43, are lunatics or idiots, of the colored population.

As different hybrids are acknowledged to be governed by different laws, is it not reasonable to believe that the human hybrid may also have its peculiar laws?—may not one of these laws be (which is a reasonable inference from foregoing data) that the mulatto is a degenerate, unnatural offspring, doomed by nature to work out its own destruction. The statistics of Philanthropist prove that the mulattoes are shorter lived, and it is an every day remark at the South, that they are more liable to be diseased and are less capable of endurance than either whites or blacks of the same rank and condition.

What then could we expect in breeding from a faulty stock; a stock which

231

has been produced by a violation of nature's laws, but that they should become more and more degenerate in each succeeding generation? We know that the parent will transmit to the child, not only his external form, character, expression, temperament, &c., but diseases, through many generations, as insanity, gout, scrofula, consumption, &c. Why then may not that defective internal organization which leads to ultimate destruction exist in the mulatto? I believe that if a hundred white men and one hundred black women were put together on an Island, and cut off from all intercourse with the rest of the world, they would in time become extinct.

It has been asserted by writers that when the grade of Quinteroon is arrived at, all trace of black blood is lost and they cannot be distinguished from the whites. Now if this be true, most of the mulattoes must cease to be prolific, before this point of mixture is arrived at—for though I have passed most of my life in places where the two races have been mingling for 8 or 9 generations, I have rarely if ever met an individual tainted with negro blood, in whom I could not detect it without difficulty—these higher grades should be extremely common, if the chain was not broken by death and sterility—how else can the fact be accounted for.

Virey, a distinguished French naturalist, states that the connections between the Europeans and women of New Holland are rarely prolific.

The different tribes in Africa, have been mixing together from time immemorial, and we have not yet any facts from which to form an opinion on the question; whether there are affinities between certain races or species which make them intermix better than others, or to what extent the law of hybrids prevails. This remark applies to other parts of the world as well as Africa.

MORAL AND INTELLECTUAL—Great as the physical differences have been shown to be, between the races of men, the intellectual and moral disparity is perhaps still greater.

I have already alluded to the fact that the brain is known to be the organ on which the mind of man, and the instinct of animals depend, and that the perfection of those faculties is commensurate with the perfect organization of this organ.—There is a marked difference between the heads of the Caucasian and the Negro, and there is a corresponding difference no less marked in their intellectual and moral qualities.

The brain of the Negro, as I have stated, is, according to positive measurements, smaller than the Caucasian by a full tenth; and this deficiency exists particularly in the anterior portion of the brain, which is known to be

232

the seat of the higher faculties. History and observation, both teach that in accordance with this defective organization, the Mongol, the Malay, the Indian and Negro, are now and have been in all ages and all places, inferior to the Caucasian.

Look at the world as it now stands and say where is civilization to be found except amongst the various branches of the Caucasian race?

Take Europe and start in the freezing climate of Russia, and come down to the straights of Gibralter, and you find not a solitary exception, not one that excites a doubt.

Take Asia in the same way, and the only approximation to civilization, is found in the mixt, or in some of the Mongol tribes. Take China which is the nearest approximation—she has for centuries had stability in her government, and many of the arts have been carried to a high state of perfection, but take her religion, her laws, her government, her literature, and how does the comparison stand? The most you can say is, that the Chinese are an intermediate link between the Negro and Caucasian.

Take Africa next and the picture presented is truly deplorable—with the exception of Egypt, and the Barbary States, which were in their palmy days occupied by Caucasian colonies, and now by their mixed descendants; and where I repeat, except here, will you find from the Mediterranean to the Cape of Good Hope, a single record or a single monument to show that civilization has ever existed? Where are the ruins of her Memphis, her Thebes, her Rome, her Athens or her Carthage. Their intellects are now as they always have been, as dark as their skins.

Carthage, once the proud rival of Rome, has often been cited as an instance of what a negro race is capable; but we now know that Carthage, like Egypt, was a Caucasian colony from Asia, and has been constantly going downwards since her people have been conquered and adulterated in blood by African hordes.

Cyprian, Augustine, Hannibal, Æsop, Euclid and others, have been brought up as evidences of African intellects; but all history would prove that they were as different from the genuine Negro, as they were from the American Indian.

Let us next look nearer home—America when discovered by Columbus, was populated by millions of Aborigines from one extreme to the other—taking in the whole range of latitude. Much has been written about the ruined cities of Central America, and endless speculations have been indulged

233

in respecting their antiquity, the people who built them, their degree of civilization, &c.

From the accumulated information of Spanish historians, and from the laborious researches of Stephens, we are forced to believe that these cities were built by the same people who inhabited these countries when they were conquered by Cortez and the Pizarros. And what was their condition then?—they lived in the cities which they had built and which are now in ruins. What was the condition amongst them of the arts, sciences, and literature? What their religion, government and laws? Every thing proves that they were miserable imbeciles, very far below the Chinese of the present day in every particular.

There is nothing in the whole history of romance, so rich in interesting incident as the conquest of these countries.—Cortez landed in Mexico with only 500 men, and determined to conquer or die, he burned his own ships to cut off all hope of retreat; he then started off for the city of Mexico, and after fighting his way with his little band, through millions of this miserable race, he entered Mexico, seized Montezuma and his palace and threw him into chains. The conquest of Peru is still more interesting if possible, but this is not the place to dwell on such topics. I merely allude to it to show what the population were, and to show that 500 Caucasian arms and heads were worth more than millions of these miserable creatures.

Many of the remains of this people are stupendous and show considerable Architectural skill, but my conviction is that too much importance has been attached to Architectural remains. The talent of constructiveness may be developed in a very high degree, but without the higher faculties of comparison and causality necessarily being in proportion. The beaver, many birds, and insects show this talent in a surprising degree.—Read the Natural history of the Honey Bee, and you will see things almost as remarkable as any thing we have spoken of in Central America—Chiapas, Yucatan, Mexico, &c. . . .

The *dwellings* of the Bee are constructed on a regular plan and on perfect *mathematical principles*. If a part of the honey-comb is cracked by the interference of man, the laborers are called up and set to work to repair the injury—a prop is constructed with all the science of a Christopher Wren, or Michael Angelo; in short, every thing in the history of the Bee shows a reasoning power little short of that of a Mexican.

But what does the history of the Caucasian show in all climes and in all

234

times—strike off the fetters of bad government, and he takes up the march of civilization and presses onward—the principle of action within him is like the life in the acorn—take an acorn which has laid in a box for a thousand years and plant it in a congenial soil, it sprouts at once and grows into the majestic oak.

History cannot designate the time when the Caucasian was a savage— Caucasian races have often been plunged by circumstances into barbarism, but never as far as we know, into savageism. Cannabalism appears to belong exclusively to the African and Oceanic Negroes—the Bushman, the Hottentots, and perhaps the Caribs; but history does not tell us when and where the Caucasian has gorged his appetite on human flesh and blood.

We can carry back the history of the Negro (though imperfectly) for 4,000 years: we know that he had all the physical characteristics then which he has now, and we have good grounds for believing that he was morally and intellectually the same then as now. One generation does not take up civilization where the last left it and carry it on as does the Caucasian— there it stands immovable; they go as far as instinct extends and no farther. Where, or when I would ask, has a negro left his impress upon the age in which he lived? Can any reasoning mind believe that the Negro and Indian have always been the victim of circumstances? No, nature has endowed them with an inferior organization, and all the powers of earth cannot elevate them above their destiny.

Imperfect as the civilization of St. Domingo now is, if you were to abstract the white blood which exists amongst them they would sink at once into savagism.

The Indian is by nature a savage, and a beast of the forest like the Buffalo—can exist in no other state, and is exterminated by the approach of civilization. You cannot make a slave of him like a negro, his spirit is broken and he dies like a wild animal in a cage.

In spite of all that has been said to the contrary, facts prove that every attempt to educate and civilize the Indian, but makes him more worthless and corrupt—they learn readily all the vices of the white man but never his virtues. Read the history of the Indians in New York and New England— numerous and well directed efforts were made to better their condition —where are they now—what has philanthropy done—let the graves of the Indian speak. Not one has been enough civilized to write the history of his unfortunate race.

235

Now let us see what truth there is in the boasted civilization of the Cherokee and Chickasaw; their destiny too is fulfilled, and their days numbered. It will be seen that whatever improvement exists in their condition is attributable to a mixture of races. Their Chiefs and Rulers are whites and mixed bloods, and the full blood Indian is now what he always has and always will be. . . .

If I had time I could multiply the proofs of the moral and intellectual inferiority of the Negro and Indian when compared with the Caucasian.

AFFINITY OF LANGUAGES AND RELIGIONS.—Volumes have been written on the affinity of languages and religions, to prove the common origin of races; but to my mind nothing can be more fallacious—the faintest resemblances in grammatical construction, or in particular words, have been seized with avidity and confidently put forth as evidence of a common origin. Is it not, however, more reasonable to believe, that in ancient times (as in the present) the nations who were most civilized, stamped their characters, both in language and religion, upon the inferior tribes with whom they held communication. We loose sight too much of the fact, that human nature has always been the same, and are too apt to believe that the present generations are wiser than their progenitors, and that important modifications now exist in men and customs which have not existed before. . . .

RECAPITULATION.—1. I have shown that it is proven beyond a doubt, that instead of one, there have been many creations, and that each successive creation has placed upon the earth entire new Genera, and species of Animals and plants, different from those which existed before.

2. I have shown that there is good reason to believe that there have been creations in the Animal and Vegetable kingdoms since the flood of Noah.

3. I have shown that these facts do not necessarily conflict with the Old or New Testament.

4. I have shown by historical facts that Negroes existed 4,000 years ago with the same physical characteristics which belong to them now.

5. I have shown, that though it may exist, no relationship can be traced between them and Noah's family.

6. I have shown that all history proves that the Negro never has nor never can live out of a warm climate, or the white man in Tropical Africa.

7. I have shown that the Caucasian and Negro differ in their Anatomical and Physiological characters, and that both written history and natural his-

tory prove that these differences could not be produced by climate and other physical causes.

8. I have shown by Analogies from the Vegetable and Animal kingdoms, that there ought to be different species in the human race.

9. I have shown that there now exists and has existed, as far as history speaks, a marked moral and intellectual disparity between the races, and that a high state of civilization never has existed in any other than the Caucasian race.

10. I have shown that there are good grounds for believing that the varieties of men seen in any particular country, and the physical approximation seen in different tribes, originate in the mingling of different races.

11. I have shown that similarity in language and religion proves nothing.

12. I have shown that there are strong facts to prove that the Mulatto is a hybrid.

Now if I have not fully demonstrated each and all of these positions, I think I have brought forward facts enough to prove that I have rational grounds for believing in the truth of the proposition with which I set out, viz: That there is a Genus, Man, comprising two or more species—that physical causes cannot change a white man into a negro, and that to say this change has been effected by a direct act of providence, is an assumption which cannot be proven, and is contrary to the great chain of Natures Laws.

The question will no doubt be asked *cui bono*? for what useful end has this vexed question of the Unity of Man, been torn open? In reply I would say that this is not a question for mere idle discussion, but one involving others of deep Political, Moral and Religious import.

If there be several *species* of the human race—if these species differ in the perfection of their moral and intellectual endowments—if there be a law of nature opposed to the mingling of the white and black races—I say if all these things be true, what an unexplored field is opened to the view of the Philanthropist! Is it not the *Christians duty* to inquire into this subject?

That the Negro and Indian races are susceptible of the same degree of civilization that the Caucasian is, all history would show not to be true— that the Caucasian race is deteriorated by intermixing with the inferior races is equally true.

The white and black races are now living together in the United States under circumstances which, if we may judge by the signs of the times cannot endure always, and it is time for the Philanthropist to do as I have done, look the question boldly in the face. What future course will be the wisest and most humane, I must leave to wiser heads than mine; but of this I am convinced, that nothing *wise can be done* without giving due weight to the *marked differences* which exist between the races.

Some no doubt will be disposed to censure me for the freedom with which I have handled this question, and for opposing opinions which time has rendered venerable and sacred; but to me the laws of God, written in the Book of Nature are more venerable, and truth more sacred than all which eminates from erring Man.

"All Nature is but Art, unknown to thee;
All chance, Direction, which thou canst not see;
All Discord, Harmony not understood;
All partial Evil, universal Good.
And spite of Pride, in erring Reason's spite,
One truth is clear, WHATEVER IS, IS RIGHT."

VI. HENRY HUGHES
Treatise on Sociology

"... the budding poetry of the all-hoping sociologist shall ripen to a fruitful history."

Born in 1829, Henry Hughes grew up in Port Gibson, Mississippi. In 1847 he graduated from Oakland College in his native state, then went on to New Orleans to study law and to Paris to pursue such varied subjects as architecture, social science, anatomy, chemistry, and moral philosophy. While abroad, Hughes encountered Auguste Comte, whose philosophy of positivism was to have a significant impact on the young Mississippian. Upon his return to Port Gibson, Hughes took up the practice of law and began to write and speak on public issues. In 1854 he published a defense of southern slavery in the form of a *Treatise on Sociology: Theoretical and Practical*, and he became a vigorous advocate for the reopening of the African slave trade. Hughes served as a state senator in the last years of the antebellum period, and during the Civil War he fought as a colonel in the Army of Northern Virginia. In 1862 Hughes died at home in Mississippi of a war-related illness.[1]

The selection below is from the second or "Practical" half of Hughes's proslavery volume.[2] In many ways, it represents an extreme example of proslavery theorists' efforts to buttress their arguments with the language and methods of social science. Hughes here adopted much of the style and vocabulary of Auguste Comte's positivism, hoping to borrow the prestige of sociology for his treatment of southern slavery. To broaden the applicability of his argument, Hughes even replaced the terminology specifically associ-

1. Except for a single diary and one scrapbook in the Mississippi Department of Archives and History, Jackson, Hughes's papers have been destroyed. I am grateful to Bertram Wyatt-Brown for bringing these to my attention. On Hughes's life, see William D. Moore, *The Life and Works of Col. Henry Hughes. A Funeral Sermon, Preached in the Methodist Episcopal Church, Port Gibson, Miss., October 26, 1862* (Mobile: Farrow and Dennett, 1863).

2. Henry Hughes, *Treatise on Sociology: Theoretical and Practical* (Philadelphia: Lippincott, Grambo and Co., 1854).

ated with human bondage in the South with the more general language of "warranteeism." Yet Hughes was unable to limit himself entirely to the self-consciously neutral vocabulary of science and erupted in the final paragraphs of the work into a romantic rhapsody. The "budding poetry of the all-hoping sociologist" seems curiously out of place amidst the sparse language of objectivity that he affected in the rest of his volume. The substance of the work similarly reflected elements of both the old and the new. Although presented as a sociological treatise, the book nevertheless followed the basic outline of a traditional tract of moral philosophy, with the emphasis simply shifted from the duties of masters and slaves to those of warrantors and warrantees. In his concern with the limitations imposed on the power of the master or warrantor by his natural interest in the warrantee, Hughes summarized the traditional doctrine of paternalism, declaring that the system's "reciprocity is absolute." The warrantor, he proclaimed, would act "as an honest father of a family acts for the good of his household."

Hughes insisted that race was not the rationalization for the warrantee system and asserted that the arrangements he described were appropriate and desirable for societies of any racial composition. His effort to provide a legitimacy for slavery beyond the circumstances of the Old South compelled Hughes to minimize the importance of race as a cause of slavery, but this in no way rendered him color-blind. The existence of blacks and whites in the South, he argued, prescribed a particular type of "ethnical" warranteeism, for the prevention of amalgamation of races was a moral and scientific necessity. While race was not the foundation of his argument for warranteeism, racism nevertheless pervaded both his writing and thinking.

Although much of what Hughes presented is notable more for the would-be scientism of its language than for its substantive innovations, his open embrace of positivism and its theories of progressive phases of social development led him to foresee a future "Slavery-Perfect Society" of man's own creation.[3] As a result, he allocated far broader power and responsibility to human agents than did the organic social philosophy of most of his fellow proslavery southerners, who railed against the Perfectionist schemes of northern abolitionists. Hughes's positivism also made him a religious scep-

3. Henry Hughes, October 24, 1852, in Diary, Mississippi Department of Archives and History.

tic. Although he tried to minimize the manifestations of this doubt in his everyday life, by, for example, offering lessons in Christianity to slaves in Port Gibson and to Confederates under his command in Virginia, a lack of personal faith certainly alienated him from the biblical and religious orientation of much of southern civilization and of much of proslavery thought. Moreover, Hughes, like George Fitzhugh, explicitly presented the arrangements of slavery as a challenge to the antagonistic social order of free labor and capitalism, thus addressing the social dilemmas posed by the slavery question in a far more iconoclastic and dangerous form than most of slavery's apologists dared.

Treatise on Sociology

The societary organization of the United States South, is Warranteeism. It is an organization both necessary and progressive. Its progress is that of accidentals only. Its essentials are both just and expedient. They are necessary. This necessity is not political and economic only: it is a moral necessity. It is a necessity of justice, humanity, purity and order. The societary organization of the United States South, is perfunctory. It is not forbidden by right. Nor this only; it is bidden by duty; it is in obedience to duty. It is an organization whose essentials, every society just to itself, must incorporate; an organization, to which every duteous society must progress.

In the United States South, there are two races. These are related. With their relations are coupled rights and duties. The organization of these States, is therefore not unqualified warranteeism; because its population is not homogeneous. The societary organization of the United States South, is warranteeism, with the ethnical qualification. This qualification is not essential to theoretical or abstract warranteeism. It is accidental. Warranteeism without the ethnical qualification, is that to which every society of one race, must progress.

Warrantees may be either, (1), Simple-laborers, or manualists only, or, (2), Skilled-laborers or manual-mentalists. In effect, the societary organization of the United States South, is Simple-labor Warranteeism, with the ethnical qualification. By the theory of this organization, all are enforced to labor. Warrantors are economically enforced: warrantees, civilly and

241

economically. This is implemental. Political enforcement is in supplement of morality and economics. This political enforcement is that of punishment for idleness or vagrancy.

The labor-obligations of warrantees are capitalized: the relations of warrantors and warrantees are public; and distribution is by the State or function of justice.

In free-labor commonwealths, the laity are divided into three states. These are, (1), the Civil, (2), the Military, and, (3), the Maritime. The relations of master and servant are private. Apprentices, menial servants, and laborers casually employed, have such rights as are secured by contract express or implied.

But in warrantee commonwealths, the laity are divided into four states. These are, (1), the Political, (2), the Military, (3), the Maritime, and, (4), the Economic. The economic relation is not private; it is public. Warranteeism in the United States South, is not an obligation to labor for the benefit of the master, without the contract or consent of the servant. That is slavery. Warranteeism is a public obligation of warrantor and warrantee to labor for the benefit of, (1), the State, (2), the Warrantee, and, (3), the Warrantor. This obligation is not unilateral; it is bilateral: it is mutual. Its reciprocity is absolute. It is an obligation with considerations to both parties. These considerations are good and sufficient: they are essentially just. They are adapted and regulated by the collective wisdom and goodness of the State. Warranteeism is a fundamental obligation enforced from a fundamental duty. That is the duty of the subsistence and progress of all. It is an obligation to which consent issues not from the will; but from the conscience, and the general reason. It is an obligation coupled to the reciprocal duties of man and society.

Warranteeism does not violate the personal liberty of the warrantee. It allows economically all rights consistent with the economic order; politically, all rights consistent with the political order; and hygienically all rights consistent with the hygienic order.

Warranteeism in the United States South does not wrong; it rights the simple-laborer: it prevents wrong. A slave is one who has no rights. A warrantee is not a slave; he has all rights. Whatever is due is awarded to him.

What therefore, are the justice and the expediency of Warranteeism in the United States South? What are the powers, rights, duties, and responsibilities of, (1), the State, (2), Warrantors, and, (3), Warrantees?

242

By the municipal law of Warrantee-commonwealths, the citizens are divided into four states or orders: the Political, Military, Maritime and Economic.

In any order are two classes. These are the, (1), Orderers or Superordinates, and the, (2), Orderees or Subordinates. This, of necessity. In the military and maritime orders, the orderers or superordinates are officers. In the political state or order, the superordinates or orderers are magistrates; the orderees or subordinates are people.

Persons are either, (1), Natural, or, (2), Artificial. Of natural persons, the relations are in the common-law, either, (1), Public, or, (2), Private. By the law of England, private relations are those of, (1), Master and Servant, (2), Husband and Wife, (3), Parent and Child, (4), Guardian and Ward. This, the law of Free-labor commonwealths.

Public relations are those of magistrates and people. Magistrates are, (1), Supreme, or, (2), Subordinate. People are either, (1), Aliens, or, (2), Citizens. And in Warrantee-commonwealths, citizens are divided into four states or orders.

The relation of Warrantors to Warrantees is public. Warrantors are magistrates; Warrantees, people. Their relation is not private; it is not the common-law relation of Master and Servant. Warrantees are neither apprentices, in their relations, nor menials, casual employees, stewards, bailiffs, or factors. . . .

In the United States South, warrantors or masters are special subordinate Magistrates, qualified for the conservation and administration of special public-peace, special public-health, special public-justice and special public-economy.

All their rights, duties, powers, and responsibilities issue from the law, pursue the law, are limited by the law; and are created, continued, modified or terminated by the law.

Their powers are compound and limited. The composition and limitations are those of the law. The warrantors are within the limits of the law, judicial, executive, and legislative. They combine the powers, in part of sheriffs, constables, and justices of the peace. They have also certain powers of health-officers and overseers of the poor. Their power is qualified and limited to those within the jurisdiction of their warranty.

The duties of warrantors are the conservation of the peace of their warranty; the conservation of the health; the administration of special justice;

243

and the administration of the economy of the warranty. They are special peace-officers, special health-officers, and special subsistence-officers. The creation of their powers, is by fundamental law. Their title to their office is from purchase or inheritance. Good-behaviour and ability to execute their warranties, are their qualifications. The termination of their office is voluntary or involuntary. If voluntary, the condition precedent to termination is the subrogation of another good and sufficient warrantor to their office. No warranty can be left vacant.

Of warrantors, the responsibilities are of both the person and the property. They are for some wrongs, according to their degree; responsible in damages to property; for others, in damage to both person and property; according to guilt.

The Duties of warrantors or masters, to warrantees, are economic, political, and hygienic. The warrantor is therefore, an orderer or superordinate of three orders, or societary systems. He is an officer to warrant three classes of societary rights; these, the economic, political and hygienic.

It is therefore the duty of the warrantor to execute the economic, political and hygienic classes of duties pertaining to his office.

Economic duties are those of, (1), Production, (2), Distribution, (3), Exchange, and, (4), Consumption. To these duties, the parties are economic orderers, and economic orderees; those, warrantors; these, warrantees.

For Production, the warrantor's duty is to execute the obligation of all to labor, according to law. It is his duty to order the productive power of his warranty; to adapt and to regulate it; and to administer as a prudent capitalist, the capital of the association.

It is his duty to prevent idleness and vagrancy.

It is his duty to adapt the labor of each to his ability; and to prevent both positive and negative waste of power, animate or inanimate.

It is the duty of warrantors to execute the statutes of the State to them directed; prescribing the hours, quantity, quality or other accidents of labor.

It is their duty to administer by all just means, the public industry of their warranty; and for this to adapt the quantity of laborers to the quantity of capital.

For Distribution, it is the duty of warrantors to execute the statutes of the

244

State to them directed, prescribing the wages or tribute to warrantees. If these wages are to be paid in necessaries, they must be of good quality. If in any commonwealth, the law by reason of its universality or from other cause, is deficient; it is their duty to execute equity in the premises. It is their duty to see that the wages of all, whether efficient or inefficient, are duly received, and that none are ever in want.

Their duty for Exchange, is to act to the best of their ability as the public exchanger and agent of the warranty. They must therefore buy and sell whatever, according to the ability of the association, is best for its welfare. They must forbid and prevent buying and selling by orderees to the detriment of industry, health, or police: exchange must be by the exchanger of the association; and production by the producers; the division of labor must be enforced.

For Consumption, the warrantor's duty is to provide consumables according to law and equity; to prevent waste consumptive or unproductive; to actualize a consumption neither deficient nor superficient, but sufficient only; to execute order, and prevent consumptive disorder. . . .

Of warrantors, the hygienic duties are both, (1), Preventive, and, (2), Curative, or sanitary and therapeutical. Warrantors as health-officers are either executive or legislative. If hygienic rules and regulations are prescribed by the State; the warrantor is executive of such as are to him directed. In default of statutory direction, it is his duty to act for the health of his warranty, as becomes the prudent head of a household. He then acts legislatively; and is to provide according to his best discretion, all hygienic necessaries. This discretion is not arbitrary; it is a legal and equitable discretion.

It is therefore the duty of warrantors to provide all sanitary necessaries for the prevention of disease. They must provide wholesome food and raiment. They must regulate the construction of all habitations in the warranty; enforce cleanliness and ventilation; and provide for purification in cases of pestilence, infection or contagion. They must execute necessary quarantines. If public quarantine is not decreed, they must, if accidentally necessary; act equitably in supplement of the law's deficiency. They must enforce such needful regularity of rest, labor, and amusements, as are sanitary. They must prevent by all due care and prudence, any violent or un-

245

forseen privation of life or bodily member. They must provide suitable work during the inclemency of seasons; and all proper clothing and other safeguards.

For the sick, it is the duty of warrantors to provide all therapeutic necessaries; and as the prudent head of a household, to act for the restoration of the warrantee's health. The warrantor must when needful, provide due medical skill, medical materials, nursing and all proper care and attention. He must provide such kind of subsistence as is adapted to the state of the sick. For such as are inefficients from chronic diseases, he must faithfully supply proper necessaries, and execute duly, his hygienic warranty.

Of warrantors, the political duties are (1), Legislative, (2), Executive, and (3), Judicial. They relate as well to the making of laws as to their adjudication and execution.

In warrantee commonwealths, warrantors are legislative representatives of warrantees. Warrantees are constituents.

It is therefore the duty of warrantors to represent in the government, the interests of warrantees. The warrantor is the political servant of the warranty. It is therefore his duty to act for the political good of the association, as an honest father of a family acts for the good of his household.

The warrantor must defend his warrantees against legislative injustice. If the laws for the benefit of warrantees are deficient; he must act for their perfection. He must act for the exhibition of their rights, and prohibition of their wrongs.

The executive political duties of warrantors are such as are prescribed by general or special laws. It is their duty to keep the peace of the warranty; and to prevent breach of law. It is their duty to execute order and to prevent disorder or insubordination. It is their duty to promulgate within their warranty, all public laws directed generally or specially to warrantors. It is their duty to prevent crimes and misdemeanors; and all offences whether against the commonwealth or individuals. It is their duty to execute according to law all judgments, in cases to which their judicial power extends. It is their duty to keep such watch and ward as a diligent magistrate ought. It is their duty to represent in court, warrantees prosecuted or prosecuting.

Warrantors' judicial duty is to hear and determine all cases over which they have lawful jurisdiction. In these cases it is their duty to decree justice without sale, denial, or delay. All their judicial duties are born of the law.

246

Their discretion is not private. It is legal and equitable, and their duty is to do that which is lawful and equitable. They must hear diligently, before determining; and render judgment according to the testimony.

The Powers of warrantors are adequate to their duties. Duty is the measure of them. They are sufficient only; they are neither deficient nor superficient. And because their duties are economic, hygienic, and political; their powers are economic, hygienic and political. Their power is that of orderers.

The fundamental power of warrantors is therefore just so much as is sufficient to execute economic, hygienic, and political order in their warranties. It is no more. That is the limit.

And because the first end of economic order is the subsistence of all; and because warrantors are responsible for the subsistence of warrantees; warrantors have the power to order the production, distribution, exchange, and consumption of their warranty. If these are regulated by special laws, they have by implication, sufficient power for their execution. If there are no special economic laws, the power of warrantors is that of an economic magistrate whose duty is to provide for the subsistence of his warrantees.

The warrantor has therefore the power to administer the public industry of his warranty. He has the power to order production. But he has not the power to check, stop, or embarrass the public industry of the warranty which he administers. Because his powers must be construed with reference to the subsistence of all; and arbitrary idleness or economic disorder, is in derogation of the public subsistence. He has the power to forbid idleness; but he has not the power to command idleness.

So also, the warrantor has power to order the distribution, exchange, and consumption of his warranty for the subsistence of all. But he has no power in derogation of this subsistence.

The warrantor is also a hygienic orderer. He has the power of order but not the power of disorder; this, the fundamental limit of his power. In the execution of powers, he must show that they are necessary to the execution of his warranties.

The warrantor has power to judge and punish irregularities in time of plague. He has power to enforce needful quarantines. He has power to punish breach of sanitary regulations. He has power to enforce regularity in food and raiment and in bodily indulgences or practices, such as eating of unwholesome provisions, sleeping in exposed places, going without suffi-cient clothing, and wandering during hours of natural rest.

The warrantor has power to punish wanton waste, idling during hours of labor prescribed by law, vagrancy, and running away, or leaving labor with-out the knowledge or permission of warrantor and in derogation of the public health, peace or industry. But the warrantor has no power to refuse this permission when such leaving or absence, will not be in derogation of the public peace, health, or subsistence.

The warrantor has the power to order and establish the arrangement of habitations; to dispose families in suitable tenements according to health, peace, and economy; and for this to visit, inspect, and superintend dwell-ing-houses, to enforce cleanliness and quiet.

He has the power to punish intemperance; and to prohibit the buying of intoxicating liquors, or their introduction into the warranty.

Warrantors have the power to punish cruelty to animals by omission or commission.

They have the power to adapt the quantity of laborers or warrantees to the quantity of the association's capital; and for this to provide for super-numeraries, other good and sufficient warrantors; and until such provision, to warrant a comfortable sufficiency of necessaries.

But warrantors have no power to terminate or qualify their warranties. Warrantees must be always warranted. A warrantor has no power to with-draw or resign his warranty otherwise than by the subrogation of another good and sufficient warrantor. This is the essence of the system. Whatever is in derogation of it, is void. Warrantors have no power to separate families, except such separation is essential to the subsistence of all. And the power then is to be strictly construed, and the presumptions against warrantors. They have under no circumstances, power to separate mothers and children under the age of ten years.

Warrantors' political power is such as is sufficient for the execution of the warranties.

They have the right to judge and punish certain offences against the pub-lic peace, and against the individual.

They have the right to judge and punish breaches of the peace within their warranty. They have the power to punish riotous assemblies of warrantees, appearing armed without permission, affrays in the warranty, riots, routs, unlawful assemblies, and challenges to fight.

They have the power to judge and punish assault and battery. But over other offences against the persons of individuals, as mayhem, rape, assault with intent to kill, forcible-abduction or wounding, they have no jurisdiction. They have judicial power over no high crimes. They have no power over felonies except to arrest the felon. They have no judicial power over offences by warrantees against the habitations of individuals, as arson and burglary.

They have no judicial power over offences against the private property of individuals; except in case of simple unaggravated larceny within the warranty, and malicious mischief not felony, and within the warranty.

Warrantors have no power to punish except after trial or fair hearing. They have no power to punish on suspicion, or to produce disclosure of guilt or criminal knowledge. That is usurpation, and against law.

Warrantors have the power to execute punishment, in cases over which they have jurisdiction. This punishment is that of the person. This, of necessity. For simple-laborers in any society cannot be punished in their property. Privation of their property is want. This want again is unhealthy or criminal, and therefore inexpedient. Only the other classes of society can be punished in their property, because the property of society is in their possession.

The personal punishment which warrantors have the power to execute, must not be cruel or unusual. They have the power to punish with stripes and blows. But these must not be such as to endanger life or limb. They must not be excessive or in derogation of the public industry. All punishment must be overt. The instruments of punishment must not be dangerous or extraordinary. Warrantors have no power over the life or limb of warrantees.

Whether warrantors have the power of punishment by imprisonment, is doubtful. Punishment by imprisonment is in derogation of public industry, and a high and sovereign power.

But such overt imprisonment or simple detention of the person as is not for punishment, but for prevention of crimes and misdemeanors, warrantors have the power to enforce. But this imprisonment must not be prolonged; power must be strictly construed. It must not be covert. It must be overt, and as for the State. Whether this would, except in case of transportation, require the place of confineement to be public, is also doubtful. But in every case, the imprisonment must not be arbitrary. It must pursue justice and the law. The burden of proof must be upon the warrantor; he must be able to show cause and justify himself like any other magistrate.

For the just execution of their duties and powers, warrantors are responsible in their person and their property. This Responsibility is both political and economic. Economic responsibility of warrantors, is that of their property only. Political responsibility is that of both person and property. This responsibility is civilly enforced. It is nothing other than punishment for breach of political laws. Such punishments are fines, confiscations, imprisonment, or any other personal or property penalty. The political responsibility of warrantors specially differs in nothing, from the responsibility of other magistrates, for misfeasance or nonfeasance in office. If either break laws directed to them; they are punished according to law. This is the method political; the political system acting with political implements. But the political system does not execute laws by political implements only. It employs the education system. It prevents breach of laws by enlightening the mind, and so lessening the desire of breaking law. Nor this system only. The economic is an agent with the political system. The societary organization of warrantee commonwealths, executes its laws not by the political system only, but by the economic, also. By the obtention of this organization, warrantors, for the just execution of their duties, are responsible to society, not politically only. They are also economically responsible. This method is in cumulation of that. Whatever therefore are the political checks to the power of warrantors; the economic checks are additional. The economic method is no other than responsibility by damage to property. By the contrivance of the warrantee economic system, the warrantor must do his duty: if he does not, he is damaged. This is damage to property. And the damage is adapted to the breach of duty. The economic system is not politically antagonistic. In warrantee organizations, the economic and political systems are syntagonistic. The syntagonism is implemental and efficient. This method of economic responsibility is self-executing and superior.

By it, and the nature of warranteeism, the labor-obligations of warrantees, are capitalized. They are values. These values express the amount of capital invested in the labor-obligation and are negotiable.

250

Whatever therefore increases or decreases the value of the labor-obligation; increases or decreases the capital of the warrantor. What affects one; affects the other. But damage to the laborer is damage to the value of the labor-obligation. Depreciation or appreciation of the obligee is depreciation or appreciation of the obligation; and this, to the warrantor, or capitalist, is loss or gain proportional. Damage to the warrantee, is hence damage to the warrantor; damage to the capitalizee is damage to the capital; and damage to the capital, damage to the capitalist.

The warrantor is economically enforced therefore to warrant health, strength, and justice, to the warrantee. Sickness, want or injustice to the warrantee, mulct the warrantor. The wrongs by their consequences right themselves. They fine the wronger, and are self-executing.

For breach of hygienic, economic or political duty to warrantee, the warrantor therefore is directly responsible in property.

If the warrantee is sick, the warrantor loses. This loss is twofold; he loses both the service of the warrantee pending illness; and the cost of his cure. The capitalist, in warranteeism, does not save the laborer's wages during illness. He pays the wages without receiving the work. So, in case of any bodily hurt. But if the sickness is mortal; the capitalist loses by the death of the laborer, not his labor only, but the entire capital invested in producing or purchasing the laborer's obligation. The warrantor therefore is by economic necessity, a health-officer. He is economically enforced to warrant the health of warrantees. That is not his duty only; it is his interest. And for breach of this duty, he is responsible in his property. Sickness is loss of expenses, and profits; death, loss of principal.

The fundamental duty of warrantors is the subsistence of all:—a comfortable sufficiency of necessaries for every one. The warrantor is enforced to actualize this. For deficiency of these necessaries, is want. Want is either unhealthy, criminal or mortal. But for unhealthy and criminal want, the warrantor is economically responsible. If the want produces crime; the warrantor is also responsible. This responsibility is both economic and political. If the crime is punished by death; the warrantor loses the principal capital invested in the warrantee's labor-obligation. In some States, this loss is divided; and the warrantor, in part indemnified. If the crime is punished by fine; the warrantor pays the fine. If the amount of the fine is greater than the value of the warrantee's labor-obligation; the warrantor has, in some States, the right to surrender his title to the labor-obligation. He thus loses its whole value. If the crime is punished by imprisonment; the warrantor loses the service of the warrantee pending imprisonment. If the crime is punished by bodily pains; this damages the orderliness and the reputation of the warrantee; and this, the negotiable value of his labor-obligation. To avoid these losses, the warrantor is economically obliged to defend the warrantee against prosecution for crimes; and in the legislation of the government, to act for justice to warrantees. If the warrantee is not wronger, but wrongee; his wrongs cannot be other than such as affect the value of the warrantee's labor-obligation. Wrong to the obligee, is wrong to the obligation; and so to the holder of the obligation. The warrantor is therefore economically enforced to defend the warrantee.

"Slaves are persons who have no rights." In the United States South, there are no slaves. Those States are warrantee-commonwealths. Their warranteeism is that with the ethnical qualification. The warrantees there, are not slaves; they are not persons who have no rights. That is error. They have substantially, whatever is due them. Their wrongs are accidental: they are not peculiar to warranteeism. That system is essentially just: injustice is alien, romantic, and unnatural to it. In the United States South, warrantees are persons who have all their rights. They are not slaves; they are not persons who have no rights. Their slavery is nominal only; and the name, a wrong to the warrantee States.

All rights are those of, (1), Existence, and, (2), Progress. Existence-rights are those of, (1), Subsistence, and, (2), Security.

In warrantee-commonwealths, the economic system is an essential part of the civil government. The civil government is a political economy: the political and economic systems are united. The union is like that of Church and State. Warrantors are magistrates, to warrantees, people. All warrantors are special government officers. Their official powers issue from the State, are subject to the State, and under review and visitation of the State. The State is supreme and supervising. It is the fountain of power.

In the United States South, the State actualizes the right of subsistence. The economic system is the implement for this. The law not only regards life and member, and protects every man in the enjoyment of them; but also furnishes him with everything necessary to their support. It provides the means by which every warrantee can earn these necessaries. This, in Free-labor societies, is "by means of the several statutes enacted for the relief of the poor;" or the right of the indigent to "demand a supply sufficient for all the necessities of life, from the more opulent part of the community." In warrantee-commonwealths, there are no indigent. Indigence is eliminated. Each warrantee earns his living. . . .

Of the compound right of existence, the component rights are those of personal subsistence, and personal security. To the right of personal security, wrongs are manslaughter, murder, mayhem, rape, assault and battery, wounding, false imprisonment, and kidnapping. Against these, warrantees are warranted. The State protects them. The law is as well for warrantees, as for other citizens. Any distinction is accidental. The political system protects all. If this protection is at any time deficient; it is amended by progress.

The master or warrantor has no power or right, to commit assault and battery on a warrantee or slave. Nobody has. The warrantor as a magistrate, has under law, judicial and executive jurisdiction over certain misdemeanors or offences against the public peace, public health, and public economy. For these offences, the warrantor has by law, the power, and it is his duty, to adjudicate and execute corporal punishment. This punishment is to be just; it is to be proportioned to the offence; it is to be overt; it is not to be cruel, or unusual, or such as endangers life or limb. For the execution of his magistracy, the warrantor is answerable to the State. He holds his power from the State. For any abuse of it, he is answerable as any other magistrate. His power is not irresponsible. It is not unlimited, unqualified, or absolute. It is checked and balanced, limited, relative, qualified and responsible. If in any commonwealth, it is abused; the abuse is like any other official abuse, to be checked. This abuse is accidental; the essence and excellence of warrantee commonwealths, is justice. . . .

Warrantees therefore, have both the right of personal-subsistence, and the right of personal-security. These rights are actualized. Warranteeism achieves the fundamental end of society. Existence-rights are warranted.

Incidental to both existence-rights and progress-rights, is the right of property. An economic system ought therefore to obtain for all, a just share of property. A just share is never less than a comfortable sufficiency of necessaries for health and strength. That is the minimum. If the obtention of a society, is less than this; there is social wrong. Progress is then a duty; the

253

privation of the right of property, must be remedied; and the first end of society, effected.

The right of property, is warranted to warrantees. The State or justice-function, is the distributor of the produce of warrantors and warrantees. Their share is never less than a comfortable sufficiency of necessaries; and the distribution is by progress, adapted and regulated to justice.

Warrantees therefore, have always the tenant-right of a comfortable dwelling; and the family-right of a comfortable sufficiency of food, fuel, raiment, and of medical and other necessaries. This is the expressed minimum of the law. That law is not political only; it is civil law, both politically and economically enforced. Over and above this subsistence-property, they have such other as is by right due. Such, the substance of their property-rights.

But warrantees are associates. Their property-right is in its forms, therefore, qualified by the fact of association. This qualification is that of the adaptation and regulation, essential to every association. But adaptation requires division of labor. Hence the warrantee-associate's right of property, must be associationally exercised. The fundamental law of the division of labor, must be observed. If one division of the associates, are producers, another exchangers, and another distributors; their functions must not be mixed; the division or adaptation must be maintained.

Warrantees have the property-right of exchange or contract. They may alien or purchase. They have the substance of the right; that is essential; but in what form exercised, is accidental. In warranteeism, the exchanges of the associates, are transacted by the head of the association. In the division of labor, that is his function. He aliens, purchases and administers for all. This conforms to the law of adaptation. Warrantees therefore, have the right of property, in association.

The right of property is incidental to the right of subsistence. Warrantees therefore, have not only the right of property; but the realization of this right is always that of the higher right to which it is incidental. Nor this only: the property distributed to them, is distributed by the State or function of justice. This also, is a method necessary to progress. Distribution of justice by the function of justice, is an essential of the production of justice. The perfection of this distribution is by the perfection of warrantee-progress. It can be by no other method.

254

Existence and Progress are ultimate rights. They are the final and supreme objects of social organization. They are its end and aim. All other rights are incidental. They are means. They are intermediate and conducive; implemental and constructive. Those rights are objective; these subjective; those, effects, these, causes.

Of ultimate rights, the compound organ is society. The ends of the societary organization, are the existence and progress of all. Ultimate rights are therefore societary. But systems compose an organization; they are means to ends. The systems of a perfect society are the economic, political, hygienic, philosophic, esthetic, moral, and religious. These are the kinds of systems. All of them are incidental to the ultimate ends of society. Rights therefore are not only societary or ultimate; they are also incidental or systematic.

Of a system, the elements are, power, order, and liberty.

The right to existence and progress, is therefore the right to societary organization; the right to societary organization is the right to societary systems; and the right to societary systems, the right to just economic, political, hygienic, philosophic, esthetic, moral, and religious, power, order and liberty.

In the United States South, warrantees have the right of economic power. That is nothing other than the right of labor and property. They have the right of economic order. Order is ordained and established. It is public; it is municipalized. Economic association, adaptation and regulation, are governed by the State or function of justice.

Nor have warrantees, the rights of economic power and order only. They have the right of economic liberty. Their economic powers, rights, duties, and responsibilities are defined; they are matter of public law. Economic license is eliminated. Of their economic freedom that only is surrendered which is inconsistent with economic order. Surrender of more than this is not orderly; it is against economic law, and unprofitable. License only is forbidden.

Warrantees have the systematic rights of hygienic power, order and liberty. The materials of health are warranted; their right to necessary hygienic power, is actualized.

For the execution of the right of hygienic order, the warrantor is appointed a special health-officer. He is specially endowed with sufficient and responsible sanitary and therapeutic power for the benefit of warrantees.

Warrantees have all hygienic freedom consistent with necessary hygienic order. This is the right of hygienic liberty. But warrantees have no right to break quarantine; to go in contagious places; to expose themselves unnecessarily. This is hygienic license, and against sanitary law. The warrantor's special duty is to prevent this.

The rights of the esthetic system, are esthetic power, order, and liberty. These are for the production of pleasure and the reduction of pain. In warranteeism, the esthetic system is not yet organized. It is natural; but not yet essential. The rights of this system will be actualized; but this will be by progress and canonically.

The esthetic is essential to the economic, political, and hygienic systems. Its actualization therefore, will not only be progressive; but the progress will be syntagonistic. The warrantor or capitalist, will supply esthetic power; and the State according to justice, order it.

When wealth therefore shall have so increased, that justice of distribution, authorizes the elements of warrantee's wages to be not only economic, hygienic and political, but also esthetic; the esthetic element will be added to wages and distributed. Esthetic wages will be esthetic power: the right to one, the right to the other. The warrantor, or some other magistrate, will then be appointed, for the execution or regulation of this right. When therefore, justice authorizes it, the right of esthetic power, order, and liberty will be systematically warranted to warrantees. This will be economic also. It will be progress executed by warrantors syntagonistic economically with warrantees esthetically: the master, by interest, enforced to justice: or injustice to the warrantee, injustice to the warrantor. But the esthetic system is both positive and negative. It is not for the production of pleasure only. It is for the prevention of pain. It is both eunesthetic and anesthetic. Warranteeism as it is, is essentially anesthetic. It systematically eliminates bodily pain. It actualizes comfort for all. Bodily pain is accidental, and such in chief, as is penal or from the execution of justice. But such pain is accidental to warranteeism.

Warranteeism as it is, actualizes warrantees' right to moral and religious power, order, and liberty. The method for the support of religion is not now that of incorporating in the wages, the expenses necessary. The religious body or church by its own means or power, distributes religion. It has the ordering of the power or means, for the religious progress of warrantees. Supplementally but not yet systematically, some warrantors support the religious service of warrantees. But the implemental method is that of religious progress by the church's capital. What is the best system of ecclesiastical polity for warrantees; how religion ought to be distributed; what are the best expedients for justice; are to be developed according to the laws of progress.

Progress will develop whether religion for warrantees should be supported by the churches; or whether when justice authorizes the increase, the religious element should be incorporated in warrantees' wages. Whichever method is best; warrantors will be syntagonistic economically with warrantees religiously. All the societary systems in warranteeism, are syntagonistic. Religion also, is economic. It is profitable. And as of the religious system, so of the ethical system. Warrantees have the right to moral power, order and liberty. This right is executed. No one has the right to violate the warrantee's progressive humanity, justice, truth, purity, orderliness or other moral duty. He has sufficient power and liberty for these. Deficiency is accidental, and by progress to eliminated.

Warrantees' right to philosophic or educational power, order, and liberty is not yet actualized. If justice economically authorized it; the educational means or power might be added to wages. If not this; any other method following justice.

But political independently of economic justice, does not now authorize the systematic education of warrantees. The warranteeism of the United States South, is that with the ethnical qualification. The existence-rights of both or of one of these races, now forbids to the other, this progress-right. The educational is at present antagonistic to the political system. This antagonism is accidental and temporary. It is not necessary or natural to warranteeism. It is due to a temporary outside fact. This fact is from an error which confounds essentials and accidentals; which is rather aggressive against the greater good essential, than progressive from the lesser bad accidental. It is bad opposition from good disposition. It is philanthropy in design, and misanthropy in deed. But between warrantors and warrantees, there is naturally no educational antagonism. The educational and economic systems, are syntagonistic. So also, the political and educational systems;

but this, only after the political fact as it is, shall be the political fact as it ought to be.

In the United States South, the rights of warrantees under the political system, are such as are just. Their political status is not wrong. It is right; it is from duty; it is a moral necessity. They have now the political power, order, and liberty to which they are rightly entitled; neither more nor less.

In the civil government of republics, the people are the sovereign. They are the supreme orderer. But republics are representative governments; the sovereign people constitute representatives. These representatives in their capacity as such, are magistrates; or supersovereign. In the political system, they are the orderers. They adapt and regulate. But all the people are not sovereign or supersovereign. Some only are sovereign. These are such alone as are peculiarly qualified. They must be males. They must be of a certain age. They must be of sound mind. They must be residents. In some commonwealths, property qualifications, are necessary; in some, religious qualifications. There may be other qualifications just or unjust.

All other people in the State, who are not sovereign people, are subsovereign. To this class belong women, minors, criminals, lunatics and idiots, aliens, and all others unqualified or disqualified.

Such, the three classes of people. In republics, all are represented. The representatives or orderers, represent and are responsible to their constituents, the sovereign people. But these are not constituents only; they likewise represent the class of subsovereign people; these are consituents of those. A man represents his family. This is special; he also represents the interests of other subsovereigns; this, his general duty.

The representation of all is thus actualized.

Duties are coupled to relations. By the common law, a natural person's relations under the civil government are public or private. By the common law, private relations are those of master and servant, husband and wife, parent and child, guardian and ward.

In warrantee commonwealths, public relations are those of magistrates and people; or orderers and orderees. Magistrates are legislators, executors and adjudicators. To these the relations of the people, are those of orderees. The people are therefore, legislatees, executees and adjudicatees. the magistrates are adapters and regulators; the people, adaptees and regulatees.

258

In republics in which the warranteeism is that with the ethnical qualification, the warrantees are subsovereign. They have not the right of sovereignty. That is not their due; it is unjust; it is wrong. Warrantees have the right of representation. But they have not the right of political constitution. Neither ought they; they are not entitled to it. Subsovereignty is the right of warrantees. Their sovereignty is the wrong of warrantors, and others.

In the warrantee commonwealths of the United States who therefore, ought to be the sovereign people? Who ought to be the supreme power in the warrantee States? There, warranteeism with the ethnical qualification is ordained and established. What is the effect of this qualification? The people are of two races. They are ethnically related to each other. But because every act has a moral quality; with every relation, duties are coupled. These races in their ethnical relations, differ from each other in beauty; in color; in the inclination, shape, and direction of the pile; in the conformation of their body, and in other physiological respects.

The black race must be civilly either (1), Subsovereign, (2), Sovereign, or (3), Supersovereign. If not subsovereign, they must be co-sovereign. The white race may also be subsovereign, sovereign, or supersovereign. If both races are promiscuously sovereign; that is co-sovereignty. The white race is now and has been sovereign; the black, subsovereign. This, the historical fact.

The black race ought not to be admitted to co-sovereignty. It is wrong: it is in violation of moral duty.

These races physiologically must be either equal or unequal. They must be either peers ethnically, or not peers. If not peers ethnically, the black race must be either superior or inferior. If superior, their ethnical progress forbids amalgamation with an inferior race. If the white race is superior; their ethnical progress forbids intermixture with an inferior race.

But races must progress. Men have not political or economic duties only. They have hygienic duties. Hygiene is both ethnical and ethical; moral duties are coupled to the relation of races. Races must not be wronged. Hygienic progress is a right. It is a right, because a duty. But hygienic progress forbids ethnical regress. Morality therefore, which commands general progress, prohibits this special regress. The preservation and progress of a race, is a moral duty of the races. Degeneration is evil. It is a sin. That sin is extreme. Hybridism is heinous. Impurity of races is against the law of nature. Mulattoes are monsters. The law of nature is the law of God. The same law which forbids consanguineous amalgamation; forbids ethnical amalgamation. Both are incestuous. Amalgamation is incest.

But the relation of the two races to each other, is moral: every relation has an ethical quality: ethics is ethnic. Moral hygienic duties must not be violated. For progress must be developed, and regress, enveloped. Polity therefore—the duty of the State—prohibits the sovereignty of the black race. Because, if the black race are sovereign, they must be co-sovereign. If not politically subordinate or superordinate; they must be politically coordinate. But the black and white race must not be co-sovereign; they must not be politically coordinate. They must be, the one subordinate, and the other, superordinate. They must not be aggregated; they must be segregated. They must be civilly pure and simple from each other. This is a hygienic ethnical necessity. It is the duty of caste to prevent amalgamation: it is, caste for the purity of races. For, political amalgamation is ethnical amalgamation. One makes the other: that is the immediate, invariable antecedent of this. Subsovereignty is necessary for segregation, and both necessary to duty.

Political amalgamation is sexual amalgamation: one is a cause of the other. There must be either caste or co-sovereignty: this is the alternative to that. For power to rule, is power to marry, and power to repeal or annul discriminating laws.

In States, the intercourse of sexes is either (1), Lawful or (2), Unlawful. Marriage is lawful intercourse. Of two races in a State, marriage may be (1), Between males and females of the same race; (2), Between males of one race and females of the other race; or, (3), Miscellaneously, between males and females of both races.

Of marriage, the motives or springs of action are such as are either (1), Matrimonial, or, (2), Extramatrimonial. Love is a matrimonial motive. Extramatrimonial motives are such as avarice or the desire of wealth; and ambition or the desire of power.

If therefore, marriage miscellaneously between two races, is lawful; the motives will be both matrimonial and extramatrimonial. Females of the inferior will elect males of the superior race. This, from natural preference, which is matrimonial; or from ambition, which is extramatrimonial. Males of the superior race will from avarice, ambition, or other extramatrimonial motives, elect females of the inferior race. These motives are certain; and

260

certainty of motive, is certainty of movement; certainty of cause, certainty of effect. If therefore, intermarriage of races, is lawful; intermarriage will be actual: the cause, certain; the effect will be certain. The law must therefore, forbid amalgamation. Intermarriage of races must be unlawful.

But law is a rule of action prescribed by the supreme-power in a State. This supreme-power is the sovereign. If it is compound; if two races are co-sovereign; the motives of legislation will be those of both races; or compound legislation, from compound legislatures. But the legislative motives of one race, will be for amalgamation; and the motives of a part at least, of the other race, not against it. That part will be those who are such from ambition, from avarice, from ignorance, from fanaticism, and from error. The power to be politically coordinate or equal, will be the power to be ethnically or matrimonially coordinate or equal. Political amalgamation will initiate sexual amalgamation. The ability for that, gives the ability for this. The duty therefore coupled to the relation of races, forbids political amalgamation or its certain effect, the lawful intermarriage of the two races. Hygienically, the two races ought not to be co-sovereign; because the obtention of co-sovereignty will be a wrong to both races. But this is immoral. If therefore the State or sovereign authorizes the cause, it authorizes the effect; it authorizes a wrong for which it is responsible; because every State is responsible for immoral polity, or non-performance of duty.

But if the sexual intercourse of two races in a State is not legitimate; it is illegitimate. The societary organization must be such therefore, as to eliminate this. If the elimination cannot be immediate; it must be proximate, and progressive. But to this, caste is necessary. For sexual intercourse follows social intercourse. In a society of two races, therefore, ethnical segregation is essential.

Between the two races in warrantee States, caste to prevent impurity, is hence, a duty. Therefore, one race must be orderers, and the other, orderees. In the political system, one race must be sovereign; and the other, sub-sovereign. In the economic system, one race must be superordinate or warrantors; the other subordinate or warrantees, and both races must have their just power, order, and liberty.

Caste of races is therefore a duty of morality. It is politically enforced; because it ought to be. This also is rightful. Subordination is not slavery; ethnical segregation is not ethical degradation. For the duties coupled to the relation of races, must be actualized. Purity of races, is right.

Caste of races is therefore the ethical qualification of warranteeism in the United States South. Sovereignty is the right and duty of one race; and sub-sovereignty, the right and duty of the other. But the class of sub-sovereigns, must not be wronged. They must not have the power of co-sovereignty; because that is not their right. But to all other just powers for existence and progress, they have rights. These rights the societary organization must actualize.

In the societary organization of the United States South, warrantees are the sub-sovereign race. That is the historic fact. All facts operate.

There, these warrantees have all the rights due them. They have essentially all the power consistent with the necessary sovereignty of one race, and sub-sovereignty of the other. Restriction of this power is accidental. It is from the accident of the political fact, and in proper adaptation to it. This is not unjust; it is dutiful.

Consistency with sub-sovereignty is therefore one test of the rights due to warrantees in the United States South. The right of primary political constituency is inconsistent with the warrantees' sub-sovereignty; it is in derogation of the sovereignty of the ruling race. Warrantees therefore have not the right of political constituency.

But the right of political representation is not inconsistent with the sovereignty of the sovereign race. Warrantees are therefore entitled to representation. That is their right. The societary organization must therefore actualize their political sub-sovereignty and representation. In the United States South, this is done. Warrantees there, are both sub-sovereign, and justly represented.

Nor this only. Warrantees have essentially all other rights, whether of legislatees, adjudicatees, or executees, due them. They have not by intention only, but by obtention, all rights incidental to existence-rights, and progress-rights.

In a republican government, all must be represented. Because, all have rights for preservation, and progression; and representation is incidental to those. Every reasonable creature in being, must be cared for; everybody must be cared for.

In the warrantee systems of the United States South, as well as in free-labor political systems, sub-sovereign people are represented by the sovereign people; as wives by their husbands; and sovereign people by the supersovereign people or magistracy. Representation is therefore both, (1), Primary, and, (2), Secondary.

In a political system, sub-sovereign people can by one method only be represented by the sovereign people. This is the method of the Unification of sovereign and sub-sovereign Interests, or NECESSARY REPRESENTATIVE SYNTAGONISM. In a political system, the interests of the sovereigns representing and the sub-sovereigns represented, must be towards each other, either, (1), Antagonistic, (2), Anagonistic, or, (3), Syntagonistic. They cannot be anagonistic, because the desire of power is not anagonistic.

If the interests of sovereigns and sub-sovereigns, are antagonistic; representation is not just. There is no check to power; and in a just government, every power must be checked and balanced.

The method of representation, therefore, by unification or syntagonism of interests, is that alone whose obtention, is just. This is the method of the United States South, whose warrantees are subsovereign, by necessity of the ethnical qualification, and for other causes temporary or perpetual, constant or variable.

In the method of representation by unification of interests, the sovereign people may be divided into two representative classes. Of the subsovereign people represented, the interests, may be divided into two classes. One class of subsovereign interests may be represented by one representative class of sovereigns. And the other class of interests, by the other representative class of sovereigns. Thus, the whole quantity of subsovereign interests, may be represented.

This is the method of the United States South. There, the sovereign people are divided into two classes. Warrantors are one class; nonwarrantors, the other.

Of the warrantees, the rights and interests are such as relate to either warantors or nonwarrantors. This relation must be that of syntagonism or of antagonism. But by the essence and nature of warranteeism, the rights of warrantors and warrantees are syntagonistic: there is a fundamental unification of their interests. This is as against wrongs by nonwarrantors. As against wrongs of warrantees by warrantors; the interests of warrantees and nonwarrantors are syntagonistic. Not the interests of warrantors only are antagonistic to warrantees' wrongs by warrantors; but in cumulation, the interests of nonwarrantors and of warrantees, are syntagonistic against such wrongs. By any wronger, wrong to warrantee is wrong to nonwarrantors. These are the highest checks of which a societary contrivance, is susceptible. Warrantors and warrantees, are affamiliated; the head of the family, is the warrantor. Damnification of the members is by the nature of the affamiliation, damnification of the head. Injury to warrantee in person, is injury to warrantor in property. . . .

Warrantors have therefore, the rights of legislatees; but not the privileges of legislators; because, for hygienic and other sufficient reasons, they ought not in morality to receive them: justice forbids it.

But warrantees have not such legislative rights only as are due them; they have judicial rights. Judicial rights are those which concern judicial actions and judicial testimony.

A judicial action is the right of claiming judicially what is due or belongs to one. It is a right incidental to existence-rights.

Actions are either (1), Public or (2), Private. Public actions are those brought by the State: private, by private persons. Actions are also (1), Civil or (2), Criminal. Civil actions are (1), Personal or (2), Real. In these, the claim is for something to be either paid or done, or not paid or done.

Of warrantees, the actions or claims are for redress of wrongs. Wrongers must be either the (1), warrantor, (2), other warrantees, or (3), nonwarrantors.

Claims of warrantees against non-warrantors, are brought by the warrantor or head of the association. If the judgment on the action, is vindictive, as for offences or quasi-offences; damages are awarded, according to the policy of the law for prevention. If the judgment orders payment on contract, restitution, or specific performance; the claim must have been for either (1), Wages, (2), Property, or (3), Damages. If for property or damages, it must be for associational property or associational wrong. The law therefore, appropriates such property or damages, to the association. Its representative or syndic in law, is the warrantor. He is the receiver. He distributes wages out of the aggregate capital. But if the judgment is for wages; these are appropriated to the warrantor. Because he warrants the warrantee's wages, and non-payment by non-warrantor, is the loss of the warrantor. The warrantee never loses his wages; he is warranted against loss.

If the action of the warrantee is against, not the non-warrantor but the warrantor; it must be for either wrongs to person or to property. But in warranteeism, these are public actions. The State brings them; it represents the warrantee. Thus, if the warrantor does not distribute to the warrantee his lawful wages, that is breach of the statute of wages. As such it is inquirable into and punishable by the State. So, if the warrantor administers cruel and unusual punishments, or in any way punishes excessively, that is a public wrong which the State prosecutes as any other crime or misdemeanor.

But if the action of the warrantor is to annul his labor-obligation; this is not brought by the State; it is a private action. It is brought by the warrantee.

All other suits by warrantees, are brought by the warrantor, or head of the association. All private suits against warrantees, are likewise brought against the warrantors. For all torts by warrantees, warrantors are responsible in damages. If one warrantee feloniously kills another; the warrantor is responsible in damages. If a warrantee robs or steals; damages are recoverable from the warrantor.

Another judicial right is that of the writ of Habeas Corpus. Warrantees are secured in this right. They have its effect and substance. Only the form of it, is peculiar. If a warrantee is unlawfully detained by one, other than his warrantor; suit for his release is brought by the warrantor, to whom his service is lost. But if the warrantor himself unlawfully detains or imprisons the warrantee, the warrantor is responsible to the State for a public wrong. Whether a writ of Habeas Corpus would lie, or what would be the nature of the remedy is not now clear. That is accidental matter for legislation, and progress.

In other courts than that of the warrantor, warrantees have the right of Appeal as other parties before courts. In the warrantor's court, warrantees have the right of appeal from the deputy-warrantor. But from judgment by the warrantor in person, no appeal is allowed. This is because (1), The jurisdiction of the warrantor is small, and because (2), The allowance of appeals now, would be in derogation of the public industry. The right is not allowed, because the allowance would be wrong. But before the court of the warranty, it is the duty of the warrantor presiding, to hear all the testimony and pleadings before rendition of judgement. Re-hearings, continuances, and new trials, are to be granted. In this court, all the fundamental rules and necessary forms, for the administration of justice, are to be observed: for warrantors are judges, and judgments must be righteous.

The power of warrantees to testify in open court, is accidental. If expedient, it may be allowed. If their competency to testify, is more conducive to justice than their incompetency; they must be allowed to testify. Their testimony is now inadmissible against those only of the sovereign race. Warrantees testify for or against warrantees. They are peers.

Warrantees have, therefore, the substance and effect of the right of Action. That is essential. What may be the mode of exercising it; how it shall be performed; that is accidental.

The right of Petitioning for redress of grievances, is secured to warrantees. They enjoy the effect and substance of the right. The mode or form of its execution, is peculiar to warranteeism with the ethnical qualification. By the essence of warranteeism, the interests of warrantors and warrantees, are affamiliated; they are syntagonistic; they are family interests. Grievance to warrantees, is grievance to warrantors; as grievance to wife is grievance to husband. Warrantors and warrantees, are wedded in interest. The sovereign warrantor is therefore, the petitioner for redress of all grievances by others than himself.

Grievances by the warrantor, are such as are either against public law, or are not. If against public law; the State redresses them. If not against public law; the petition is for new laws declaratory, enabling, restraining or remedial.

Here it is not clear what is the form in which the right of petition should be substantiated. Nor ought this to be hastily determined. It is not well settled what justice and policy require. Justice affirms the substance of the right; but denies some forms of its execution. Right and expediency to both races are consistent. Justice and expediency to the sub-sovereign, cannot be by injustice or inexpediency, to the sovereign race. This is wrong. It must always be forbidden.

For redress of grievances by their warrantor, the warrantees may petition either by (1), Themselves, or by (2), Others. Their personal petitioning is more or less unjust and inexpedient; because it is more or less amalgamative. Petitioning by others, in the place of warrantees, is a method either sufficient or deficient, as it now is. By the method as it now is, petitioning is by any of the sovereigns. This is the general vicarious method. Wrong or grievance to warrantee is wrong to some of the sovereign people. It is in derogation of either the public peace, industry, health, or trade. If a wrong

266

to warrantees, it is a wrong to either warrantors or non-warrantors. Such grievance is either economic, political, hygienic, philosophic, esthetic, moral, or religious. Whatever is its kind; it is by the nature of warranteeism, a grievance as well to non-warrantors and warrantors as to warrantees. There is a syntagonism. Grievance to sub-sovereigns, is grievance to some sovereigns. The sovereigns therefore, petition. The other method is that of special vicarious petitioning. This, by the appointment of a special representative of warrantees, with sufficient responsibilities and inducements. Than these two methods of general and special vicarious petitioning, there can be no others.

Petitioning is a right of legislatees. The right of having and using Arms for self-defence, belongs to executees. By the Common-Law of England, this is secondary or incidental to absolute rights. Warrantees have the right. But it is subject to the effects of the ethnical qualification, and the nature of associations. In the warrantee association, warrantees have not the right of having arms proper to themselves. Because arms are association-property. They belong to the association and are therefore administered by the administrator or head of the association. The warrantor orders the association not for its subsistence only, but for its protection. The arms of the association are therefore subject to his order. Warrantees have not the right to have and use arms as against the warrantor; because he is their officer or magistrate and represents the majesty of the State. The entire warranty is the precincts of his court. But as against other warrantees, if the necessity arose, warrantees would have the right of using and having arms. So, if about to leave the protection of the warranty and go into strange, dangerous, and unfrequented places, they would have the right. In what cases, they would have it, as against sovereign non-warrantors, is not yet well settled, except in the case of overt felony, as to prevent murder.

The relations of legislatees, adjudicatees, and executees, to legislators, adjudicators, and executives, are public. By the Common-Law of England, private relations are those of master and servant, husband and wife, parent and child, guardian and ward.

In warranteeism, the relation of warrantor and warrantee, is not that of master and servant. It is not a private relation. It is the relation of magistrate and people. It is a public relation. This is the essence of warranteeism.

267

It is the fundamental difference between warrantee and free-labor organizations. Warrantors are not private masters. They are public masters, orderers or magistrates. Their rights, duties, powers, and responsibilities, are adapted and regulated by law. They are not in derogation but in favor, and of necessity, to the conservation and progress of all, and their inalienable rights of life, liberty, and property.

Marriage is both (1), a Civil contract and (2), a Religious union. Of the civil contract, the objects, are amongst other things the administration of the wife's property, the protection of her person, and the maintenance, education, and protection of the children. By the Common Law, "the holiness of the matrimonial state, is left entirely to the ecclesiastical law; the temporal courts not having jurisdiction to consider unlawful marriage as a sin, but merely as a civil inconvenience." In this light, the law treats it, as it does all other contracts. . . .

In the United States South, the marriage of warrantees is not a perfect civil contract. It is a religious union, and a natural obligation. In warranteeism, all marriages of warrantees performed by a minister of religion, or under the ceremonies of the Church, are lawful. This constitutes in law, a natural obligation. Whether the consent of both parties, willing and able to consent; with a public and overt acknowledgment of each other, as husband and wife, would constitute a valid marriage, is not certain; but it seems that it would. What should be the effect in law, of the natural obligation of the marriage; whether the State should intervene and make it a perfect civil contract; whether it should regulate the law of divorce or leave it free; whether bigamy and adultery of warrantees, should be civilly punished; or whether as now, the Church instead of the State, should have complete jurisdiction of the marriage of warrantees, is matter for development by progress. Sundering of husband and wife, except for subsistence, is a public wrong, and to be remedied, if needful. As warranteeism now is, marriage of warrantees is not a perfect civil contract; it is a natural or moral obligation, and a religious union. Any other voluntary intercourse of the sexes, is or is not, in law, a crime or misdemeanor.

The relation of parent and child, is not in warranteeism, as in the Common Law, economic. The parents do not divide wages with the children. They do not maintain them. The association is the economic father of the children. Such duties only as result from nature belong, in warranteeism, to the parents. But to the natural relation all the natural rights are coupled.

The parents cannot be separated from their children. Children cannot be disobedient or disrespectful. The parents have the right of correction.

Wherefore;—in the United States South warrantees have all their rights. Wrongs are accidental and remediable. Warranteeism is an economic, political, and hygienic organization. It is consistent with morality and religion. It is necessitated by them. It is a duty of humanity, justice, and order. Its justice is inherent, self-executing, and positive. . . .

In the economic system of the Free-labor form of societary organization, order is not ordained and established. Association, adaptation, and regulation are free. They are not essential; they are accidental. They are not fundamental. They are not publicly instituted. The relation of capitalist and laborer, or of master and servant, is private. Their interests are not syntagonistic.

Systematic quantitative adaptation of laborers and capital, is not actualized. Laborers are not appreciated. They have not the value produced by circulation; the value of local production from where they are not in demand to where they are. To the capitalists, superficiency or excess of laborers, is desirable; because more than a sufficiency, is more orderly.

Distribution is not by the function of justice or the State. It is accidental. The distributor may be either the capitalist or the laborer. Their interests are antagonistic. Their antagonisms are not equipollent. Injustice is actualized. Wages may vary below the standard of comfortable sufficiency. Inefficients are not warranted subsistence. None are warranted. Want is not eliminated. Wages are variable to unhealthy, criminal, and mortal want. The young, the old, and other inefficients are supported not by the capital of capitalists, but by the wages of the laborers. The amount of these wages, is not adapted to the amount of the consumers; there is no discrimination. Pauperism is not eliminated.

The consumption of laborers is not the least possible. The capitalist has no preservation-interest in the laborer. Loss of a laborer is not the capitalist's loss.

Subsistence is not warranted to the laborers; neither is work or the means of subsistence.

In the Free-labor hygienic system, hygienic necessaries are not an element of laborers' wages. Capital is not supplied for the production of his health. The capitalist is not hygienically syntagonistic. Medicine, medical atten-

dance, nursing, and therapeutical necessaries, are not warranted to laborers. They are not treasured. Their sickness or death, is not a direct economic injury to the capitalist.

In the Free-labor political system, the interests of classes are not syntagonistic. Taxes are not an element of wages paid by the capitalist. Crime
from economic causes, is not eliminated. There are no economic methods,
for the prevention of offences. There are no economic general and special
securities. The magistracy are expensive and political only. The rich and
poor, conflict. Agrarianism is not eliminated. The fundamental laws for the
public health, public peace, public industry and public subsistence, are not
executed. The interest is deficient, and the order. Strikes and riots are not
eliminated. The expediencies of the political system, are political only; the
economic system is not civilly ordained and established. It is not a civil
implement.

Both Free-labor and Warrantee forms of society, are progressive. Free-labor progress is a progress by antagonisms. Warrantee progress is a progress
by syntagonisms. The Free-labor form of society, must be abolished; it must
progress to the form of mutual-insurance or warranteeism. It must progress
from immunity to community. It must necessitate association. It must warrant the existence and progress of all. Men must not be free-laborers; they
must be LIBERTY-LABORERS. LIBERTY MUST BE THE SUBSTITUTE OF FREE-
LABOR. That must be abolished. But the abolition must not be sudden, or
disorderly. It must not be that kind of abolition, which is mere destruction.
It must be canonical. It must be humane, just, truthful, pure, and orderly;
the envelopment of the evil, by the development of the good.

The economic system in the United States South, is not slavery. IT IS WAR-
RANTEEISM WITH THE ETHNICAL QUALIFICATION. It is just. It is expedient. It
is progressive. It does not progress by antagonisms. It progresses by syntagonisms. It is in no way slavery. Religiously, it is Ebedism; economically,
Warranteeism. The consummation of its progress, is the perfection of
society.

And when in other generations, this progress, which is now a conception
and a hope of all, shall be a memory and a fact; when what is now in the
future, shall be in the present or the past; when the budding poetry of the
all-hoping sociologist, shall ripen to a fruitful history; that history will be
thrice felicitous; for it shall unroll the trophied poem, the rhapsody of a

270

progress epic in its grandeur; pastoral in its peace; and lyric in its harmony. Such shall be its fulfilment. And then on leagued plantations over the sun-sceptred zone's crop-jeweled length, myriad eyes, both night-faced and morning-cheeked, shall brighten still the patriot's student glance and fondly pore upon the full-grown and fate-favored wonder of a Federal banner in whose woven sky of ensign orbs, shall be good stars only, in such happy constellations that their bonds and beams, will be sweeter than the sweet influences of the Pleiades, and stronger than the bands of Orion; unbroken constellations—a symbol sky—a heaven which also, shall declare the glory of God, and a firmament which shall show His handiwork. Then, in the plump flush of full-feeding health, the happy warrantees shall banquet in PLANTATION-REFECTORIES; worship in PLANTATION-CHAPELS; learn in PLANTATION-SCHOOLS; or, in PLANTATION-SALOONS, at the cool of evening, or in the green and bloomy gloom of cold catalpas and magnolias, chant old songs, tell tales; or, to the metred rattle of chattering castanets, or flutes, or rumbling tamborines, dance down the moon and evening star; and after slumbers in PLANTATION-DORMITORIES, over whose gates Health and Rest sit smiling at the feet of Wealth and Labor, rise at the music-crowing of the morning-conchs, to begin again welcome days of jocund toil, in reeling fields, where, weak with laughter and her load, Plenty yearly falls, gives up, and splits her o'erstuffed horn, and where behind twin Interest's double throne, Justice stands at reckoning dusk, and rules supreme. When these and more than these, shall be the fulfilment of Warranteeism; then shall this Federation and the World, praise the power, wisdom, and goodness of a system, which may well be deemed divine; then shall Experience aid Philosophy, and VINDICATE THE WAYS OF GOD, TO MAN.

VII. GEORGE FITZHUGH
Southern Thought

"... to defend and justify mere negro slavery, and condemn other forms of slavery, is to give up expressly the whole cause of the South."

George Fitzhugh was born in 1804 in Prince William County, Virginia. Although he was descended from one of Virginia's oldest and most prominent families, Fitzhugh himself was never prosperous. The agricultural decline of the 1820s forced the sale of the family plantation, and Fitzhugh received almost no formal education. Self-taught, he was admitted to the bar and entered the practice of law in Port Royal, a country town near Fredericksburg.[1]

Preoccupied with local and personal concerns, Fitzhugh for years rarely traveled outside his own neighborhood and played little role in public life. In 1849, however, with the publication of *Slavery Justified, by a Southerner*,[2] this isolation ended. During the next decade, Fitzhugh produced an extraordinary stream of writing on the social issues of his day. He became a regular editorialist for the Richmond *Enquirer* and a frequent contributor to *De Bow's Review*, for which he wrote more than one hundred articles. Fitzhugh's greatest renown, however, arose from his publication of two of the best-known volumes on the slavery question, *Sociology for the South; or the Failure of Free Society* and *Cannibals All! or Slaves Without Masters*.[3]

1. Twentieth-century historians have written extensively on Fitzhugh. See, for example, Eugene Genovese, *The World the Slaveholders Made: Two Essays in Interpretation* (New York: Pantheon, 1969); Louis Hartz, *The Liberal Tradition in America* (New York: Harcourt, Brace, and World, 1955), Chapters VI and VII; Harvey Wish, *George Fitzhugh: Propagandist of the Old South* (Baton Rouge: Louisiana State University Press, 1943); C. Vann Woodward, "George Fitzhugh: *Sui Generis*," in George Fitzhugh, *Cannibals All! or Slaves Without Masters*, ed. C. Vann Woodward (Cambridge: John Harvard Library, 1960).

2. George Fitzhugh, *Slavery Justified, by a Southerner* (Fredericksburg, Va.: *Recorder* Job Office, 1851). See also George Fitzhugh, *What Shall be Done with the Free Negroes?* (Fredericksburg, Va.: *Recorder* Job Office, 1851).

3. George Fitzhugh, *Sociology for the South; or the Failure of Free Society* (Richmond: A.

In 1856 Fitzhugh made a lecture tour of the North, where his professed support for white as well as black slavery attracted horrified attention. Despite his public success, Fitzhugh was constantly pressed for funds to meet the needs of his growing family, and he urged friends to find him a remunerative government post that would support him while he continued to write on the South's behalf. With the inauguration of Buchanan, Fitzhugh received a minor appointment in the office of the attorney general and moved to Washington.

When the Civil War broke out, Fitzhugh returned to Port Royal. Menaced by marauding troops, he soon departed with his family to Richmond, where he secured a livelihood as a minor government functionary. After the Confederate defeat, Fitzhugh moved to a post at the Freedman's Bureau, the department of the Union army responsible for protection and relief of the former slaves. Fitzhugh took up his pen in protest against the conditions of Reconstruction and the horrors of emancipation. Although he had consistently argued before the war that race was no justification for slavery, his postbellum writings expressed a virulent racism.

In 1866 his employment with the Freedman's Bureau ended, and Fitzhugh returned to his war-ravaged home in Port Royal. For the remaining years of his life, he was plagued by poverty. After 1870 his publications ceased, and he died in 1881 after a long period of illness and growing incapacitation.

"Southern Thought" appeared as two articles in *De Bow's Review* in 1857. In them, Fitzhugh both summarized his own proslavery position and commented upon the defense of human bondage as it had evolved in the South during the preceding two and a half decades.[4] Although the region had earlier "had no thought," Fitzhugh proclaimed, she had begun at last to understand her system of domestic slavery as the most desirable and benevolent of social arrangements. Having rejected the social contractual theories of Locke and the "absurd" and "dangerous" principles of the Declaration of Independence, southern slaveholders had begun to find that they lived in the "most prosperous and happy country in the world."

But Fitzhugh called upon the South to go still further in her ideological

---

Morris, 1854); George Fitzhugh, *Cannibals All! or Slaves Without Masters* (Richmond: A. Morris, 1857).

4. George Fitzhugh, "Southern Thought," *De Bow's Review*, XXIII (1857), 338–50, and George Fitzhugh, "Southern Thought Again," *ibid.*, XXIII (1857), 449–62.

progress, to recognize the implications of the positions she had already taken by mounting an all-out attack on free society. Slavery, he insisted, could not be effectively defended for blacks alone. The proslavery argument must not only justify the southern system, but should actively condemn the arrangements of free labor in the North and elsewhere. "Domestic slavery must be vindicated in the abstract, and in the general, as normal, natural, and, *in general* necessitous element of civilized society, without regard to race or color." Human bondage, Fitzhugh argued, was an ideal form of social security, ensuring subsistence to all and eliminating the poverty and suffering experienced by free laborers of England and the industrialized North. The murderous competition endemic to capitalist or "free" society must be replaced by a system that established common interests between employer and worker, as slavery did through the master's ownership of the slave.

Fitzhugh readily acknowledged in these articles for *De Bow's* that southern opinion did not in general coincide with his radical position; he recognized and criticized a proslavery mainstream that did not take as "general" or as "abstract" a stance as his own. Fitzhugh sought here, as throughout his writing, to dramatize the contradictions in southern thought—and in the proslavery argument—and thereby compel others to accept his resolution of these inconsistencies. Working from the proslavery theories accepted by his fellow southerners, Fitzhugh pushed these assumptions to their logical extreme, then demanded that the South confront and accept the implications of her position. But most southerners were reluctant to take such an uncompromising stance, for Fitzhugh's conclusions embodied a challenge to the intellectual and social *status quo* that most of the South was unwilling seriously to entertain.[5]

Southern Thought

Twenty years ago the South had no thought—no opinions of her own. Then she stood behind all christendom, admitted her social structure, her habits, her economy, and her industrial pursuits to be wrong, deplored

---

5. See, for example, De Bow's review of Fitzhugh, "Cannibals All! or Slaves without Masters," *De Bow's Review*, XXII (1857), 543–49, in which he hailed Fitzhugh as a daring thinker but expressed reservations about Fitzhugh's attacks on existing social arrangements. For other southern attacks on Fitzhugh, see G. C. Grammer, "Failure of Free Society," *De Bow's Review*,

them as a necessity, and begged pardon for their existence. Now she is about to lead the thought and direct the practices of christendom; for christendom sees and admits that she has acted a silly and suicidal part in abolishing African slavery—the South a wise and prudent one in retaining it. France and England, who fairly represent the whole of so-called free society, are actively engaged in the slave-trade under more odious and cruel forms than were ever known before. They must justify their practices; and, to do so, must adopt and follow Southern thought. This, of itself, would put the South at the lead of modern civilization.

In the sneering ridicule of the false and fallacious philanthropy of Lord Brougham by the London Times, the leading paper of Western Europe, we see that they are breaking ground to condemn and repudiate the "rosewater philanthropy" of Clarkson, Wilbeforce, Howard, and Hannah More, that nursed scoundrels and savages at the expense of the honest, industrious, laboring whites.

The next inevitable step will be to approve and vindicate the conduct of Hercules, and Moses, and Joshua, and the discoverers and settlers of America, who have conquered, enslaved, and exterminated savages, just as fast as might be necessary to make room for free civilized whites. This is the only philosophy that can justify the subjugation of Algiers or the hundred southern conquests and annexations of England; and this philosophy is consistent with Southern thought and practices, but wholly at war with the maudlin sentimentality of Hannah More, Wilbeforce, and Lord Brougham. Southern thought alone can justify European practices, and Southern practices alone save Western Europe from universal famine; for cotton, sugar, rice, molasses, and other slave products are intolerably dear and intolerably scarce, and France and England must have slaves to increase their production, or starve. They have begun to follow in our wake, instead of our humbly imitating them. It is true they are still impertinent and presumptious, and loud in their abuse of our form of slavery, whilst they are busily adopting worse forms. But the veil of hypocrisy with which they would conceal their conduct is too transparent to avail them long. Besides, they can use no arguments to justify their conduct that will not equally justify ours. In any

---

XIX (1855), 29–38; George Frederick Holmes, "Failure of Free Society," *Southern Literary Messenger*, XXI (1855), 129; E. Etheridge, Speech of the Honorable Representative from Tennessee in the House of Representatives, February 21, 1857, *Congressional Globe*, 34th Cong., 3rd Sess., App.

view of the subject Southern thought and Southern example must rule the world.

The South has acted wisely and prudently, acted according to the almost universal usage of civilized mankind, and the injunctions of the Bible, and she is about to gather her reward for so doing. She flourishes like the bay tree, whilst Europe starves, and she is as remarkable for her exemption from crime as her freedom from poverty. She is by far, very far, the most prosperous and happy country in the world. Her jealous and dependent rivals have begun to imitate her. They must soon openly approve her course in order to vindicate themselves.

But there is no narrow philosophy to justify slavery. No human or divine authority to vindicate mere negro slavery as an exceptional institution. All the authority is the other way. White slavery, not black, has been the normal element of civilized society. It is true that the authorities and the philosophy which approve white slavery, are still stronger authorities in favor of negro slavery, for the principle and the practices of mankind in the general have been to make inferior races and individuals slaves to their superiors. How fortunate for the South that she has this inferior race, which enables her to make the whites a privileged class, and to exempt them from all servile, menial, and debasing employments.

But we must force the reluctant admission from Western Europe that the emancipation of the white serfs or villians was a far more cruel failure, so far as those serfs were concerned, than West India emancipations. In truth, the admission is made in fact, though not in form, in almost every review, newspaper, and work of fiction, that emanates from the press of Western Europe or our North. They concur in describing the emancipated whites as starving from year to year, and from generation to generation, whilst nobody pretends that the liberated negroes of the West Indies are starving. As for crime and ignorance, we suspect that the laboring liberated poor of Western Europe may well claim to rival, if not surpass, the negroes of Jamaica. But the liberated whites work harder and cheaper as freemen, or rather as slaves to capital, than they did as serfs; and, therefore, the rich who employ them think white emancipation a successful experiment, a glorious change for the better. Because, although it starves and brings to untimely graves some half million of the laboring poor annually, it nevertheless makes labor cheaper, and increases the profits of the rich.

We despise this flood of crocodile tears which England is shedding over

276

the free negroes of the West Indies, whilst she has not one tear to shed on account of her laboring poor at home, who are ten times worse off than the free negroes.

In the absence of negro slavery there must be white slavery, else the white laboring class are remitted to slavery to capital, which is much more cruel and exacting than domestic slavery.

Southern thought must justify the slavery principle, justify slavery as natural, normal, and necessitous. He who justifies mere negro slavery, and condemns other forms of slavery, does not think at all—no, not in the least. To prove that such men do not think, we have only to recur to the fact that they always cite the usages of antiquity and the commands of the Bible to prove that negro slavery is right. Now if these usages and commands prove anything, they prove that all kinds of slavery are right.

By Southern thought, we mean a Southern philosophy, not excuses, apologies, and palliations.

The South has much work before her, for to justify her own social system, she will have to disprove and refute the whole social, ethical, political, and economical philosophy of the day. These philosophies have grown up in societies whose social relations are different from hers, and are intended to enforce and justify those relations. They all inculcate selfishness and competition as the great duties of man, and success in getting the better of our fellow beings in the war of the wits as the chiefest, if not the only merit. The opposite or protective philosophy, which takes care of the weak whilst it governs them, is the philosophy of the South.

The free trade or competitive philosophy is an admitted failure, and most of the literature of Europe is employed in exposing and condemning it. From the writings of the socialists, (and almost everybody is a socialist in Western Europe,) we can derive both facts and arguments quite sufficient to upset the whole moral philosophy of the day. From the Bible and Aristotle we can deduce (added to our own successful experiment) quite enough to build up a new philosophy on the ruins of the present false and vicious system.

The South is fulfilling her destiny and coming up to her work beautifully. She is multiplying her academies, her colleges, and her universities, and they are all well patronised and conducted by able professors. Several of these professors have written works defending slavery with great ability, on general and scientific principles. All of them are true to Southern institutions.

From these schools thousands of educated and influential men annually proceed to every quarter of the South. They will mould and control thought and opinion, whether they settle down as private citizens or become editors, lawyers, divines, or politicians.

Female schools and colleges are also rapidly increasing in numbers, and this is an important gain, for it is the mother who first affects opinions, and it is difficult in after life to get rid even of erroneous principles which have been taught by the mother in the nursery. It is not safe, wise, or prudent, to commit the education of our daughters to Northern schools, nor to female teachers brought from the North.

Fashion is one of the most powerful engines in controlling opinion, and fashion will soon cease to be borrowed from the North. Southern watering places are full to overflowing, and few go to the North to be insulted by the helps in their hotels. These Southern watering places annually bring together intelligent and influential persons from the various States of the South, who form friendships, unite various sections in stronger bonds of amity, and confirm each other in the support of Southern institutions, by comparison and concurrence of opinion. People do not like to be out of the fashion in thought any more than in dress, and hence the prevalent anti-slavery doctrines at Northern watering places, must exercise a baleful and dangerous influence on Southerners who visit them.

The educational conventions held in various parts of the South exercise a similar influence to our watering places, but a far more important and potent one, for they are attended by the ablest men in the nation, whose every day business, duty, and occupation, is to form opinion, and to inaugurate a Southern thought. The importance of these conventions in cutting us off from imitative allegiance to the North and to Europe can hardly be overrated. Nay, they will do more; they will teach our revilers to respect, admire, and imitate us, by the unanswerable facts and arguments which they will adduce to justify our institutions.

Another fact for congratulation to the South is, that our people are beginning to write books—to build up a literature of our own. This is an essential prerequisite to the establishment of independence of thought amongst us. All Northern and European books teach abolition either directly or indirectly. The indirect method is more dangerous than the direct one. It consists in inculcating doctrines at war with slavery, without expressly assailing

278

the institution. Now, all authors who write about law, religion, politics, ethics, social or political economy, if not pro-slavery men themselves, are continually inculcating doctrines accordant with their own social forms, and therefore at war with ours. Hence it follows, that all books in the whole range of moral science, if not written by Southern authors, within the last twenty or thirty years, inculcate abolition either directly or indirectly. If written before that time, even by Southern authors, they are likely to be as absurd and as dangerous as the Declaration of Independence, or the Virginia Bill of Rights.

It is all important that we should write our own books. It matters little who makes our shoes. Indeed, the South will commit a fatal blunder, if, in its haste to become nominally independent, it loses its present engines of power, and thereby ceases to be really independent. Cotton is king; and rice, sugar, Indian corn, wheat, and tobacco, are his chief ministers. It is our great agricultural surplus that gives us power, commands respect, and secures independence. The world is pinched now for agricultural products. The rebellion in India will increase the scarcity. Then, take away our surplus from the world's supply, and famine and nakedness would be the consequence. We should not jeopard this great lever of power in the haste to become, like Englishmen, shop-keepers, cobblers, and common carriers for the universe. Our present pursuits are more honorable, more lucrative, and more generative of power and independence than those we fondly aspire to. We cannot do double work. If we become a commercial and manufacturing people, we must cease to be an agricultural one, or at least we shall cease to have an agricultural surplus. We should become as feeble, as isolated and contemptible as Chinese or Japanese. Actual independence would be bartered off for formal independence, which no one would respect. An increase in our commerce and manufactures, so gradual as not to affect the amount of our agricultural surplus, would be desirable, provided that increase never extends so far as to make us a commercial and manufacturing people. That we can be all three is one of the most palpable absurdities ever conceived by the human brain. Foreigners cannot buy from us unless we buy an equivalent amount from them. If they should do so, our agricultural surplus would absorb the whole currency of the world in less than a century, and we should be oppressed with a plethora of money that would necessitate the carrying about a cart-load of silver to buy an ox.

279

We can afford to let foreigners be our cobblers, and carriers, and trades-men for a while longer, but we cannot safely delay writing our own books for an hour.

In Congress, and in the courts of Europe, in the conflict of debate, and in the war of diplomacy, Southerners have always shown themselves the equals, generally the superiors, of the first intellects of the world. This is easily accounted for.

All true power, whether in speaking, writing, or fighting, proceeds quite as much from strength of will as from power of mind or body; and no men have half the strength of will that Southerners possess. We are accustomed to command from our cradle. To command becomes a want and a necessity of our nature, and this begets that noble strength of will that nerves the mind for intellectual conflict and intellectual exertion, just as it nerves the body for physical contest. We are sure to write well, because we shall write boldly, fearlessly, and energetically.

We have already made a start. A great many Southern books have been written within the last three or four years. They are almost all distinguished by that boldness of thought, and close and energetic logic, which character-izes the Southern mind. The North surpasses us in taste and imagination, equals us in learning, but is far behind us in logic. No doubt our greater intensity of will gives us this advantage, for in no intellectual effort is force of will so absolutely necessary as in moral reasoning. It is the most difficult intellectual exercise, and therefore the most perfect self-control and self-command are required to nerve to high effort in this direction.

Several of our distinguished professors are employed in preparing school books for academies and common schools, and text books for our colleges. It is all important to "teach the young idea how to shoot," and to give it, in early life, a Southern bent. We have been guilty of great remissness on this subject, but we shall speedily repair it, and soon no more school books from Europe or the North will be seen south of Mason's and Dixon's line.

Last, not least, of the causes, in busy operation to beget a Southern thought, are our annual commercial conventions. We have little practical acquaintance with trade or commerce, and do not know that conventions can direct industry, or control trade, any more than they can stop or divert the tide. We shrewdly suspect, however, that despite of conventions, private individuals will direct their industry and invest their capital in such manner as they think most profitable. Nay, more—we are so irreverent as to believe that each man is the best judge in such matters for himself. Besides, we think it far more dignified to let a starving and naked world come to our Egyptian granaries, as Joseph's brethren came to him, than for us to be hawking, peddling, and drumming like Englishmen through the universe. The character of drummer, hawker, and peddler, does not suit Southern taste or Southern talent. We have no turn whatever for swapping, drumming, and bargaining; and if we went from home with our products, might get cheated out of our eyes. Besides, we should neglect our crops, and in a short time would have nothing to employ our commerce.

But poorly as we think of these conventions as commercial stimulants or agencies, we know that they are invaluable as a means, and by far the most potent means, of uniting the South, begetting a common public opinion, and preparing us for any crisis or emergency that may arise. Let the South but be prepared and united, and her rights will always be respected, and the Union secure. But apathy and inertness beget aggression; and any further aggression by the North will precipitate disunion. The cup of our endurance is filled to the brim.

These conventions are composed of able, patriotic, and conservative men. Their proceeding, though firm, are calm, dignified, and moderate. They represent Southern feeling and opinion correctly, and excluding Russia, the South is the only conservative section of civilized christendom. The democracy of the North, it is true, are conservative, but there Black Republicanism is in the ascendant, and that is radical and revolutionary in the extreme. The Pope of Rome is a radical reformer. Louis Napoleon and Victoria are half-way socialists, and Henry the Fifth, the Bourbon heir to the French throne, is a thorough socialist. So desperate is the condition of the people throughout Western Europe, that no one in power dare tell them that there shall be no change, that all things shall remain as they are. The South is the only conservative section of christendom, because it is the only section satisfied with its own condition. Every where else, except in our North, the people are suffering intolerable ills, and ripe, at any moment, for revolution. There is no occasion for radicalism and revolutionary spirit at the North. Next to the South, it is the most prosperous, and should be the most contented country in the world. All of its discontent, and its political, moral, and religious heresies have grown out of abolition. Men who begin by assailing

281

negro slavery find that all government begets slavery in some form, and hence all abolitionists are socialists, who propose to destroy all the institutions of society.

That slavery to capital, so intolerable in densely settled countries, where lands are monopolised by the few, can never be felt at the North, until our vast possessions in the West are peopled to the Pacific, and a refluent population begins to pour back upon the East. Then, like Western Europe, the North would have a laboring population slaves to capital, "slaves without masters." Famine would become perennial, and revolution the common order of the day, as in Western Europe. Nay, the condition of the laboring class of the North-east, would be far worse than in Europe, because there would be no checks to competition, no limitations to the despotism of capital over labor. The spirit of trade and commerce is universal, and it is as much the business of trade to devour the poor, as of the whales to swallow herrings. All its profits are derived from unjust exacting or "exploitation" of the common poor laboring class; for the professional and capitalist, and skilful laboring classes, manage to exact five times as much from the poor, as they pay to the tradesmen in way of profit. The poor produce everything and enjoy nothing. The people of the North are hugging to their breasts a silly delusion, in the belief that the poor can tax the rich, and thus prevent those evils that are starving and maddening the masses in Western Europe. You can't tax a rich man unless he be a slave-holder, because he produces nothing. You can't tax property, except in slave society, because it does not breed or produce anything itself. Labor pays all taxes, pays the rich man's income, educates his children, pays the professional man's fees, the merchant's profits, and pays all the taxes which support the Government; a property tax must take a part of the property proposed to be taxed, and such a tax never will be imposed; a property tax would soon divest all men of their property.

Gerrit Smith said most truly in Congress: "The poor pay all taxes, we (meaning the rich) are the mere conduits who pass them over to government." This was the noblest and the grandest truth that ever was uttered on the floor of legislative hall. It is this awful truth that is shaking free society to its base, and it will never recover from the shock. 'Tis now tottering to its fall. Property and not labor is taxed in slave society. 'Tis true the negro produces the wherewithal to pay the tax, but he loses nothing by it. Neither his food or his raiment are abridged. Both humanity and self-interest prevent the master from lowering his wages. The master pays the tax by abridging his own expenses. He has less of food and raiment, not the slave. The capitalist charges higher rents and profits to meet increased taxation, and lives as expensively as ever. The employer reduces the wages of his laborers for the same purpose, and dines and sups as luxuriously as ever.

Labor pays all taxes, but labor in slave society is property, and men will take care of their property. In free society, labor is not property, and there is nothing to shield the laborer from the grinding weight of taxation—all of which he pays, because he produces everything valuable.

We have made this digression to show that if the North ever becomes densely settled, there is no mode of escaping from the evils of free competition and from the taxing power or exploitation of skill and capital. In Europe, competition is not so fierce, the spirit of trade not so universal. They have still kings, nobles, and established churches, stripped, it is true of their fair proportions, reduced somewhat to the semblance of shadowy "phantasms;" yet, still, as the natural friends of the poor, interposing some check to the unfeeling exactions of the landholder, the tradesman, and the employer. In the palmy days of royalty, of feudal nobility, and of catholic rule, there were no poor in Europe. Every man had his house and his home, and both his brave and his pious protectors. The baron and the priest vied with each other in their care of the vassal. This was feudal slavery; and what is modern liberty? Why, quietly, slowly, almost insensibly, the poor have been turned over from the parental and protective rule of kings, barons, and churchmen, to the unfeeling despotism of capitalists, employers, usurers, and extortioners; and this was called emancipation!

Although, in the event of a dense population cooped up in the North, without means of escape, the evils which we have depicted, would occur more virulently there than in Europe; yet, it is not worth while to anticipate evils that may never happen. The North is now doing well. Her poor are not the slaves of capital, and never will be whilst there are vacant lands in the North. Population does not always increase. It has its ebbs and flows. Very large countries, such as America, are not likely to be overstocked with inhabitants. Secret causes at work will diminish population in some sections, whilst it is increasing in others. The situation of the North is natural, healthful, and progressive, but for the abolitionists and other agrarian isms. 'Tis treason in them to disturb society by the unnecessary agitation of questions as to contingent and future evils. But this is not their only treason. They propose, in their conventions, to dissolve the Union, not for any evils with which it afflicts them, but because the South hold slaves. Now, Black Republicans, who are under the rule of abolitionists, if not all abolitionists themselves, are radical and revolutionary in their doctrines, and dangerous to the Union; whilst Southern Commercial Conventions are composed entirely of men of the opposite character, of enlightened conservatives.

We differ from what are called the extremists of the South; but would not shoot down the sentinels of our camp. If not the wisest, most far-seeing, and most prudent, they are the most zealous friends of the South. They believe, that eventually, the aggressions of Northern abolition will force disunion upon us, and look to disunion as probably the only ultimate redress for the wrongs inflicted on us. We think a victory may yet, perhaps, be won by the South, not by arms, but by Southern thought and European necessities. Thought, by means of the press and the mail, has now become almost omnipotent. It rules the world. Thought, with hunger and nakedness to prompt, stimulate, and direct it, will prove irresistable. That thought has commenced and begotten a counter-current in Europe, that impels France to renew the slave-trade under a new form, and induced a debate in the British Parliament which evinces a universal change of opinion as to abolition and squints most obviously towards the renewal of the slave-trade. Revolutions of opinion do not go backwards, nor do they stand still in a half-way course. England sees, admits, and deplores the error of West India emancipation. This admission is but a step in a chain of argument, which must ultimately carry her further from abolition, and bring her nearer to slavery. For a while, she will try to maintain some middle ground between emancipation and slavery, and substitute coolies, and African apprentices, for negro slaves. But there are two reasons why she cannot long occupy this ground. First, its falsity and hypocrisy are too obvious; and secondly, coolies and apprentices do not answer the purpose of slaves. Her necessities will compel her to reinstate African slavery in its old and mildest form. Thus will Southern thought triumph, Southern morality be vindicated, and Southern wisdom, prudence, and foresight, be rendered apparent. The crusades lasted for a century. Those who conducted them had stronger convictions, and a clearer sense of duty, than modern abolitionists, for they laid down their lives by the million in the cause, whilst modern abolitionists, from Wilbeforce to Greely, have not evinced the slightest taste for martyrdom. All Europe then believed the crusades a righteous and holy undertaking. Abolition has never commanded such universal assent, nor such self-denying sacrifices. So far from marching a thousand or more miles to fight for their cause, they have not been willing to give up a cup of coffee, an ounce of sugar, or a pound of cotton, to speed it; no, they have been encouraging slavery, whilst abusing it, by consuming slave products. Europe and the North can any day abolish slavery by disusing slave products. They should try the experiment, for should they succeed in abolishing it, they will have none of those products thereafter—Jamaica and Hayti prove this.

The crusades lasted for a century, and their signal failure opened men's eyes to the folly and wickedness of such expeditions; and soon men began to wonder at the infatuation of their crusading ancestry. So it will be with abolition. It has lasted nearly a hundred years. It has failed as signally as the crusades, and brought hunger and nakedness on its votaries, or at least on the laboring poor at their doors. As in the case of the crusades, abolition will soon be considered a mad infatuation—for want, brought on by it, combines with failure, to open men's eyes.

Southern thought must be a distinct thought—not a half thought, but a whole thought. Domestic slavery must be vindicated in the abstract, and in the general, as a normal, natural, and, *in general*, necessitous element of civilized society, without regard to race or color.

This argument about races is an infidel procedure, and we had better give up the negroes than the Bible. It is a double assertion of the falsity of the Bible—first, as it maintains that mankind have not sprang from a common parentage; and, secondly, as it contends that it is morally wrong to enslave white men, who, the Bible informs us, were enslaved by the express command of God. But it is also utterly falsified by history. The little States of Greece, in their intestine wars, made slaves of their prisoners, and there was no complaint that they did not make good slaves; whilst the Macedonians, an inferior race, were proverbially unfit for slavery. The Georgians and Circassians, the most beautiful of the human family, make excellent slaves, whilst the Bedouin Arab and American Indian are as unfit for slavery as the Bengal tiger, or those tribes in Palestine whom God commanded Moses and Joshua to put to the sword without discrimination or mercy.

Again: to defend and justify mere negro slavery, and condemn other forms of slavery, is to give up expressly the whole cause of the South—for

285

mulattoes, quadroons, and men with as white skins as any of us, may legally be, and in fact are, held in slavery in every State of the South. The abolitionists well know this, for almost the whole interest of Mrs. Stowe's Uncle Tom's Cabin, arises from the fact, that a man and woman, with fair complexion, are held as slaves.

We are all in the habit of maintaining that our slaves are far better off than the common laborers of Europe, and that those laborers were infinitely better situated as feudal serfs or slaves than as freemen, or rather as slaves to capital. Now, we stultify ourselves if we maintain it would be wrong to remit them back to domestic slavery, which we always argue is much milder and protective than that slavery to capital, to which emancipation has subjected them. They have been wronged and injured by emancipation, would we not restore them to slavery? Or are we, too, to become Socialists, and coop them up in Greely's Free-Love phalansteries? There are no other alternative.

Again: every Southern man in defending slavery, habitually appeals to the almost universal usages of civilized man, and argues that slavery must be natural to man, and intended by Providence as the condition of the larger portion of the race, else it could not have been so universal. What a ridiculous and absurd figure does the defender of mere negro slavery cut, who uses this argument, when the abolitionist turns round on him and says— "why, you have just admitted that white slavery was wrong, and this universal usage which you speak of has been white, not black slavery. The latter is a very recent affair."

We must defend the principle of slavery as part of the constitution of man's nature. The defence of mere negro slavery, will, nay, has involved us in a thousand absurdities and contradictions. We must take high philosophical, biblical, and historical grounds, and soar beyond the little time and space around us to the earliest records of time, and the farthest verge of civilization. Let us quit the narrow boundaries of the rice, the sugar and the cotton field, and invite the abolitionists to accompany us in our flight to the tent of Abraham, to the fields of Judea, to the halls of David and of Solomon, to the palaces and the farms of Athens and of Rome, and to the castles of the grim Barons of medieval time. Let us point to their daily routine of domestic life. Then, not till then, may we triumphantly defend negro slavery. "You see slavery everywhere, and throughout all times: you see men

286

subjected to it by express command or by permission of God, with skins as white and intellects as good as yours. Can it be wrong to enslave the poor negro, who needs a master more than any of these?" Less than this is inconsiderate assertion, not Southern thought; nay, not thought at all.

The temptation to confine the defence of slavery to mere negro slavery is very strong, for it is obvious that they require masters under all circumstances, whilst the whites need them only under peculiar circumstances, and those circumstances such as we can hardly realize the existence of in America. May the day never arrive when our lands shall be so closely monopolized, and our population become so dense, that the poor would find slavery a happy refuge from the oppression of capital.

In the South, there is another and a stronger reason for the feeling of indignation at the bare suggestion of white slavery—that is pride of caste. No man loves liberty and hates slavery so cordially as the Southerner. Liberty is with him a privilege, or distinction, belonging to all white men. Slavery a badge of disgrace attached to an inferior race. Accustomed from childhood to connect the idea of slavery with the negro, and of liberty with the white man, it shocks his sensibilities barely to mention white slavery. 'Tis vain to talk to him of the usages of mankind, for his prejudices and prepossessions were formed long before he heard of history, and they are too strong to be reasoned away.

This peculiarity of Southerners, and other slaveholders, is admirably described by Burke, who was the most philosophic and farseeing statesman of modern times. He says, "in Virginia and the Carolinas they have a vast multitude of slaves. Where this is the case in any part of the world, those who are free are by far the most proud and jealous of their freedom. Freedom is to them not only an enjoyment, but a kind of rank and privilege. Not seeing then that freedom, as in countries where it is a common blessing, and as broad and general as the air, may be united with much abject toil, with great misery, with all the exterior of servitude, liberty looks among them as something more noble and liberal. I do not mean to commend the superior morality of this sentiment, which has at least as much pride as virtue in it; but I cannot alter the nature of man. The fact is so; and those people of the Southern colonies are much more strongly, and with a more stubborn spirit attached to liberty, than those to the Northward. Such were all the ancient commonwealths; such were our Gothic ancestry; such, in our days, were the Poles; and such will be all masters of slaves who are not slaves themselves. In such a people, haughtiness of domination combines with the spirit of freedom, fortifies it, and renders it invisible."

Southern Thought Again.

When a public opinion is formed on a state of existing facts, and of anticipated results, and an entire change of facts and anticipations takes place, public opinion itself must also change.

Fifty years ago all christendom believed that if the negroes were emancipated, they would become more moral, intelligent, and industrious. The experiment of emancipation has been tried in every form, and on the large as well as the small scale.

Whether in South America or the West Indies, in our Southern or Northern States, in Liberia or Sierra Leone, the free negro is an idler and a nuisance. Besides, his emancipation has so diminished Southern tropical products, that the poor laboring whites cannot afford to purchase the common necessaries of life. Moreover, to obviate this great evil, we see France and England reviving the slave-trade, under new forms, and Cuba actively engaged in it, under its old form, rendered far more cruel, however, by the abortive attempts to suppress it.

Now, we say that, with the experience of the last fifty years, it is impossible for public opinion, in any part of christendom, to remain on the subject of negro slavery, what it was fifty years ago. Mistaken philanthropy has had full sway, and its entire failure must give rise to new doctrines on this subject.

These doctrines begin to be openly preached, and practiced on, too. The South leads opinion; she virtually proposes a renewal of the old slave trade. But the North and Europe are ahead of her in practice, for they are carrying on the trade, whilst she is only discussing its propriety. Yet, even in the British Parliament, regret is expressed for the great blunder of negro emancipation; and some speakers went on to palliate, if not to justify, the old slave-trade. One of them saying in debate, that only five per cent of the negroes died on the middle passage, whilst ten per cent of English troops sent to India perished on their way.

The latest accounts from Marautius show that she is flourishing. Because near two hundred thousand Asiatic slaves, or coolies, have been introduced into that single little colony within a few years past.

Abolitionism is dying out, because it is deprived of its old arguments and golden expectations, because it has done no good, and stands convicted before the world of infinite mischief.

The extreme pro-slavery men are the last to discover this state of facts; because a Northern sectional party is on the increase, they think abolition is increasing. But the origin and growth of that party has been all owing to the advance of pro-slavery doctrines at the South, and the consequent, seeming, aggressions of the South. At the time of the ordinance of 1789, the South seemed willing to give up all share in the territories. Under the Missouri Compromise she claimed more; and now she claims equal right in all the territories with the North, and she is successfully maintaining her claim. She leads public opinion everywhere, because she is in advance of that new counter-current of opinion, that has set in everywhere, about slavery. Soon the Democratic party will be in a majority again at the North. The South will take some other advance step on the subject of slavery, and then a new Northern party will be formed to resist Southern aggression. But nature is sure in the long run to conquer, and nature is on the side of the South. Negro slavery is as indispensable to the North as to us. They begin to see it, and to feel it, too. The introduction of more negroes, and the extension of slave territory, are new doctrines with us. Give the North a little time, and she will eagerly adopt them. We are her slave colonies, and she will command the commerce of the world. In the conduct of France and England about coolies and apprentices, we have a foretaste of what the North will do. Those nations need slave colonies, and if Northern fanatics are tired of union with the South, France or England will be ready to unite with us on favorable terms.

The world sadly needs works on the general subject of slavery—on slavery in the abstract—a history and philosophy of the institution.

Though it has been through all time the most common condition of mankind, little is to be found in the literature of the world about it, except a few pages of Aristotle and our own crude suggestions.

The attempts to defend negro slavery as exceptional, have been written with signal ability by the ablest men in the South. But it is vain to preach against the prejudices of mankind, especially where those prejudices have some foundation in truth. Negro slavery gave rise to abolition, (which never existed before,) because, in its inception, it was attended with much that was odious and cruel, and continues so to be attended in Cuba and Brazil. There, slaves are still worked to death, and it requires large annual importations to keep up the supply.

The strongest argument against slavery, and all the prejudice against it, arise from the too great inferiority of race, which begets cruel and negligent treatment in the masters, who naturally feel little sympathy for ignorant, brutal savages. Inferiority of race is quite as good an argument against negro slavery as in its favor.

We, of the South, have most successfully shown that, as the negro advances in civilization, the master becomes attached to him; and that, eventually, this attachment secures to him kind treatment and an abundant supply of the necessaries of life. But the whole history of the institution shows, that, in giving up slavery in the abstract, we take the weakest position of defence that we could possibly select. We admit it to be wrong, and then attempt to defend it in that peculiar form which has always been most odious to mankind.

We set out to write something of a rambling essay, and, indeed, the subject of Southern Thought is so large and suggestive, that it is difficult to write otherwise.

The first great Southern thought will be to refute the political economy of the "let alone" Free Trade School, and adopt some more social, protective, and humanitarian, in its stead. We make no war on political economy in its large and extended sense, for we indulge in disquisitions ourselves on national and social wealth, and what will best promote social and national well-being; but only on that Adam Smith School, who encourage unlimited competition, beget a war of the wits, and propose to govern mankind by "letting them alone, and encouraging the strong, skillful, and rich, to oppress the weak and ignorant." The science of political economy, strictly understood, has but one principle, or at least one distinctive principle. This is variously expressed by the terms, "Pas trop gouverner," "Every man for himself," "Laissez-faire," "Demand will regulate supply," &c. It is this narrow and selfish philosophy which the South must refute; and, yet, which it is teaching in all its higher schools. It leads directly to the "No Government" doctrines of the abolitionists and socialists, and only involves slavery, in one common ruin, with all the other institutions of society.

Nothing is so directly adverse to slavery as a philosophy, which teaches that society succeeds best, when all are let alone to make their own way in the world. In truth, "Political Economy is the philosophy of universal liberty," and the outgrowth of that competitive society where the few wallow in luxury, and the unprotected masses, without masters to provide for them, are left to the grinding, unfeeling oppression of skill and capital, which starve them by the million. We must teach that slavery is necessary in all societies, as well to protect, as to govern the weak, poor, and ignorant. This is the opposite doctrine to that of the political economists.

Again: We should show that slave society, which is a series of subordinations, is consistent with christian morality—for fathers, masters, husbands, wives, children, and slaves, not being equals, rivals, competitors, and antagonists, best promote each others selfish interests when they do most for those above or beneath them. Within the precincts of the family, including slaves, the golden rule is a practical and wise guide of conduct. But in free society, where selfishness, rivalry, and competition are necessary to success, and almost to existence, this rule cannot be adopted in practice. It would reverse the whole action of such society, and make men martyrs to their virtues.

Here we may pause awhile, and consider that new system of ethical philosophy and of moral duties which slavery naturally suggests and gives rise to. Outside the Bible, the christian world has now no moral philosophy, except that selfish system, which teaches that each individual most promotes the good of others, and of the whole of society, by a continuous struggle for his own selfish good, by making good bargains, and by giving as little of his own labor as possible for as much as he can obtain of other peoples.

The scale of moral merit is nicely graduated, and he is universally considered most meritorious, who works least and gets best paid. The difference between honesty and dishonesty being, that the latter takes short cuts, whilst the former gets greater advantages, appropriates more of other people's labor, by deliberately bleeding all with whom it deals a little, than dishonesty does by grabbing at too much at once.

Lawyers, merchants, artists, mechanics, and professional and skillful men, of all kinds, are considered more honorable and meritorious than common laborers, because they work but little, and exchange a little of their light labor for the results of a great deal of common labor. All merit, in free society, consists in getting the advantage in dealing: all demerit and disgrace, in laboring more for others than they labor for you. This system is

291

called by the French philosophers "exploitation," which means taking honest advantages. In the general, no other moral rule of conduct is practicable in free society, because separation of interests and competition arm men against each other, and keep up a continual social war of the wits. It is true, the doctrines of the Bible are as extensively known as those of the political economists, and those doctrines touch and mollify the hearts of men, and neutralize in some degree the poison of the selfish system.

We, of the South, can build up an ethical code, founded on the morality of the Bible, because human interests with us do not generally clash, but coincide. Without the family circle it is true competition and clashing interests exist, but slavery leaves few without the family, and the little competition that is left is among the rich and skillful, and serves to keep society progressive. It is enough that slavery will relieve the common laborers of the evils of competition, and the exactions of skill and capital.

We have thus attempted to show that Southern thought must build up an entire new system of ethical philosophy. The South must also originate a new political science, whose leading and distinctive principle will be, "the world is too little governed." Where government restraint and control and protection are most needed, modern politicians propose to have, and in practice have, no government. They express a holy horror of sumptuary laws, of Roman censors, of Jewish and Catholic Priests, and of all interference with the family. Ignorant fathers must riot in unrestrained despotism. They have "a right divine to govern wrong," and maltreat wives and children as much as they please. Modern, so called liberty, robs three-fourths of mankind, wives and children, of all rights, and subjects them to the despotism of brutal and ignorant fathers and husbands. The most important part of government is that which superintends and controls the action of the family, for society is composed of families; and if the parts be rotten, the whole cannot be sound. Slavery secures intelligent rulers, interested in the well-being of its subjects, and they never permit the maltreatment by slaves of their wives and children. Every mail teems with accounts of wife murders at the North, and yet we have never heard or read of a negro murdering his wife at the South. Nothing but the strong arm and inquisitorial superintendence of a master, can restrain their wife murderers; they need "more of government."

Southern thought will teach that protection and slavery must go hand in hand, for we cannot efficiently protect those whose conduct we cannot control. (Hence, the powers and obligations of husbands and fathers.) We can never be sure that our charities will not be misapplied, unless we can control their expenditure.

It is the duty of society to protect all its members, and it can only do so by subjecting each to that degree of government constraint or slavery, which will best advance the good of each and of the whole. Thus, ambition, or the love of power, properly directed, becomes the noblest of virtues, because power alone can enable us to be safely benevolent to the weak, poor, or criminal.

To protect the weak, we must first enslave them, and this slavery must be either political and legal, or social; the latter, including the condition of wives, apprentices, inmates of poor houses, idiots, lunatics, children, sailors, soldiers, and domestic slaves. Those latter classes cannot be governed, and also protected by mere law, and require masters of some kind, whose will and discretion shall stand as a law to them, who shall be entitled to their labor, and bound to provide for them. This social organization begets harmony and good will, instead of competition, rivalry, and war of the wits.

Slavery educates, refines, and moralizes the masses by separating them from each other, and bringing them into continual intercourse with masters of superior minds, information, and morality. The laboring class of Europe, associating with nothing above them, learn nothing but crime and immorality from each other, and are well described by Mr. Charles Dickens as "a heaving mass of poverty, ignorance, and crime." Slavery is necessary as an educational institution, and is worth ten times all the common schools of the North. Such common schools teach only uncommonly bad morals, and prepare their inmates to graduate in the penitentiary, as the statistics of crime at the North abundantly prove.

There certainly is in the human heart, under all circumstances, a love for all mankind, and a yearning desire to equalize human conditions. We are all philanthropists by force of nature, for we are social beings, tied to each other by invisible chords of sympathy. Nature, which makes us members or limbs of the being society, and affects us pleasantly or painfully, as any of those members or limbs, however distant from us, are affected, would teach us how to promote the well being of each and all, if we would but attend to her lessons. The slaveholder feels quite as sensibly the vibrations of the nervous system of humanitarian sympathy which makes society one being, as the abolitionist, the socialist, or the christian. They are all in pursuit of one object—the good of the whole—feeling that the good of each is indissolubly connected with the good of all. By observing and studying the habitudes of the bees and the ants, of flocking birds and gregarious animals, we must become satisfied that our social habits and sympathetic feelings are involuntary, a part of our nature, and necessary to our healthful and natural existence. This induces us to reject the social contract of Locke, which presupposes a state in which each human being has a separate independent existence; and also the philosophy of Adam Smith, which grew out of Locke's theory, and goes still further by insisting that "every man for himself" is the true doctrine of government.

Now, the question arises, how are man's social wants and habitudes to be satisfied, after rejecting the philosophy which dissociates him? How is that equality of social happiness and enjoyment to be attained which we all involuntarily desire? Has not nature, which made us social and gregarious, taught us ere this our best governmental policy? Has man no instincts, no divine promptings and directions; or is he accursed of God, and been left to grope and blunder in the dark for six thousand years, whilst other social animals have understood the science and practice of government from the first?

We, of the South, assume that man has all along instinctively understood and practiced that social and political government best suited to his nature, and that domestic slavery is, in the general, a natural and necessary part of that government, and that its absence is owing to a decaying and diseased state of society, or to something exceptional in local circumstances as in desert, or mountainous, or new countries, where competition is no evil, because capital has no mastery over labor. But how does slavery equalize human conditions, whilst it vests with seemingly unlimited and despotic power a few, and subjects the many to all the ills or evils which that power may choose capriciously to inflict?

First: There is no such thing as despotic power in the moral world, for human beings act and re-act on each other, and affect each other's course of action, just as in the physical world all bodies, by the laws of gravitation, mutually attract and control each other's motions. The difference being, that in the moral world, the smaller and weaker bodies not only neutralize the despotism of the larger, but often control and rule them. The wife, the infant, the slave, by virtue of that nervous, social sympathy, which connects us together, by means of domestic and family affection, which shield and

294

protect the weaker members of the household, and by that singular influence which compassion and pity for the helpless and dependent exercises most especially over the conduct of the strong, the brave, and the powerful, are in the general far more efficiently shielded from tyranny and ill treatment than they could be by the interposition of any human laws and penalties. Within the family circle it is impossible to interpose usefully many such laws and penalties; hence, Providence has abundantly supplied those checks to power which man in vain attempts to fabricate. "I am thy slave, deprives me of the power of a master!" All acknowledge and admire the truth and beauty of this sentiment, and thus tacitly admit the correctness of our theory.

But another step in the argument is necessary. This only proves that the despotic power of the master, the husband, and the father is no engine of tyranny, but usually and naturally a tie of affection, and a means of support and protection. Yet, it does not prove that the condition of the inferiors is equally desirable with that of superiors.

The labors of life devolve on inferiors, its cares on superiors. Their obligations are mutual, and each in a broad sense equally slaves, for the superior is as much bound by law, natural feeling, self-interest, and custom, to take care of, govern, and provide for inferiors or dependents, as they to labor for him. Which is the happier condition, in general, none can determine.

Faith in God, which establishes and perpetuates the two conditions, should make us bow in humble submission to his will, and with reverential respect for his wisdom, benevolence, and justice, be ready to believe that in a naturally constituted society, high and low are equally happy. . . .

But the free laborer has nightly care superadded to incessant daily toil, whilst his employer is exempted as well from the labor of life, as from most of its cares. The former is a slave, without the rights of a slave; the latter, a master, without the obligations of a master. What equality of condition can there be in free society?

Socially, slavery is quite as promotive of human happiness as it is morally and politically. "It is not good for man to be alone." His nature is social, and most of his happiness and enjoyment is reflected, and proceeds from his sympathy with the pleasures of others. Too small a family circle is injurious to happiness, as well because it circumscribes the pleasures of association, and prevents much interchange of ideas, as because it brings us nearer to that state of helplessness to which the solitary man is subjected. We cannot conceive of much pleasure or enjoyment in the life of a man and wife, with five or six infant children, living to themselves and cultivating their own lands. The sickness of either parent would render the situation of the whole family desperate. The healthy parent could not nurse the sick one, attend to the children, and to all domestic concerns, and also cultivate the land. The apprehension of this common event would suffice to mar enjoyment. But such a family, as we have described, would have scarcely any sources of social enjoyment at any time, for the constant drudgery of labor would confine them at home, and deprive them of the opportunity to acquire subjects for conversation, or ideas for interchange. Such a life is solitary and monotonous, begets cruel and despotic exercise of power on the part of the husband, who is not brought in contact with public opinion, negligence and slovenliness in the wife, and ignorance with the children. The boasted independence of such a life will not bear examination. The wife and six children are the slaves often of a cruel, capricious husband, who treats them badly, and provides for them insufficiently.

All this was obviated by the admirable slave institutions of the Romans, and other nations of antiquity. Society was divided into circles sufficiently large to insure against want, and to secure social enjoyment and intellectual improvement. These circles revolved around a common central head, thus securing order, concert and cooperation, and promoting kind and sympathetic feelings, instead of jealousy, rivalry, and competition. The Roman patrician had hundreds of followers, or clients, bound by hereditary ties to his house. For six hundred years, it is said, there never occurred an instance of faithlessness to the tie of patron and client. The nobleman never failed to protect, and the client never proved recreant to his duties when his patron needed his services. Next in the circle came the freedmen, who, although liberated from slavery, rarely forgot their allegiance to their late master— for they still needed his powerful protection. Lastly, were the slaves, who performed all common labor, but were relieved from the cares of life, and from the perils and privations of war. We can see in such society all the elements of social order, and of social happiness, and adequate *insurance* against casualties, sickness, injustice from without, and from hunger, nakedness, and poverty. Insurance is the business of government. Insurance is the object of society, and necessitates society. Modern free society neglects it, and foolishly says "the world is too much governed," thus forcing mankind to supply the deficiency of government, by thousands of forms of insurance, such as the Odd-Fellows, the Masons, the Sons of Temperance, Rappites, Mormons, Shakers, and Socialists of every hue; besides, the regular insurance companies, from fire and other casualties. Ancient slave society insured all its members, and so, in a great degree, does modern slave society—for master, mistress, and slaves, will never be all sick, or die at once, so that the weak and infirm are always secure of sufficient provision and attention.

Economically, slavery is necessary to bring about association of labor and division of expenses. Labor becomes far more efficient when many are associated together, and the expenses of living are greatly diminished when many families are united under a common government. The socialists are all aiming to attain these ends by an unnatural association, let them adopt the natural one, slavery, and they would show themselves wise and useful men.

We will cite a single example to illustrate our theory, that of farming. A single family, man, wife, and two or three children, under twenty-one years of age, cannot carry on farming profitably. Indeed, we believe their labors *on their own lands* would not support them, if mere grain producers, as well as slaves are usually supported. At least, where the family consisted of husband and wife and four or five young children, their labor would be inadequate to their support.

The expenses of small farms are proportionately much greater than those of large ones. To make and keep up an enclosure around a five acre field, of ordinary land, would cost more than the gross amount of sales of crops. Farmers of fifty acres must have a wagon, a fan, granary, and many other things quite as costly as those on a farm of three hundred acres. The labor or expense of sending to mill, to the blacksmith's shop, to stores, and to market, and the general labor of providing and superintending, are as great on a small farm as on one of much larger size. Every day's experience of the world shows the great economy of carrying on business on a large scale. Mammoth steamships are taking the place of sail vessels, mammoth hotels of ordinary taverns, and railroads and omnibuses are supplanting common roads and carriages. Now, slavery, as an industrial institution, bears the same relation to independent, separate, free labor, that these modern improvements do to those which they have supplanted. But we have proof incontestible of the superior availability of slave labor in the fact, that the South, with a thin soil, is now producing a larger agricultural surplus than

297

any other population of the same amount in the world, whilst the general comfort of its people, and its domestic consumption, exceed that of any other people.

We have thus attempted to show that Southern thought must inaugurate a new philosophy of ethics or morals, (in the restricted sense of the term morals,) because the present system resulting from the competition, and every man for himself, theory of free society, is selfish and anti-scriptural. That it must originate a new theory in politics, because the present system proposes to govern men by "letting them alone," and encouraging the strong, astute, and wealthy, to make a continual war of the wits and of capital, upon the weak, poor, and ignorant.

That we must have a new social philosophy, because man is by nature helpless when alone, and social from taste, feeling, and necessity; and yet, political economy proposes to disintegrate society, and set every man up for himself.

And lastly, that we must have a new economic philosophy, because association of labor and division of expenses is the true secret of national and individual wealth, and that this is brought about by slavery, and prevented by free society. We know that after such society has lost its liberty, though still retaining its name, after a few have monopolized all capital, their power over the masses is greater than that of slave-owners. Then, association of labor and division of expenses is more perfect than in slave society. Then is (so called) free society more productive than slave society; but it is because slavery to capital has taken the place of domestic slavery. The employers profits become greater than those of the slaver-holder, because he pays less wages to his laborers.

The Black Republicans and Abolitionists, with Sumner at the head, have displayed a degree of intellectual imbecility on the subject of the settlement of the public lands, that is absolutely marvellous and astounding, especially in a party, who, for thirty years, have done little else than study, write, speak, and agitate about sociological questions.

They boast that lands are dearer and labor cheaper at the North than the South. They say, (and say truly,) if you introduce white labor into Kansas, lands will be more valuable than if it be settled by slaveholders. Now, is it possible that they are such simpletons as not to see that they are asserting that the white laborers of the North, as slaves to capital, get less wages than our slaves? Lands do not breed produce of themselves nothing valuable, and, if as common to all as air and water, would be as valueless as air and water. Their value is the amount which land monopoly enables the land owner to exact from the laborer. Where the laborer is allowed most of the proceeds of his labor, there lands are cheapest. Where he is allowed least, there lands are most valuable. Dogberry wished to be "written down an ass;" these men write themselves down asses twice in one sentence. Say they, "lands are dearer and labor cheaper at the North." If either proposition be true, their white laborers are more of slaves than our negroes. If it be true, as the abolitionists assert, that, lands are dearer North than South, then our negroes are freer than their white laborers, for the price of land is the thermometer of liberty. But there is a vast deal more of knavery and hypocrisy than idiotcy about these men. They are deliberately planning the enslavement of white men. . . .

The South should daily remind the abolitionists that they, themselves, in effect, are continually asserting that the condition of our slaves is better than that of their free laborers—for if lands be dearer and labor cheaper with them, it only proves that their laborers, who cultivate the soil, get less of the proceeds of their labor than our slaves, and the land-owner more of those proceeds than our slaveholders.

But the abolitionists are mendacious and hypocritical, for it is not possible, constituted as the human mind is, that since the universal and disastrous failure of negro emancipation, they can hold the same opinions that they did thirty years ago, when they were sanguinely expecting the entire success of the emancipation experiment. Many were then sincere—all are now false and hypocritical.

Selected Bibliography of
Secondary Works on the Proslavery Argument

Albert, Peter Joseph. "The Protean Institution: The Geography, Economy, and Ideology of Slavery in Post-Revolutionary Virginia." Ph.D. dissertation, University of Maryland, 1976.

Allen, Jeffrey Brooke. "The Debate over Slavery and Race in Antebellum Kentucky, 1792–1850." Ph.D. dissertation, Northwestern University, 1973.

Bach, Julian S., Jr. "The Social Thought of the Old South." *American Journal of Sociology*, XLVI (September, 1940), 179–88.

Bailor, Keith M. "John Taylor of Carolina: Continuity, Change and Discontinuity in Virginia's Sentiments Towards Slavery, 1790–1820." *Virginia Magazine of History and Biography*, LXXV (July, 1967), 290–304.

Bellot, Leland J. "Evangelicals and the Defense of Slavery in Britain's Old Colonial Empire." *Journal of Southern History*, XXXVII (February, 1971), 19–40.

Bennett, Jon B. "Albert Taylor Bledsoe: Social and Religious Controversialist of the Old South." Ph.D. dissertation, Duke University, 1942.

Berwanger, Eugene H. "Negrophobia in Northern Proslavery and Antislavery Thought." *Phylon*, XXXIII (Fall, 1972), 266–75.

Bishop, Charles C. "The Proslavery Argument Reconsidered: James Henley Thornwell, Millennial Abolitionist." *South Carolina Historical Magazine*, LXXIII (January, 1972), 18–26.

Booker, H. Marshall. "Thomas Roderick Dew: Forgotten Virginian." *Virginia Cavalcade*, XIX (Winter, 1969), 20–29.

Bozeman, Theodore Dwight. "Joseph LeConte: Organic Science and a 'Sociology for the South.'" *Journal of Southern History*, XXXIX (November, 1973), 565–82.

———. "Science, Nature and Society: A New Approach to James Henley Thornwell." *Journal of Presbyterian History*, L (Winter, 1972), 307–325.

Brace, C. Loring. "The 'Ethnology' of Josiah Clark Nott." *Bulletin of the New York Academy of Medicine*, L (April, 1974), 509–528.

Brugger, Robert. *Beverley Tucker: Heart over Head in the Old South*. Baltimore: Johns Hopkins University Press, 1978.

Burke, Joseph C. "The Proslavery Argument and the First Congress." *Duquesne Review*, XIV (Spring, 1969), 3–15.

Caravaglios, Maria Genoino, "A Roman Critique of the Pro-Slavery Views of Bishop Martin of Natchitoches, Louisiana." *American Catholic Historical Society of Philadelphia Records*, LXXXIII (1972), 67–81.

Carsel, Wilfred. "The Slaveholders' Indictment of Northern Wage Slavery." *Journal of Southern History*, VI (November, 1940), 504–520.

Cash, Wilbur J. *The Mind of the South.* New York: Alfred Knopf, 1941.

Cooke, J. W. "Albert Taylor Bledsoe: An American Philosopher and Theologian of Liberty." *Southern Humanities Review*, VIII (Spring, 1974), 215–28.

Craven, Avery O. *Edmund Ruffin, Southerner: A Study in Secession.* Baton Rouge: Louisiana State University Press, 1923.

Daniel, W. Harrison. "Virginia Baptists and the Negro in the Ante-Bellum Era." *Journal of Negro History*, LVI (January, 1961), 1–16.

Davis, David Brion. *The Problem of Slavery in the Age of Revolution, 1770–1823.* Ithaca: Cornell University Press, 1975.

———. *The Problem of Slavery in Western Culture.* Ithaca: Cornell University Press, 1966.

Donald, David. "The Proslavery Argument Reconsidered." *Journal of Southern History.* XXXVII (February, 1971), 3–18.

Dorfman, Joseph. "George Fitzhugh and Slavery as Ideal Communism." In *The Economic Mind in American Civilization*, II, pp. 929–34. 5 vols. New York: Viking, 1946–59.

Duncan, H. G., and Winnie Leach Duncan. "The Development of Sociology in the Old South." *American Journal of Sociology*, XXXIX (March, 1934), 649–56.

Durden, Robert F. "J. D. B. De Bow: Convolutions of a Slavery Expansionist." *Journal of Southern History*, XVII (November, 1951), 441–61.

Faust, Drew Gilpin. "Evangelicalism and the Meaning of the Proslavery Argument: The Reverend Thornton Stringfellow of Virginia." *Virginia Magazine of History and Biography*, LXXXV (January, 1977), 3–17.

———. "A Southern Stewardship: The Intellectual and the Proslavery Argument." *American Quarterly*, XXXI (Spring, 1979), 63–80.

———. *A Sacred Circle: The Dilemma of the Intellectual in the Old South, 1840–1860.* Baltimore: Johns Hopkins University Press, 1977.

Fredrickson, George M. *The Black Image in the White Mind: The Debate on Afro-American Character and Destiny, 1817–1914.* New York: Harper and Row, 1971.

Freehling, Alison Harrison Goodyear. "Drift Toward Dissolution: The Virginia Slavery Debate of 1831–1832." Ph.D. dissertation, University of Michigan, 1974.

Freehling, William W. *Prelude to Civil War: The Nullification Controversy in South Carolina, 1816–1836.* New York: Harper and Row, 1965.

Gardner, Robert. "A Tenth Hour Apology for Slavery." *Journal of Southern History*, XXVI (August, 1960), 352–67.

Genovese, Eugene. *The World the Slaveholders Made: Two Essays in Interpretation.* New York: Pantheon, 1969.

Gillespie, Neal C. *The Collapse of Orthodoxy: The Intellectual Ordeal of George Frederick Holmes.* Charlottesville: University of Virginia Press, 1972.

Gravely, William B. "Methodist Preachers, Slavery, and Caste: Types of Social Concern in Antebellum America." *Duke Divinity School Review*, XXXIV (Fall, 1969), 209–229.

Greenberg, Kenneth S. "Revolutionary Ideology and the Proslavery Argument: The Abolition of Slavery in Antebellum South Carolina." *Journal of Southern History*, XLII (August, 1976), 365–84.

Guillory, James D. "The Pro-Slavery Arguments of Dr. Samuel A. Cartwright." *Louisiana History*, IX (Fall, 1968), 209–227.

Hall, Claude H. *Abel Parker Upshur: Conservative Virginian*. Madison: Wisconsin State Historical Society, 1964.

Hall, Kermit L. "Federal Judicial Reform and Proslavery Constitutional Theory: A Retrospect on the Butler Bill." *American Journal of Legal History*, XVII (Spring, 1973), 166–84.

Hart, Albert Bushnell. *Slavery and Abolition, 1831–1841*. New York: Harper and Bros., 1906.

Hartz, Louis. *The Liberal Tradition in America*. New York: Harcourt, Brace, and World, 1955.

Hesseltine, William B. "Some New Aspects of the Pro-Slavery Argument." *Journal of Negro History*, XXI (January, 1936), 1–15.

Higham, John. "The Changing Loyalties of William Gilmore Simms." *Journal of Southern History*, IX (May, 1943), 210–23.

Hite, James C., and Ellen J. Hall. "The Reactionary Evolution of Economic Thought in Antebellum Virginia." *Virginia Magazine of History and Biography*, LXXX (October, 1972), 476–88.

Hubbart, Henry Clyde. "Pro-Southern Influence in the Free West, 1840–1865." *Mississippi Valley Historical Review*, XX (June, 1933), 45–62.

Jenkins, William Sumner. *The Pro-Slavery Argument in the Old South*. Chapel Hill: University of North Carolina Press, 1935.

Kolchin, Peter. "In Defense of Servitude: American Proslavery and Russian Proserfdom Arguments, 1760–1860." *American Historical Review*, LXXXV, No. 4 (October, 1980), 809–827.

Lloyd, Arthur Young. *The Slavery Controversy, 1831–1860*. Chapel Hill: University of North Carolina Press, 1939.

Longton, William H. "Some Aspects of Intellectual Activity in Ante-Bellum South Carolina, 1830–1860." Ph.D. dissertation, University of North Carolina, 1969.

Loveland, Anne C. "Richard Furman's 'Questions on Slavery.'" *Baptist History and Heritage*, X (June, 1975), 177–81.

Lyons, Adelaide Avery. "The Religious Defense of Slavery in the North." *Trinity College Historial Society Papers*, XIII (1919), 5–34.

McCardell, John. *The Idea of a Southern Nation: Southern Nationalists and Southern Nationalism, 1830–1860*. New York: Norton, 1979.

McColley, Robert. *Slavery in Jeffersonian Virginia*. Urbana: University of Illinois Press, 1964.

McKitrick, Eric L., ed. *Slavery Defended: The Views of the Old South*. Englewood Cliffs, N.J.: Prentice-Hall, 1963.

McPherson, James M. "Slavery and Race." *Perspectives in American History*, III (1969), 460–73.

Maddex, Jack P., Jr. "Proslavery Millennialism: Social Eschatology in Antebellum Southern Calvinism." *American Quarterly*, XXXI (Spring, 1979), 46–62.

———. *The Reconstruction of Edward A. Pollard: A Rebel's Conversion to Postbellum Unionism*. Chapel Hill: University of North Carolina Press, 1974.

———. "'The Southern Apostasy' Revisited: The Significance of Proslavery Christianity." *Marxist Perspectives*, II (Fall, 1979), 132–41.

Mansfield, Stephen S. "Thomas Roderick Dew: Defender of the Southern Faith." Ph.D. dissertation, University of Virginia, 1968.

Marshall, Mary Louise. "Samuel A. Cartwright and States' Rights Medicine." *New Orleans Medical and Surgical Journal*, XCIII (1940–41), 74–78.

Merritt, Elizabeth. *James Henry Hammond, 1807–1864*. Baltimore: Johns Hopkins University Press, 1923.

Morrison, Larry. "The Proslavery Argument in the Early Republic, 1790–1830." Ph.D. dissertation, University of Virginia, 1975.

Morrow, Ralph E. "The Proslavery Argument Revisited." *Mississippi Valley Historical Review*, XLVII (June, 1961), 79–94.

O'Brien, Kenneth. "The Savage and the Child in Historial Perspective: Images of Blacks in Southern White Thought, 1830–1915." Ph.D. dissertation, Northwestern University, 1974.

Onwood, Maurice. "Impulse and Honor: The Place of Slave and Master in the Ideology of Planterdom." *Plantation Society*, I (February, 1979), 31–56.

Perkins, Howard C. "The Defense of Slavery in the Northern Press on the Eve of the Civil War." *Journal of Southern History*, IX (November, 1943), 501–531.

Peterson, Thomas Virgil. *Ham and Japheth: The Mythic World of Whites in the Antebellum South*. Metuchen, N.J.: Scarecrow Press, 1978.

Purifoy, Lewis. "The Southern Methodist Church and the Proslavery Argument." *Journal of Southern History*, XXXII (August, 1966), 325–41.

Rogers, Tommy W. "Dr. F. A. Ross and the Presbyterian Defense of Slavery." *Journal of Presbyterian History*, XLV (June, 1967), 112–24.

Rosenberg, Morton Melvin, and Dennis V. McClung. *The Politics of Proslavery Sentiment in Indiana, 1816–1861*. Muncie: Ball State University Press, 1968.

Schmidt, Frederika Teute, and Barbara Ripel Wilhelm. "Early Proslavery Petitions in Virginia." *William and Mary Quarterly*, 3rd. ser., XXX (January, 1973), 133–46.

Seal, Albert, ed. "Notes and Documents: Letters from the South: A Mississippian's Defense of Slavery." *Journal of Mississippi History*, XI (October, 1940), 212–31.

Sellers, Charles G., Jr. "The Travail of Slavery." In *The Southerner as American*. Edited by Charles G. Sellers, Jr. Chapel Hill: University of North Carolina Press, 1960.

Shalhope, Robert. "Race, Class, Slavery, and the Antebellum Southern Mind." *Journal of Southern History*, XXXVII (November, 1971), 557–74.

Silbey, Joel H. "Pro-Slavery Sentiment in Iowa, 1836–1861." *Iowa Journal of History*, LV (October, 1957), 289–318.

Skipper, Ottis Clark. *J. D. B. DeBow, Magazinist of the Old South*. Athens: University of Georgia Press, 1958.

Smith, Harmon L. "William Capers and William A. Smith: Neglected Advocates of the Pro-Slavery Moral Argument." *Methodist History*, III (October, 1964), 23–52.

Smith, H. Shelton. *In His Image, But . . . : Racism in Southern Religion, 1780–1910*. Durham: Duke University Préss, 1972.

Stampp, Kenneth M. "An Analysis of T. R. Dew's *Review of the Debate in the Virginia Legislature*." *Journal of Negro History*, XXVII (October, 1942), 380–87.

———. "The Southern Refutation of the Proslavery Argument." *North Carolina Historical Review*, XXI (January, 1944), 35–45.

Stanton, William. *The Leopard's Spots: Scientific Attitudes Toward Race in America, 1815–1859*. Chicago: University of Chicago Press, 1960.

Stein, Stephen J. "George Whitefield on Slavery: Some New Evidence." *Church History*, XLII (June, 1973), 243–56.

Takaki, Ronald T. *A Pro-Slavery Crusade: The Agitation to Reopen the African Slave Trade*. New York: Free Press, 1971.

Tandy, Jeannette Reed. "Pro-Slavery Propaganda in American Fiction of the Fifties." *South Atlantic Quarterly*, XXI (January and April, 1922), 41–51, 170–79.

Taylor, William R. *Cavalier and Yankee: The Old South and American National Character*. New York: George Braziller, 1957.

Temperley, Howard. "Capitalism, Slavery, and Ideology." *Past and Present*, LXXV (May, 1977), 94–118.

Tise, Larry Edward. "The Interregional Appeal of Proslavery Thought: An Ideological Profile of the Antebellum American Clergy." *Plantation Society*, I (February, 1979), 58–72.

———. "Proslavery Ideology: A Social and Intellectual History of the Defense of Slavery in America, 1790–1840." Ph.D. dissertation, University of North Carolina, 1975.

Tucker, Robert C. "James Henry Hammond: South Carolinian." Ph.D. dissertation, University of North Carolina, 1959.

Vassar, Rena. "William Knox's Defense of Slavery." *Proceedings of the American Philosophical Society*, CXIV (August, 1970), 310–26.

Wakelyn, Jon L. "The Changing Loyalties of James Henry Hammond: A Reconsideration." *South Carolina Historical Magazine*, LXXV (January, 1974), 1–13.

———. *The Politics of a Literary Man: William Gilmore Simms*. Westport, Conn.: Greenwood Press, 1973.

Wander, Philip C. "The Savage Child: The Image of the Negro in the Pro-Slavery

Movement." *Southern Speech Communication Journal*, XXVII (Fall, 1972), 335–60.

Wilson, Edmund. "Diversity of Opinion in the South: William J. Grayson, George Fitzhugh, Hinton R. Helper." In *Patriotic Gore: Studies in the Literature of the American Civil War*. New York: Oxford University Press, 1962.

Wilson, Harold. "Basil Manly, Apologist for Slavocracy." *Alabama Review*, XV (January, 1962), 38–53.

Wiltshire, Susan Ford. "Jefferson, Calhoun, and the Slavery Debate: The Classics and the Two Minds of the South." *Southern Humanities Review*, XI (Special Issue, 1977), 33–40.

Wish, Harvey. *George Fitzhugh: Propagandist of the Old South*. Baton Rouge: Louisiana State University Press, 1943.

———. "George Frederick Holmes and Southern Periodical Literature of the Mid-Nineteenth Century." *Journal of Southern History*, VII (August, 1941), 343–56.

———., ed. *Ante-Bellum: Writings of George Fitzhugh and Hinton Rowan Helper on Slavery*. New York: G. P. Putnam, 1960.

Woodward, C. Vann. "George Fitzhugh: *Sui Generis*." In George Fitzhugh, *Cannibals All! or Slaves Without Masters*. Edited by C. Vann Woodward. Cambridge: John Harvard Library, 1960.

Wright, Benjamin Fletcher, Jr. "George Fitzhugh on the Failure of Liberty." *Southwestern Political and Social Science Quarterly*, VI (December, 1926), 219–41.

Wyatt-Brown, Bertram. "Proslavery and Antislavery Intellectuals: Class Concepts and Polemical Struggle." In *Antislavery Reconsidered: New Perspectives on the Abolitionists*. Edited by Lewis Perry and Michael Fellman. Baton Rouge: Louisiana State University Press, 1979.